The Atlantic Alliance Under Stress

US–European Relations After Iraq

edited by

David M. Andrews

CAMBRIDGE
UNIVERSITY PRESS

PUBLISHED BY THE PRESS SYNDICATE OF THE UNIVERSITY OF CAMBRIDGE
The Pitt Building, Trumpington Street, Cambridge CB2 1RF, United Kingdom

CAMBRIDGE UNIVERSITY PRESS
The Edinburgh Building, Cambridge, CB2 2RU, UK
40 West 20th Street, New York, NY 10011-4211, USA
477 Williamstown Road, Port Melbourne, VIC 3207, Australia
Ruiz de Alarcón 13, 28014 Madrid, Spain
Dock House, The Waterfront, Cape Town 8001, South Africa

http://www.cambridge.org
Information on this title: www.cambridge.org/9780521614085

First published 2005

Printed in the United Kingdom at the University Press, Cambridge

Typeset in 10/12pt. Plantin   *System* Advent 3B2 8.07f [PND]

A catalogue record for this book is available from the British Library
1005 496410
ISBN-13-978-0-521-84927-2 hardback
ISBN-10-0-521-84927-6 hardback
ISBN-13-978-0-521-61408-5 paperback
ISBN-10-0-521-61408-2 paperback

The Atlantic Alliance Under Stress

Can the political institutions of the transatlantic alliance endure the demise of
the Soviet enemy? Did the Iraq crisis of 2002–3 signal the end of the Atlantic
partnership? If so, what are the likely consequences? In this book, a distinguished
group of political scientists and historians from Europe and the United States
tackles these questions. The book examines the causes and consequences of the
crisis in Atlantic relations that accompanied the invasion of Iraq in March 2003.
The authors' collective focus is not on the war itself, or how it was conducted,
or even the situation in Iraq before or after the conflict. Instead, the crisis over
Iraq is the starting point for an examination of transatlantic relations and specifically the Atlantic alliance, an examination that is crossnational in scope and
multidisciplinary in approach.

DAVID M. ANDREWS is Associate Professor in the Department of Politics and
International Relations at Scripps College, California, Adjunct Professor at the
Claremont Graduate University, and founding Director of the European Union
Center of California.

Contents

III   Prospects for the Alliance

Contributors

DAVID M. ANDREWS (EDITOR) is Associate Professor of Politics and International Relations at Scripps College, the Claremont Colleges, and Director of the European Union Center of California. During 2002–4, he was Senior Research Fellow in Transatlantic Relations at the European University Institute in Florence, Italy.

WADE JACOBY is Associate Professor of Political Science at Brigham Young University and Director of the BYU Center for the Study of Europe.

MILES KAHLER is Rohr Professor of Pacific International Relations at the Graduate School of International Relations and Pacific Studies, University of California, San Diego, and Director of the Institute for International, Comparative, and Area Studies at UCSD.

GEIR LUNDESTAD is Director of the Norwegian Nobel Institute, Secretary of the Norwegian Nobel Committee 1990, and Adjunct Professor of International History at the University of Oslo.

LEOPOLDO NUTI is Professor of History of International Relations at the Università degli Studi Roma Tre.

TIM OLIVER is a Ph.D. student in the Department of International Relations at the London School of Economics.

ELIZABETH POND is editor of *Transatlantic Internationale Politik* and a member of both the US Council on Foreign Relations and the German Council on Foreign Relations.

GEORGES-HENRI SOUTOU is Professor of Contemporary History at the University of Paris IV-Sorbonne.

MARC TRACHTENBERG is Professor of Political Science at the University of California at Los Angeles.

WILLIAM WALLACE (Lord Wallace of Saltaire) is Professor of International Relations at the London School of Economics and Liberal Democrat spokesman on foreign affairs in the UK House of Lords.

HUBERT ZIMMERMANN is DAAD Visiting Professor in the Department of Government, Cornell University.

Preface

This book arises out of a series of seminars hosted by the European University Institute beginning in spring 2002 and concluding in spring 2004. These seminars were organized by the Transatlantic Programme of the Robert Schuman Centre for Advanced Studies, with generous funding for the series provided by BP. The seminars addressed the political, economic, cultural, and ideological dimensions of the crisis in Atlantic relations associated with the 2003 war in Iraq. The seminars benefited from the contributions of distinguished participants from both sides of the Atlantic.

For an American, the EUI is an unusual vantage point from which to observe Atlantic relations. As Senior Research Fellow in Transatlantic Relations, I was in residence as the Atlantic relationship sharply deteriorated in the months immediately before the war. It was from this self-consciously European institution that I witnessed the rising tensions that accompanied the final move towards hostilities and the mutual recriminations that later accompanied Iraq's occupation. During the seminar series that addressed these topics, the views expressed were sometimes controversial and the discussions often vigorous. Always, however, the seminars were marked by a seriousness of purpose, an attention to intellectual rigor, and a generosity of spirit. These qualities are in the best tradition of academic discourse, and I commend both our visitors and my Institute colleagues for adhering to such high standards.

I was especially grateful for the intellectual leadership demonstrated by Yves Meny, President of the European University Institute, and Helen Wallace, Director of the Robert Schuman Centre for Advanced Studies. Thanks go as well to the entire staff of the Schuman Centre, and in particular to Mei Lan Goei, Filipa de Sousa, Angelika Lanfranchi, Catherine Divry, Laura Jurisevic, Francesca Parenti, and Laura Burgassi. Able research assistance in support of this and related projects was provided by Melinda Baker, Monica Boduszynksi, Jennifer Boyd, Elizabeth Hillman, John Reilly, and William Talbott. I am also grateful to Scripps College, and especially to Michael Deane Lamkin, for arranging a leave of absence allowing me to be in residence at the EUI.

Finally but most importantly, I am grateful to the contributors to this project. Hailing from six nations and a variety of disciplinary backgrounds, their commitment to this project was a model of transatlantic cooperation.

Introduction

This book examines the causes and consequences of the crisis in Atlantic relations associated with the invasion of Iraq in March 2003. The contributors' collective focus is not on the war itself, or how it was conducted, or the situation in Iraq either before or after the conflict. Instead, the crisis over Iraq is the starting point for an examination of transatlantic relations and specifically the Atlantic alliance.

We believe that the project of building and maintaining an Atlantic community is at risk as never before. The Alliance's strategic purpose is unclear; its domestic support in key countries is, if not altogether unraveling, at least greatly weakened by historical standards. To understand these problems better, our study focuses in large measure on the nexus of domestic and international politics in the Alliance's major partners: how changes in the international environment – sometimes in conjunction with unrelated changes in patterns of domestic politics – have tended to undermine support for Atlanticism in both the United States and Europe.

The Atlantic community has many aspects; nevertheless, for almost fifty years, it was sustained by a set of calculations regarding how best to manage the Soviet threat. Beyond the specifics of those security calculations or of the accompanying Atlantic economic framework, there was a broader and largely unspoken political agreement: European governments supported, or at least refrained from actively opposing, American policy activism around the world, while the United States supported, or at least refrained from actively undermining, a series of regional and global arrangements that underwrote Europe's regional prosperity and international influence. The resulting arrangement was far more complex than simply a free hand for a free ride, but at the same time this phrase reflects certain underlying truths. The United States was for the most part at liberty to pursue a strategic global vision; though west European capitals frequently criticized US policy, they rarely challenged it directly (and certainly not in crisis situations). Meanwhile, Europe was in parallel fashion able to develop a framework for regional prosperity that, though likewise criticized by Washington, was never seriously challenged by it, despite that framework's reliance on systematic barriers to the most competitive US exports.

In short, an implicit bargain emerged: the United States enjoyed a privileged role in international security matters while acquiescing to aspects of European integration that challenged its own economic interests. Whatever the merits of such an arrangement, it was bound to irritate substantial segments of the population in each of the Alliance's members. The partnership endured, however, because counterbalancing domestic interests held a real stake – whether security, economic, or political – in Atlanticism. When participating governments chose at key junctures to put support for the Alliance ahead of particular domestic interest groups, there were generally other constituencies prepared to offset, at least in part, the resulting political costs; preserving the anti-Soviet partnership therefore remained within the sphere of the politically possible. It was for this reason that the White House managed to resist periodic congressional pressure to reduce the American troop presence in Europe, for example, and that west European governments agreed to install medium-range nuclear weapons in the 1980s despite considerable public ire.

Underlying this complex state of affairs was the Cold War confrontation with the Soviet Union. The disappearance of the Soviet threat therefore put all these calculations at risk; but the consequences of this changed environment were not fully apparent during the 1990s, as several mitigating factors helped to keep tensions within the Alliance, though at times considerable, nevertheless broadly manageable. The crisis over Iraq was, at least in this sense, quite different. Tensions rose; critics of the Alliance's underlying precepts became increasingly vocal; offsetting constituencies either mobilized very slowly or failed to mobilize at all; and the costs of managing the Alliance were not successfully contained. While Atlantic relations have since improved, the deep divisions revealed by this episode between the United States and several of its major European allies – especially France and Germany – suggest that the Alliance's continued cohesion is in real peril.

Purpose and organization of the volume

The analysis provided in this volume is crossnational in scope and multi-disciplinary in approach. The contributors come from six countries and three different disciplinary backgrounds: history, political science, and international relations. While differing in perspective and prescription, they share a longstanding commitment to the study of the Atlantic partnership. Each offers an essay, original to this project, examining the sources and the consequences of the crisis in transatlantic relations provoked by disagreements over Iraq.

All too often, discussions of this subject – on both sides of the Atlantic – have been excessively introverted. Our aim here has been to open these essentially national discourses to a broader public, and to submit them to more rigorous examination. We have tried to avoid, at least to the extent possible, the controversies of the moment and have focused instead on enduring questions. Our efforts are motivated by the hope that a more cooperative transatlantic relationship can emerge. But enhanced collaboration will depend on a more realistic understanding of what the Atlantic partners can expect of one another, and of the Alliance as a whole. This book is intended to advance such an understanding.

The book's organization reflects our analysis. Part I provides a historical and theoretical framework for addressing why the Iraq War was so divisive for the Atlantic allies. Part II provides studies of Atlantic policy in the United States, France, Germany, Italy, and the United Kingdom in light of that framework. Part III offers contrasting visions of the implications of the crisis for the Atlantic partnership, together with a synthetic concluding chapter.

We begin with a look at the crisis of 2002–3. In part I of the volume, Geir Lundestad provides a broad historical background to this debacle, contrasting the recent crisis to previous difficult episodes faced by the Alliance over the past half-century. He argues that both heightened American unilateralism and fundamental shifts in the policies of France and Germany were key drivers of the crisis, with the growing role of the European Union as a security and foreign policy actor a contributing factor. In her contribution, Elizabeth Pond focuses on the Atlantic diplomacy that immediately preceded and followed the war in Iraq. In her view, primary responsibility for the crisis lies with the George W. Bush administration's unnecessarily muscular and alienating approach to its allies. David Andrews then examines the policy preferences of the governments in Berlin, London, Paris, and Washington. He argues that, while the absence of a strategic rival did not foreordain the crisis, it did enable Alliance members (especially the United States and Germany) to pursue more adventurous policies than would have been imaginable during the Cold War.

Part II of the volume examines more closely different national policies towards the Alliance. Miles Kahler considers how changes in the political strategies of the two major parties in the United States have undermined the influence of the political center and opened the door to much greater swings in American foreign policy than occurred during the bipolar conflict. Georges-Henri Soutou argues that, while the Franco-American relationship has always been crisis-prone, recent changes in French politics and political discourse will make reconciliation with Washington even more difficult than in times past. For Hubert Zimmermann, Germany's transformation from a net importer to a net exporter of security has implications for the Alliance that have yet to be fully digested on either side of the Atlantic. Britain's support of the United States during the Atlantic crisis is unlikely to garner any long-term benefits for the United Kingdom, according to William Wallace and Tim Oliver; instead, London has become increasingly alienated from its European partners without having demonstrated any genuine leverage over policy in Washington. In Rome, as Leopoldo Nuti explains, the Italian state's affinity for a strong Atlantic partnership is a strategic response to both domestic and foreign policy needs. Those needs remain substantially in place despite the Cold War's end; hence, the end of the East–West conflict was less destabilizing to Italian foreign policy than it was elsewhere.

Part III of the volume engages the consequences of the Atlantic crisis. Marc Trachtenberg maintains that the Bush administration's policy, if unnecessarily clumsy, nevertheless represented a serious and responsible reaction to the new strategic situation in which the United States finds itself, and that the decisions of Paris and Berlin to lead international resistance to this policy suggest that the Alliance is in deep peril. In Trachtenberg's view, a strategic rethink, in some ways echoing John Foster Dulles' promised "agonizing reappraisal," is therefore in order. Wade Jacoby suggests that such a fundamental reappraisal may be premature. Focusing on central Europe, he argues that NATO has produced salutary effects both for the region and for the Alliance's senior partners. The Alliance may be imperfect, but its alternatives are worse; relying on "coalitions of the willing" as primary means of addressing future security problems will fail to secure the interests of either the United States or those governments whose views are, at least for the present, most congenial to Washington. David Andrews concludes with a synthesis of the project as a whole, including an adjudication of these contending viewpoints regarding the Alliance's future.

Prospects for the partnership

Of late, discussions of Atlantic relations have almost inevitably gravitated toward questions about the war in Iraq. Attention tends to focus on issues such as responsibility for the war's initiation, its conduct, and developments after the end of "major hostilities." This tendency is certainly understandable and, in democratic societies where leaders must account for their actions to their publics, even laudable. Certainly the contributors to this project were not of one mind about how best to allocate blame for the recent crisis.

Beyond these disputes, however, and irrespective of their resolution, certain core issues face the Alliance. These issues may have been highlighted by the war in Iraq, but they do not derive from that conflict. Principal among these concerns are the continued enthusiasm of Europeans for the United States to play a major role in continental security matters, and Washington's attitude towards continued European integration. Writing at a similar crossroads in the Atlantic relationship, a senior American foreign policy official once put it this way:

> We have sought to combine a supranational Europe with a closely integrated Atlantic Community under American leadership. These objectives are likely to prove incompatible.

That senior official was not Paul Wolfowitz but Henry Kissinger.[1] Writing shortly after the Nixon administration assumed office in 1969, Kissinger confronted circumstances not entirely unfamiliar to us today. A US president sought to distinguish his policies from those of the previous eight years of Democratic administration, and to prove himself personally after a closely contested national election. A Social Democratic government in the Federal Republic of Germany pursued a foreign policy that, at least in Washington's view, was more attuned to domestic opinion than to international realities. In France, after a period of national indecisiveness, a reasonably strong president had assumed a key brokering role at both the European and international levels.

How did these governments get along? Under the leadership of Kissinger and Nixon, the United States promulgated a foreign policy based on a strategic worldview and the forceful projection of American military power against perceived threats. That policy was deeply unpopular abroad, and especially in Europe. It was counterpoised by a European predilection for greater policy nuance and the maximum utilization of civilian power – a prescription that appealed to both intellectuals and street demonstrators, but that the US government regarded as naive.

The Nixon administration sought to reshape the Atlantic partnership in a fashion that better suited American interests, including a reconsideration of the very bases of US engagement with Europe. But the end result of that reconsideration was reaffirmation of central aspects of the Atlantic partnership. Costs and benefits of the partnership were rebalanced, and ultimately the United States did gain an enhanced measure of autonomy (especially in its economic relations – a somewhat ironic outcome, inasmuch as this was hardly Kissinger's strong suit). But Washington also confirmed, even if reluctantly, its support for

---

[1] "What Kind of Atlantic Partnership?," *Atlantic Community Quarterly* 7 (1969), p. 30.

multilateralism in general and for the process of European integration in particular. When push came to shove, the Atlantic partners had too much to lose not to make the necessary efforts to accommodate one another's core interests.

Whether present-day national leaders will similarly choose to revitalize the Alliance is unclear. The challenges they face in doing so are immense, and the benefits that might result are in dispute, leading some observers – including some of this project's contributors – to wonder if Atlanticism is a lost cause. I will return to these questions in the conclusion. First, however, we provide our analysis of the recent crisis and of national policy towards the Alliance in the leading Atlantic partners.

Part I

The Iraq War and the Atlantic alliance

1   Toward transatlantic drift?

Geir Lundestad

The Cold War years are nowadays sometimes seen as a golden period in American–west European relations. There is of course some truth to this assessment, since NATO was in many ways a stunning success. Yet it bears pointing out that crises were a nearly constant feature of the NATO relationship even during the Cold War, so in that sense one might argue that there has never really been a golden period in the Atlantic relationship. Strangely enough, September 11 may have represented the climax of Atlantic cooperation. For the first time, NATO invoked its famous Article 5. Everybody had always assumed this would happen over some crisis in Europe; now it was invoked to show unlimited solidarity with the United States. But this was not to last.

The following chapter, by Elizabeth Pond, describes in some detail the events leading up to the transatlantic crisis of 2002–3 and developments in its immediate aftermath. Here I am going to take a longer view, placing these events in historical context. Taken as a whole, the diplomacy in the run-up to the war in Iraq suggests a fundamental break with the practice of the preceding fifty years. Previously, especially in the most serious crises, France in the end sided with Washington on critical matters: German rearmament, Berlin, Cuba, to a lesser extent Afghanistan and Poland in the early 1980s, and the 1990–1 Gulf War. But in 2003, Paris became the champion of opposition to the United States in a crisis that the administration in Washington considered of supreme importance. For half a century, Germany had been the most loyal of US partners in Europe. Yet in this instance, Berlin sided firmly with the French; in fact, it took an even more anti-American position than did the French. With the country no longer divided, with only friendly neighbors, and with no Iron Curtain running down its middle (making its security almost entirely dependent on the United States), Germany was free to act; and for the first time it chose to go directly against the United States.

For its part, US policy had likewise undergone a fundamental change. Following the horrors of September 11, the United States preferred to conduct the war in Afghanistan completely on its own terms. Then came

Iraq; and France, far from renewing President Jacques Chirac's earlier calls for "total support" of the United States, became Washington's main antagonist in the United Nations Security Council, preventing the administration of George W. Bush from getting the world organization's explicit support for a military campaign against Saddam Hussein and his alleged weapons of mass destruction. In this new environment, traditional American enemies (Russia and China) simply hid behind the French. And, in the run-up to national elections in the fall of 2002, German chancellor Gerhard Schröder made it perfectly clear that he would offer no military or economic assistance to the United States in Iraq even if Washington's campaign gained the eventual support of the UN.

The situation was of course more complicated than this brief summary suggests. For one thing, the Bush administration's Iraq policy received the support of half the governments of the European Union (with Britain in the lead) and was also backed by almost all the former Warsaw Pact members in central and eastern Europe on their way to joining both NATO and the EU. Thus, US policy was not as universally rejected by Europeans as is sometimes argued. Even so, three qualifiers to any suggestion of widespread support for the United States should be stressed as well.

First, while Britain again made the choice in 2003 not to challenge the United States on an overriding policy issue, this did not mean that the two sides shared broad agreement about their foreign policy aims. Tony Blair clearly disagreed with George W. Bush on Kyoto, on the International Criminal Court (ICC), and on how to balance relations between Israelis and Palestinians. Much the same considerations applied to the other European leaders who sided with the United States over Iraq, including Silvio Berlusconi in Italy and José María Aznar in Spain. And, like the central and east European governments that similarly supported the Bush administration, these leaders had a tactical motive for supporting the United States as well: to challenge the French and German assumption that these two states could decide the policy of the EU more or less on their own.

Second, except during brief periods (particularly in Britain right after the war started), public opinion in virtually every European country was clearly skeptical about the Bush administration's foreign policy – not only toward Iraq, but in more general terms. This was true even for the central and east European countries. Such a broad European consensus represented something new in transatlantic relations. Not even during the Vietnam War had public attitudes been so universally negative toward Washington.

Finally, the failure to identify weapons of mass destruction after the war caused enormous problems for US allies in western Europe, and in particular for the most crucial ally of all, Tony Blair. For a time, the lack of public support for the war, the missing weapons, and the furious subsequent debate about the Blair government's credibility threatened the very political survival of the prime minister.

What does this all mean? While it is still far too early to draw definitive judgments, I am inclined to believe that these developments signal something new and deeper than the many transatlantic crises that preceded them. I see three primary reasons for concern about the continued close relationship between the United States and western Europe. First, the Cold War is over, and terrorism is not the unifying factor many think. Second, American unilateralism, while always an element of that country's foreign policy, is definitely growing. And, third, attitudes are changing in Europe, particularly in France and Germany, and the EU is slowly but steadily taking on an ever greater role. The combined weight of these three factors has contributed to a proliferation of transatlantic political, economic, and even cultural disputes. Some of these many issues are more divisive than others, but the sum of them is bound to effect significant change.

The net result of these developments – changes in the direction and tenor of US policy, in both the substance and articulation of European interests, and in the global environment that conditions the Atlantic partnership – appears to be, and is likely to remain, a fundamental shift in the character of relations between the United States and western Europe. That shift is from a relationship characterized by periodic crises of high politics toward a greater overall drift and distance between the Alliance partners. But before sketching out the nature of that drift, I briefly remind readers of the problematic nature of the NATO partnership during its supposed heyday.

Always a crisis

During the Cold War, hardly a year passed without a crisis of one sort or another in Atlantic relations.[1] In the aftermath of World War II, there was great confusion about what role the United States would eventually play in Europe. Would Franklin Roosevelt turn out to be another Woodrow Wilson, a president who sought the active involvement of the United States in European politics but who saw his course undercut by the

---

[1] The story of all these crises is told in my book *The United States and Western Europe Since 1945: From "Empire" by Invitation to Transatlantic Drift* (Oxford: Oxford University Press, 2003). See also Philip H. Gordon and Jeremy Shapiro, *Allies at War: America, Europe, and the Crisis over Iraq* (New York: McGraw Hill/Brookings Institution Press, 2004), pp. 19–45.

Senate and the American people? Many European governments, including especially the British, were concerned that Washington would not take a sufficiently active interest in their affairs. And there seemed to be plenty of evidence to vindicate these fears. Anglo-American cooperation in atomic weapons development was quickly ended by the Truman administration once the war was over; the American loan to Britain in 1945–6 was less generous than London had expected; the United States was repatriating its occupation forces from the continent. Only the international crisis in the spring of 1948 made the Truman administration agree to create an Atlantic security organization instead of simply supporting a European system.

On European integration, Washington was pushing hard for as supranational a unit as possible, but it quickly met with disappointment. Under the Marshall Plan, the Europeans refused to integrate their national economies to the extent the Truman administration wanted. On the political side, Britain was firmly opposed to any supranational framework, and France hesitated to take the lead without Britain's involvement. Later, no sooner was NATO created than the crisis over German rearmament erupted. Paris proposed a European army in 1950, only to reject its own initiative four years later. The rearmament question was not solved until 1955, with West Germany's entry into NATO.

During the following year, the United States had a bitter conflict with its two main European allies, Britain and France, over Suez. The fact that Washington forced its two partners to stop their joint invasion of Egypt in mid-track was to cast long shadows over future relations between the three capitals. The British decided that never again would they rebel directly against the United States; the French concluded that they had to rely more on Europe and less on the USA. Beginning soon after Charles de Gaulle's 1958 ascent to power in France, disputes between the United States and France proliferated. The most serious ones occurred in 1963, as discussed by Marc Trachtenberg in this volume (chapter 9), when *le général* said "non" to British membership in the EEC and concluded a German–French treaty that briefly made the Kennedy administration panic and apply rather direct pressure to keep the Germans in their loyal place vis-à-vis the United States; and in 1966, when de Gaulle decided that France should leave NATO's military structure.

Soon the Vietnam War led to considerable tension between Americans and Europeans. *Ostpolitik* likewise created problems, especially between Richard Nixon and Willy Brandt; but the American president was not the only one who felt that the Germans were becoming too independent in their approach to Moscow and the east European capitals. Later, when Nixon and Henry Kissinger themselves began to cooperate intimately with the Kremlin's leadership, many Europeans feared that their détente would go too far. And when Washington tried to mend fences in 1973 with the "Year of Europe" initiative, relations deteriorated even further.

Along came Jimmy Carter with the best of intentions, only to find himself in a bitter dispute with many Europeans over the deployment of the neutron bomb in Europe; the bitterness was particularly pronounced between Carter and German chancellor Helmut Schmidt. Then came the prolonged crisis about the deployment of American intermediate-range nuclear missiles in Europe. Virtually every European leader, including to some extent even Margaret Thatcher, initially found Ronald Reagan just too tough with the Soviets (particularly when he wanted the Europeans to curtail their trade with Moscow); for his part, Reagan was irked when François Mitterrand included the Communists in his 1981 government. Later, when Reagan began his lovefest with Mikhail Gorbachev, the Europeans became concerned that this would go much too far. Thatcher worried that Reagan would undermine the US strategic deterrent; the French feared another Yalta, a division of Europe over the heads of the Europeans, as Paris alleged (incorrectly) had taken place in 1945. When George Bush, Sr., joined forces with Helmut Kohl and the East German people in supporting the rapid unification of Germany, this too led to worries in London and Paris; lacking practical alternatives, however, Thatcher and Mitterrand had to move with the course of events.

If these were the golden years, what would the future hold? Indeed, following the end of the Cold War, tensions continued. During Bill Clinton's tenure in office (which has benefited from some nostalgic retrospection), the Alliance partners faced a host of crises. The two sides of the Atlantic were soon at odds over Bosnia, where the USA's emerging "lift-and-strike" policy differed dramatically from Europe's reluctance to take sides in ex-Yugoslavia's civil wars. No sooner had the allies recovered at Dayton than the Kosovo conflict again threatened unity. As if this were not enough, there were the differences over NATO enlargement, Kyoto and the environment, the ICC, and a host of increasingly complex economic issues. On the question of the "rogue states" of the world – then defined by the United States as including Iran, Iraq, Libya, North Korea, and Cuba – Washington favored coercion and sanctions while Europe argued for engagement and dialogue. Sound familiar?

September 11 prompted a dramatic resurgence of Atlantic cooperation, or at least of expressions thereof. President Jacques Chirac was the first foreign leader to visit Washington and New York after the attacks, and he expressed his "total support" for the United States. *Le Monde*, generally quite skeptical of the United States, declared that "we are all Americans" now. In Germany, Chancellor Gerhard Schröder announced his "unlimited solidarity" with the United States; he indicated that Germany actually expected to be asked for military assistance. In Britain, Prime Minister Tony Blair emphasized that the United Kingdom would cooperate with the United States to the full extent permitted.

This moment of transatlantic solidarity proved fleeting. I have already recounted the broad outlines of its breakdown in the run-up to the 2003 war in Iraq. As for the conflict itself, the war against Saddam Hussein was certainly an impressive demonstration of the revolution in military affairs that had taken place in the United States. But in other ways, the war was considerably less of a triumph. Saddam's downfall was followed by a limited outpouring of support for the United States, but even more by looting, terrorism, and chaos. American casualties have been much higher since George W. Bush declared the end of "major hostilities" on May 1, 2003, than they were during the war. Saddam himself was not caught until eight months after the end of combat operations; more important, the weapons of mass destruction have yet to be found. This last point was especially troubling for Atlantic relations. In Europe, these weapons had been seen as the main reason for the war, although it must be admitted that in the United States the emphasis had been at least equally on "regime change," an objective that was after all achieved.

Leaving aside for a moment the precise differences over the war – which were as vivid within Europe as across the Atlantic – as well as the intense controversies surrounding Iraq's status after the conflict, the question remains whether these developments signal something new and deeper than the many transatlantic crises that preceded them. As suggested earlier, I am inclined to think so. I see three primary reasons for concern about the continued close relationship between the United States and western Europe.

The Cold War's end

First and foremost, the end of the Cold War has reduced NATO's cohesion. Lingering suspicions about Russia and the new challenges faced by the allies are hardly likely to measure up to the old and constant fear about Soviet intentions. David Andrews focuses on this point in his contribution to this volume (chapter 3), and I am inclined to accept the main thrust of his argument. At least in the long run, the traditional momentum working in NATO's favor is likely to peter out.[2]

---

[2] The remainder of this section follows quite closely my argument in *The United States and Western Europe Since 1945*, pp. 281–293. Statements that are documented there will not generally be documented again here.

In fact, NATO's emphasis is already being redefined away from its military side and to more general political functions, and this process has accelerated with the addition of the many new members from central and eastern Europe (see in this regard chapter 10). To exaggerate the point only mildly, NATO could become "an OSCE with an integrated military structure." And this outcome is likely to be reinforced as new generations assume leadership roles on both sides of the Atlantic. Those who matured during and immediately after World War II have already disappeared from the scene; Helmut Kohl was probably the last of that generation. Born in 1930, he fondly recalled that his first dark suit, the one he wore on the night of his prom, had come out of an American CARE package, as had the gown of his future wife. Today the German government is instead dominated by "1968ers" who cut their political teeth in the streets, protesting against *inter alia* the United States. Schröder himself was head of the Social Democrats' youth wing when it still described itself as Marxist, and acted as a defense lawyer to a member of the terrorist Red Army Faction. The Bushes, the Blairs, the Chiracs, and the Schröders of today tend to have less emotional and instead far more coldly pragmatic reasons for supporting (to varying degrees) Atlantic cooperation; yet even they experienced the Cold War and still see that period as the more or less automatic historical backdrop for thinking about international relations. The next generation of leaders will lack even that framework.

Of course, it is possible that terrorism or some other new threat could become as important in holding the two sides of the Atlantic together as the Soviet threat was during the Cold War, although Hubert Zimmermann (chapter 6 in this volume) is more optimistic on this point than I am. Certainly more terrorist incidents in Europe such as the one in Madrid on March 11, 2004, could lead to national responses similar to those seen in the United States after 9/11. So far, however, the responses to terrorism are developing along different lines in the USA and in most of Europe.

Why is this? First, the urgency in fighting terrorism is clearly greater in the United States than in Europe. September 11 remains a huge event in American thinking, a much smaller one in European thought. In fact, several European countries have lived with terrorism for decades. Second, while the United States is emphasizing military means of combating terrorism, most European governments want to address what they see as the political and economic causes of the problem. As Bulgarian political scientist Ivan Krastev has stated, "The Americans feel they are engaged in a war, the Europeans feel they are engaged in preventing one." In fact, the single most disturbing finding for Atlantic cooperation in the flood of polls taken on both sides of the Atlantic during 2002 was probably that a majority of Europeans (55 percent) thought that US policies contributed to the terrorist attacks on New York and Washington, DC.[3] Third, the Bush administration sees the war in Iraq and the war on terrorism as one and the same. In their collective view, there is no war in Iraq; there is only a war against terrorism. Most Europeans see them as separate, and believe that the war in Iraq has actually made the fight against terrorism much more difficult.

Furthermore, while there remains a feeling that the two sides of the Atlantic are facing at least some common threats and vulnerabilities, the sources of these new potential conflicts are for the most part located outside Europe – and hence outside NATO's traditional geographic focus. While NATO's strategy (though not the treaty itself) was redefined in 1999 at Washington's insistence to include the entire "Euro-Atlantic" region, the historical truth remains that it has generally been easier for the Alliance to cooperate on matters close at hand than on those at a distance. Out-of-area missions frequently meant conflict within the Alliance, and Europe has tended to dislike the US focus on non-European crises at least since the Vietnam War. Certainly the substantial transatlantic differences with respect to the Middle East exemplify this problem. Even with regard to Europe's near abroad, that is to say ex-Yugoslavia, Atlantic relations in the early 1990s were very strained until Washington finally took charge and sorted matters out at Dayton.

In any event, the American definition of security is much more absolutist than the European one. Washington wants to eradicate threats many European capitals are prepared to live with, and its vast military arsenal gives Washington options the Europeans quite simply do not have. Most Europeans instead emphasize the options they have at their disposal: diplomatic negotiation and economic instruments.[4] As Zimmermann notes in this volume (chapter 6), this is changing; but it is not changing very quickly. And, as I argue in the following sections, these changes are just as likely to lead to increased transatlantic tensions as to enhanced cooperation.

American unilateralism

A second deep factor affecting the Atlantic relationship is the increasing unilateralism of the United States. Although unilateralism has always

[3] Craig Kennedy and Marshall M. Bouton, "The Real Trans-Atlantic Gap," *Foreign Policy* 133 (November–December 2002), p. 70.

[4] This is the somewhat overstated argument made by Robert Kagan in *Of Paradise and Power: America and Europe in the New World Order* (New York: Knopf, 2003). After all, in the 1990s and in the first decades after 1945 – when it was even stronger in relative terms than today – the United States exercised its options in quite different ways.

been part of US foreign policy, it has definitely been gaining strength in recent years; and the stronger this impulse becomes, the greater the chances of conflict with Washington's European allies.

The reasons for unilateralism's renewed appeal are many. While in some historical periods unilateralism, and particularly its feebler variant, isolationism, has been associated with weakness, in recent years it springs from US strength. The Soviet Union has collapsed; the United States is clearly the world's only military superpower; in the 1990s, the United States witnessed stronger economic growth than any other great power except China (which started from a much lower base); the military triumphs of the Gulf War, ex-Yugoslavia, Afghanistan, and, initially, Iraq finally chased the memories of Vietnam and Somalia away; and so forth. If the twentieth century belonged to the United States, the twenty-first will presumably be even more American.

US military power is indeed colossal. It now spends as much on defense as the rest of the world added together. Americans are clearly willing to spend substantially more on defense than are Europeans. With its vast lead, particularly in the new technologies, the United States is presumably more able to go it alone; with its global concerns, its allies will vary from event to event; and even these temporary partners will have less to offer, at least in purely military terms, and will have difficulty in keeping up with the new US way of warfare.

Still, American unilateralism derives as much from a heightened sense of vulnerability as from relative strength. The United States is uniquely powerful, but now it also feels itself to be uniquely vulnerable. As a result, the Bush administration has reserved to itself the right to strike preemptively against anything that might threaten the USA's rapidly expanding security interests. Indeed, this new security doctrine aims rather more at prevention than preemption, since Saddam was clearly not about to strike out directly against the United States.[5] Thus the heightened sense of vulnerability after September 11 may help the United States to appreciate allies, but also drives it to dominate them. This is reinforced by a political culture that "seems to see security as a series of zero-sum absolutes: one either has it or one does not."[6] Presumably, missile defense and the prosecution of the war against terrorism will restore US security; Europeans, with their entirely different

---

[5] Arthur Schlesinger, Jr., "Eyeless in Iraq," *New York Review of Books*, October 23, 2003, pp. 24–27.

[6] Julian Lindley-French, *Terms of Engagement: The Paradox of American Power and the Transatlantic Dilemma Post-11 September* (Paris: Chaillot Papers, European Union Institute for Security Studies, May 2002), pp. 27–31, 77–78. The quotation is from p. 77.

geography and history, find such an ambition difficult to grasp. They have never felt really secure; they never controlled their surroundings in the way that Americans did.

At the same time, terrorism is only the newest and most dramatic example of the fact that globalization has finally begun to challenge the sovereignty even of the United States. The outside world is intruding more and more on the United States, in a variety of ways. Economically, the United States is much more dependent on exports and imports than it used to be, and new organizations such as the World Trade Organization (WTO) have more "bite" than their predecessors. Similar developments are taking place in the environmental and cultural fields. Congress and the American public often respond negatively to these encroachments, thus strengthening the unilateralist impulse still further. All kinds of international conferences are held in which measures are adopted that the United States has to address, but it cannot impose its own views in such meetings. Many Americans find it puzzling that the United States is voted down in many international forums when it is so powerful and despite the fact that, as most Americans automatically assume, its intentions are so good. The result is an increasing sense of frustration.

A related but different point has been the US swing to the right. As Miles Kahler points out in this volume (chapter 4), the particular strength of recent American unilateralism obviously has had much to do with the Republican control of Congress since 1994 and of the presidency since 2000. As these leaders saw it, Bill Clinton had sacrificed the USA's true interests at the multilateralist altar; now US power was to be used to pursue US interests, presumably different from those of the rest of the world. While the American public may not necessarily be so unilateralist in orientation, it is simply not particularly interested in foreign policy. Gone are the leaders in Congress who took a strong interest in foreign affairs, often in a spirit of bipartisanship; the new leaders are generally more partisan and have their eyes sharply focused on domestic matters.[7]

It is difficult to predict what course the renewed American unilateralist impulse will assume in the future. Iraq threatens to revive the specter of Vietnam; on the other hand, the United States could simply come to see that a variety of global concerns, terrorism being perhaps the most prominent, require broad international cooperation and hence a fair amount of give-and-take. Certainly if the United States is to lead effectively, it must reorient itself toward the global community and not automatically

---

[7] For a study underlining the moderate nature of American public opinion, see Steven Kull and I. M. Destler, *Misreading the Public: The Myth of a New Isolationism* (Washington, DC: Brookings Institution Press, 1999), as well as chapter 4 in the present volume.

assume that the American standard is the world standard.[8] But, at the moment, basic trends still appear to point in the opposite direction. The United States is likely to remain "number one" among powers, it will be increasingly influenced by global forces to which many of its citizens will respond negatively, and domestic considerations will probably continue to take precedence over foreign policy issues for both political leaders and voters. If so – if the United States is to ignore the principled concerns of the rest of the world – this will dramatically reduce its international legitimacy. Such a development would, in fact, make it a more traditional imperial power, and no longer the special "empire by invitation" of my earlier accounts.[9]

On the other hand, it is important not to present an unbalanced analysis. Despite all the shifts outlined above, Americans and Europeans continue to like each other. When Americans are asked to measure the depth of their positive feelings toward various countries, the leading European countries (with the exception of France) still come out significantly higher than countries in any other part of the world, save only Canada. For their part, Europeans are definitely much more skeptical of the United States than before, but continue to express warm feelings toward Americans if not toward the Bush administration.[10] Importantly, the climate of German–American relations has improved since the war in Iraq, and it may improve further. Italy's generally positive orientation toward the United States has deep foundations quite independent of security considerations, as Leopoldo Nuti demonstrates in this volume (chapter 8). And finally the central and east Europeans, who will steadily count for more in European politics, are bound to be relatively sympathetic to the United States. After decades under Soviet domination, they are eager for all forms of cooperation with the United States – military, economic, and cultural.

These are important offsetting factors. But even in unison they will tend to mitigate the central tendency, not to reverse it. And that central tendency is for American political leadership to be more responsive to the unilateralist impulse now than was the case for the previous half-century.

---

[8] See for instance Joseph S. Nye, Jr., *The Paradox of American Power: Why the World's Only Superpower Can't Go It Alone* (Oxford: Oxford University Press, 2002).

[9] Andrew J. Bacevich, *American Empire: The Realities and Consequences of US Diplomacy* (Cambridge: Harvard University Press, 2002). For my own views, in addition to *The United States and Western Europe Since 1945*, see particularly my book *The American "Empire"* (Oxford: Oxford University Press, 1990).

[10] Kennedy and Bouton, "The Real Trans-Atlantic Gap," p. 68; Meg Bortin, "European Distrust of US Role Sharpens," *International Herald Tribune*, March 17, 2004.

European political change

The final source of deep change in the Atlantic relationship has been on the European side. These changes emanate primarily from three sources: France, Germany, and the EU itself.

Under the deep layers of French nationalist rhetoric, it is easy to forget that since 1919 France has more or less consistently sought a security guarantee from the United States – first against Germany, then against the Soviet Union. After World War I, the guarantee disappeared with the Senate's rejection of US membership in the League of Nations. After World War II, Paris got its guarantee in multilateral form, with NATO. During the Cold War, de Gaulle in particular wanted to limit American influence on developments in Europe, but even *le général* favored the American nuclear guarantee and a US troop presence in Europe (although not in France itself). In times of crisis, France therefore virtually always ended up supporting the United States. Now, with France leading the opposition to the United States, this long historical line seems to have come to an end; Georges-Henri Soutou's contribution to this volume (chapter 5) underlines this point.

Similarly, during the Cold War, the massive Soviet troop presence in East Germany made Bonn's support for the American security guarantee virtually automatic. Germany's slowly growing assertiveness would have been limited by the underlying need to have the Americans in place in case anything dramatic happened on the security front. But now Germany is united, it is on good terms with all its many neighbors, the Russian troops are back in Russia, and Germany's freedom of action has increased dramatically. And, over Iraq, Germany used this freedom to side decisively with Paris against Washington. Thus, another long-term historical line has come to an end.

On the European side more generally, the regional integration process is progressing steadily if often slowly. This process has always been driven to a very considerable extent by France and Germany. Historically, the EU has been able to combine "widening" and "deepening." It has increased its membership (or widened) from the EEC of the Six to the EC of the Nine, and then of the Twelve, to the EU of Fifteen; in spring 2004, it was joined by an additional ten new members. It has at the same time expanded the number and depth of European functions (or deepened) by evolving from the Coal and Steel Community to the Treaties of Rome, to the Single Market, to the single currency and the European Security and Defence Policy. The progress in the last decade on both fronts, widening and deepening, has been particularly impressive. The pattern has often been the same: ambitious goals were established, goals that many felt were in fact too ambitious, but that were still largely reached if not by all then certainly by most of the EU's members.

That said, the EU has far to go before it will have developed a genuinely common foreign and defense policy. Beneath the constant meetings and consultations, there are still widely diverging national interests that were on full display in the different responses to the situation over Iraq. Still, European mechanisms are slowly being developed and national interests gradually redefined. A common foreign economic policy has long been in existence; increasingly, development assistance is also coordinated (and together the EU countries are by far the world's leading foreign aid donor). Not only humanitarian assistance but also crisis management and peace-keeping, the so-called Petersberg tasks, are becoming EU matters. Slowly the EU is beginning to take on even more difficult security tasks, as we have most recently seen in Macedonia, the Democratic Republic of Congo, and Bosnia.

Many impatient people, such as Americans and journalists, have made a habit of underestimating the force of European integration, since progress has tended to be so slow and has been accompanied by so many acrimonious meetings. If and when the EU is able to develop a truly common foreign and defense policy, however, it is bound to change the US–EU relationship dramatically. The EU already has a population that is one hundred and fifty million larger, and a gross national product somewhat larger, than that of the United States (depending particularly on how one accounts for exchange rates). Despite the EU's problems in working out its proposed new constitution, in the end it will undoubtedly strengthen the EU's supranational nature in many fields and improve coordination even in foreign and security policy. In fact, if the Europeans really accepted the American exhortations about even modestly increasing their military capabilities, this could come to mean that there would be little or no need for American forces in Europe. And this is not to mention what would happen if the EU countries developed a military strength commensurate with their economic position.

But these are big "ifs." The EU has shown great willingness to develop the institutions necessary for a common security policy; less progress has been made on the substance of such a policy, and particularly on the means to carry it out. The conflict over Iraq has shown how deep the rift is between Britain and the Atlantic-oriented members of the EU on the one side, and France, Germany, and their supporters on the other: the EU's governments were divided right down the middle on this critical question.

The crucial issue in this regard remains how willing the EU countries will be to develop their defensive capabilities. In the late 1980s and early 1990s, defense expenditures in Europe actually fell at a slower rate than in the United States, but compared with the European objective of a more independent defense this was still not very satisfactory. When defense expenditures rose sharply in the United States after 1997 and particularly after September 11, while most European countries showed little sign of reversing their declining expenditures, the Europeans became in some ways more rather than less dependent on the United States. This was certainly the lesson of the wars in ex-Yugoslavia and in Afghanistan. In several crucial fields of warfare, the Europeans still rely almost entirely on the United States.

It is true that the necessary increase in defense spending would be somewhat smaller if the national armed forces of the EU members were indeed integrated. But, again, while there is definitely movement in this direction, the process is slow. With the EU countries feeling a continued need for some 100,000 US troops in Europe, European independence in foreign policy is bound to be limited. Plainly, the Europeans have at least so far found it easier to continue their reliance on the United States than to increase their own defense budgets.

What, then, is happening to the European "invitations" for the United States to play a leading role in European security affairs – invitations that have played such a prominent part in Atlantic relations until the present?[11] The Europeans clearly do not want any dramatic reduction in the American position and are afraid of the repercussions of any significant weakening in the American military role. Thus, when the US military suggested that they reduce the number of troops in Europe substantially and move many of the remaining ones from Germany to eastern Europe, the German government reacted negatively and saw this as punishment for its stand on Iraq.[12] American investment in the troubled economies of Europe is still highly desired, as are most aspects of American popular culture.

Nevertheless, the emphasis is now definitely on what the Europeans can and must do for themselves, not what the Americans can do for them. Comfortable majorities in European countries want the EU to become a superpower like the United States, although one generally cooperating with the latter.[13] In fact, some argue (particularly in the United States) that the Europeans have been so busy organizing themselves that they are

---

[11] My original article on this topic was "Empire by Invitation? The United States and Western Europe, 1945–1952," *Journal of Peace Research* 23:3 (1986), pp. 263–277. See also my "'Empire by Invitation' in the American Century," *Diplomatic History* 23:2 (Spring 1999), pp. 189–217.

[12] Michael R. Gordon, "US Weighs Cutback in Forces in Germany," *International Herald Tribune*, June 4, 2004.

[13] Kennedy and Bouton, "The Real Trans-Atlantic Gap," pp. 68, 70.

unable to give the outside world the attention that its many problems deserve. European governments understand that they have to cooperate much more closely if the EU is to develop a credible foreign policy. With Paris and to some extent Berlin in the lead, these governments are defining "Europe" more and more as an alternative to the United States. Tony Blair obviously views the situation differently but, as the prime minister himself has pointed out, "Europe's citizens need Europe to be strong and united. They need it to be a power in the world. Whatever its origin, Europe today is no longer just about peace. It is about projecting collective power."[14] For Blair and for his successor (from whatever party), pressing forward with this European agenda while maintaining the United Kingdom's close collaboration with the United States will be a real challenge; William Wallace and Tim Oliver express their doubts in their contribution to this volume (chapter 7).

But even if the concrete new contributions of the EU have been meager and the Europeans remain badly divided, the integration process has already started to influence security policy at the margins – and this process will likely continue. The constant meetings on foreign and security policies, even if held in part to paper over the disagreements over Iraq, will probably end up shifting the focus somewhat away from Atlantic and toward European cooperation. France and Germany will not be able to impose their will in these forums, but neither will Britain and its supporters. Instead, a compromise will eventually emerge.

The proliferation of disputes

The new climate between the United States and western Europe has led to a proliferation of economic and even cultural disputes, which have in turn soured political relations still further. True, there have almost always been economic disputes between the United States and various European countries. But, with the end of the Cold War and the globalization of the world economy, such disputes have taken on added prominence and importance. During the Cold War, political-military considerations almost always took precedence over economic ones; that is unlikely to remain the case. Meanwhile, globalization increases the number of potential conflicts dramatically, as we can see from the flood of issues both large and small. US steel duties are but a single example: the Bush administration, though claiming to be strongly in favor of free trade,

---

[14] Quoted from Charles A. Kupchan, "The Rise of Europe, America's Changing Internationalism, and the End of US Primacy," *Political Science Quarterly* 118:2 (Summer 2003), p. 211; Bortin, "European Distrust of US Role Sharpens."

imposed restrictions on foreign steel for the most blatantly obvious electoral reasons. The result was howls of protests from all corners of the world. Meanwhile, agriculture remains the most contentious economic issue on both sides of the Atlantic. As the saying goes, "all politics is local," and agricultural interests have deep local political organizations.

With globalization bringing so much change, the protection of jobs has become a crucial concern for voters in most countries. Globalization wipes out the traditional separation between foreign and domestic matters; consider legislation on tax, competition (anti-trust), and environmental policy. Many Europeans now see globalization as synonymous with Americanization, and they do not like it – particularly in France. But many Americans are also responding negatively. Though still somewhat less affected by globalization, Americans are also less accustomed to foreigners intruding in their affairs. For many, it is simply not acceptable that various international institutions – the WTO, the ICC, or the Kyoto Protocol, for example – should determine the actions of the United States.

Nevertheless, if there ever were a time when an Atlantic economic community existed, that would seem to be today. The economies of the United States and Europe are so inextricably linked that permitting economic disputes to grow out of control would be extremely costly; note for example that Washington eventually dropped the steel duties. Exports between the United States and the European Union are also much more balanced than is the case of American trade with China and Japan, with which the United States runs large and (to many Americans) irritating deficits. And investment is even more important than trade. Here, in relations with nearly every west European country, the value of American exports is far surpassed by the sales of American affiliates based within that country. In 1998, US affiliate sales from Britain amounted to US$224 billion, compared to US$39 billion in goods exported to Britain – a ratio of almost six to one. Overall, the many American companies doing business in Europe represent 50 percent of total US affiliate sales.[15]

It is difficult to assess how the proliferation of economic disputes balances against the undoubted fact that the United States and the European Union are becoming more and more economically dependent on each other. Judging from the media and political chatter, conflict predominates; but for political and business leaders the calculations must be far more complex. Still, the general downturn in the economy in the United States and western Europe that took place in 2001–2 threatened Atlantic relations by strengthening protectionism and making

[15] Joseph Quinlan and Marc Chandler, "The US Trade Deficit: A Dangerous Obsession," *Foreign Affairs* 80:3 (May–June 2001), pp. 87–97, particularly pp. 94–95.

the necessary free trade compromises more difficult. The eventual outcome of the WTO's Doha Round will be a very important indicator in this context. With strengthened economies, particularly in the United States, there is renewed optimism about the negotiations.

Traditionally, culture has been a field of transatlantic cooperation. And although the impact of American cultural hegemony has not resulted in Europeans becoming Americans, they have become somewhat more like Americans than they were in the past. This can easily be seen in many areas: cinema, television, popular music, literature, clothing, etc. More and more the English language has become the *lingua franca*, first for scientists, then for tourists and people more generally. Today even some of France's biggest corporations are using English as their business language.[16]

But a deep split is developing even in this area of traditional cooperation between the United States and western Europe. Now, rather suddenly, Americans are increasingly blamed by Europeans not for what they do, but for who they are. The United States is alleged to be morally retrograde for failing to respect international law abroad (as Trachtenberg laments in chapter 9 of this volume), for practicing the death penalty at home, for its sometimes violent opposition to abortion, and for a gun culture that most Europeans find senseless. The country is likewise castigated as socially retrograde for its neglect of the poor, the inner cities, and public infrastructure. It is supposedly culturally retrograde as it "gorges itself on fatty fast food, wallows in tawdry mass entertainment, starves the arts and prays only to one God, which is Mammon."[17] In opposition to all this stands Europe, with its alleged tolerance, sense of community, taste, and manners.

Obviously, much of this is caricature. Unemployment is still almost twice as high in major European countries as in the United States; most of the vulgar new television concepts sweeping the airwaves have been developed in Europe, not in the United States; and, although the European television industry and to some extent even national movie industries are becoming stronger, American popular culture remains on average as popular in Europe as a whole as it has ever been. Even American high culture, ranging from its world-leading universities to its literature and music, remains very strong. So the pat American response to these criticisms is obvious: if Europe is so superior, why then is it so

---

[16] For a good historical account of cultural relations, see Richard Pells, *Not Like Us: How Europeans Have Loved, Hated and Transformed American Culture Since World War II* (New York: Basic Books, 1997).

[17] Josef Joffe, "Who's Afraid of Mr. Big?," *The National Interest* 64 (Summer 2001), p. 44.

dependent on the United States for everything from its security and economic well-being to its cultural activities?

The point is not who will win this fruitless debate, but that Europeans and Americans appear to be moving apart even culturally. And, in the long run, public opinion on these and related issues will matter. Returning to high politics, there have been several instances in the past when public opinion in one or more European countries was skeptical of US policies; but now public opinion in every European country, however pro-American its government, is deeply mistrustful of the administration in Washington. Such a situation has not existed before; it will likely have serious ramifications for the future.

Still, on the whole, the United States and western Europe remain closely bound together, even in cultural terms. Compared to the differences with most of the rest of the world, it could even be argued that one common Atlantic culture exists, characterized by democracy, relatively free markets, Christianity (at least residually), and a high-consumption popular culture. Whether these ties will be sufficient to bind the Atlantic partners together as their perceptions of self-interest drift apart remains to be seen.

The more distant future

If history repeated itself, historians would be experts not only of the past but of the future as well. But history does not really repeat itself; only historians do. While the central trends I have identified are generally negative for the transatlantic relationship, there are additional counterbalancing factors beyond those I have enumerated. Thus, were I to hazard a guess for the more distant future, I would certainly not be predicting any direct confrontation between the United States and western Europe as a whole. Instead, what seems more likely is an extensive political conflict between the United States and some European countries, accompanied by a more general slow drifting apart of the two continents. The two sides of the Atlantic are just not as important to each other as they were during the Cold War, particularly in military terms. And they are considerably farther apart on many of the crucial issues of the post-Cold War world.

However gradually, the EU is growing closer together, even in its foreign and security policies. Again, France will most likely continue to emphasize Europe's institutional autonomy and Britain increased European capabilities, but slowly the EU is improving its defense coordination. Despite NATO's continuing predominance, this is bound to have significant long-term consequences.

The Atlantic structure has proved remarkably resilient and long-lasting. Recall that Eisenhower always insisted that the American troops in Europe were there on a "temporary or emergency" basis. As the supreme commander of NATO, he frequently expressed the hope that they would go home in three to four years.[18] In this sense NATO and the American troop commitment have already lasted much longer than anyone could have expected in the early years of the Cold War. But nothing lasts forever, and the changes in Atlantic cooperation in the past decade have been dramatic, particularly during the past few years.

While the economic and to a much lesser extent the military balance between the two sides of the Atlantic have changed dramatically since the Atlantic system was set up, the overall relationship has never really been redefined. Consider first the changes in the two sides' structural positions. In 1945, the United States was producing almost as much as the rest of the world added together; now the EU is producing as much as the United States. In 1945 the United States was the world's largest creditor; now it is running increasingly bigger balance-of-payments deficits. While the EU is still dependent on the United States militarily, with the Cold War over, this dependence is seen as less significant than it used to be. Now the EU countries are preparing, however slowly, to take on new tasks that will reduce their dependence still further.

Repeated attempts have been made to redefine the Atlantic relationship to reflect these changing realities, most explicitly by Kennedy, Kissinger, and George Bush, Sr. In each case, the point of these efforts was always that, in return for greater influence, the Europeans should be paying more toward the common defense. These efforts never met with any more than limited success, although in fact events were moving in the desired direction anyway. The Europeans *were* becoming more influential and they *were* paying somewhat more, at least in a long-term perspective. Yet it could be argued that, as far as the basic situation is concerned, little has actually changed. Indeed, the Bush administration has insisted on a leadership role for the United States that is even more explicit than it was during the Cold War.

Sooner or later, there has to be a true redefinition of the American–European relationship. This will be difficult since the United States has never had a truly balanced relationship with western Europe. Under isolationism, the United States stayed away; it feared that the New World would inevitably be corrupted by the Old. For years after World War II, the United States was so strong that it did not need to worry about

---

[18] Stephen E. Ambrose, *Eisenhower: The President* (New York: Simon & Schuster, 1984), pp. 143–144.

being unduly influenced by the Europeans; influence went almost entirely in the other direction. Even in the more balanced state of affairs today, the USA remains the undisputed leader: it is impossible for Europe to be equal to the United States as long as it remains militarily dependent on the latter. Still, the need to define a new basis for Atlantic cooperation is rising, as several of the chapters in this volume discuss.

The jury is still out on whether the United States and western Europe are capable of a truly balanced relationship. While many have argued that a balanced relationship will be more harmonious than the existing one, there would seem to be good reason to doubt this. Slowly the day is approaching, however, when we will find out. In the many decades when the United States pushed hard for European integration, it was always assumed that this integration would take place within an Atlantic framework, which was really code for continued American leadership; Washington never favored an independent European third force in international relations, alongside the United States and the Soviet Union.[19] A stronger EU would presumably have no need for American troops in Europe; once they had left, this would have significant consequences for the relationship between the two sides of the Atlantic. Indeed, such a development might strike even at Washington's relationship with its favorite Atlantic partner, London. After all, Anglo-American relations became "special" only when, after 1945, Britain became so clearly inferior to the United States; before 1940, when Britain was relatively much stronger than it has been since, there was no special relationship.[20]

But despite the continued weakening of Atlantic ties, most likely there will be limits to future transatlantic conflict and the drifting apart of Europe and the United States. NATO, the preeminent symbol of Atlantic cooperation, is likely to survive, although in much modified form compared with the Cold War years. From Washington's point of view, especially given NATO's new and more global orientation, the organization remains useful, for instance in its significant role in postwar Afghanistan. Even more important, NATO has been the USA's primary instrument for taking charge in Atlantic affairs. The EU is really the only power that, in the foreseeable future, could challenge the United States for the top position in international affairs; it would therefore be self-defeating for the Bush or any other administration to abandon such a useful instrument, particularly when there is nothing to take NATO's

---

[19] Lundestad, *The United States and Western Europe Since 1945*, pp. 77–86; but compare Marc Trachtenberg's analysis in this volume, chapter 9.

[20] See Robert Skidelsky, "Imbalance of Power," *Foreign Policy* 129 (March–April 2002), pp. 46–55, and also chapter 7 in the present volume.

place. We have already seen how the American position was weakened by the struggle with France and Germany; a deeper and more lasting falling-out with the entire EU would obviously have even more dramatic consequences for the position of the United States in the world.

Nor are the key European powers likely to abandon NATO completely. It is possible that France has now abandoned its policy, going all the way back to 1919, of wanting guarantees from the United States for its protection; certainly Paris's on-again, off-again desire to lead the fight for a multipolar world suggests that it has. Yet even France probably has no desire to make NATO disappear entirely. Germany definitely does not: Berlin has even made it abundantly clear that it does not want the American troops in Germany to leave the country, for a variety of military, political, and economic reasons. Indeed, most European countries in NATO and in the EU still want a firm link to the United States.

Thus, while the relationship between the two sides of the Atlantic has cooled considerably, it is simply not possible to unite Europe in a policy of confrontation with the United States. Too many countries are too dependent upon the United States government, and have too much residual respect for its people, for that to occur. A more united Europe will therefore have to maintain fairly close ties with the United States; a more divided Europe will mean that at least some European countries will be maintaining even closer ties with Washington. Either way, some continuation of present arrangements seems likely. But the golden years of Atlantic cooperation – although never as golden as now presumed – are gone forever.

2 The dynamics of the feud over Iraq

Elizabeth Pond

The feud that erupted in late 2002 and early 2003 over war in Iraq was the worst US–European crisis in half a century. The scale of the confrontation was wide, the polemics vitriolic, and the associated ill-will deep. The clash was a real test of the new Pax Americana and the new hegemonic style of the Bush administration. Indeed, that style itself was the biggest single variable in the schism. The neoconservative policy shift after 9/11 transformed the United States from being the guarantor of the status quo, its traditional role, into a revolutionary power and supplanted the USA's collaborative Cold War leadership with a more muscular, unilateral, and crusading exercise of hegemony.[1] Both the shape and substance of American foreign policy during the run-up to the war alienated many of Washington's traditional allies and helped undermine support for the United States among European governments and publics alike.

The preceding chapter, by Geir Lundestad, outlines the broad context of these developments. The immediate background included a wide variety of mutually reinforcing transatlantic policy disputes and increasingly acrimonious claims about US and European identities. Muscular Americans mocked craven Europeans[2] and objected strenuously to what they saw as a surge in anti-Americanism, anti-Semitism, ingratitude, and disloyalty in Europe.[3] Conversely, the European political class felt

---

[1] See Ivo H. Daalder and James M. Lindsay, *America Unbound: The Bush Revolution in Foreign Policy* (Washington, DC: Brookings Institution Press, 2003); Robert J. Art, *A Grand Strategy for America* (Ithaca: Cornell University Press, 2003); and Lawrence F. Kaplan and William Kristol, *The War over Iraq: Saddam's Tyranny and America's Mission* (San Francisco: Encounter Books, 2003).

[2] Most famously Robert Kagan, in his seminal essay on "Power and Weakness" in *Policy Review* 113 (June–July 2002, http://www.policyreview.org/JUN02/kagan.html, accessed June 2004); but see also Seymour Martin Lipset, *American Exceptionalism* (New York: W. W. Norton, 1996), and Walter Russell Mead, *Special Providence: American Foreign Policy and How It Changed the World* (New York: Century Foundation, 2002), for interesting variants.

[3] E.g., Charles Krauthammer, "Europe and 'Those People,'" *Washington Post*, April 26, 2002; George F. Will, "'Final Solution,' Phase 2," *Washington Post*, May 2, 2002; Thomas

degraded by the sheer contempt for Europe it encountered in the administration of George W. Bush.[4]

Still, but for the catalyst of 9/11 and the subsequent American determination to attack Iraq, it is possible that US and European authorities might have accommodated their growing differences without real crisis. The destruction of the World Trade Center towers on September 11, 2001, by al Qaeda suicide militants, however, and the never-solved anthrax attacks that followed, shattered Americans' assumption of US invulnerability and left the superpower with a sense of unbearable threat not shared by most Europeans.[5] Hence the analysis that follows begins with 9/11, and the long trail that eventually led not only to war in Iraq but also to rupture within the Atlantic alliance.[6]

L. Friedman, "Nine Wars Too Many," *New York Times*, May 15, 2002; William Safire, "The German Problem," *New York Times*, September 19, 2002; Michael Ledeen, "A Theory/What If There's Method to the Franco-German Madness?," *National Review*, March 11, 2003; and Ralph Peters, "Hitler war wenigstens ehrlich" [Hitler Was At Least Honest], *Frankfurter Allgemeine Zeitung*, May 15, 2003. Refutations of the charges of anti-Semitism may be found in Michael Lind, "The Israel Lobby," *Prospect* 73 (April 2002), pp. 22–29; Antony Lerman, "Sense on Antisemitism," *Prospect* 77 (August 2002), pp. 34–39; John Lloyd, "Rowing Alone," *Financial Times*, August 3, 2002, and "Sign of Life from the Past?," *Financial Times*, November 16, 2002; Linda Grant, "America's Liberal Jews," *Prospect* 84 (March 2003), pp. 52–54; Tony Judt, "The Way We Live Now," *New York Review of Books*, March 27, 2003, pp. 6–10; Anatol Lieven, "Speaking Up," *Prospect* 86 (May 2003), pp. 24–27; and Michael Brenner, "Juden und Normalität" [Jews and Normality], *Süddeutsche Zeitung*, August 14, 2003.

[4] Timothy Garton Ash, "Anti-Europeanism in America," *New York Review of Books*, February 13, 2003, pp. 32–34; and Richard Lambert, "Misunderstanding Each Other," *Foreign Affairs* 82:2 (March–April 2003), pp. 62–74. On the sense of European identity, at least among European elites, see Robert Cooper, *The Post-Modern State and the World Order* (London: Demos, 1996), written when he was still a senior British diplomat. Now, as the director-general of the staff of Javier Solana, the EU's high representative for foreign policy, he has developed his analysis further in *The Breaking of Nations: Order and Chaos in the Twenty-First Century* (London: Atlantic, 2003).

[5] Compare Francis Fukuyama, "Has History Restarted Since September 11?" (John Bonython Lecture at the Centre for Independent Studies, Melbourne, Australia, August 8, 2002), with Pierre Hassner, "The United States: The Empire of Force or the Force of Empire?" (Paris: Chaillot Paper 54, European Union Institute for Security Studies, September 2002), www.iss-eu.org, and Hassner, "Friendly Questions to America the Powerful," *In the National Interest* 1:2 (Fall 2002), www.inthenationalinterest.com/.

[6] For a more detailed exploration, see my *Friendly Fire: The Near Death of the Transatlantic Alliance* (Washington, DC: Brookings Institution Press, 2004); and also Philip H. Gordon and Jeremy Shapiro, *Allies at War: America, Europe, and the Crisis over Iraq* (New York: McGraw-Hill/Brookings Institution Press, 2004). For indications of the American souring on the Iraq War and the Arab world's souring on the United States, see "Collateral Damage," *Time*, May 24, 2004, pp. 24–28; and "Moubarak: les Américains häis dans le monde arabe," *Le Monde*, April 21, 2004.

9/11 and the war in Afghanistan

Immediately after 9/11 there was a groundswell of European sympathy for the United States. *Le Monde* proclaimed, "Nous sommes tous américains."[7] NATO invoked its Article 5 for the first time ever to declare this attack on the United States an attack on all Alliance members. Some 200,000 Germans gathered spontaneously at the Brandenburg Gate for a pro-American rally. In the Bundestag, Chancellor Gerhard Schröder pledged "unlimited solidarity" with the United States, then risked his post on a vote of confidence to carry the war-averse Germans further than ever before in military engagement to send Special Forces to help the US operation in Afghanistan. The German Embassy in Washington established a fund to aid 9/11 victims, expecting to collect several tens of thousands of dollars – and was overwhelmed by the $42 million that poured in. And the Bundesnachrichtendienst swiftly provided its counterpart Central Intelligence Agency with the clue that led to the arrest of the alleged "twentieth hijacker," Zacarias Moussaoui.[8] Berlin's reaction was especially important, not only because today's Germans resemble Americans more than do any other Europeans, but also because Bonn/Berlin had for half a century been the quiet intermediary between the United States and an often anti-American France.

Along with this wave of very human pro-American emotion, there was strong political support for the initial policy responses of the Bush administration. European governments viewed American pressure on Pakistan as necessary to force Islamabad to stop harboring al Qaeda networks and promoting Wahhabi *madrasas* that preached hatred of the West. They also appreciated Washington's warding off of a nuclear confrontation between Pakistan and India over Kashmir. They welcomed too Bush's restraint in resisting both the notion of a Christian–Islamic clash of civilizations and the war on Saddam Hussein that administration hardliners were already promoting, without any proof of Iraqi collusion with al Qaeda or possession of nuclear weapons.[9] They were relieved by what they interpreted, despite Washington's rebuff to NATO's offers of help,

---

[7] September 13, 2001, p. 1.

[8] The downside for bilateral relations was that Americans lost no time in blaming the Germans for not having broken up the al Qaeda cell in Hamburg that many of the suicide hijackers came from. The German retort that the United States had allowed the inconspicuous Hamburg cell members to take very conspicuous and suspicious pilot training in the United States hardly succeeded in deflecting the accusation.

[9] News spread quickly that President Bush had rebuked Deputy Secretary of Defense Paul Wolfowitz for advocating war on Iraq out of turn at the first Camp David war council after 9/11 once this was reported by Bob Woodward, *Bush at War* (New York: Simon & Schuster, 2002), pp. 84–85. What took much longer to seep out of the highly secretive

as a return from unilateralism to multilateralism in efforts to build a large anti-terror coalition much as President George Bush, Sr., had done in his Gulf War a decade earlier. The European governments' only objection to the American military campaign in Afghanistan was that they were allowed only a minor role in it.[10]

Above all, at this fraught moment, Europeans accepted and even craved US leadership, as they had for the previous half-century. If the United States did not lead, no one did in the community of industrialized democracies. As the Cold War axiom had it, the Europeans loved to be led by the United States – in the direction the Europeans wanted to go. In late 2001, they thought, Bush was taking them in the direction they wanted to go.

To be sure, Europeans already had misgivings about Bush's black-and-white views and seeming certitude that he was sent by God to lead the United States in its time of need, about the almost exclusive reliance of the administration on military countermeasures, and about its zealous guardianship of Washington's monopoly on determining how to vanquish evil. Almost more distressing to the Europeans, however, was their own disarray in the crisis. Instead of rallying to forge their much-vaunted Common Foreign and Security Policy (CFSP), Prime Minister Tony Blair of Britain rejuvenated the old Anglo-Saxon special relationship, while other European leaders elbowed each other to win their own individual invitations to Crawford, Texas.

The long road to Baghdad

It was at the beginning of 2002 that transatlantic relations deteriorated palpably.[11] From the European point of view, the triggers of the quarrels

administration was Vice President Dick Cheney's early fixation on invading Iraq and the administration's subordination of the war on terror to this priority, to the extent of diverting scarce commandos and other resources from the search for Osama bin Laden in Afghanistan to Iraq. See Woodward, *Plan of Attack* (New York: Simon & Schuster, 2004); Richard A. Clarke, *Against All Enemies* (New York: Free Press, 2004); and Seymour Hersh, "The Gray Zone,"*New Yorker*, May 24, 2004, http://www.newyorker.com/fact/content/?040524fa_fact.

[10] The United States did permit a NATO task force to monitor the Horn of Africa, let five NATO AWACS surveillance aircraft patrol American skies to free their US equivalents for duty in Asia, and also took on some allies' Special Forces and marines to join in Operation Enduring Freedom in Afghanistan. NATO allies wanted to do much more, but Washington, rating its allies' military capacities as far inferior to its own, rebuffed them and furthermore made it clear that allied participation would not win a policy voice for contributors.

[11] The bulk of the account that follows is based on the author's background interviews with sixty-nine senior officials of Germany, France, Britain, the United States, the EU, Poland, Canada, NATO, and other organizations. A full list of these sources is available from the author upon request.

were Bush's State of the Union address at the end of January and Deputy Secretary of Defense Paul Wolfowitz's conduct at the blue-ribbon Munich Security Conference in early February. From the American point of view, the triggers were European dissent from American leadership and a surge of anti-Americanism and anti-Semitism in Europe, as North African immigrants in France in particular desecrated Jewish synagogues and memorials.

For US allies, the most dismaying elements in Bush's State of the Union address were its downgrading of Europeans as not even worthy of mention, and the lumping together of Iraq, North Korea, and Iran as an "axis of evil."[12] The speech presaged possible American attacks not only on Iraq, but also on Iran, a country the Europeans had been cultivating in an effort to support its many young would-be reformers, modernizers, and liberalizers. Treating Tehran as a pariah, they feared, would only strengthen the hardline ayatollahs.

The most dismaying element for Europeans in Wolfowitz's performance in Munich was his emphatic repetition of Secretary of Defense Donald Rumsfeld's admonition that from then on the mission would determine the coalition in any American military operation, not vice versa. The clear message, as the deputy secretary authoritatively lectured the NATO defense ministers above his rank, was that the transatlantic alliance they had come to think of as immutable was, for Washington, expendable. It could and now would be replaced by *ad hoc* assemblies of American subordinates.

On Iraq, Americans and Europeans agreed that President Saddam Hussein was an oppressor of Iraqis and a would-be megalomaniac threat to his regional neighbors. Europeans thought, however, that, in the dozen years since he had been pushed out of Kuwait, Hussein had been effectively contained by United Nations embargos and enforcement of Iraqi no-fly zones by American and British planes – and had been successfully prevented from acquiring nuclear weapons or again firing chemical weapons on enemies in a repetition of his barbarity in the 1980s. Nor, despite their pleas for such information, were the Europeans given any evidence by the United States of a link between Iraq and terrorists. They therefore saw no urgency in running the high risks of unintended consequences in invading Iraq. Their own intelligence, and what they saw of US intelligence, seemed to indicate that, while Baghdad was working hard to acquire nuclear weapons, it was still several years away from getting the crucial fissile materials, and could be

---

[12] George W. Bush, State of the Union address, January 29, 2002, www.whitehouse.gov/news/releases/2002/01/20020129-11.html, accessed June 2004.

kept equally far away in the future.[13] Europeans contended that the one thing that might induce the rational Hussein to a desperate launch of the chemical weapons he was still thought to possess – perhaps against Israeli targets – would be an invasion that threatened his existence and made him think he had nothing left to lose.

The political dangers, they continued, were that an attack on Iraq could break up this crucial Arab country, with Iran taking over parts of the south and Turkey the Kurdish territory to the north. Especially if an invasion were mounted with the Israeli–Palestinian confrontation still at a boil, they feared, the consequences could destabilize the entire Middle East. They found naive the American expectation that defeat of Hussein would make Iraqis democratic and then spread democracy throughout the region. Instead, it was far more likely that an occupied Iraq would be the best possible breeding ground for al Qaeda, would draw resources away from the more essential fight against terrorists, and perhaps even enable fundamentalists to get their hands on Pakistan's nuclear weapons. More basically, they accepted the precept inculcated in them over two generations (not least by the Americans) that use of force in defense of stability and the status quo was moral, but use of force in a revolutionary gamble was not; they therefore found it alarming to hear their mentors increasingly singing the praises of democratizing the medieval Islamic world by the sword. Historical memories of the devastation of the Thirty Years War and of Napoleon's "revolution in boots" – the very kind of bloodshed they had worked so assiduously to escape after 1945 – returned.

A number of American generals and foreign policy veterans from the administration of President Bush, Sr., shared these worries, it seemed; in the summer of 2002, leaks about military planning in the US media and op-ed columns by former National Security Council advisor Brent Scowcroft, former secretary of state James Baker III, and even the delphic former secretary of state Henry Kissinger obliquely challenged administration assumptions about Iraq.[14] George W. Bush's own Middle East envoy, General Anthony Zinni (who subsequently lost his pro bono post), was characteristic in the direction of his comments but uncharacteristic in his bluntness in saying, "Attacking Iraq now will cause a lot of

[13] Author's background interviews with German and other European officials. At that point no official yet suspected that Saddam Hussein might in fact have halted his nuclear program.

[14] James A. Baker III, "The Right Way to Change a Regime," *New York Times*, August 25, 2002; Brent Scowcroft, "Don't Attack Saddam," *Wall Street Journal*, August 15, 2002; Todd S. Purdum and Patrick E. Tyler, "Top Republicans Break with Bush on Iraq Strategy," *New York Times*, August 16, 2002; and Nicholas Lemann, "The War on What?," *New Yorker*, September 16, 2002.

problems ... It might be interesting to wonder why all the generals see it the same way, and all those that never fired a shot in anger and [are] really hell-bent to go to war see it a different way ... The Middle East peace process, in my mind, has to be a higher priority. Winning the war on terrorism has to be a higher priority ... Our relationships in the region are in major disrepair [and] we need to quit making enemies we don't need to make enemies out of."[15]

Cheney's call for regime change in Iraq

At the end of August, 2002 Vice President Dick Cheney silenced the doubters with a speech advocating a war on Iraq to effect regime change and thus preempt a potential future threat from Baghdad.[16] At this point, the new American strategy of "preemption" – which Bush had adumbrated at his West Point graduation address in June and would shortly be enshrined in the new National Security Strategy – took on concrete form. In principle, European diplomats acknowledged the need to expand the leeway for preemption allowed under international law in an age when a single unblocked chemical or nuclear weapon could obliterate thousands or even millions in an instant. In practice, however, they saw no imminent threat in the wily, secular Saddam Hussein and viewed the intervention Cheney was promoting as at best an optional war. On this point, as former British foreign secretary Robin Cook's subsequent diaries and testimony about the suicide of British government scientist David Kelly revealed, there was far more consensus between the skeptical governments across the Channel and the pro-American British government than was publicly apparent at the time.[17] Europeans wondered how many other regimes Washington might now decide to topple, and whether the American

---

[15] Comments of Gen. Anthony Zinni (ret.) during a speech to the Florida Economic Club, August 23, 2002, http://www.npr.org/programs/morning/zinni.html, accessed June 2004.

[16] "Vice President Speaks at VFW 103rd National Convention," www.whitehouse.gov/news/releases/2002/08/20020826.html, accessed June 2004.

[17] David Cracknell, "Blair 'Knew Iraq Had No WMD,'" *Sunday Times* (London), October 5, 2003; and Philip Stephens, "Bush and Blair's Differing Designs for a Secure World," *Financial Times*, March 21, 2003. Many British commentators conclude, somewhat more cautiously, that, while Blair considered the potential combination of terrorists and WMD a grave threat, his overriding motivation was to keep a United States determined to invade Iraq from doing so alone. See, for example, Charles Grant's review of books about Blair by two British journalists, John Kampfner and Peter Riddell, "Blair's Five Wars," *Prospect* 91 (October 2003), pp. 40–43. Blair's own speech to Parliament on the eve of war, by contrast to earlier government statements, claimed neither that Iraq was on the verge of acquiring nuclear weapons nor that Hussein had links with al Qaeda; instead, Blair stressed Hussein's defiance of seventeen UN resolutions, the leader's repugnant

voters' patience would last long enough to complete real reconstruction after such coups.

In late summer of 2002, Gerhard Schröder was in the run-up to an election the polls predicted he would lose. He had already picked up the anti-war theme on August 5 (in violation of a promise to Bush not to touch the subject, US officials complained). After the Cheney speech, Schröder's rejection of German military or financial participation in any "adventure" in Iraq joined the down-home issue of coping with summer floods as the staples in his campaign. The chancellor advocated a "German way," a vague phrase he never defined and seemed to apply interchangeably to domestic and foreign policy – but one that evoked in American listeners the historical ghosts of a German *Sonderweg*, or "special way," between East and West. Washington understood this as a summons to German defiance of American foreign policy. Moreover, unlike the more ambiguous French at the time, Schröder allies said categorically that Berlin would not join any war on Iraq even if the UN Security Council blessed it.[18] For a country that put so much stock in multilateralism in general and the United Nations in particular, this was an oddly unilateralist stance. It appealed to anti-war east German voters in particular, however, and with the help of their ballots Schröder's Social Democratic–Green coalition narrowly won reelection – trouncing maverick extremist-right candidates, as usual,[19] and, more unusually, wiping out the east German postcommunist Party of Democratic Socialism after its decade as a party on the national level.

Washington censured Schröder for running against the United States for the first time in the electoral history of the Federal Republic. And after the German justice minister – talking with several dozen constituents three days before the election – said both Bush and Hitler resorted to foreign wars to divert attention from domestic problems, National Security Advisor Condoleezza Rice accused the Germans of having "poisoned" relations.[20] The White House demanded that the chancellor fire his minister within twenty-four hours, before the election – and when he

repression of Iraqis, concern that if the United States and Britain backed down after their military buildup in the Gulf, this would only embolden Hussein to commit worse deeds, and, of course, that Britain must stand by the United States.

[18] The most detailed account of this issue in English is Stephen Szabo, *Parting Ways: The Crisis in German–American Relations* (Washington, DC: Brookings Institution Press, 2004).

[19] Since its founding in 1949, the Federal Republic has never had any significant right populist movement of the sort led by Jean-Marie Le Pen, Jörg Haider, Pim Fortuyn, Christoph Blocher, and others in neighboring countries.

[20] Note that it was permissible for Bush's campaign manager Karl Rove to compare the adulation of Bush by baseball fans with Nazi adulation of Hitler (see Woodward, *Bush at War*, p. 277), but comparisons of this sort by a German official were considered off limits.

did so only on the day after the election, Bush ostracized Schröder for the next year, refusing to congratulate him on his election victory, to meet with him, or even to take his phone calls.[21] Reflecting administration anger, influential Pentagon advisor Richard Perle declared publicly that Schröder should resign.

After his September 22 reelection, the chancellor followed the customary pendulum of politics. While still rejecting any German combat role in the impending war, he toned down his anti-war rhetoric and reemphasized Berlin's commitment to all NATO obligations. These were considerable, including full American use of German airspace and bases, logistical support, assumption by Bundeswehr soldiers of guard duty at US bases in Germany to free American troops for war, continued German participation in airborne AWACS surveillance flights, and loan of Patriot anti-missile systems and armored Fuchs biological and chemical weapons detectors and decontaminators to Israel, Turkey, and Kuwait.[22] In a notable shift for a country that on constitutional grounds had had no combat troops abroad just a decade earlier, the Germans now had almost 10,000 peacekeeping troops abroad – a small number compared with US forces, but more than any other nation. In Kabul, they would further shortly assume co-command, with the Dutch, of the International Security Assistance Forces.[23]

In the poisoned bilateral atmosphere, this contribution did not assuage Washington. As one German official put it, Bush made it clear that, while he deemed Russia's Vladimir Putin a man he could trust, he deemed Gerhard Schröder a man he could not trust. For Washington, the central issue of the contretemps seemed to be German betrayal of the United States. The burden of proof was not on the United States to demonstrate the imminent threat that would justify a drastic resort to war; instead, the administration maintained that a potential growing threat sufficed to require preventive war. Thus it was incumbent on the Germans to demonstrate their loyalty to the United States, a country to which they owed so much from 1945 on through reunification in 1990.

---

[21] Throughout that year, this personal insult to the US president received as much as or even more stress from US officials interviewed by the author than did Schröder's opposition to the war.

[22] The Patriots were sent to Turkey via the Netherlands, picking up Dutch crews in order to keep Schröder's campaign pledge of abstention from the war.

[23] See, for example, Christian Wernicke and Christoph Schwennicke, "Bundeswehr muss mit Grösserem Türkei-Einsatz rechnen" [Bundeswehr Must Count On Larger Operation in Turkey], *Süddeutsche Zeitung*, February 20, 2002; "Awacs-Besatzungen bleiben vorläufig im Einsatz" [AWACS Crews Remain in Operation for Now], *Frankfurter Allgemeine Zeitung*, March 24, 2003; and chapter 6 in this volume.

For several months after the Cheney speech, Europeans remained confused. On first hearing – even though they had been given no advance notice of the speech, as normal diplomatic practice would prescribe before a major foreign policy announcement – they regarded the vice president's speech as a statement of official US policy and responded accordingly. They were reproached by administration contacts, however, for jumping to conclusions without giving Washington the benefit of the doubt. American policy was shaped in the rough and tumble of competing voices, the Europeans were told; no decisions about going to war had yet been made.[24]

The Europeans, adapting to this admonition, then shifted, underestimated the vice president's importance, and accepted the judgment of Bush's insider biographers, Bob Woodward and David Frum, that Cheney's role was just a subordinate one of saluting the president.[25] They had not yet caught on to the policy-setting power of what Zbigniew Brzezinski later called Cheney's own parallel "national security council."[26] And anyway, if the vice president's drumbeat of war was the official American position, why had not the president himself proclaimed such a departure from previous policy? Why did US officials continue to maintain (as they would throughout the massive US troop buildup in the Gulf that began shortly, right up to a few days before war started in March 2003) that the whole issue of Iraq was wide open and the administration had not yet made up its mind?[27] And since Bush, at Blair's urging, went to the UN in September to seek an imprimatur for enforcing UN

---

[24] Author's interviews with senior German officials, September through December 2002. See also reporting by Stephen Erlanger in "Traces of Terror," *New York Times*, September 1, 2002, that the issue of war in Iraq was still wide open. He wrote, "Senior officials in Washington are angry at his [Schröder's] presumption that the American debate over Iraq is finished and his failure to give his closest ally the benefit of the doubt."

[25] Woodward, *Bush at War*, p. 38; and David Frum, *The Right Man* (New York: Random House, 2003), p. 62.

[26] When George W. Bush took office in 2001, the US media widely assumed that the experienced Cheney would be the foreign policy heavyweight in the administration. Administration spokesmen rejected this view, however, and by mid-2002 they had certainly convinced Europeans that the president himself determined foreign as well as domestic policy, and that only his voice was authoritative. It was only as the Iraq War broke out in 2003 that the media consensus in Washington (and thus perceptions in Europe) shifted back to focus on Cheney as the driving force in administration foreign policy; one of the first columnists to pinpoint this was Jim Hoagland, "How He Got Here," *Washington Post*, March 21, 2003; see also Zbigniew Brzezinski, "Where Do We Go from Here?," *Transatlantic Internationale Politik* 4:3 (Fall 2003), p. 4.

[27] Even as late as mid-January 2003, German officials could not tell whether the Bush administration had "already decided that war with Iraq was inevitable," wrote James Kitfield in "Damage Control,"*National Journal*, July 19, 2003 (as carried in the NATO Enlargement Daily Briefs, Op-Eds, July 18, archived at http://yahoo.com/group/nedb/ messages, and distributed on the listed date by e-mail). Kitfield writes that German

prohibitions on Iraqi weapons of mass destruction (WMD) programs, didn't this mean that the president was turning multilateral after all and would seek a diplomatic solution?

Only half a year later would a senior White House official inform the Germans that a decision to go to war had already been made prior to Cheney's speech; only then would Europeans learn that the United States had already begun softening-up military strikes against Iraqi fiber-optics communications in June 2002.[28] And only as insurgent violence escalated to weekly targets on Americans, foreign civilian contractors, and those Iraqis who collaborated with the occupation in spring of 2004 would it become known that the Iraqi invasion was set on course as early as November 2001.[29]

Resolution 1441 and the Prague Summit

On November 8, after a two-month French–American minuet about the wording, the UN Security Council agreed unanimously on Resolution 1441 calling on Saddam Hussein to allow international inspections in Iraq to resume and threatening unspecified "serious consequences" if Baghdad were found to remain in "material breach" of longstanding UN bans on Iraqi WMD programs. UN teams under the former head of the International Atomic Energy Agency, Hans Blix, immediately took up the task. In the deliberate ambiguity that usually attends such compromises, the United States interpreted the French signature on 1441 and its lobbying for unanimous adoption of the resolution as a promise that

officials "felt they had to divine the answer using troop-deployment schedules like so many tea leaves – rather than accept Secretary of State Colin L. Powell's assurances that no such decision had been made." Other summary narratives of the turbulent diplomatic run-up to the Iraq War in US media appeared in the *Wall Street Journal* on March 27, 2003, and the *New York Times* on March 17, 2003.

[28] Author's interviews with senior German officials, September 2002 through September 2003; Michael R. Gordon, "US Air Raids in '02 Prepared for War in Iraq," *New York Times*, July 20, 2003. Richard Haass, director of the State Department policy planning staff throughout this period, dated the decision to invade Iraq at July 2002, as cited in Nicholas Lemann, "How It Came to War," *New Yorker*, March 31, 2003, p. 9. Thomas L. Friedman, a vocal supporter of the war, agreed with the July date, writing in "Chicken à la Iraq" in the *New York Times* on March 5, 2003, that the administration's "small group of war hawks" had created a fait accompli by then by "persuading Mr. Bush to begin a huge troop buildup in the Gulf back in July – without consulting Congress or the country – [and] knew it would create a situation where the US could never back down without huge costs."

[29] On November 21, 2001, President Bush ordered Defense Secretary Rumsfeld to draw up a plan of attack. Bush gave the final green light to the campaign the first week of January 2003; see Woodward, *Plan of Attack*, pp. 1–30, 253–258. In retrospect (spring 2004), Richard Haass personally reaffirmed his earlier deduction that the trajectory had been set by at least July 2002.

Paris would eventually sign a second resolution, as war approached, that would specifically authorize the threatened "serious consequences." And, indeed, all the diplomatic signals seemed to indicate that France was simply playing hard to get, planning to join the American action at the last minute after extracting the highest political price it could from Washington. In mid-December 2002, a senior French general informed the Pentagon that, if the Security Council approved, France would send 15,000 troops, 100 planes, and an aircraft carrier to join in the invasion.[30]

At this point – even though Washington and Paris clearly had quite different scenarios in mind – the eventual US–French schism was not inevitable. In late November, an upbeat NATO summit in Prague agreed amicably on two shifts to keep the Alliance relevant to the new security threats. In a major departure from its fifty-year precept that NATO was a defensive status quo alliance that was noninterventionist outside its own territory, the Alliance approved the principle of out-of-area operations.[31] And to carry out intervention in future Afghanistan-like crises, it created a NATO Reaction Force (NRF). At first, some Europeans feared that the NRF might be a disguised American Foreign Legion; but eventually the view prevailed that this was a credible American offer to give NATO a role in the asymmetrical fight against terrorism and help strengthen the EU's projected reaction force.[32]

Then on December 13 – after a European Union summit promised Ankara serious consideration of Turkish EU membership by the end of 2004 – a landmark agreement was reached between NATO and the European Union on coordinating their security efforts. In cases where NATO itself was not engaged, it would give planning, command, and logistical support to the European Rapid Reaction Force (ERRF) of 60,000. This would ensure that the ERRF did not take on operations it could not carry out, while preserving NATO's "escalation dominance" and avoiding "renationalization" of security (i.e., European countries acting on their own). The EU had been jolted into a "strategic re-awakening," as veteran analyst Julian Lindley-French put it. In the deal, the Europeans acknowledged that they could not just tend their own Garden of Eden and

---

[30] According to Kitfield, "Damage Control."

[31] In 1999 NATO had redefined its territory as the "Euro-Atlantic region," thus permitting various operations that previously would have been considered "out of area" to proceed; but the Prague Summit took this process an important step further.

[32] For a European assessment of the summit, see "Prager Nato-Gipfel: Meilenstein der Atlantischer Allianz" [Prague Nato Summit: Milestone of the Atlantic Alliance], *Neue Zürcher Zeitung*, November 20, 2002, http://www.nzz.ch (accessed November 2002). For a positive European view of the NRF, see Alyson J. K. Bailes, "NATO's New Response Force," *Transatlantic Internationale Politik* 4.1 (Spring 2003), pp. 25–29.

let the United States take care of global strategic threats, while the United States acknowledged that the EU might be helpful to it after all.[33]

The Franco-German embrace and the pan-European split

Despite these hopeful developments, the lull in transatlantic tensions did not last long. By January 2003, the (then) three-month-long US ostracism of Gerhard Schröder pushed him into the arms of a colleague for whom he had previously shown no particular liking, French president Jacques Chirac.[34] This unwonted embrace by the previously staunch Atlanticist Germans in turn tempted Chirac to go further in baiting Washington than he had hitherto done. Washington reacted by staging a showdown over the issue of NATO solidarity with Turkey. Tempers rose.

The stage was set in the razzmatazz leading up to the celebration in January of the fortieth anniversary of the Elysée Treaty of post-World War II French–German reconciliation. Chirac and Schröder hardened their opposition to the coming war, and to the second UN resolution that the United States hoped would brand Iraq as being in "material breach" of Resolution 1441. Washington held that it required no such finding to justify an invasion of Iraq, but it sought the second resolution at the urging of Tony Blair, who said he needed it to convince the skeptical British public of the war's legitimacy.

To the mounting frustration of Washington, Chirac now argued that all Resolution 1441 authorized at this stage was more intensive international inspections in Iraq. He threatened to veto any UN resolution that would help the United States and began mobilizing, successfully, a majority of other Security Council members against the United States. And he began this campaign in a way that embarrassed and alienated even the moderate American secretary of state, Colin Powell. The French insisted that Powell skip the important political appearances he was scheduled to make in the United States on Martin Luther King Day, January 20, to come to the UN instead and discuss what was billed as a session on countering terrorism. French foreign minister Dominique de Villepin used his press conference after the Security Council meeting, however, to make a pointed attack on Washington.

---

[33] Julian Lindley-French, "The Ties That Bind," *NATO Review* (Autumn 2003, http://www.nato.int/docu/review/2003/issue3/english/art2.html, accessed June 2004).

[34] This interpretation comes both from German officials and from Wolfgang Schäuble, the deputy head of the conservative parliamentary caucus who is best known as a sharp critic of the chancellor. The author's interview with Schäuble took place on June 17, 2003, in Berlin. Relevant interviews with senior German officials took place from December 2002 through June 2003.

If the United States invaded Iraq, he said, this would be "a victory for the law of the strongest."

Powell felt ambushed, by all Washington accounts, and thereafter pleaded the hardline case for war in the UN with full passion.[35] Rumsfeld promptly scorned the "old Europe" of France and Germany and welcomed the "new Europe" of Poland and other enthusiastic American allies in central Europe. Next, leaders of EU members Britain, Spain, Italy, Portugal, and Denmark, along with aspirants Poland, Hungary, and the Czech Republic, wrote a major opinion essay in the *Wall Street Journal* (without informing France and Germany beforehand) that implicitly backed the approaching US war in Iraq. Ten NATO and EU candidates followed with an American-drafted, somewhat more explicit pro-US declaration.[36] Memorably, the angry Chirac told reporters that the central European candidates for EU membership had missed a good opportunity to shut up, and threatened to veto their entry into the union.[37]

The American government lauded the eighteen "courageous" European signers of the statements, aware that the American public supported war, according to opinion polls, only if allies joined the United States in the expedition. "France and Germany do not speak for Europe," a bipartisan Sense of the Congress resolution stated, praising "the majority of Europe's democracies" that endorsed the war. Democratic Congressman Tom Lantos decried the "blind intransigence and utter ingratitude" of the old Europeans for their rescue by Americans from Hitler and Stalin and asserted that the failure of Paris and Berlin to

---

[35] Serge Schmemann, "The Quarrel over Iraq Gets Ugly," *New York Times*, January 26, 2003. Various observers speculated that Powell, reading the handwriting on the wall in Washington, was ready to yield to the juggernaut to war in any case, and chose the moment of French affront to do so; the latter view gained credence when Bob Woodward revealed that Bush informed Powell on January 13, 2003 that the United States was going to go to war (*Plan of Attack*, pp. 269–270).

[36] José María Aznar, José Manuel Durão Barroso, Silvio Berlusconi, Tony Blair, Václav Havel, Peter Medgyessy, Leszek Miller, and Anders Fogh Rasmussen, "United We Stand," *Wall Street Journal*, January 30, 2003; Alan Cowell, "European Leaders Divide Between Hawks and Doves," *New York Times*, January 31, 2003; Glenn Frankel and Keith B. Richburg, "8 Leaders in Europe Back Bush On Iraq," *Washington Post*, January 31, 2003; William Safire, "Surprising Germany," *New York Times*, February 10, 2003. For a Polish view that this alignment of central Europeans with the United States against Germany and France represents enduring interests, see Radek Sikorski, "America's Friends in Europe, and What They Understand," *National Review*, March 31, 2003; for a Polish view that Poland and central Europe's longer-term interests will be aligned to Germany and France, see Adam Krzeminski, "Poland's Home Is Europe," *Transatlantic Internationale Politik* 4:3 (Fall 2003), pp. 65–68.

[37] Craig S. Smith, "Chirac Scolding Angers Nations That Back US," *New York Times*, February 19, 2003.

"honor their [NATO] commitments is beneath contempt." George F. Will wrote off NATO as "a thing of ridicule" and asked why any American troops should remain "in an unsympathetic country such as Germany." The Congressional restaurant renamed French fries "freedom fries"; some Republicans sought a boycott of Perrier and French wines if the EU continued to ban imports of genetically modified American foods. Rumsfeld savored telling a congressional hearing that some countries were not helping the United States – like Cuba, Libya, and Germany.

To the dismay of his own foreign ministry and the editorial pages of the major German newspapers, on the left as well as on the right, Chancellor Schröder now declared flatly that Germany would not vote for any UN resolution that would be taken as justifying war.[38] This was no longer campaign rhetoric – or at least it had no positive impact on voters, who gave the Social Democrats their worst showing ever in regional elections in early February. Instead, the chancellor's defiance of the United States this time was a deliberate policy choice to magnify rather than minimize differences. US ambassador to Germany Daniel Coats dismissed Germany as no longer relevant.[39]

Berlin did indeed pay a huge price in loss of "relevance" for Schröder's Gaullist lurch and estrangement from the United States. The chancellor forfeited yet again any chance of cutting the exorbitant EU farm subsidies that, in essence, German citizens pay for and French farmers consume. He abandoned the traditional German championing of the smaller EU states' interests to embrace the kind of big-state directorate the French had long sought. He dropped Germany's post-Cold War tutoring of the new central European democracies for EU membership, which the French had long tried to deny to the newcomers. The isolated Schröder had to pay so much, he told confidants, because he now needed Chirac and feared that Paris would side with the American war at the last minute, leaving Berlin utterly alone in its anti-war stance.[40] The precept that had governed German foreign policy ever since the signing of the Elysée Treaty – that US–German relations must always

[38] German diplomats had widely assumed that the rhetoric of the autumn electoral campaign would be toned down as the real political maneuvering began at the UN Security Council. Schröder put them on a tight leash in January 2003, however, and would not let them soften the edges of the German stance: author's interviews with senior German officials, December 2002 and June 2003. See also Stefan Kornelius, "Joschka Fischer's Long Journey," *Transatlantic Internationale Politik* 4:3 (Fall 2003), pp. 49–54.

[39] Szabo, *Parting Ways*; Thomas Hanke, "Coats Rechnet mit Neubewertung der Beziehungen" [Coats Counts on a New Evaluation of Relations], *Financial Times Deutschland*, March 17, 2003; author's interview with Coats, March 19, 2003.

[40] Author's background interviews with senior German officials, January and April 2003.

take precedence even over the crucial French–German relationship – seemed to be at an end.[41]

Schröder's anti-war stance was certainly popular throughout Europe, even among the publics of Britain, Spain, Italy, and other countries whose governments supported the USA's Iraq War. Across Europe, public opinion opposed the war, majorities ranging from clear to overwhelming, while general public approval of the United States plummeted correspondingly.[42] But this hardly compensated for Schröder's constriction of Berlin's room for diplomatic maneuver.

Meanwhile, by the end of January, Washington gave up trying for a second UN resolution.

Showdown within NATO

The NATO partners now embarked on one of the most bizarre confrontations in the history of the Alliance. The issue was endorsement of advance military planning to help Turkey defend itself in case of war. Formal authorization was hardly needed; such contingency planning occurs continuously, and various Turkish scenarios were already under discussion in the planning staff, according to a senior officer at Supreme Headquarters Allied Powers Europe (SHAPE) headquarters.[43] But the United States wanted to maximize the pressure on Iraq by recruiting the fledgling new Islamic government in Ankara to the cause of the war on Iraq. The Turkish parliament balked, with an eye to the 94 percent of Turks who opposed the war; Washington presented Ankara with carrots and sticks in promises of NATO and US military and financial assistance – and in open speculation about the reduced strategic importance of Turkey once the United States had occupied Iraq.[44] France and

---

[41] For background on the bilateral relationship at this stage, see Robert Graham and Haig Simonian, "After 40 Years Together, France and Germany May Be Struggling to Keep the Spark in Their Close Relationship," *Financial Times*, January 20, 2003; Thomas Klau, "France and Germany: A Re-Marriage of Convenience," US–France Analysis Series, Brookings Institution, January 2003, available at http://www.brookings.edu/usfrance/analysis/index.htm, accessed June 2004; and Ulrike Guérot, Karl Kaiser, Martin Koopmann, Maxime Lefebvre, Thierry de Montbrial, Philippe Moreau Defarges, and Hans Stark, "Deutschland, Frankreich und Europa: Perspektiven" [Germany, France, and Europe: Perspectives], DGAP-Analyse No. 21 (German Council on Foreign Relations and the French Institute of Foreign Relations, January 2003).

[42] Pew Research Center for the People and the Press, "America's Image Further Erodes, Europeans Want Weaker Ties," opinion survey released March 18, 2003, and *Views of a Changing World*, June 2003, http://people-press.org.

[43] Conversation with author, February 7, 2003.

[44] Dexter Filkins, "In Defeat of US Plan, Turks See a Victory for Democracy," *New York Times*, March 5, 2003; Leyla Boulton, "A Hopeful Picture Turned on Its Head," *Financial Times*, April 1, 2003, special section.

Germany opposed formal NATO approval of allegedly defensive aid to Turkey – in clear preparation for an American and British invasion of Iraq – as a thinly disguised effort to get NATO sanction for the impending war itself, a point Washington in fact seemed to have very much in mind. Indeed, the United States gave every sign that it wanted to make Schröder eat crow publicly. Personally, the chancellor assured the Turks that he would help them; but at the same time he was showing the 71 percent of Germans who opposed the war that he could say no to the United States. Germany, France, and Belgium refused to go along with the required unanimous vote in the NATO Council. There must be no automatism, they argued, no NATO prejudgment that the looming war was justified.

Securing the imprimatur of the political North Atlantic Council of permanent ambassadors to NATO headquarters quickly became a test of wills. The United States kept threatening that the Alliance would be dead if a statement of solidarity with Turkey were not forthcoming. After a month of wrangling, language acceptable to Berlin about "defensive" assistance for Turkey was found – and the decision was whisked out of the Council and into NATO's Defense Planning Committee, a body to which France, as a political but not military member of the alliance, did not belong.

However ridiculous the issue, what was at stake was the survival of the Alliance. After half a century of defending Europe against the twenty Soviet divisions in East Germany, instituting unprecedented confidence-building in open shared medium-term military planning, socializing American and German and Turkish and Greek officers to mutual trust, and helping the new central European democracies to bring their armies under civilian control, NATO now faced possible extinction. Americans saw the French and Germans as the villains; not a few Europeans saw the Americans as the villains in putting the world's longest-lasting alliance at risk in their compulsion to invade Iraq. Americans thought the French were trying to declare Europe's independence from the United States; the French and Germans thought it was the United States that was trying to declare independence from the fetters of alliance. Only the powerful hegemon that had once invented cooperative institutions to maximize American influence, they believed, had the power to dissolve these institutions, on the presumption that as the only remaining superpower it was now strong enough to steer the globalized world alone.

These sentiments were echoed in Europe's leading newspapers, including the generally pro-American press. "The prospect of war has divided the United Nations Security Council, riven the most enduring military alliance of modern times, and split the European Union," the

Financial Times pronounced somberly as war approached.[45] The United States had carried out "wilful destruction of the international security system during the past few months," concluded the paper's columnist Philip Stephens shortly thereafter.[46] "The Iraq War is not legitimate self-defense. It is not humanitarian intervention. And it is not crisis control," added a representative German editorial in the *Süddeutsche Zeitung*. "The war hollows out the international ban on violence; it leaves war to the whim of the stronger. The power of this negative model leads to geopolitical destruction; if it is legitimate for the USA to conduct a preventive war, then it will be easy for other states to do so too."[47]

Countdown to war

In the final weeks before war began, there was further French–American sparring over the inconclusive UN inspections of Iraqi nuclear programs. The French wanted to prolong the inspections; the United States, now that its military buildup in the Gulf was complete, did not want to relax the pressure on Saddam Hussein. Secretary of State Colin Powell and Prime Minister Tony Blair took their evidence about the threat of Iraqi WMD to the UN and Westminster respectively; their governments' string of public presentations would soon turn out to have been riddled with forgeries, plagiarism from a student paper, misrepresentation of the use of some cylinders imported by the Iraqis, and hearsay reports from Iraqi exile groups close to the Pentagon hawks.[48] On March 7, the United States and Britain gave Baghdad a deadline to disarm or be disarmed. On March 11, as Blair faced rebellious back-benchers, Secretary of Defense Rumsfeld set off a storm in Britain by remarking that, even if Blair couldn't get a majority, British forces didn't really matter anyway since the United States could handle this task on its own.

---

[45] "Blix Speaks – and the Stakes Could Not Be Higher for the Transatlantic Allies Bitterly Divided over War with Iraq," *Financial Times*, February 14, 2003.

[46] Philip Stephens, "The Transatlantic Alliance Is Worse Off than the Coalition," *Financial Times*, March 28, 2003.

[47] "Den Krieg aufhalten" [Block the War], *Süddeutsche Zeitung*, February 14, 2003.

[48] See, for example, Seymour Hersh, "The Stovepipe," *New Yorker*, October 27, 2003, www.newyorker.com/fact/content/?031027fa_fact, accessed June 2004; "Intelligence on Iraq," web page for the Carnegie Endowment for International Peace, accessed first week of November 2003, http://www.ceip.org/files/projects/npp/resources/iraqintell/home.htm; and Walter Pincus, "US–British Differences Show Iraq Intelligence Gap," *Washington Post*, September 30, 2003, carried in NATO Enlargement Daily Brief of October 1, 2003, archived at http://yahoo.com/group/nedb/messages.

Westminster, after the only serious debate about the war in any allied parliament, at last gave the prime minister his majority. In what was widely regarded as the best speech of his career, Tony Blair reviewed "Saddam's lies, deception and obstruction" in a decade of flouting UN bans on Iraqi development of WMD. He refuted the "absurd" claim that Hussein might have destroyed these weapons. He reprimanded France for placating the Iraqi tyrant in the face of the "two begetters of chaos" in the twenty-first century – "tyrannical regimes with WMD and extreme terrorist groups who profess a perverted and false view of Islam." The great "danger to the UN is inaction" and loss of credibility in the next confrontation, he said. The current state of affairs was "the consequence of Europe and the United States dividing from each other." Failure of Europeans to stand by the United States now, he warned, would "be the biggest impulse to unilateralism there could ever be."[49]

A third of the prime minister's own Labour MPs defected on the vote. Their concern was voiced by Robin Cook, the former foreign secretary and one of two members of Blair's cabinet to resign over the war. In his emotional resignation speech, Cook declared, "A US administration visibly dominated by Vice President Richard Cheney and Donald Rumsfeld ... scorns the multilateralism at the core of Mr. Blair's strategic vision ... The shredding of international support for America's stance over recent months has represented the biggest foreign policy defeat since the Vietnam War. Worse still, Messrs Cheney and Rumsfeld scarcely care .... We are back ... to the Hobbesian world in which right is measured only by might. That's what frightens me."[50]

On March 19 war began; within three weeks Baghdad fell. American and British troops, constituting 99 percent of the expeditionary force, won on their own.[51] There was no contingent of 160,000 troops from thirty-two Arab, European, and Asian states as there had been in George Bush, Sr.'s war; on the contrary, in mid-April, Schröder and Chirac added insult to injury by enlisting Russia's Vladimir Putin to join them in calling for international rather than unilateral US supervision of Iraq's postwar reconstruction.[52] And in late April, Schröder, Chirac, and their

---

[49] Tony Blair, Speech in Parliament, March 18, 2003, www.number-10.gov.uk/output/Page3294.asp, accessed March 2003.

[50] Quoted in Philip Stephens, "Bush and Blair's Differing Designs for a Secure World," *Financial Times*, March 21, 2003.

[51] Ivo Daalder, "Bush's Coalition Doesn't Add Up Where It Counts," *Newsday*, March 24, 2004.

[52] Michael Wines, "Three War Critics Want UN Effort to Rebuild," *New York Times*, April 12, 2003. Condoleezza Rice's tart riposte was that the United States should "punish France, ignore Germany, and forgive Russia"; see Jim Hoagland, "Three Miscreants," *Washington Post*, April 13, 2003.

Belgian and Luxembourg counterparts ostentatiously met in what was nicknamed derisively "the chocolate summit" to start a European defense avant-garde that the United States understood as a challenge to NATO and American leadership.[53] As the triumphant George W. Bush landed on an aircraft carrier on May 1 to declare the war over in front of a banner proclaiming "Mission Accomplished," he saw as yet little reason to seek reconciliation with the Germans and French.

On the battlefield, Rumsfeld's gamble on a fast, light, 21st-century cavalry with night-sight goggles, laser-guided munitions, and laptops paid off. The skeptics' fears did not materialize; there were no blazing oilfields, no streams of refugees, no house-to-house fighting with high American casualties, no seizure of northern Kurdish territory by Turks or of eastern territory by Iranians, no eruptions on the Arab street, no worsening of *intifada* violence. The biggest prize of all, a disheveled, disoriented, and visibly aged Saddam Hussein who had survived the war by hiding ignominiously in tiny holes in the ground near his native Tikrit, was captured alive nine months after the war began.

In stabilizing postwar Iraq, however, Rumsfeld's lean dream army did not perform as well. Deterioration in civilian security and the American failure in nation-building would thwart administration hopes of bringing democracy to the Arab world and frustrate efforts to persuade European critics that Washington had been right all along.

The bloody aftermath

In his speech to Parliament just before the war began, the ever-optimistic Blair set forth the hope that after the conflict the transatlantic community could put the bitter differences of the preceding months behind it and unite

---

[53] Elaine Sciolino, "4-Nation Plan for Defense of Europe," *New York Times*, April 30, 2003. The French intent may well have been to emancipate Europe from NATO, but this was certainly not the German intent. Nor was the subsequent row over establishment of a small EU military planning unit interpreted by the British as an attempt to defy the United States, although much of official Washington understood it this way. See Jolyon Howorth, "France, Britain and the Euro-Atlantic Crisis," *Survival* 45:4 (Winter 2003/4), pp. 173–192; and Marc Champion and Christopher Cooper, "Bush–Blair Alliance Faces New Strains: As US President Prepares to Visit His Strongest Ally, Tensions Come to the Fore," *Wall Street Journal Europe*, November 10, 2003; NATO Enlargement Day Brief, November 10, 2003, archived at http://yahoo.com/group/nedb/messages. Javier Solana too contended that there was no cause for American concern in this small team of thirty, which would certainly not preempt the 1,000 officers on SHAPE's own planning staff. In an interview with the author (November 13, 2003, Berlin), he concluded that the real problem was American suspicion that behind this there might be a hidden agenda (by the French, he implied, but did not say) to separate an eventual EU defense union from NATO.

in two common projects. The first would be rebuilding Iraq, with the Europeans joining the United States wholeheartedly in the reconstruction, and with the United States ceding a major political role to the international community as represented by the UN. The second – following the pattern of President George Bush, Sr.'s action after the defeat of Iraq in the early 1990s – would be advancing the Israeli–Palestinian peace process toward a two-state solution as outlined in the "roadmap" sketched out by the "Quartet" of the United States, Europe, the UN, and Russia.[54]

Neither of these projects has succeeded. In the view of Europeans, Bush, while stating his support for the Israeli–Palestinian peace process, never put his own representative on the ground to keep the process going, and did not give Secretary of State Powell adequate negotiating authority.[55] The attempt had barely gotten underway when *intifada* bombers once again derailed the peace process with violence, and Israelis responded in kind and proceeded to build a security wall on occupied territory that split many Palestinians from their fields and from each other.

Nor did any of the postwar Iraqi issues serve as a transatlantic unifier. The first major postwar dispute arose from the embarrassing failure of elite US teams to find any weapons of mass destruction in Iraq, despite thousands of man-hours of searching. The impression hardened that, contrary to the prevailing Western assumptions, Hussein had probably not had any significant WMD programs since international inspectors found and destroyed more weapons in the mid-1990s than all those destroyed in the 1991 Iraq War.[56] The absence of WMD – the strongest reason cited for going to war in the first place – confirmed the instincts of European critics of the United States and put Tony Blair through his second domestic trial by fire (on this, see chapter 7 in this volume). In Washington, a blame game for the fiasco of prewar intelligence pitted the White House against CIA analysts, though it had little immediate impact on transatlantic relations.

---

[54] Blair speech in Parliament, March 18, 2003, www.number-10.gov.uk/output/Page 3294.asp, accessed March 2003; "Why Blair Fears America," *Economist*, March 22, 2003, 40; and author's background interviews with senior German officials and European diplomats in Berlin, March and April 2003.

[55] EU High Representative for Foreign Policy Javier Solana made this point in his interview with the author on November 13, 2003. Other European officials, less diplomatically, said on background that Bush undercut Powell and strongly backed Israeli prime minister Ariel Sharon's hard line – especially as the president's 2004 election campaign drew nearer. One EU official even denied that the "Quartet" was indeed a quartet, sarcastically saying that it was more like a three-on-one.

[56] See Richard W. Stevenson, "Iraq Illicit Arms Gone Before War, Departing Inspector States," *New York Times*, January 24, 2004, accessed at http://www.nytimes.com on day of publication.

Meanwhile, the US administration reluctantly accepted that it was now responsible in Iraq for the same sort of nation-building it had in the past so publicly detested. But the Defense Department, persuaded that the Iraqi population would welcome its American liberators as the Afghanis had welcomed them, discarded the detailed State Department planning for reconstruction; it chose instead to rely on the assurances of Iraqi exiles that democracy would blossom once Saddam Hussein was gone. The military was not directed to secure hospitals, museums, or electricity infrastructure against the initial rampage of looting. By the end of 2003, public water and electricity had still not been restored to prewar levels in Iraq, and popular complaints were mounting.[57] Worse, the Coalitional Provisional Authority soon disbanded the Iraqi army, turning loose thousands of unemployed young men with weapons. The US army turned out to be both undermanned and untrained for the job of civilian security and administration it now faced. Soldiers' repatriation was repeatedly postponed; the call-up of reserves reached its highest level since the Korean War; uniformed officers worried that so much of their combat capability was being tied down in Iraq that they could not fulfill all their other global commitments. Worst of all was the security situation, both for Iraqis and for foreigners. Reported murders, rapes, and abductions of women rose.[58] Two key moderate Shiite clerics were murdered in the first months after victory. GIs in tanks, with no knowledge of Arabic or local customs, proved to be poor urban policemen.

The guerrilla war, as US Central Command General John P. Abizaid called it, soon claimed more lives from the United States and its allies than had "major hostilities." Suicide and stand-off attacks on the local UN headquarters, the Red Cross, Italian soldiers, the embassies of US allies, and Iraqi policemen cooperating with the United States drove most of the staff of the United Nations and nongovernmental organizations out of the country. The attacks also drove American (rather more than British) soldiers behind barricades and made them appear more like occupiers than liberators to many Iraqis. The presumed culprits were Hussein loyalists and fundamentalist Arabs from other countries drawn

---

[57] As of November 2003, only 80 percent of prewar telephone and electricity services had been restored, while oil production had not yet been restored to the prewar 2,500,000 barrels per day. The rate of reported attacks on US soldiers rose from five to ten a day in April to between thirty and thirty-seven in November, with fatalities among coalition soldiers rising from fourteen in August to thirty-three in October to fifty in the first half of November (BBC World Service News Hour [radio], 17:00–18:00 GMT, Europe broadcast, November 14, 2003, citing official coalition figures).

[58] Jimmy Burns, "US Told Stance May Spur Anarchy in Iraq," *Financial Times*, July 11, 2003; "Walking on Eggshells," *Economist*, July 5, 2003, p. 1.

by the rich Western target opportunities in Iraq – and some of those hundreds of thousands of disbanded, unemployed Iraqi soldiers. Bombs also began exploding for the first time in Saudi Arabia.

In this environment, Iraqi reconstruction too failed to become a catalyst for transatlantic reconciliation. In September 2003, the first face-to-face meeting between Bush and Schröder in over a year seemed like a good omen. Yet there was no meeting of minds. Germany and France both refused to send their troops to get killed in the embers of Bush's war in Iraq. (Poland, by contrast, was initially proud to step in, take over command of a military sector, get paid by Washington to do so, and enjoy a bit of one-upmanship over the Germans.) Berlin and Paris likewise refused to underwrite the second American–Iraqi war the way they had the first war a decade earlier. They also declined to contribute substantially to the reconstruction effort under an American monopoly on political authority and pressed instead for a major role for the UN. This the United States was initially unwilling to grant – and after top members of the UN team in Iraq were blown up in the suicide bombing at UN headquarters in Baghdad, Secretary-General Kofi Annan also became reluctant to have the world body take on that task. Once again, various American columnists fumed at European disloyalty to Washington and refusal to pay up;[59] only as the drawn-out occupation of Iraq threatened to become a liability for Bush's reelection campaign did the administration again turn to the UN.

Wary rapprochement

By then, both diplomacy and autonomous events were nudging the two sides of the Atlantic – and new and old Europe – together. The overstretched United States was no longer contemplating further military interventions that might set off new quarrels, and in summer 2004 even started on a new pragmatic course in Iraq by turning the local administration over to a UN-brokered interim government. The EU approved, in December 2003, a strategy paper that went some way toward accepting American definitions of global threats. Bush's close ally, Prime Minister José María Aznar, was voted out of office three days after the first major Islamist attack in Europe killed more than 200 commuters in Madrid in March 2004. Two months later, the "new European" countries became

---

[59] See, for example, the scathing put-down of old European ingrates by Karl Zinsmeister in the *Chicago Tribune* of October 28, 2003, "It's Time for New Allies," http://www. chicagotribune.com/news/opinion/oped/chi-0310280074oct28,1,6389123.story?coll= chi-newsopinioncommentary-hed, accessed November 2003.

official members of the EU – and were experiencing some disillusionment with the United States. These developments helped to recalibrate the US–EU relationship, as the European threat assessment became more like the American one at the same time as US triumphalism was belatedly toned down.[60]

The EU's first-ever strategy statement identified much the same dangers as Washington's National Security Strategy of a year earlier in the mix of terrorism, WMD proliferation, failed states, and organized crime. The document, largely the work of Javier Solana and his team, counseled Europe to extend its immediate zone of security to its nearest neighbors including, insofar as possible, the Balkans, the Middle East, and the Caucasus. It further recommended spending more on defense and spending it more intelligently, and taking unspecified preventive (though not "preemptive") action when necessary.[61]

Within the EU, the next summit the following June finally approved the draft "constitutional treaty" that aspired to a more unified foreign policy in calling for a single EU "foreign minister." At the European Council, the new Spanish prime minister was Socialist José Luis Rodriguez Zapatero, who had fulfilled his campaign promise to pull Spain's 1,800 soldiers out of Iraq. The dominant interpretation of the election in the American media was that the Islamist attack in Madrid – and the threat of more to come if Spain did not repudiate the Americans and the war in Iraq – had cowed voters into dumping Aznar. The dominant European reading, by contrast, was that Aznar had angered voters one time too many by falsely blaming the bombings on violent Basque separatists rather than Islamist extremists.[62] In any event, Zapatero not only immediately joined Madrid to the old Europe of Paris and Berlin in opposing the security role that Washington was seeking for NATO in Iraq; he also stopped blocking the new constitution over concerns about Spain's voting weight in the European Council.

At that point the EU complexion was further altered by the graduation of the new Europeans to full membership, as the union's biggest

---

[60] For an early harbinger of the Bush administration's newfound appreciation of the UN and the legitimacy its support might confer, see Robert Kagan, "A Tougher War for the US Is One of Legitimacy," *New York Times*, January 31, 2004; and Kagan, "America's Crisis of Legitimacy," *Foreign Affairs* (March–April 2004), pp. 65–87.

[61] The summit also prepared for imminent EU assumption of primary responsibility for security in Bosnia and, in a less-noticed move, set up the organization's first-ever joint military procurement agency.

[62] See Charles Krauthammer, "Spaniards Capitulating," *Washington Post*, March 19, 2004; and Leslie Crawford and Joshua Levitt, "'A Place in the History of Infamy' – How the Government's Assumption and Misjudgment Shook Spain," *Financial Times*, March 26, 2004.

enlargement ever finally reunited Europe after the decades of enforced separation. Overnight, the number of members shot up from fifteen to twenty-five, vastly complicating decision-making. This changed the tenor of US–European relations surprisingly little, however, in part because of waning central European enthusiasm for the Iraq War. "None of those countries would sign that letter today," commented a west European diplomat, referring to the Letter of Eight of February 2003 backing the American invasion of Iraq.[63] The desire of central Europeans to retain American reinsurance against any resumption of Russian bullying remained; their romanticism about the United States did not.

The Poles, as the commanders of an Iraqi sector, were emblematic.[64] To begin with, they realized that at the end of the day they would need to sell their cherries and computers in Frankfurt, not Houston. And they followed Spain in socializing into the EU's consensus system and dropping their now solo resistance to the draft constitution over Warsaw's voting weight. In addition, after a year in the desert, they discovered that, as a very new member of the Alliance, they were in over their heads with this magnitude of responsibility, even with full NATO support and US funding of their efforts. They discovered as well that they received little reward from Washington for their efforts, and certainly not the visa-free travel to the United States that Warsaw craved. By spring 2004, some 63 percent of Poles wanted their 2,500 soldiers too to be withdrawn from Iraq as soon as possible.[65]

Most fundamentally, by spring 2004, the spread of violence by Iraqi insurgents and the rise in popular Iraqi disapproval of the American occupation[66] strengthened the aversion of both old and new Europeans to sending troop reinforcements that would have little hope of restoring security and might harden the perception of a Muslim–Western clash of civilizations. The antipathy only increased as the ugly torture and humiliation by American soldiers of Iraqi prisoners at Abu Ghraib jail became known in April.[67]

---

[63] Conversation with the author, May 19, 2004, Aachen.

[64] For more on the experience and perspectives of the central European states, see chapter 10 in this volume.

[65] According to a CBOS poll published May 21: "General Praises Handover of Falluja," *Financial Times*, May 22, 2004.

[66] Thomas E. Ricks, "80% in Iraq Distrust Occupation Authority," *Washington Post*, May 13, 2004.

[67] See, for example, Hersh, "The Gray Zone"; Amnesty International, "Iraq: Memorandum on Concerns Relating to Law and Order," July 2003, http://web. amnesty.org/library/Index/ENGMDE141572003?open&of=ENG-IRQ, accessed June 2004; "Report of the International Committee of the Red Cross (ICRC) on the Treatment by the Coalition Forces of Prisoners of War and Other Protected Persons

By then, many Europeans felt vindicated in their original opposition to the war. After all, Saddam Hussein had not had WMD. He had not had links with al Qaeda – though after the war very strong new links pulled *jihadis* to Iraq to fight the infidel occupiers. The Iraq War had diverted substantial resources from the war on terror.[68] Israel had become less safe, not more so, as Palestinian and Iraqi grievances blended and the once stable Iraq threatened to erupt into civil war. The American invasion did not secure more oil for world markets, but bumped oil prices up to a level that threatened the global economy. And now it appeared that the Americans, far from launching the democratization of the Arab world that was the last remaining rationale for the war, had instead brutalized themselves and turned the world's pro-American sympathy after 9/11 into profound anti-American mistrust and even hatred.[69]

In effect, the transatlantic allies have now agreed to disagree and to look to the future rather than the past. But wary rapprochement is not yet reconciliation. The lingering legacy of the Iraq feud is eroded European trust in Washington's judgment and leadership, and eroded American confidence in Europe's solidarity.

---

by the Geneva Conventions in Iraq During Arrest, Internment and Interrogation," February 2003, 24; and Scott Higham and Joe Stephens, "New Details of Prison Abuse Emerge," *Washington Post*, May 21, 2004.

[68] See Hersh, "The Gray Zone."

[69] See John Vinocur, "Concerned, NATO Is Not Gloating on Iraq," *International Herald Tribune*, May 12, 2004; Martin Wolf, "The Saviour of Democracy Is Run by a Unilateral Bully," *Financial Times*, May 12, 2004; Philip Stephens, "Iraq Is a Disaster But The World's Future Looks Worse," *Financial Times*, May 14, 2004; and "Busted Neo-con Icon," *Financial Times*, May 22, 2004.

3   The United States and its Atlantic partners

David M. Andrews

As Geir Lundestad reminds us in chapter 1, the Atlantic alliance has known recurrent controversy since its inception. Still, the diplomatic crisis of 2002–3 was of a different character than its predecessors. Prior to the war to dislodge Saddam Hussein from power, the USA's key NATO partners had never adopted as a matter of official, publicly stated policy the aim of thwarting the United States on a matter Washington had described as of supreme importance; but that is precisely what took place in the fall of 2002 and spring of 2003. The behavior of the George W. Bush administration prior to the invasion of Iraq was likewise extraordinary. Many senior US policy officials seemed not merely to accept that many of the United States' chief allies were opposed to the action; they appeared to revel in that fact. The diplomatic conflict with European opponents of the war, and especially the French, at times appeared more exhilarating than the prospect of removing the "butcher of Baghdad" from power.

The subject of this chapter is the evolution of US grand strategy and especially American policy toward its leading Atlantic partners, France, Germany, and the United Kingdom.[1] In addressing these subjects I will draw attention to structural considerations, or in other words to the distribution of power in the international system. The bipolar distribution of power that reigned throughout the Cold War encouraged certain behaviors; the shift to a different distribution of power encourages

An earlier and somewhat shorter version of this chapter appeared in the *Cambridge Review of International Affairs* 17:3 (October 2004), pp. 421–436. I am grateful to numerous friends and colleagues for excellent and sometimes demanding suggestions for revision; remaining errors of fact or interpretation are entirely my own. Special thanks are in order to Rasmus Bertelsen, Benjamin Cohen, Scott Cooper, Richard Gardner, Wade Jacoby, Joseph Jupille, Richard Morningstar, Hugo Paemen, Michael Smith, Georges-Henri Soutou, Pascal Vennesson, Helen Wallace, Kenneth Waltz, S. Linn Williams, and Hubert Zimmermann.
[1] Attention to Washington's bilateral relations with other European partners would complicate the presentation without changing the underlying analysis. For an assessment of US relations with Italy, see chapter 8 in this volume; for relations with Poland, Hungary and the Czech Republic, see chapter 10.

others.[2] Nevertheless, as structural theory is ill suited to explaining the actions of particular states at particular times, attention to the intellectual, ideological, and political circumstances that have informed recent developments in the American strategic outlook is also in order. Put differently, attention to system structure provides a backdrop to a wider analysis.

Considered in light of the dramatic structural change brought on by the end of the Cold War, it is the resilience of the Atlantic alliance, not tensions within it, that requires explanation. Beginning around 1947, the United States government chose to develop a system of close and continuous political and security relations with a number of Atlantic partners. Why did it do so? The resulting arrangements, after all, violated longstanding American practice and inclination. American ideology rested on an aversion to entangling alliances, and especially entangling alliances with European powers; American diplomatic history reflected that aversion.[3] Why then did the United States reverse its traditional orientation in the wake of World War II?

The answer lies in the postwar European security situation, which had some particularly vexing qualities. The North Atlantic Treaty Organization (NATO), and the larger transatlantic relationship in which it became embedded, reflected a particular solution to those problems. That solution proved stable for a number of reasons, some of them deriving from the security situation itself and others from larger, self-reinforcing features of the resulting partnership. These circumstances – the closely intertwined political, economic, and security fates of the members of the Alliance during the Cold War – helped a series of US administrations overcome the doubts and misgivings harbored by many Americans about close collaboration with partners they regarded as dubious or unreliable.

Of course, politics within the Atlantic alliance remained difficult during this period, with important controversies over decolonization, the war in Vietnam, the October 1973 Arab–Israeli war, and the installation of intermediate-range nuclear forces missiles during the 1980s. These crises were accompanied by mass political protests in western Europe against American policy, similar to those seen in early 2003. Indeed, the expression of dissatisfaction with American leadership by

---

[2] For the classic statement of structural realist theory, see Kenneth Waltz, *Theory of International Politics* (New York: McGraw-Hill, 1979).

[3] For an examination of American attitudes toward France in particular and Europe more generally, see Thierry de Montbrial, "Franco-American Relations: A Historical-Structural Analysis," *Cambridge Review of International Affairs* 17:3 (October 2004), pp. 451–466.

large segments of the European public has been a hardy perennial of the Alliance. But street protests and associated political posturing are one thing; the strategic commitments of governments are quite another. The fall of the Berlin Wall and subsequent collapse of the Soviet Union dramatically altered the strategic attitudes of governments within the Alliance, and specifically their tolerance for transatlantic tension. This should hardly be surprising. The post-Cold War international environment was "permissive" to a degree unknown during the preceding forty years; that is, the discipline once imposed by the competition between Eastern and Western blocs was relaxed. This change in structural context is an important key to understanding both the depth and character of the recent crisis in transatlantic relations.

If the end of the bipolar struggle was so crucial, why didn't it result in immediate challenges to the vitality of the Alliance? In fact it did; but a variety of factors, many of them temporary, conspired to mask this structural shift for the next decade. In the rest of this chapter, I describe those factors, and especially the slow pace of change in American strategic thinking during the 1990s. I then return briefly to the Atlantic crisis of 2002–3 before addressing the likely outlines of American foreign policy in the wake of that crisis, and especially policy toward Washington's major European allies.

But I begin with a description of the Atlantic alliance as it developed after World War II, partly in order to debunk the view that transatlantic cooperation is either a normal or reflexive habit for the United States. In fact the opposite is true. The United States is in some senses ill suited to sustained international leadership.[4] Blessed by nature and history with two maritime frontiers, American foreign policy tends to lack the necessary discipline to sacrifice immediate interests to longer-term considerations. The Cold War was an exception in this regard, the product of circumstances described below. But those exceptional circumstances no longer obtain.

Thus, there are two arguments I wish to advance here. The first is that, absent a common foe, previously suppressed tensions within the Atlantic community were bound to play a more prominent role than in the past, and they remain likely to do so. Second, even when faced with that common and deadly opponent, the United States was at times barely able to sustain its commitments to its Atlantic partners. The conjunction of these two points – that interests, and especially security interests, within the Alliance

---

[4] This formulation raises the question of whether any other candidate, better suited to this role, is currently on offer. This is doubtful; the United States remains, in Madeleine Albright's memorable phrase, "the indispensable nation."

are less convergent now than during the Cold War, and that in any event US foreign policy tends to lack discipline – suggests stormy seas are ahead.[5]

In making this argument, I do not mean to insist that the Atlantic partnership will necessarily deteriorate further; indeed, the breakdown in Atlantic relations surrounding the invasion of Iraq in spring 2003 was in many ways a stunning aberration. As amply demonstrated in the contribution by Elizabeth Pond (chapter 2), the governments of the United States, France, and Germany behaved very foolishly in the months before the war; the government of the United Kingdom much less so, though it has little to show for its greater prudence. One can only hope that this episode will produce a sobering effect on future leaders on both sides of the Atlantic. But the point is that Washington, Paris, and Berlin could afford to indulge in such cavalier behavior precisely because the stakes of their partnership were so greatly reduced. That is the structural logic of the situation. The challenge for the allies in the future, therefore, will be to cooperate absent the discipline once imposed by their respective international situations.

The strategic foundations of the Atlantic alliance

The great anti-Nazi coalition of the middle of the twentieth century did not long survive the defeat of Hitler's Germany. Within months of the end of World War II, the alliance between the United States, the USSR, and the United Kingdom was under enormous strain; a few years later it collapsed altogether. The Cold War ensued, a great contest between rival blocs centered around Washington and Moscow that went on for some forty years. The new anti-Soviet alliance, though initially built on delicate foundations, eventually developed characteristics that allowed it to become remarkably enduring. Not only did the Western allies share a common foe, to a substantial extent they shared common values as well – certainly to a much greater extent than had the anti-Nazi coalition.

The foundations of this community of values can be traced back at least to World War II. Then, despite tensions between Washington and London,[6] there were substantial efforts – from the signing of the Atlantic

---

[5] In chapter 4 in this volume, Miles Kahler also notes the breakdown of the bipartisan consensus over foreign policy that had characterized American politics during much of the Cold War period. He argues that this shift toward greater policy volatility derives primarily from changes in partisan competition rather than changes in the international environment; I regard these as complementary rather than competing explanations.

[6] Tensions were real between imperial Britain and the anti-imperialist Roosevelt administration, although FDR in essence ordered his subordinates on occasion to ignore difference in the postwar aims of the two governments; on the latter point, see Jon Meacham, *Franklin*

Charter in August 1941 through the series of wartime conferences aimed at designing a framework for the conduct of postwar political and economic relations[7] – to develop a shared moral foundation to the anti-Nazi campaign.[8] The Allies self-consciously engaged their Axis foes in a battle of rival ideologies, a battle that both reflected and reinforced the clash of arms.

After the war, the great and remarkably successful experiments in converting Japan and western Germany into functioning democracies were likewise fundamental to the construction of a politically durable anti-Soviet alliance. This was especially true in the case of the Federal Republic, since the recent victims of Nazi aggression across western Europe had to be persuaded to accept not only the political but eventually the partial military revival of a German state.[9] The institutions of NATO were a critical aspect of this transformation, and a key to the sometimes reluctant agreement of Bonn's neighbors to countenance German rearmament. In addition to these shared political and security interests, however, the NATO partners and especially the members of the incipient European Community became coupled by numerous economic ties, ties that were carefully nurtured and grew ever deeper with the passage of time.[10]

Nevertheless, the core political bargain among the Atlantic partners concerned security. To better understand this, we have to reexamine the

---

and Winston: An Intimate Portrait of an Epic Friendship (New York: Random House, 2003). These frictions subsided in part following Britain's eventual decision to permit, and then to promote, decolonization.

[7] Indeed, one of the motivations for the Bretton Woods conference on the postwar international monetary system was to counter Nazi propaganda concerning the new European order that the Third Reich would usher in. Consider for example this extract from the so-called White Plan, written in April 1942: "serious discussion of specific proposals ... will be a factor toward winning the war ... The people of the anti-Axis powers ... must be assured that something will be done in the sphere of international economic relations that is new, that is powerful enough and comprehensive enough to give expectation of successfully filling a world need" (in J. Keith Horsefield [ed.], *The International Monetary Fund, 1945–1965*, vol. III, Documents [Washington, DC: International Monetary Fund, 1969], pp. 38–39).

[8] Roosevelt's efforts to include Stalin as a partner in this shared moral crusade, for example his characterization of the Soviet leader as "Uncle Joe," were decidedly less successful. For a clear precedent, see Woodrow Wilson's remarks about Russia in his War Message of April 2, 1917: Wilson, *War Messages*, 65th Congress, 1st Session, Senate Doc. No. 5, Serial No. 7264 (Washington, DC, 1917), pp. 3–8.

[9] On the democratic transformation of western Germany, see John Gimbel, *The American Occupation of Germany* (Stanford: Stanford University Press, 1970); and Klaus-Dieter Henke, *Die amerikanische Besetzung Deutschlands* [The American Occupation of Germany] (Munich: Oldenbourg, 1995).

[10] On the role of the United States in promoting European integration in these early years, see Geir Lundestad, *"Empire" by Integration: The United States and European Integration, 1945–1997* (Oxford: Oxford University Press, 1998).

characteristics of the NATO alliance more closely, and here one can do little better than to begin with Lord Ismay's famous dictum. The Alliance's first secretary general reportedly said that the organization's function was "to keep the Russians out, the Americans in, and the Germans down." The first element of Ismay's formulation, keeping the Russians out, is of course the most obvious: NATO was an anti-Soviet alliance. But the second and third elements – keeping the Americans in and the Germans down – were of central importance as well.

In the most comprehensive study to date of the official documents of the period, Marc Trachtenberg[11] concludes that the division of Europe after World War II, painful as it was for the peoples of central and eastern Europe within the Soviet sphere of influence, was nevertheless broadly stable. The Western powers and the USSR were, again broadly speaking, prepared to allow each other a free hand to act on their respective sides of the line of demarcation. But there was one major exception to this rule: the Soviets were not prepared to let West Germany become too strong or too independent. Such an outcome – especially a politically independent and nuclear-armed West Germany – would have been sufficiently provocative to prompt an armed response from Moscow. The principal task of the early Cold War years, therefore, was to enmesh the Federal Republic firmly into Western security and economic systems in a manner that satisfied not only the United States and its west European allies but also the Soviet Union. The solution involved an extended US military presence in Europe, and especially in the Federal Republic. Keeping "the Americans in" and "the Germans down" were therefore not secondary to keeping "the Russians out": they were the central means by which the Russians were persuaded to stay out.

In Trachtenberg's view, this essential task was not fully accomplished until the mid-1960s.[12] By that time, a second abiding political problem of the transatlantic relationship had emerged: Franco-American rivalry. Though France was greatly weakened by World War II, French leaders retained global aspirations in a way that the leadership of the nascent Federal Republic of Germany could not, and they chose to pursue these objectives in ways that British leaders, at least after the Suez crisis, did not – that is, by openly contesting American leadership. The United Kingdom certainly retained a global role and, by means of its close

---

[11] *A Constructed Peace: The Making of the European Settlement, 1945–1963* (Princeton: Princeton University Press, 1999).

[12] Specifically in 1963, when "the elements of a political system fell into place ... [that] would provide the basis for a relatively stable peace for the balance of the Cold War period, and beyond": ibid., p. 352.

relationship with the United States (as well as the two countries' shared language), benefited from American hegemony in ways that France did not. But successive British governments progressively unwound many of the United Kingdom's more far-flung interests, and at least after 1956 tended to define their interests in close parallel to those of the United States.[13]

Calculations in Paris were entirely different. Strategically, the French government refused to align itself decisively with the Western powers, culminating in the 1966 withdrawal from NATO's integrated military command structure. Culturally, French leaders tended to conceive of France as not merely a rival power but, at least on occasion, as a rival civilization in sharp contrast to the Anglo-Saxon alignment of London and Washington.[14] Little wonder, then, that – especially after 1956 – a recurrent tendency of French foreign policy has been to resist, rather than to complement, the influence of the United States.[15]

While this competitive impulse was most pronounced in the policies of de Gaulle, it has been evident in every French president since the founding of the Fifth Republic. As is described by Georges-Henri Soutou (chapter 5), Pompidou was bitterly frustrated that his efforts to restore Franco-American cordiality after de Gaulle's resignation were met not with enhanced status for Paris in Washington, but instead by the Nixon administration's policy of promoting a tight bipolar framework. Giscard was put off both by Jimmy Carter's moralizing tone and by his apparent strategic indecision. Mitterrand would have been only too happy to retire NATO to the ash heap of history following the end of the Cold War. In short, former French foreign minister Hubert Vedrine's desire to balance the American "hyperpower" has a long pedigree.[16]

Despite these recurrent tensions, during the Cold War three factors tended to mitigate Franco-American rivalry. The first such factor was the restraining influence exercised by the Federal Republic of Germany on French policy. West Germany's reliance on the US security guarantee, and equally importantly the promise of American support for eventual

---

[13] For a cogent critique of Britain's reliance on the "special relationship" with the United States, see Rodric Braithwaite, "End of the Affair," *Prospect* (May 2003).

[14] The tendency to think of Franco-American rivalry in cultural and even civilizational terms has deep rhetorical foundations – see again de Montbrial, "Franco-American Relations" – but probably had only limited effects on policy until François Mitterrand's term in office and, especially, the present.

[15] See, for example, Charles Cogan, *French Negotiating Behavior: Dealing with La Grande Nation* (Washington, DC: United States Institute of Peace Press, 2003).

[16] On "hyperpower," see Hubert Vedrine with Dominique Moïsi, *France in an Age of Globalization*, translated by Philip H. Gordon (Washington, DC: Brookings Institution Press, 2001).

reunification with the German Democratic Republic, constituted an important buffer against the sometimes latent, sometimes active French tendency to conceive of geopolitics in anti-American terms.[17] The second factor was self-restraint on the part of France, which profited handsomely from the American security guarantee (against both the Soviets and the Germans) and did not wish to undermine it, merely to alter its terms. The third was a corresponding self-restraint on the part of successive US governments, which regarded NATO as the leading security arrangement, and Europe as the most important theater of operations, of the Cold War conflict with the Soviet Union.

It bears reiterating why American leaders formed this judgment. The simultaneous rearmament and pacification of Germany – its continued entrenchment within Western military structures, including the absence of a genuinely independent German foreign policy – was a key to avoiding armed conflict with the Soviet Union. Continued German pacification depended in large measure on Franco-German reconciliation, undertaken partly within the context of NATO and partly within the context of European integration.[18] Thus, while French withdrawal from NATO's integrated military command had no apparent impact on the overall balance of power between the United States and the Soviet Union,[19] it nevertheless represented a deep political crisis within the Alliance. Accordingly, while American administrations were periodically exercised by French policy, given the complex politics of the Atlantic partnership, it was normally accommodation, not confrontation, that was the order of the day.

The result of these interlocking interests was a stable if continuously tense constellation of relationships among the Western allies. Keeping the Russians out necessitated keeping the Germans down by keeping the Americans in – and this despite the desire of significant political factions in the United States, West Germany, and France to repatriate American military forces. Successive German governments came to accept this policy, even if they did not always warmly embrace it and sometimes tested it at the margins. London, in its self-defined role of transatlantic "bridge" (on this point, see chapter 7), had a similarly strong vested

---

[17] Witness, for example, the decision of the Kennedy administration to target the more vulnerable FRG to express its displeasure over the January 1963 announcement of the Franco-German Friendship Treaty. "There is not much we can do about France," Kennedy said, "but we can exert considerable pressure on the Germans": cited in Trachtenberg, *A Constructed Peace*, p. 374.

[18] Despite the initial reaction of the Kennedy administration, the Elysée Treaty ultimately provided a framework for bilateral relations that reinforced this process.

[19] As noted by Waltz, *Theory of International Politics*, p. 169.

interest in the success of these arrangements, and often played a crucial role in facilitating the resolution of disputes among the other Atlantic partners.[20]

But the point is that the Soviet threat provided the major motive for the Western alliance, while Soviet attitudes toward West Germany helped shape the eventual form that the Alliance assumed. The result was neither simple nor predetermined. Ultimately, a complex equilibrium of interests between London, Paris, Washington, and Bonn emerged that helped preserve the Atlantic partnership, even when aspects of the NATO framework were subject to almost continual questioning in each of these capitals. The essential background condition for the emergence of this equilibrium, however, was the threat from Moscow.

A further point bears underlining as well, especially in light of recent tensions, and that was the role of alliance management in American grand strategy during this period. By "alliance management", I simply mean the regular attention that must be paid to the concerns of allies in order to sustain their useful participation in a political and military alliance. Once the United States became committed to a long-term policy of deterrence and containment, Washington's grand strategy necessitated active attention to alliance management within NATO. Deterring the Soviets was not only a contest of rival wills and capabilities; it also required close attention to the special role of Germany, and because of that to the rest of Europe. Relations within the Alliance were perennially challenging, and occasionally quite frustrating for all concerned. But successive US governments found it to be in their interest to accommodate European concerns, sometimes merely in form but often in substance as well. Why? Because management of the Western alliance was not a secondary concern of US grand strategy during this period; it was part and parcel of that strategy. As with all other strategic aspects of the Cold War, the remission of the military threat from Moscow has called this practice into question.

The end of the Cold War: muted effects

Given the preceding analysis, it should hardly be surprising that the Western alliance proved much more enduring than the old anti-Nazi

---

[20] For example, the substantial British troop presence in the Federal Republic, second only to the American presence, played an important role in persuading both US and West German publics to accept the long-term stationing of foreign troops on German soil. See, e.g., Hubert Zimmermann, *Money and Security: Troops, Monetary Policy, and West Germany's Relations with the United States and Britain, 1950–1971* (Cambridge: Cambridge University Press, 2002).

pact. Especially within the Atlantic community, the geopolitical imperative of balancing Soviet power went largely hand in hand with the more
liberal objectives of democracy promotion and the construction of international institutions aimed at facilitating cooperation and shared prosperity
within the West.[21] Thus for half a century the realism of Theodore
Roosevelt was married to the idealism of Woodrow Wilson, a union
that survived (if only barely, on occasion) many a crisis.[22] But could it
survive success?

Indeed, if the complex series of relationships described above was
driven primarily by the geopolitical logic of balancing Soviet power,
then the end of the Cold War should have changed everything. With
the Cold War's end, and especially following the collapse of the Soviet
Union, the chief reason for the Atlantic alliance – security against a hostile
superpower actively bent on expansion – no longer existed. The strategic
rationale that underpinned the complex Atlantic bargain was therefore
no longer operative. From Washington's perspective, Europe was unlikely
to remain the focus of US geopolitical concerns, nor was it likely that
NATO would remain the primary vehicle for achieving American political and military objectives. In Bonn (and then Berlin), the previously
tight constraints on German foreign policy should have been relaxed.
The value of the "special relationship" between the United States and the
United Kingdom should have come under close examination, in both
Washington and London. In Paris, the buffers on Franco-American
rivalry should have been removed.

In short, the whole strategic basis of the transatlantic relationship
should have come undone. Prominent theorists of international relations
from the US realist tradition therefore predicted, and awaited, the
Alliance's imminent collapse.[23] Their reasoning was simple: no common
threat, no common purpose – such was the lesson of history, repeated

---

[21] See, e.g., John Ikenberry, *After Victory: Institutions, Strategic Restraint, and the Rebuilding of
Order After Major Wars* (Princeton: Princeton University Press, 2001).

[22] Henry Kissinger (*Diplomacy* [New York: Simon & Schuster, 1994], pp. 29–55) empha-
sizes Theodore Roosevelt and Woodrow Wilson as representative of alternative
approaches to American foreign policy, as does John Gerard Ruggie ("The Past as
Prologue? Interests, Identity, and American Foreign Policy," *International Security* 21:4
[Spring 1997], pp. 89–125). Walter Russell Mead employs a variant of this approach in
Special Providence: American Foreign Policy and How It Changed the World (New York:
Century Foundation, 2002).

[23] Powerful early statements along these lines came from John J. Mearsheimer, "Back to the
Future: Instability in Europe After the Cold War," *International Security* 15:1 (July–August
1990), pp. 5–56, and Kenneth Waltz, "The Emerging Structure of International Politics,"
International Security 18:2 (Autumn 1993), pp. 44–79. For a later analysis with good
references to the ensuing debate, see Kenneth Waltz, "Structural Realism After the Cold
War," *International Security* 25:1 (Summer 2000), pp. 5–41.

again and again.[24] But NATO proved durable, at least in the short term, due to a combination of institutional robustness, attitudinal inertia, and the favorable confluence of a number of temporary conditions.

Not least among these temporary mitigating factors was the election of a US president in 1992 who was supremely able to persuade his European interlocutors that he understood and agreed with them, even while pursuing policies that were sometimes extremely difficult for them to accept. In addition, the military conflicts that arose during the 1990s tended to distract attention from the underlying changes in the Atlantic partnership. Consider policy toward the Middle East, normally a "focus of discord" between the United States and its European partners.[25] But Saddam's inept diplomacy, followed by George Bush, Sr.'s extraordinary efforts to marshal international opinion against Baghdad, resulted in an unprecedented display of not merely Western but global solidarity against a regional villain, culminating in the Persian Gulf War of 1991.

Later, the temporary absence of strategic conflicts elsewhere in the globe allowed the allies to focus on NATO's enlargement and transformation. These changes to the Alliance were driven at least in part by domestic politics: in the United States, for example, the Clinton administration did not support NATO's enlargement until the Republicans threatened to make the subject an electoral issue.[26] Still, the addition of central and east European states to the Alliance could at least plausibly be said to address what many regarded as the major security challenge of the post-Cold War era: containing ethnic rivalries, especially in the former Soviet sphere of influence.[27]

Finally, one additional factor helped mask the inherent strains within the Alliance: the slow evolution of US grand strategy. Despite belated American leadership on NATO's transformation, no clear formulation of

---

[24] For an interesting counterargument, see James W. Davis, "Victims of Success? Post Victory Alliance Politics," NATO Research Fellowship Final Report (2000), available at http://www.nato.int/acad/fellow/98-00/davis.pdf.

[25] William Wallace and Costanza Musu, "The Focus of Discord? The Middle East in US Strategy and European Aspirations," in John Peterson and Mark A. Pollack (eds.), *Europe, America, Bush: Transatlantic Relations in the Twenty-First Century* (London: Routledge, 2003), pp. 99–114.

[26] A clear majority of American experts opposed NATO enlargement on strategic grounds, especially with respect to the Baltic states; see for example John Gaddis' condemnation of the policy in his "History, Grand Strategy, and NATO Enlargement," *Survival* 40:1 (1998), pp. 145–151. For a retrospective defense of the policy by one of its chief advocates, see Ronald D. Asmus, *Opening NATO's Door* (New York: Columbia University Press, 2002).

[27] Certainly the Balkan wars helped catalyze NATO's post-Soviet evolution. On this and related points, see chapter 10 in this volume.

a new general philosophy toward global security was evident during the Clinton years.[28] This subdued pace of change, as described in the next section, further reduced pressure on the Alliance.

American strategic thought: the implications of primacy

Well before the events of September 11, 2001, American understanding of the strategic position of the United States had changed, at least within its expert community. This change necessarily affected perceptions, even among Atlanticists, of the strategic significance of the American partnership with Europe. Overall, it was clear that these changes boded ill for a stable transatlantic relationship.

During the 1990s, a lengthy discussion took place in the American academy and in leading think tanks concerning the bases and implications of US power preponderance after the Cold War.[29] In particular, the shift from a bipolar to a unipolar distribution of military power gave rise to two questions: whether American military dominance was likely to prove enduring or ephemeral, and (closely related) where the major threats to American security lay.

On both these questions, there was initially a wide range of expert opinion. Analysts varied between arguing that American primacy was likely to prove both enduring and beneficial;[30] that primacy was threatened but beneficial, and therefore worth preserving;[31] that eventual

---

[28] Barry R. Posen and Andrew L. Ross, "Competing Visions for US Grand Strategy," *International Security* 21:3 (Winter 1996), pp. 5–53, especially pp. 5–6 and 44–50.

[29] A parallel discussion was more narrowly focused on the military lessons of the 1991 Gulf War, Somalia, and the Balkan conflicts; hence, the questions were more technically defined, for example in terms of the relative significance of air versus land power. My remarks in the text are confined to the questions of possible peer competitors and the changing nature of security threats. It bears noting, however, that American analysts involved in this second, more technical debate were deeply concerned about the difficulties of conducting an effective military operation without clear lines of command. The sustained discussion on this topic helps explain the resonance of Secretary of Defense Donald Rumsfeld's later dictum that the mission should determine the coalition, not the reverse, despite the fact that this formulation elevated a tactical principle to the level of strategy.

[30] This view gained greater ascendancy late in the decade. See, for example, William C. Wohlforth, "The Stability of a Unipolar World," *International Security* 21:1 (Summer 1999), pp. 1–36.

[31] There were two important variants of this argument, quite at odds with one another in terms of policy prescription. The first, advocated by many traditional realists as well as liberal internationalist theorists, held that potential rivals needed to have their fears of American preeminence assuaged; the second, championed by neoconservatives, held that potential rivals to American preeminence needed to be intimidated. An example of the latter thinking can be found in the Draft Policy Guidance produced by the Defense Department during the administration of George Bush, Sr., in March 1992; see "Extracts

American decline was inevitable, and therefore the United States should be preparing for a stable transition to a multipolar world;[32] and that withdrawal from an active role in international affairs was in order.[33] As for the nature of future security threats, some pointed to threats from a resurgent Russia;[34] others to emerging powers (typically China);[35] some to current US allies, including members of the European Union;[36] still others to rogue states, especially those armed with weapons of mass destruction; and, finally, some to nonstate terrorist networks fueled by anti-Western ideologies and rendered increasingly capable of inflicting harm by the global diffusion of technology.

Limitations of space do not permit a thorough examination of how this debate evolved. Suffice it to say that, by the end of the 1990s, most of the serious thinkers in the US foreign policy community were persuaded that threats to American primacy, if any, were at best distant: no peer competitors were on the immediate horizon.[37] On the other hand, debates about the nature of existing and future threats to American security continued to rage unabated.

Despite these differences, what was increasingly plain was that alliance management and, in closely related fashion, American involvement in

from Pentagon's Plan: 'Prevent the Emergence of a New Rival,'" *New York Times*, March 8, 1992. Authored primarily by Paul Wolfowitz, its contents foreshadowed policies to be adopted a decade later during the administration of George W. Bush.

[32] See, e.g., Christopher Layne, "The Unipolar Illusion: Why New Great Powers Will Arise," *International Security* 17:4 (Spring 1993), pp. 5–51.

[33] This perspective had little appeal within the American academy, Eric Nordlinger being the chief exception (Nordlinger, *Isolationism Reconfigured: American Foreign Policy for a New Century* [Princeton: Princeton University Press, 1995]). It did, however, resonate with a segment of the American population; witness the popularity of Patrick J. Buchanan's later treatise on the subject (*A Republic, Not An Empire: Reclaiming America's Destiny* [Washington, DC: Regnery Publishing, 2002]).

[34] Henry Kissinger, "Expand NATO Now," *Washington Post*, December 19, 1994; Zbigniew Brzezinski, "The Premature Partnership," *Foreign Affairs* 73:2 (March–April 1992), pp. 67–82.

[35] This was certainly one of the leitmotifs of foreign policy discussion within the administration of George W. Bush prior to 9/11. For example, shortly prior to the election of 2000, Condoleezza Rice, soon to be named national security advisor, wrote that "For America and our allies, the most daunting task is to find the right balance in our policy toward Russia and China"; the next seven paragraphs dealt exclusively with China: Rice, "Promoting the National Interest," *Foreign Affairs* 79:1 (January–February 2000), pp. 45–62. For an earlier formulation of this concern, see Zalmay Khalizad, *From Containment to Global Leadership? America and the World After the Cold War* (Santa Monica: RAND Corporation, 1995), especially p. 30.

[36] This was originally an outlier position; see for example Jeffrey T. Bergner, *The New Superpowers: Germany, Japan, the US and the New World Order* (New York: St. Martin's Press, 1991). It has since become more respectable; see Charles Kupchan, "The End of the West," *Atlantic Monthly* 290:4 (November 2002), pp. 42–44.

[37] This was the starting place of the analysis in John G. Ikenberry, *America Unrivaled: The Future of the Balance of Power* (Ithaca: Cornell University Press, 2002).

international organizations would play different roles in future US foreign policy than they had in the past. No longer was there the sharp disciplining effect associated with a rival superpower threatening nuclear war if American relations with its allies proved unsatisfactory. As a consequence, even the strongest advocates of preserving and further developing American commitment to international institutions[38] were obliged to argue that the function of these commitments was to augment American power and influence – which was merely desirable – rather than, as in days gone by, to avert nuclear war – which had been essential.

In short, the passing of the Cold War confrontation with the Soviet Union meant that the United States had greater liberty with respect to its foreign commitments than at any time in the preceding half-century. Attention to the NATO alliance could be justified on a number of strategic grounds, but it was no longer a geopolitical imperative in the same sense that it had been during the Cold War. It was in this context that George W. Bush assumed office in January 2001.

The Alliance under stress

To summarize the preceding argument, for roughly a decade after the Cold War's end the happy conjuncture of a number of temporary factors trumped the effects of diverging national interests within the Alliance.[39] But the effects of structural change were delayed, not averted; and later the situation was reversed, with temporary conditions drawing attention to divergent Atlantic interests rather than away from them. Among these new conditions were George W. Bush's election in 2000 and Saddam's relatively successful diplomatic gambits of the late 1990s and early twenty-first century, as opposed to his reckless military adventures of the early 1990s. But the supreme catalytic event was September 11, which helped galvanize changes in the USA's strategic self-understanding.

Of course, strains within the Alliance were evident prior to the terrorist attacks on New York and Washington, and even prior to George W. Bush's election. The Kyoto Protocol, the International Criminal Court, and other initiatives – many of them emanating largely from Europe – were bound to test the Atlantic framework regardless of the American administration of the day. These, however, were exacerbating circumstances,

---

[38] For example, Joseph S. Nye, Jr., *The Paradox of American Power: Why the World's Only Superpower Can't Go It Alone* (Oxford: Oxford University Press, 2002).

[39] There were also more enduring institutional characteristics that likewise contributed to NATO's durability; see, e.g., Celeste A. Wallander, "Institutional Assets and Adaptability: NATO After the Cold War," *International Organization* 54:4 (2000), pp. 705–735.

not the source of the transatlantic crisis of 2002–3. During the weeks and months following the end of "major hostilities" in Iraq, there was ample opportunity for governments – regardless of their initial support for or opposition to the war – to reflect on just what those underlying sources were.

To begin with, Paris and Berlin realized (much to their dismay) that their threats to undermine European public support for American policy had lost much of their previous traction. Absent the interlocking concerns that once united Washington and Moscow in supporting a substantial armed American presence in Germany, Europe is no longer the center-piece of American grand strategy. As a consequence, even the active opposition of some leading European states to the Iraq War, though damaging, was not fatal. As Helga Haftendorn has noted, the United States no longer requires European support in the same way it did during the Cold War.[40] During those forty years, the implementation of American grand strategy required German (and to a lesser degree French) consent precisely because that strategy was focused on keeping the Germans down in order to keep the Russians out. But that logic no longer obtained, and in its absence neither the Franco-German threat to oppose the war nor the execution of that threat was serious enough to deter American action in Iraq.

But a learning process was likewise underway in the United States. There, at least among the chattering classes, lingering triumphalism regarding the Soviet Union's demise was slowly replaced with the realiza-tion that in the post-Cold War environment, European support for US foreign policy was likely to be much more conditional than had previously been the case. Despite the focus of both the media and the White House on disagreements with Paris, it was the articulation of a German critique of American policy that was most striking. While difficult relations with France had come to be expected (and largely accepted), it was a new experience to have a central feature of US foreign policy forcefully rejected by a German government.

From a structural perspective, the key change in postwar European politics is Germany's newfound capacity for policy maneuver. As Hubert Zimmermann argues in this volume (chapter 6), Germany is now an important net security exporter rather than, as was the case during the Cold War, a substantial net security importer. This fact alters the underlying politics of the bilateral relationship with the United

---

[40] Helga Haftendorn, "One Year after 9/11: A Critical Appraisal of German–American Relations," Thyssen German American Dialogue Seminar Series, AICGS (2002, http://www.aicgs.org/publications/PDF/haftendorn.pdf).

States. For example, while future governments of the Federal Republic may not follow the lead of Gerhard Schröder in actually courting confrontation with Washington, it is evident that they are capable of doing so.

Thus the Cold War's end has ushered in a new era of "permissiveness" for Germany that parallels the changes experienced by the United States. The ability of governments from these two states to disregard the consequences of their actions for the Atlantic alliance – even if that capacity for neglect remains unexercised – represents a fundamental change in transatlantic relations.

The implications of this shift are far-reaching. For example, tensions within Europe during the run-up to the Iraq War – especially those between Britain and France – made a mess of the European Union's pretensions to behave as a coherent actor on the world stage. But it bears underlining that the orientation of French and British policies toward the United States did not fundamentally change with the passing of the bipolar system. Quite the opposite, in fact: Atlantic policies in Paris and London have been reasonably consistent with their Cold War precedents, and far more so than is the case in either Washington or Bonn/Berlin. During the whole of the Iraq crisis, Tony Blair and Jacques Chirac adopted policies fully conforming to Britain's historic affinity for, and France's reflexive skepticism of, close partnership with Washington. Certainly the crisis exposed the underlying divisions between the UK and France – divisions, by the way, that Charles de Gaulle understood only too well. But the heightened tensions between these traditional rivals were primarily the result of changes of policy in the United States and Germany, not in Britain or France.

To put it bluntly, Washington and Berlin are at liberty to pursue far more foolish policies in the early twenty-first century than either the US or West German governments could afford to imagine during most of the late twentieth century. In the weeks and months preceding the invasion of Iraq, both these governments (joined by Paris and, to a much lesser degree, London) explored and exploited the international system's new tolerance for policy error.

Policy in the unipole

What then lies ahead? Andrew Moravcsik speaks for many American analysts when he argues that "Washington must shift course and accept multilateral conditions for intervention" while Europeans must "be prepared to pick up much of the burden of conflict prevention and postconflict engagement."[41] But while such an approach is superficially rational, this moderately revamped version of the old Atlantic bargain is unlikely to prove stable. The old framework was at perennial risk even in the context of the Cold War struggle: that is to say, even when there was a clearly recognized mutual foe, a commonly agreed strategy to engage that foe, and a credible threat by that foe to punish instances of alliance failure. Absent these enabling conditions, the domestic costs of compliance with such a revamped agreement are likely to swamp the perceived strategic benefits. This is the sort of arithmetic that elected governments understand.

Especially after the Iraq crisis, reheating this plate of Cold War leftovers will regularly arouse resistance, and not only in the United States.[42] Self-restraint has not been a defining characteristic of foreign policy during George W. Bush's presidency.[43] But even if a more disciplined administration were to assume office, it would have to address the changed interests of the United States resulting from its changed position in the international system. While the associated threat assessment continues to vary, it is far from clear that this uncertainty bodes well for the Alliance. Future administrations will likely continue to hedge their bets, probably with greater attention to international legitimacy than the first administration of George W. Bush but certainly with a continued focus on the capacity to respond to threats flexibly and autonomously.

Such a slow transition to a new security doctrine on the part of the world's leading power is of course fairly natural. It takes time to adjust to new challenges, and the combination of stateless terrorism, nuclear

---

[41] Andrew Moravcsik, "Striking a New Transatlantic Bargain," *Foreign Affairs* 82:4 (July–August 2003), p. 75. For a prescient analysis that offers a similarly pragmatic prescription, see Malcolm Chalmers, "The Atlantic Burden-Sharing Debate: Widening or Fragmenting?", *International Affairs* 77:3 (2001), pp. 569–585.

[42] On the difficulties of swapping American moderation for European aid in reconstruction, Ronald Asmus concludes that "no American leader of any political persuasion will accept the proposition that the basis for a US–European partnership should be containment of US ability to act," while Douglas Hurd notes that "out of Kosovo came the bitter saying that the Americans fight the wars while Europe does the dishes. That is not a sound basis for an alliance": Asmus, "Rebuilding the Atlantic Alliance," *Foreign Affairs* 82:5 (September–October 2003), p. 29; Hurd, "Europe Must Respond to the Arc of Danger," *Financial Times*, March 28, 2001.

[43] On the foreign policy peregrinations of the Bush administration, compare Condoleezza Rice's "Promoting the National Interest," published in early 2000, in which she argued that the administration of George W. Bush would distinguish itself from its predecessor by focusing on the United States' strategic relations with other great powers, with her remarks in the summer of 2003, when she began arguing that bringing freedom and democracy to the Middle East was "the security challenge – and moral mission – of our time" ("Remarks to Veterans of Foreign Wars," August 25, 2003, http://www.whitehouse.gov/news/releases/2003/08/20030825-1.html, accessed July 12, 2004).

proliferation, and the widespread availability of biological weapons raises difficult intellectual conundrums. Some fifty years ago, the development of an intellectual consensus among elites about the appropriate response to the nuclear revolution took well over a decade; the current security environment, with its multiplicity of both weapons and actors, is at least as complex. This suggests that we are entering a new era in which not only US foreign policy but the policies of its allies and adversaries, both current and potential, will be characterized by the probing of alternative approaches unless and until a new strategic consensus emerges. During the Cold War, a reasonably stable situation did not arise until after the development of such a consensus, its firm embrace by the national security establishment in Washington, and its successful promotion abroad.[44] That stability derived from a shared understanding among leading actors of international roles, responsibilities, and appropriate behavior; no such consensus exists today.[45]

Put differently, while shared fears of terrorism may eventually lead to the development of a new strategic consensus within the Alliance, they have not done so yet.[46] In the meantime, alliance management does not and likely will not occupy the central space on the American strategic agenda that it once did, and that it had to, during the Cold War. This is so despite the fact that the Alliance can play an important and perhaps even critical role in international policing efforts in the fight against terrorism. But given the diverse nature of the security threats facing the United States, there is no longer any logically compelling case for management of the Atlantic alliance to play the same central role it once did; this is one of the consequences of the passing of the Soviet threat. Absent a geopolitical imperative to devote substantial resources (including the time and attention of senior officials) to resolving transatlantic crises as they arise, there is greater scope for small problems to fester and for larger problems occasionally to explode, as they did during spring 2003. That crisis

---

[44] On the evolutionary development of nuclear strategy, see Marc Trachtenberg, *History and Strategy* (Princeton: Princeton University Press, 1991). The complexity of the current security environment is a major theme of Trachtenberg's contribution to the present volume (chapter 9).

[45] While the Bush administration's National Security Strategy of September 2002 (http://www.whitehouse.gov/nsc/nss.html) might be regarded as a first step in this direction, that eclectic document was not the result of a consensus among leading American strategic thinkers nor has it been successfully marketed abroad.

[46] The strategy document adopted by the European Council in December 2003 (retrievable at http://www.ueitalia2003.it/EN/, accessed July 12, 2004) was groundbreaking; the EU had never previously developed a statement of its strategic framework, and the resulting document had many points in common with its US counterpart from the previous year. But this is best understood as an early exchange in what is likely to be a long dialogue.

need not serve as a paradigm for future behavior, but on the whole one can expect that the United States – at least intermittently and probably on average – will be a more difficult partner than in times past, regardless of the administration of the day.

US relations with the "Big Three"

What, then, of US relations with Europe's three "great powers"? Let us consider France, Germany, and the United Kingdom in turn.

In France, senior officials of the French government – including the president of the Republic – have since the mid-1990s explicitly framed discussions of foreign policy in terms of balancing American power. On the face of it, this desire is not necessarily inconsistent with continued Franco-American partnership; there is, after all, an important precedent in the earlier NATO aim of containing the political and military independence of West Germany, another Alliance member. But the French pursuit of "double security" against both the USSR and Germany normally remained implicit, and the foreign policy establishment in Paris wisely exercised sustained discretion throughout the Cold War in pursuing one agenda while proclaiming another.[47] In the longstanding French debate about global politics that preceded the Iraq crisis, on the other hand, no such discretion was apparent.

Quite the opposite, in fact: the establishment of a multipolar world system in which American political and military preeminence could be effectively challenged has now been an avowed objective of French foreign policy for almost ten years. Since it is not hard to imagine how the public articulation of such a vision would be received by American citizens and their elected representatives, this suggests either that the French stance is not serious – that is, that the senior officials who engage in this rhetoric do not really desire this outcome, except in a wistful sort of way – or else that the government intends to pursue this policy outside NATO. Neither conclusion bodes well for the bilateral relationship or for the Alliance.

More generally, episodic but substantial crises can be expected as long as the principal interlocutors of the Atlantic relationship remain Paris and Washington. In neither of these capitals does a critical mass of the political establishment believe any longer that accommodation with the other should be a guiding principle of foreign policy. While such accommodation was never popular, during the Cold War a sufficient

---

[47] See once again chapter 5.

number of elites held that it was essential, and their will generally prevailed; that outcome is considerably less likely to obtain in the future.

In Germany, now that the genie of anti-Americanism has been let out of the bottle of German domestic politics by a sitting German government, it is not clear that it can be locked up once more. Future debates within the Federal Republic will take place within a much more elastic international policy environment, as discussed earlier, but also against the historical backdrop of Schröder's precedent. Thus not only have structural circumstances changed; the German electorate's awareness of those circumstances has changed as well. Cooperation across a wide range of measures should nonetheless be expected, given the deep and ever-growing economic ties that reach across the Atlantic. But the prospects for periodic clashes of the Schröder–Bush variety cannot be dismissed, and will therefore color calculations on both sides.

In the United Kingdom, Tony Blair is paying a heavy personal and political price for his government's role as the USA's chief ally in the war against Saddam Hussein.[48] Blair was always a special case. On the one hand, he had publicly articulated a moral argument about the necessity of removing Saddam long before George W. Bush assumed office;[49] on the other, he argued before the House of Commons that a principal reason for joining the Americans in the invasion of Iraq was to prevent the much greater possible damage to international affairs that would result from a truly unilateral US action.[50] Whatever his motivations, there is precious little evidence that he secured more than marginal influence over the course of US policy, either in the "greater Middle East" or elsewhere, in exchange for his loyalty.

Still, it is unclear that any superior strategy was available to the British prime minister. First Schröder and then an increasingly intransigent Chirac rejected Blair's efforts at transatlantic mediation, allowing the Bush administration to simply ignore the same. Since World War II, Britain has made much of its potential influence over both Washington and continental Europe by virtue of its bridging role between the two; but

---

[48] As did José María Aznar in Spain. Leszek Miller in Poland did not appear to gain any substantial dividend from Warsaw's relationship with Washington, although in fairness his political star had already faded. In Italy, the political consequences of Silvio Berlusconi's support for the war remain unclear.

[49] Tony Blair, "Doctrine of the International Community," April 23, 1999, http://www.number-10.gov.uk/output/Page1297.asp.

[50] "And if our plea is for America to work with others, to be good as well as powerful allies, will our retreat make them multilateralist? Or will it not rather be the biggest impulse to unilateralism there could ever be": Tony Blair, "PM Statement Opening Iraq Debate", March 18, 2003 (http://www.number-10.gov.uk/output/Page3294.asp., accessed 12 July 2004).

the changes of policy in Washington and Berlin outlined earlier – changes that were enabled by the new international environment – made such a role impossible to play, at least in this instance. Whether it can be resumed in the future remains to be seen.

Ultimately, however, any discussion of American bilateral relations with each of the "Big Three" that fails to take into account the larger and dynamic relationship among all four states is misleading. As a global superpower, Washington has an interest in a relationship with Europe as a whole in addition to its component parts; hence its interest in how the European Security and Defence Policy (ESDP) plays out, and the uneasy relationship of ESDP with NATO. It is in the context of these larger concerns that American policy must be understood.

Thus, while American efforts to preserve and perhaps even enhance the "special relationship" with Britain are likely, these are essentially rearguard or defensive actions; for the Alliance to be truly revitalized, wooing Germany firmly back into the political fold is essential. Conversely, for Europe to emerge as a genuine counterweight to American policy, it will not be sufficient for Paris to sustain or even to upgrade its relationship with Berlin. The Franco-German partnership may be necessary, but it is plainly insufficient to address French ambitions; only by removing the UK from its American orbit can Europe begin to develop a security capacity able, even in the long term, to challenge Washington.

Any decisive resolution of this quadrilateral tug-of-war would have profound consequences for the larger Atlantic relationship, and for world politics more generally. But such a decisive break from present dynamics is unlikely. France will normally be willing to make whatever occasional concessions to Germany are necessary to prevent Berlin's long-term defection to Washington; and Washington will (or at least should) be willing to make similar concessions to Britain in order to prevent its wholesale defection to Paris. These outcomes, dictated by objective interests, are the more likely because they largely coincide with cultural proclivities. Many Britons were aggravated by the policies of the Bush administration, but they are extremely unlikely to trust their future security to Paris; both the Atlantic capabilities gap and their own history suggest too strongly that such a course would be unwise. Meanwhile, despite accumulating evidence that the German government and especially the larger German political establishment have had second thoughts about realigning Berlin decisively away from Washington and toward Paris, it is nonetheless difficult to imagine any fundamental break between the European Union's core couple. This is not to say that a future German government may not one day decide that it is able to challenge the French in a dramatic, public way on some major policy issue without threatening the project of European integration – a development that would in itself revolutionize the European political scene. But Germany has been even more thoroughly "Europeanized" than it has been "Atlanticized," so a decisive German break with Paris and toward Washington is simply not in the cards.

Structure and statecraft

If the long-term logic of international politics is to balance against preponderant power, then the eventual formation of an anti-American alliance is inevitable, and European states may well form part of that coalition. But other formulations of realist theory maintain that states balance against rival threats, not power per se, in which case such an outcome is far from assured.[51] Following the tragedy of September 11, Europe was confronted with the most bellicose American administration of at least the previous twenty years. Even so, it was hardly clear that the United States represented a threat to Europe or to European interests, occasionally heated rhetoric notwithstanding.

Previously such rhetoric, and accompanying policy actions, were restrained by the desire to present a united front to the Soviet Union. That restraint is now gone; so likewise is the favorable confluence of temporary circumstances that once postponed a post-Cold War crisis across the Atlantic. A skilled and attractive US president was replaced by one who, at least in European eyes, was profoundly unsympathetic, and a series of military conflicts meeting with Europe's general approval was followed by a contest that was deeply unpopular. As a result, the deep rifts at the heart of the Atlantic community, rifts that were previously latent, have been laid bare.

These rifts are the result of changing state interests flowing in part from a changed international distribution of power. But structural factors have never been sufficient to determine foreign policies, only to discipline them – or to fail to do so. The relative absence of disciplining effects has been evident in the experimentation (a term I employ charitably) that characterized foreign policy-making on both sides of the Atlantic during 2002 and 2003. Since then, no consensus on the strategic agenda – on the nature of shared threats and especially on the appropriate steps to address them – unites the United States and its major European partners. Absent such an intellectual consensus and the structural circumstances to sustain it, the challenge for the Atlantic partners will be to cooperate without a

---

[51] See, for example, Stephen M. Walt, *The Origins of Alliances* (Ithaca: Cornell University Press, 1987).

stable and comprehensive framework for cooperation. Can this be done? Of course. Will it be difficult? Undoubtedly. Cooperation was difficult when the strategic circumstances of the partnership were both propitious and relatively stable; at present this is not the case. The prospects for cooperation will therefore rely more than ever on statecraft, in an era when this precious human resource is in unusually short supply.

Part II

National policies within the Alliance

4 US politics and transatlantic relations: we are all Europeans now

Miles Kahler

Forty years ago, at the height of the Cold War, a popular and sophisticated president was in the White House. The French ambassador commented at the time, "Never before have the misunderstandings between France and the United States been as profound."[1] American escalation of the war in Vietnam two years later produced judgments in Europe as harsh as any heard during the Iraq War. President Lyndon Johnson was considered by nearly one-third of the French population as the "most dangerous threat to peace"; the president of France, Charles de Gaulle, labeled Johnson "the greatest danger in the world today to peace."[2] Similar levels of distrust and anxiety could be found at other times in the half-century of the Atlantic alliance. Given this history of sharp conflict and multiple misunderstandings, how does the current transatlantic crisis differ?

Many explanations for the pattern of transatlantic relations rely on the international environment or changes in relative power to explain oscillation between cooperation and conflict. For those on either side of the Atlantic who view the current post-Iraq conflict between the United States and Europe as unprecedented, two such changes are awarded a central place. The end of the Cold War was the source of many premature predictions of NATO's demise, on the basis of a simple, realist explanation for alliances: end of Soviet threat, end of alliance. Now the absence of a common threat and, more important, divergent strategies for meeting agreed threats appear to signal a deeper level of discord.[3] A second change, European unification, has been translated by some observers into the birth of a new international power that will inevitably challenge the United States, or the source of a foreign policy orientation that will distance a

---

[1] Richard Barnett, *The Alliance* (New York: Simon & Schuster, 1983), p. 249, cited in Thomas Alan Schwartz, *Lyndon Johnson and Europe: In the Shadow of Vietnam* (Cambridge: Harvard University Press, 2003).

[2] Schwartz, *Lyndon Johnson and Europe*, p. 84; Frank Costigliola, *France and the United States: The Cold Alliance Since World War II* (New York: Twayne, 1992), p. 142, cited ibid., p. 93.

[3] The chapters by Andrews and Zimmermann in this volume involve variants on this theme, admittedly more nuanced than this generalization suggests.

multilateralist Europe from the more muscular posture of the United States.[4] Another explanation, more idiosyncratic than the first, relies on the beliefs and actions of George W. Bush, a president who arouses particular hostility in parts of the European population. The foreign policy changes that have elicited such hostility across the Atlantic are labeled the "Bush revolution."[5] For those with a less charitable view of the president and his grasp of foreign policy, the revolution is portrayed as more of a coup d'état, one in which a neoconservative cabal has seized control of foreign policy.

These candidate explanations for the current transatlantic rift – structural and personal – have limited scope, since they fail to explain past episodes of conflict. Two patterns emerge in reviewing those conflicts. First, a surprising number have centered on areas outside Europe. A divergence between the United States and Europe in threat perception was more likely outside the main arena of confrontation with the Soviet Union. The European ex-colonial powers, particularly Britain and France, continued to claim influence in these areas, and the United States was easily seen to be dislodging them. Among these "out-of-area" regions, the Middle East has always loomed particularly large as a site of conflict, beginning with Algeria and Suez, key episodes in the collapse of British and French power in the region. Tensions arose over relations with postrevolutionary Iran, and over the Israeli conflict. With the exception of the ill-fated 1983 intervention by the United States in Lebanon, however, neither the United States nor the Europeans took unilateral military action between decolonization and the post-9/11 Afghanistan and Iraq wars. Diplomatic tensions remained subdued, despite different domestic perceptions of the Middle East, since the resulting divergence in views was not exacerbated by the use of force. In many ways, Afghanistan and particularly Iraq replay and continue this long tradition of divisive conflict over the Middle East. In a mirror image of Suez, the United States now views the region as a source of mortal threat and a site for informal empire. The heated rhetoric of the Bush administration toward Saddam Hussein echoes Anthony Eden's inflation of the threat from Nasser.[6]

---

[4] The first position is taken by Charles A. Kupchan in *The End of the American Era: US Foreign Policy and the Geopolitics of the Twenty-First Century* (New York: Knopf, 2002); the second by Robert Kagan in his *Of Paradise and Power: America and Europe in the New World Order* (New York: Knopf, 2003).

[5] Ivo H. Daalder and James M. Lindsay, *America Unbound: The Bush Revolution in Foreign Policy* (Washington, DC: Brookings Institution Press, 2003).

[6] In a telegram to President Eisenhower early in the crisis, Eden claimed that, if the two did not take a "firm stand" against Nasser, "our influence and yours throughout the Middle East will, we are convinced, be finally destroyed." In a later letter to Eisenhower, Eden

If the site of conflicts partially explains their intensity over time, political context has contributed as well. At least since the Vietnam War, Republican administrations in the United States have had more troubled relations with European allies than Democratic administrations. From the Nixon–Connally monetary shock to the Reagan administration's extraterritorial claims and nuclear weapons policies, American unilateralism has been particularly prominent under Republican presidencies; the more conservative the administration, the sharper the conflict.

Awarding American politics a prominent place in any explanation for transatlantic conflict suggests a different explanatory perspective on the current crisis. Both structural and personal explanations for conflict between Europe and the United States are notably apolitical. Charles Kupchan, for example, traces many of the long-term changes in American political life that might undermine American internationalism, but, at its core, his argument rests on claims about the position of the United States in the international system. The proponents of a Bush revolution also describe this former governor from a populous and fractious state as curiously inattentive to the political implications of his actions.

A different and more realistic perspective on both structural international change and presidential imprints would not deny their importance but would view their influence through the lens of domestic politics. Systemic change – such as the collapse of the Soviet Union – may permit a more direct expression of domestic politics in foreign policy. The actions of individual politicians will reflect domestic political calculations as well as foreign policy beliefs. Presidents, prime ministers, and their advisors are concerned with domestic political survival as well as foreign policy goals. Domestic political change has direct effects on the external orientation of Europe and the United States; it also filters international developments and shapes policy responses.

Domestic politics, foreign policy, and transatlantic relations

For much of the Cold War, transatlantic relations rarely produced deep divisions in domestic politics. In American politics, relations with Europe were arguably the most consensual and least controversial element in American foreign policy. NATO quickly became a bipartisan sacred cow; trade conflict with the European Community seldom exploded

closed with the statement "it would be an ignoble end to our long history if we accepted to perish by degrees": Hugh Thomas, *The Suez Affair* (Harmondsworth: Penguin Books, 1970), pp. 41, 76.

with the rancor directed toward Japan. In Europe, the United States was sometimes a convenient political target on the anti-nuclear left and the Gaullist and imperial right, but, with the important exception of the communists, anti-Americanism did not become a persistent line of political cleavage in the politics of any major European country. Even at moments of intense disagreement between elites on either side of the Atlantic, these core relations were rarely exploited for domestic political gain. As Schwartz notes, Lyndon Johnson did not target the manifestly unpopular Charles de Gaulle during the Vietnam War, even though such a strategy might have deflected some of the domestic opposition to that conflict.[7] Domestic politics served to stabilize transatlantic relations, rather than deepening elite conflict.

This insulation of transatlantic relations from the vagaries of domestic politics began to change during the Reagan administration, as the Cold War consensus in the United States began to break down. At least until the Iraq War, Europe was not a defining issue in American politics, but domestic political trends in the United States now have clear and, on balance, negative implications for the stability of transatlantic relations. What is presented here is a balance sheet of two types of developments in domestic politics, concentrating on the United States, where change has been most significant. On the one hand, certain domestic political patterns – notably public opinion and the political consequences of economic interdependence – provide substantial elements of continuity in transatlantic relations and pull elites on either side toward cooperative behavior. They provide ballast for the relationship in a changing international environment. A second change, political polarization in the United States, threatens past cooperative relations and could serve as a catalyst for future volatility and possible disruption. Change in the ethnic composition of electorates in Europe and the United States has more ambiguous implications for foreign policy.

What seems to have occurred in recent years, and particularly during the George W. Bush administration, is not a change of underlying foreign policy *preferences* on either side of the Atlantic. As large, democratic, and capitalist societies, the United States and Europe continue to share similar underlying views about a desirable global order. Choices of external *strategy* have diverged – unilateralism versus multilateralism, the utility of diplomacy versus military force, and short-run versus long-run remedies. Transatlantic conflict over strategy in turn is rooted in domestic politics – and not simply a domestic political reaction to 9/11 in the

---

[7] Schwartz, *Lyndon Johnson and Europe*, p. 104.

United States – and has been driven primarily by changes in American politics. One final irony will become apparent: politics in the United States has become *more* European – that is to say, more partisan and more ideologically coherent – and that trend may present a major threat to stability in transatlantic relations.

Stabilizers in transatlantic relations: American public opinion

American public opinion continues to stabilize and provide continuity to US–European relations. Although observers have emphasized different dimensions of American public opinion during and after the Cold War, its outlines are clear. Since the mid-1940s, the balance between internationalism and isolationism in the attitudes of the American public has been remarkably stable. Although elite opinion has been consistently more internationalist than broader public opinion, on certain dimensions, such as attitudes toward the United Nations, the public has demonstrated stronger support.[8] The end of the Cold War did not affect this balance significantly; in fact, the peak of isolationist sentiment in the past four decades came in 1982.[9]

The American public's support for international engagement has been labeled "qualified internationalism"[10] or "apathetic internationalism,"[11] since the public also awards domestic issues and policies a higher priority than foreign policy. Equally important, the American public as a whole rarely acts on its internationalist beliefs, leaving the field to more intensely committed interest groups: "Americans endorse internationalism in theory but seldom do anything about it in practice."[12] Such lack of mobilization on foreign policy issues among the public is hardly new. Support for

---

[8] Miroslav Nincic, Roger Rose, and Gerard Gorski, "The Social Foundations of Adjustment," in Peter Trubowitz, Emily O. Goldman, and Edward Rhodes (eds.), *The Politics of Strategic Adjustment: Ideas, Institutions, and Interests* (New York: Columbia University Press, 1999), pp. 176–209; Ole R. Holsti, "Public Opinion and US Foreign Policy After the Cold War," in James M. Scott (ed.), *After the End: Making US Foreign Policy in the Post-Cold War World* (Durham: Duke University Press, 1998), pp. 138–169; Steven Kull and I. M. Destler, *Misreading the Public: The Myth of a New Isolationism* (Washington, DC: Brookings Institution Press, 1999); Ole R. Holsti, "Public Opinion and Foreign Policy," in Robert J. Lieber (ed.), *Eagle Rules? Foreign Policy and American Primacy in the Twenty-First Century* (Upper Saddle River, NJ: Prentice Hall, 2002), pp. 16–46. These attitudes have been measured in a consistent way over time.
[9] Measured by those who support "stay[ing] out of world affairs."
[10] Nincic, Rose, and Gorski, "The Social Foundations of Adjustment."
[11] James M. Lindsay, "The New Apathy: How an Uninterested Public Is Reshaping Foreign Policy," *Foreign Affairs* 79:5 (September–October 2000), pp. 2–8.
[12] Ibid., p. 4.

foreign involvement is also conditioned by perceived costs, particularly the sacrifice of valued domestic goals. The American public's qualification of activism abroad extends to the content of its internationalism. Few, for example, express a strong interest in promoting American values or democratic institutions abroad.

The American public's consistent preference for multilateralism seems to be based on the same pragmatic considerations as its support for internationalism. Since the public tends to overestimate the burden of overseas commitments for the United States (particularly foreign aid), multilateralism and alliances are viewed as desirable instruments of burden-sharing. With regard to the transatlantic relationship, surveys indicate opposition to American dominance and support for power-sharing between the United States and Europe. As recently as five years ago, only 32 percent of Americans favored unilateralism as the preferred policy stance of the United States, and strong majorities in both Europe and the United States backed the continuation of NATO nearly a decade after the end of the Cold War.[13] In the late 1990s, substantial majorities endorsed increased international cooperation and a strengthening of international institutions, ranging from the United Nations and the World Trade Organization to the proposed International Criminal Court. During this period, party affiliation affected only the degree of support for multilateral options. Regional differences were also relatively narrow (with somewhat more skepticism regarding international organizations in the Southern and Midwestern states).[14]

The terrorist attacks of September 11, 2001, are often portrayed as a turning point in American attitudes toward the international environment. As early as 1995, international terrorism had ranked among the top three international threats in public opinion surveys.[15] The events of 9/11 sharply and understandably increased perceptions of this external threat among the American public. The public's perception of a more threatening international environment was associated with *increased* attachment to multilateral action, however.[16] Two years after the attacks on the World Trade Center, a majority of the public felt that the Bush

[13] Steven Kull, *Seeking a New Balance: A Study of American and European Public Attitudes on Transatlantic Issues* (Washington, DC: Program on International Policy Attitudes, Center for International and Security Studies, University of Maryland, June 26, 1998).

[14] Program on International Policy Attitudes, *Americans on Globalization* (Washington, DC: Center for International and Security Studies, University of Maryland, March 28, 2000); see also Nincic, Rose, and Gorski, "The Social Foundations of Adjustment."

[15] Nincic, Rose, and Gorski, "The Social Foundations of Adjustment," p. 192.

[16] Marshall Bouton and Benjamin I. Page (eds.), *Worldviews 2002: American Public Opinion and Foreign Policy* (Chicago: Chicago Council on Foreign Relations, 2002).

administration should place more emphasis on cooperation, nonmilitary methods, and multilateral action in the battle against terrorism. And in the wake of the Iraq War, a greater percentage of citizens agreed that the most important lesson of 9/11 was the need for intensified American collaboration with other countries in the fight against terrorism.[17]

As a result, allies, particularly the major European allies, became more important to the American public after the 2001 attacks. The US public viewed Europe as the most reliable partner in combating the new terrorist threat; substantially more Americans perceived a "vital interest" in Germany, France, and Great Britain in 2002 than in 1994. The public's estimate of the importance of Asia relative to Europe had increased during the 1990s, but Europe's priority rebounded after 9/11. The stability of the American public's commitment to NATO remained impressive, reaching its highest point in recent decades in 2002.[18] Counter to predictions of an emerging rivalry between the United States and a unifying Europe, an overwhelming majority of the American public (79 percent) endorsed as "desirable" or "somewhat desirable" the exercise of "strong leadership" by the European Union in world affairs.[19]

Overall, the portrait of American public opinion since 9/11 does not indicate a radical revision in American attitudes toward international affairs. In fact – and in direct contrast to the rhetoric of the Bush administration – the American public seem more attached to international organizations and to European allies than they were before the terrorist attacks on New York and Washington. As described in the next section, however, by 2003 the American public began to reflect a much deeper partisan and ideological polarization that had been long evident among elites.[20] That polarization could have more serious implications for transatlantic relations than any overall shift in American public opinion following the Cold War or the terrorist attacks of September 11, 2001.

If the American public has become more entrenched in its support of international institutions and alliances as well as more convinced of the importance of Europe, how does one explain its support for the foreign

---

[17] Steven Kull, *Americans on Terrorism: Two Years after 9/11*, Program on International Policy Attitudes (PIPA) and Knowledge Networks, September 9, 2003, pp. 4–5.

[18] Support for NATO was decidedly lower in 1974, in the wake of the Vietnam War: Marshall Bouton and Benjamin I. Page (eds.), *Worldviews 2002: Topline Data from US Public Survey* (Chicago: Chicago Council on Foreign Relations, 2002), p. 122, question 610.

[19] Bouton and Page, *Worldviews 2002: American Public Opinion and Foreign Policy*, p. 8.

[20] Elite polarization is described below; on the partisan gap in public opinion, see Pew Research Center for the People and the Press, *The 2004 Political Landscape: Evenly Divided and Increasingly Polarized* (November 5, 2003, http://people-press.org/reports/display.php3?ReportID=196).

and security policies of the first administration of George W. Bush? First, even before the September 11 attacks, the public was consistently more apprehensive about external threats than was the foreign policy elite. That apprehension facilitated acquiescence in the Bush administration's policies, as it would have for any presidency. Also, despite substantial divergence between the Bush administration's policies and several core public attitudes, Republicans were still viewed as more likely than Democrats to manage foreign and security policy successfully. The latitude awarded by the public is also highly contingent on the costs of external policy: low costs tend to reinforce acquiescence. Most important, however, the political strategies of both the administration and its opponents have shifted from appealing to an often apathetic public to mobilization of the party faithful in a polarized political setting. One important implication of polarization – explored further below – has been a widening gap between the views of the electorate taken as a whole and the programs promoted by US political parties and politicians.

A second stabilizer: economic interdependence

A dense network of politically powerful economic interests serves as a second key stabilizer in transatlantic relations. Even during the years of US "isolation" in the 1920s and 1930s, economic ties between the United States and Europe were strong: financial centers were closely linked by American lending to Europe during the 1920s, and central bank cooperation persisted during a period of relative diplomatic disengagement. After World War II, the *défi américain* of the 1960s – US multinational investment in Europe – became a flood of foreign direct investment in both directions during the 1980s and 1990s. The European and United States economies are now more deeply intertwined through trade and investment than any other economies that do not share regional economic institutions.

In contrast to the often stormy economic relations between the United States and Japan, transatlantic economic exchange is firmly based on large-scale cross-investment. That enormous island of cross-investment is unique in its scale within the world economy. Transatlantic investment not only dwarfs US–Japanese investment; it has become relatively symmetric, as more European firms have invested in North America.[21] This

---

[21] From 1972 to 1985, US investment in Europe grew by 216 percent, compared to 132 percent in the rest of the world; another period of growth ensued with the Single Market Initiative. By the early 1990s, the total volume of two-way foreign direct investment across the Atlantic was four times the volume of US–Japan investment at the peak of the

economic base also has important political ramifications: the representatives of multinational corporations constitute a potent business lobby in Washington, in US state capitals, and in Brussels. For example, Peterson and Cowles identify the EU Committee of the American Chamber of Commerce as "one of the most effectively organized groups in Brussels," serving as an important window on European decision-making for US business as well as ensuring that the interests of resident US firms are incorporated into EU policy.[22] Such business lobbies exert influence in both directions: shaping EU policies toward foreign investors as well as American policy toward Europe.

More novel than the US presence in Europe is the powerful European investor presence in such regions as the American South, where European manufacturing plants have provided important offsets to the loss of more traditional manufacturing employment (such as textiles). How this internationalization of regional economies in the United States will be reflected in American politics remains an important question for the future of transatlantic relations. Overall, the scale of US–European investment and the political power of the multinational corporations that drive investment flows have served as a powerful stabilizer in transatlantic relations. The economic relationship has typically been undisturbed by conflict in other arenas; reciprocal investments tend to dampen the conflict that has often surrounded trade disputes. The relative symmetry of the relationship has also served to restrain temptations to seek unilateral advantage.

Even in the climate of distrust following the Iraq War, the economic relationship has remained relatively unthreatened. The combined weight of this economic stabilizer and (relatively passive) internationalist public opinion may not serve to offset other, more disruptive trends in domestic politics, however: the polarization of political conflict in the United States and, with more uncertain effects, the shifting balance of ethnicities in both the United States and Europe.

Catalyst of change: political polarization

As the quintessential centerpiece of elite foreign policy during the Cold War, transatlantic relations relied upon a strong political center in the conduct of American foreign policy. Even under the conservative presidency of Ronald Reagan, the personnel and policies dominating

Japanese boom in the late 1980s: John Peterson and Maria Green Cowles, "Clinton, Europe and Economic Diplomacy: What Makes the EU Different?," *Governance* 11:3 (July 1998), pp. 253–254.
[22] Ibid., p. 261.

American foreign policy seemed to represent a stable consensus: few significant differences separated George Shultz, James Baker, and Warren Christopher on major foreign policy issues, particularly those affecting Europe. Equally important, the congressional leadership, including the chairs of key committees, was typically dominated by centrist figures in both parties until the 1990s. The center appeared to hold, at least in the first years after the end of the Cold War. The 1990s demonstrated, however, that political dynamics in the United States could quickly undermine the foreign policy center, a polarized outcome that threatened severe consequences for transatlantic relations.

Ideological divisions within the foreign policy elite sharpened at the time of the Vietnam War and became particularly evident during the Reagan administration. Underlying this conflict over foreign policy were shifts in the partisan orientation of particular elite groups and regions. The neoconservatives, although small in number, were visible and influential intellectual partisans of a worldview that was sharply critical of communist regimes and expansive in its view of American power and ideological purpose in the world. Many of the neoconservatives were former Democrats who had migrated to a new political home in the Republican Party of Ronald Reagan after the nomination of George McGovern and the presidency of Jimmy Carter. Despite their merger with Republicans in the 1980s, they remained distinct from traditional conservatives in their "northeastern roots, combative style, and secularism."[23]

The Reagan administration also consolidated the shift of many conservative Southern Democrats into the Republican coalition. Peter Trubowitz attributes much of the renewed ideological conflict over foreign policy issues in the 1980s to sectional conflict, a battle between the assertive internationalism of the Republican Sunbelt and the defensive and protectionist stance of the Northeast and Midwestern Rustbelt.[24] The internationalist coalition of Northeast and South embodied in the New Deal coalition was shattered. Conflict between "polarized internationalists" over such issues as the defense budget, Nicaragua, and ballistic missile defense was played out between a Republican executive and an assertive Democratic Congress.[25] Although conclusive presidential defeats on central foreign policy issues were very rare, increasing partisanship on

---

[23] John Ehrman, *The Rise of Neoconservatism: Intellectuals and Foreign Affairs, 1945–1994* (New Haven, CT: Yale University Press, 1995), p. 174.

[24] Peter Trubowitz, *Defining the National Interest: Conflict and Change in American Foreign Policy* (Chicago: University of Chicago Press, 1998).

[25] I. M. Destler, "Congress and Foreign Policy at Century's End: Requiem on Cooperation?," in Lawrence C. Dodd and Bruce I. Oppenheimer (eds.), *Congress Reconsidered*, 7th edition (Washington, DC: CQ Press, 2001), pp. 315–333.

foreign policy issues became the norm for congressional leaders, particularly in the House of Representatives.[26]

In part because of the Cold War and in part because internationalists dominated both sides of the partisan divide, transatlantic relations were not disrupted by partisan polarization during the 1980s. Nevertheless, conflicts between the Reagan administration and European elites (backed by a powerful European peace movement) in many ways foreshadowed the outlines of conflict during the first administration of George W. Bush. An American administration that had a more threatening view of the international environment was intent on reclaiming American power and leadership after a period of perceived American weakness. Its new strategy produced an evident impatience with multilateral niceties and alliance consultation.[27] The turn in Soviet policy under Mikhail Gorbachev reduced this threat-driven division, however, and the George Bush, Sr., and early Clinton administrations saw a reduction in alliance discord.

The politics of American foreign policy would take a further turn toward polarization, however, with the congressional elections of 1994. Those elections, which swept the Republicans into power in both houses of Congress, witnessed two significant changes that would mark the politics of foreign policy for a decade. First, the elections produced a generational and leadership change in Congress, in which members who did not recall World War II or the early Cold War years assumed power. Atlanticism for this political generation was no longer a reflex. More ideological conservatives from the South and the West replaced moderates from the Northeast and Midwest in leadership positions and committee chairmanships. I. M. Destler characterizes these new congressional Republicans as "noninternationalists," not isolationists. Military service – characteristic of the World War II political generation – was not typical of their ranks, and most had little experience of or engagement with the world outside the borders of the United States.[28] Many espoused a unilateralist and nationalist skepticism or hostility toward international organizations and other constraints on American military power. This orientation had long been a presence in the Republican Party, but it had been a minority faction since the Eisenhower

---

[26] David W. Rohde, "Partisanship, Leadership, and Congressional Assertiveness in Foreign and Defense Policy," in David Deese (ed.), *The New Politics of American Foreign Policy* (New York: St. Martin's Press, 1993), pp. 76–101.

[27] Miles Kahler, "The United States and Western Europe: The Diplomatic Consequences of Mr. Reagan," in Kenneth A. Oye, Robert J. Lieber, and Donald Rothchild (eds.), *Eagle Resurgent? The Reagan Era in American Foreign Policy* (Boston: Little, Brown and Company, 1987), pp. 297–333.

[28] Destler, "Congress and Foreign Policy at Century's End," p. 322.

administration. Now conservatives – traditional and neo – became the dominant voice in the party; and, with an internationalist Democrat in the White House, partisan calculations reinforced these growing ideological predispositions. Their political style was "militantly partisan and confrontational."[29]

Although the Cold War had provided some residue of consensus in an ideologically charged environment during the Reagan administration, few issues escaped the polarization between parties and branches of government during the Clinton administration. Nonmilitary instruments of United States foreign policy, supported by a bipartisan center, now came under attack. Restrictions were placed on US participation in United Nations peacekeeping operations. Funds for the United Nations were cut and held hostage to conservative policy goals. The State Department and foreign aid budgets were also cut sharply. Congressional rank-and-file opposition prevented an initial attempt at financial rescue during the Mexican peso crisis; replenishment of resources at the International Monetary Fund was delayed at a time of global financial crisis. Even foreign policy issues of central importance to the president were defeated in an atmosphere of partisan conflict: fast-track authority, which would have permitted the negotiation of additional trade agreements, and the Comprehensive Nuclear Test Ban Treaty, the most recent in a long line of arms control agreements.[30] Ideology and partisanship were principal drivers of foreign policy decisions by members of Congress. Ideology was "usually the single, most important factor in members' decision making on foreign and defense issues."[31]

The polarization of the parties in Congress was easily documented. Conservative Democrats and liberal Republicans nearly disappeared.[32] Party organizations in Congress strengthened, as did the centralization of power in party leaderships (particularly in the House of Representatives). Party unity increased sharply, and the number of centrists in each party declined, from 25 percent of all members in 1980 to 10 percent in

---

[29] Destler, "Congress and Foreign Policy at Century's End."

[30] Ibid.; Jürgen Wilzewski, "Back to Unilateralism: The Clinton Administration and the Republican-Led Congress," in Matthias Dembinski and Kinka Gerke (eds.), *Cooperation or Conflict? Transatlantic Relations in Transition* (New York: St. Martins Press, 1998), pp. 23–43.

[31] Ralph G. Carter, "Congress and Post-Cold War US Foreign Policy," in James M. Scott (ed.), *After the End: Making US Foreign Policy in the Post-Cold War World* (Durham: Duke University Press, 1998), p. 127.

[32] Gary C. Jacobson, "Party Polarization in National Politics: The Electoral Connection," in Jon R. Bond and Richard Fleisher (eds.), *Polarized Politics: Congress and the President in a Partisan Era* (Washington, DC: CQ Press, 2000), pp. 9–30.

1996.[33] Growing ideological and partisan polarization in Congress was mirrored in the widening divide over domestic and foreign policy issues between party activists and opinion leaders. This parallel development was predictable since, as David King points out, nearly all politicians are drawn from the ranks of "strong partisans" who make up about 30 percent of the electorate and are "more extreme in their ideological and policy views than most voters."[34] This group is reflected in the responses of opinion leaders surveyed for their foreign policy views. Among that group, large gaps between Democrats and Republicans had opened on a wide range of issues by the 1990s. On the need to maintain superior military power worldwide, thirty-four percentage points separated partisans (Republicans over Democrats); on strengthening the UN, twenty-seven percentage points (Democrats over Republicans); and on arms control, environmental policy, and development, Democrats favored an active policy by a wide margin over Republican opinion leaders. All of these differences had implications for transatlantic relations (with the Democrats closer to the European median), even though attitudes on European policy itself did not diverge so sharply. Foreign policy attitudes among opinion leaders came to be linked closely in ideological and partisan clusters; they also overlapped with domestic policy cleavages.[35] Trade was the only major policy exception to growing partisan polarization: proponents and opponents of trade liberalization bridged the partisan divide.[36]

With the election of a Republican president in 2000, the executive branch was no longer immune to the ideological shift that had taken place within the congressional parties and among party activists. The new president himself, with no experience in foreign policy, seemed to share many of the new ideological positions. Ideological conservatives and neoconservatives assumed prominent positions in directing foreign and defense policy in the first George W. Bush administration.

---

[33] Over a longer period of time, the decline of the moderate center is even more striking; see Sarah A. Binder, "The Dynamics of Legislative Gridlock, 1947–1996," *American Political Science Review* 93:3 (September 1999), p. 526.

[34] David C. King, "The Polarization of American Parties and the Mistrust of Government," in Joseph S. Nye, Jr., Philip D. Zelikow, and David C. King (eds.), *Why People Don't Trust Government* (Cambridge: Harvard University Press, 1997), pp. 164, 165.

[35] Ole R. Holsti and James N. Rosenau, "Liberals, Populists, Libertarians, and Conservatives: The Link Between Domestic and International Affairs," *International Political Science Review* 17:1 (1996), pp. 29–54; Ole R. Holsti and James N. Rosenau, "The Political Foundations of Elites' Domestic and Foreign Policy Beliefs," in Eugene R. Wittkopf and James M. McCormick (eds.), *The Domestic Sources of American Foreign Policy* (Lanham, MD: Rowman & Littlefield, 1999), pp. 33–50.

[36] Holsti, "Public Opinion and Foreign Policy," pp. 37–39.

Colin Powell, who represented the center of past Republican administrations, was now very much on the moderate flank of a nationalist and
conservative national security team.[37] In part, the administration's ideological coloration reflected the regional shift within the Republican Party
that had been underway for three decades. As Michael Lind points out,
George W. Bush was the first Southern conservative to be elected
president since before the Civil War, and had the strong backing of
Protestant fundamentalists.[38]

Although the ideological tilt within the Republican Party had the most
direct effect on foreign policy issues that implicated transatlantic relations, the center of gravity in the Democratic Party had also moved to
match its activist base. A strong anti-globalization current among the
labor and environmental movements pressured Democratic presidential
and congressional candidates toward positions that were skeptical or
hostile toward trade liberalization and foreign direct investment.
Mirroring movement within the Republican Party, an ideological point
of view that had been a vocal part of the party coalition since the 1970s
now assumed a dominant position. The implications for transatlantic
relations were less significant, however, since European societies, with
their stringent environmental standards and protections for labor, could
hardly be accused of social or environmental "dumping." Trade conflict
with the European Union on issues such as beef hormones and genetically
modified foodstuffs placed the Europeans in positions *favored* by
Democratic interest groups. The international targets for Democratic
activists were successful exporters in the developing world, such as
China and India, as well as the multinational corporations whose activities promoted global economic integration.

With the election of George W. Bush, the polarization of American
politics seemed complete: the last bastions of the Cold War consensus
within the executive branch were now beleaguered outposts. Party activists and politicians in both parties had become far more ideologically
committed, and consequently more distant on a range of issues from
their political opponents. The electorate also showed signs of following
the parties into their polarized corners: consistency in voting behavior
increased (evidenced by less ticket-splitting) and the constituencies of the
two parties became "politically more homogeneous and more dissimilar."[39]

---

[37] Daalder and Lindsay, *America Unbound,* p. 57.

[38] Michael Lind, *Made in Texas: George W. Bush and the Southern Takeover of American Politics* (New York: Basic Books, 2003), pp. 130, 145.

[39] Jacobson, "Party Polarization in National Politics," pp. 19–21; King, "The Polarization of American Parties," pp. 170–171.

Nevertheless, polarization in Congress and the political parties had moved well beyond a simple reflection of the political views of American voters. The electorate remained considerably less polarized than political activists and party politicians. On foreign policy and national security issues, however, three years of the Bush administration and the Iraq War sufficed to produce a polarization of views among the electorate that also surpassed previous levels. By 2004, Republican attachment to "peace through military strength" surpassed that of the Democrats by twenty-five percentage points (69 percent to 44 percent). When ideology is added to partisanship (conservative Republicans and liberal Democrats), the gap on such issues as preemptive use of military force widens further.[40]

As partisanship among the electorate approaches the polarized stance of political activists and the congressional parties on foreign policy issues, the role of the public as a stabilizer in transatlantic relations could be impaired. Even if the electorate at large remains less polarized than the more politically active, its influence on foreign policy is called into question: how could the political parties drift farther apart ideologically than the electorate appeared to desire? Electoral competition might reverse the trend toward polarization as the parties seek moderate and independent voters at the center of the political spectrum, a political journey taken by Bill Clinton after the 1994 congressional defeat. On the other hand, political parties may spend many years in the political wilderness, failing to move to the center despite repeated electoral defeats: the British Labour Party, pre-Tony Blair, is only one example. David King suggests a final possibility: as the political and party elites grow more distant from the public's political concerns, public mistrust and apathy grow. Participation declines, and the relative power of activists and ideologues grows, deepening political polarization. The evidence available in advance of the 2004 elections suggests that the dynamic of ideological polarization is dominant, as parties aim to mobilize their respective bases rather than aligning their appeals to the median voter.

The bipartisan Cold War consensus that had sustained the transatlantic relationship narrowed but persisted after the Vietnam War. During the 1990s, however, political polarization threatened the political base that had sustained those policies. Transatlantic relations suffered from this polarization in two ways. The foreign policies endorsed by Republican activists and the Republican congressional party shifted from a Cold War (and European) emphasis on multilateralism and close collaboration with allies in favor of reliance on military instruments and unilateral action.

[40] Pew Research Center, *The 2004 Political Landscape*.

At the same time, transatlantic relations were not a core foreign policy issue for committed partisans on either side of the widening ideological divide. Political polarization in the United States threatened to produce increased volatility in American foreign policy on issues of concern to Europeans, as well as persistent neglect of what had once been the core relationship in American foreign policy.

A second catalyst of change? Ethnic ties and the politics of foreign policy

A second development that might affect the politics of American foreign policy has been a shift in ethnic balance during a period when the strategic environment permits the expression of particularistic interests in American foreign policy. The wave of new immigration – both legal and undocumented – that has occurred since the 1965 revision of US immigration laws has produced a steady increase in immigration from areas outside Europe, particularly Asia and Latin America. European observers, extrapolating from the fractious pluralism of American politics, often assume that foreign policy will inevitably shift in the direction of the new immigrants' home countries as the new groups mobilize to influence policy. Europe, in this view, will inevitably suffer a decline in influence and centrality in American foreign policy. Such a conclusion, however, takes into account neither the history of foreign policy involvement on the part of immigrant groups nor their attitudes toward foreign policy.

The past history of politically organized ethnic groups and their foreign policy interventions is complex; their influence can hardly be traced in a straightforward fashion to particular outcomes. In the first half of the twentieth century, when most mobilized groups were of European origin, the lobbying of different groups was often in direct opposition to one another. Before American entry into both world wars, some groups urged American intervention on the side of the Allies while others pressed for neutrality or isolationism.[41] In similar fashion, contemporary ethnic groups that mobilize to influence foreign policy are often countered by others who support another country or cause.

Few of the new immigrant groups of electoral importance, with the exception of Cuban-Americans, have demonstrated a clear foreign policy orientation or a deep political attachment to their homelands. Mexican-Americans, for example, have participated only episodically in the foreign

---

[41] Tony Smith, *Foreign Attachments: The Power of Ethnic Groups in the Making of American Foreign Policy* (Cambridge: Harvard University Press, 2000), p. 51.

policy arena, frustrating the efforts of Mexican governments to mobilize them on issues such as the North American Free Trade Agreement.[42] Mexican-Americans have demonstrated little interest in the Central American issues that have so absorbed Cuban-Americans. Within the Mexican-American community, differences also emerge between the native-born and immigrants, with immigration as the only major foreign policy issue that brings the two groups together.[43] Although they are hardly a new immigrant group, African-Americans have also demonstrated only a sporadic involvement in the politics of foreign policy. Their influential intervention in policy toward South Africa, where a regime of racial discrimination summoned memories of domestic segregation, stood in contrast to other cases of massive human rights violations in Africa, such as Rwanda.[44]

The new ethnic politics may weaken any electoral incentive to strengthen ties to Europe on the grounds of identity, but those incentives were fading in any case, as ties to former European homelands weakened. These groups are unlikely to lobby for issues and causes that are important in sustaining transatlantic ties or institutions such as NATO. Such ethnic lobbying was seldom of central importance to the transatlantic relationship in any case. Perhaps the most important effect of the new ethnic balance in American politics may be reinforcement of domestic priorities and a dilution of activist internationalism. Surveys of Latino leaders, for example, suggest that foreign policy issues do not rank high on their political agendas. In their increasing domestic preoccupation, they are essentially similar to other Americans before 9/11. Rather than fragmenting American foreign policy or tugging it away from Europe to other regional preoccupations, the new ethnic politics seems most likely to reinforce an orientation of "apathetic internationalism" among the American public.

European political change and transatlantic relations

Although the effects of political change on European foreign policies appear less dramatic than those caused by the transformation in American

[42] Michael Jones-Correa, "Latinos and Latin America? A Unified Agenda?" in Thomas Ambrosio (ed.), *Ethnic Identity Groups and US Foreign Policy* (Westport, CT: Praeger, 2002), p. 119.

[43] Louis DeSipio, *Counting on the Latino Vote: Latinos as a New Electorate* (Charlottesville, VA: University of Virginia Press, 1996), p. 55; Jones-Correa, "Latinos and Latin America?," p. 126.

[44] Fran Scott and Abdulah Osman, "Identity, African-Americans, and US Foreign Policy: Differing Reactions to South African Apartheid and the Rwandan Genocide," in Ambrosio, *Ethnic Identity Groups and US Foreign Policy*, pp. 71–91.

[handwritten marginalia: US = pro-Israel]

politics, recent immigration patterns have shifted political incentives in Europe as well.) During the post-2000 conflict between Israel and the Palestinians, growing Muslim populations in Europe weighed in favor of the Palestinians and against the Israelis.[45] The relative political balance between Arabs and Jews in the contest for public support in Middle East policy was a mirror image of the United States, where a growing Arab-American lobby could not offset the political influence of Israel's supporters.

A second political change followed the end of the Cold War. During the era of US–Soviet rivalry, the European political base for the NATO alliance and alignment with the United States lay in political coalitions ranging from the center-right to the center-left; the communist left in particular was excluded from political power until the French Socialist–Communist victory in 1981. The end of the Cold War added former communists to the political spectrum throughout Europe as their parties were transformed into socialist or social democratic parties. In Germany, reunification brought former Communist Party members and prospective voters into the German political order. Although the ex-Communist Parties have become respectable shadows of their former Leninist selves, their voters are at the very least likely to remain skeptical of American motives and policies. The ex-Communist electorate therefore remains open to foreign policy appeals that run counter to American policies, from their own leaders or from other political formations on the extreme left or extreme right.

Political change and transatlantic conflict

The end of the Cold War opened an era of greater ambiguity in the international strategic environment for both Europe and the United States. The disappearance of the Soviet Union did not dictate greater conflict in transatlantic relations or the end of common institutions such as NATO. Interpreting the Soviet threat and agreeing on an appropriate response were also sources of conflict throughout the Cold War. Rather, international change opened space for greater expression of *domestic* political change in foreign policy on either side of the Atlantic.[46] Given a history of involvement by both sides in the Middle East, a region fraught

---

[45] See especially the observations by Georges-Henri Soutou on this subject in his contribution to this volume (chapter 5).

[46] In addition to the chapter by Soutou (focusing on France), the contribution by Hubert Zimmermann to this volume (chapter 6) explores the consequences of this opening for German foreign policy.

with imperial nostalgia, ethnic and religious resonance, and strategic and economic importance, it was hardly surprising that the latest manifestation of transatlantic conflict was centered there.

One axiom is required for claims that domestic politics drives cycles of transatlantic conflict and cooperation: politicians respond to political incentives on foreign policy issues just as they do on other issues. Two powerful forces have served to stabilize transatlantic relations over the decades by shaping the incentives faced by political leaders from both parties. The first is a broad internationalist majority among the American public – one that values Atlantic institutions such as NATO, even in the post-Cold War era, and that is committed to multilateral instruments whenever possible. Skeptics point to the shallow nature of this "apathetic" internationalism and to the growing importance of domestic political and economic issues on the public's agenda. Nevertheless, the consistency of this internationalism and Atlanticism is striking. The heightened threat perceived after 9/11 only increased these attachments, rather than pointing the public in a unilateralist direction. Although the attention of the electorate to foreign affairs and its unwillingness to mobilize around foreign policy issues may grant considerable latitude to political elites, these attitudes do set certain bounds to foreign policy choice, particularly if costly tradeoffs against valued domestic goals are involved.

A second stabilizer has been the deepening and largely symmetric economic interdependence between Europe and the United States. The growth in foreign direct investment across the Atlantic, which implicates the largest corporations in each economy, has particular political significance. Skeptics will point to the persistent stream of trade conflicts that divide the European Union and the United States, from beef hormones to steel tariffs. Such conflicts are a constant, however, and the institutions of the World Trade Organization have so far assisted in their management, if not their resolution. Before any of those conflicts are allowed to endanger the economic relationship, the political stabilizers of corporate power will be brought to bear in Washington and Brussels.

These longstanding stabilizers are now under considerable pressure from changes in American politics, particularly the ideological and partisan polarization that has grown over the past three decades. That polarization does not directly implicate the transatlantic relationship or institutions such as NATO: no powerful political force in the United States (or in Europe) aims to undermine the relationship. Instead, transatlantic cooperation has suffered collateral damage from the growing weight of unilateralist and nationalist policies in the Republican Party. The Republican mainstream that emerged in the 1990s sharply disagrees with the European mainstream on a range of foreign policy issues – from global environmental agreements (the Kyoto accord) and human rights violations (the International Criminal Court) to the value of the United Nations in dealing with threats such as proliferation of weapons of mass destruction. Although disagreement surrounds the substance of many of these issues, the sharpest disagreements have emerged over the instruments that are chosen: military versus diplomatic or economic, unilateral versus multilateral. Conflict is heightened by the absence of a clear political analogue to conservative Republican ideology in the European political spectrum. The Conservative Party once led by Margaret Thatcher is a shadow of its former self; even those European politicians who align themselves with the Bush administration, such as Berlusconi in Italy and Aznar in Spain, seldom share the combined Republican attachments of religiosity, nationalism, and unfettered capitalism.

The latest round of conflict between the United States and Europe, then, does not arise from the dissimilar backgrounds of Martians and Venusians or from any fundamental disagreement between all Europeans and all Americans – a widespread misreading that pervades many of the treatments of contemporary transatlantic conflict. Claims regarding the attitudes of "Americans" should be viewed with considerable suspicion in an era when political divisions run so deep. Conflict between the United States and Europe arises, paradoxically, from the Europeanization of American politics. After decades of complaint regarding the ideological incoherence of American political parties, the United States has arrived at a party system that is as unified, at least among party activists and congressional parties, as European systems.[47] That very polarization and ideological consistency, however, has hollowed out the center of the American foreign policy consensus which supported transatlantic bonds and close collaboration.

The ethnic transformation of the United States may also produce strains on transatlantic relations in the longer run. A simple equation of ethnic background with foreign policy attitudes, often voiced by European observers, does not capture the intricate filtering of immigration patterns into political action. The era of uniform European ancestry

---

[47] The classic statement of the case for responsible parties in the United States was made by an American Political Science Association Committee on Political Parties in 1950 ("Toward a More Responsible Two-Party System: A Report of the Committee on Political Parties," *American Political Science Review* 44:3 [1950], Part 2, Supplement). With considerable optimism (in light of recent developments), the committee concluded that "needed clarification of party policy will not cause the parties to differ more fundamentally or more sharply than they have in the past" or "to erect between themselves an ideological wall" (p. 2).

among the politically active American electorate ended with the civil rights revolution and the enfranchisement of African-Americans. The more recent immigration of Asian and Latin American populations may reduce positive identification with Europe, but European identities had mixed effects on American foreign policy in the past, reinforcing isolationism as often as spurring internationalist engagement. Given the episodic engagement of most ethnic groups with foreign policy issues and the overriding importance of domestic issues that affect their economic and social status, any immediate and direct effect of changing ethnic composition of the United States on transatlantic relations seems unlikely. More unpredictable are situations in which European immigration patterns run counter to ethnic or religious mobilization in the United States. The Arab–Israeli conflict is the major – and most troubling – exemplar of such ethnic crosscurrents.

International relations between Europe and the United States – as dense and complex as any in the world – rest on a domestic political base. Partisan polarization in the United States, evident since the Vietnam War and accelerating in the 1990s, has served to provoke change by increasing volatility in American foreign policy, toward Europe as well as other parts of the world. That volatility – and the conflict that has ensued between the United States and Europe – would be reduced if partisan oscillation were offset in one of several ways. The Republican Party could be pulled back toward the electoral median – internationalist and multilateralist – by electoral punishment meted out by an American public confronting the costs of a unilateral and militarized policy toward the Middle East. Disruption of transatlantic relations could also be minimized by pressure from the business allies of the Republican Party, if conflict with Europe on security issues threatened to spill over into economic relations. Since all signs point to a harshly partisan electoral battle in 2004, relations between the United States and Europe are likely to face continuing strains based on the new, European-style American politics. The existing ideological alignment within the Republican Party and the polarization between that party and its Democratic adversaries will continue to shape transatlantic relations at least as profoundly as the shifting post-Cold War international environment.

5   Three rifts, two reconciliations: Franco-American relations during the Fifth Republic

Georges-Henri Soutou

There is a widespread view that Franco-American relations have been consistently difficult at least since the presidency of Charles de Gaulle, but not so difficult as to prevent the two countries from joining together in times of crisis. The reality is more complex: the state of relations between France and the United States has not been a stable quantity but has instead oscillated over time, with a series of rifts and reconciliations. But the current crisis is more severe and goes deeper than previous ones, and is therefore likely to last longer – or even to become permanent.

To understand this, it is essential to realize that the French have recently experienced a major change in their worldview: they no longer see close bilateral Franco-American cooperation, even on terms favorable to France, as a central interest. The reasons for this change of heart are manifold, including the transformation of geopolitics, ideological shifts within French society, and changes in the structure and conduct of French domestic politics. But the inescapable result of these various changes is that maintaining positive relations with the United States is no longer a priority for a large portion of the French political class. Thus, while maintaining Franco-American relations on an even keel has never been an easy task, repairing the breach in bilateral relations occasioned by the Gulf War of March 2003 will therefore be even more difficult than in times past.

To make this point, I begin this chapter with an overview of the efforts of Georges Pompidou and Valéry Giscard d'Estaing to broker reconciliations with the Americans following bilateral crises during their respective presidencies. The success of their efforts, I will argue, was due in large measure to the substantially convergent interests of Paris and Washington during the Cold War. Absent that convergence, the efforts of Jacques Chirac during the mid-1990s to upgrade Franco-American relations did not succeed; underlying motivations were now too divergent on both sides. I then turn to the characteristics of the current situation that militate against successful reconciliation following the recent war in Iraq, or at least reconciliation along the lines of past efforts. I conclude

with some observations about the conditions under which a genuine
improvement in relations between France and the United States might
be possible.

Franco-American relations during the Cold War

The legacy of de Gaulle for the French political system was immense,
especially with respect to foreign affairs. After 1962, Franco-American
relations entered a continuing crisis, climaxing with the French withdrawal from the NATO integrated command structures in 1966. But
during 1969–70 President Georges Pompidou largely succeeded in
restoring positive relations, and managed to do so without renouncing
the basic tenet of Gaullist foreign policy: national independence. Later,
President Valéry Giscard d'Estaing similarly managed to repair breaches
in the bilateral relationship that had developed during the late
Nixon–Kissinger years, particularly 1973–4. To understand these developments it is necessary to consider the strategic orientation of these two
French presidents as well as the domestic political constraints under
which they operated.

Pompidou and the first Franco-American reconciliation

Unlike de Gaulle's, Pompidou's worldview and foreign policy agenda did
not directly collide with those of the Americans. He believed that the
American guarantee to Europe against the Soviet menace was essential.
He therefore wanted American troops to remain in Europe, and he stated
so publicly; he believed that Franco-American cooperation was necessary
to prevent German *Ostpolitik* from going astray. He understood the need
for American help in developing the French *force de frappe*. Whereas de
Gaulle had tried to capitalize on American difficulties in Vietnam,
Pompidou was discreetly helpful, convinced as he was that opposition
to the Vietnam War on the internal French scene had been seminal for
the outburst of 1968.[1] As for the Middle East, he believed that France
should not try to insist on a special role that might undercut American
peace efforts.

In short, Pompidou's preferred policies did not differ as sharply from
those of Washington as had been the case with de Gaulle. On top of that,
President Pompidou had to rely on a governing majority that included the
two Atlanticist parties, the Républicains indépendants and the Centrists.

---

[1] Raymond Marcellin, *L'importune vérité* (Paris: Plon, 1978), pp. 165–180.

Repairing Franco-American relations was part of the mandate that got him elected in 1969, even while he had to take into account still another (and the most important) component of his majority, the Gaullists, and therefore to strike a fine balance among the three.[2]

But, while electoral considerations reinforced Pompidou's Atlanticism, they were not its source. De Gaulle had believed that the great ideologies were on the decline, that nationalism was reasserting itself in eastern Europe and Russia, and hence that communism was in long-term decline. But Pompidou was much less sanguine. The Soviet system was certainly evolving, but it would be a long process; meanwhile, the West should do nothing that might hamper its collective resistance to communism. Whereas de Gaulle believed in a new European order, based on Franco-Soviet cooperation and with the United States pushed to the periphery as a sort of guarantor of last resort, Pompidou would have none of it. He neither believed in nor favored such a new order, especially because in his view such a system would end up relying on cooperation between the USSR and Germany, rather than France. He resisted all attempts by the Soviets (and by parts of his own government) to establish a contractual Franco-Soviet relationship akin to the Franco-German Elysée Treaty of 1963.[3] For all those reasons, and with ready cooperation from Nixon and Kissinger, Pompidou oversaw the restoration of positive Franco-American relations that endured for the three years following his assumption of office in 1969. On several important issues, the two countries cooperated quite closely.[4] A new balance was struck: France would not return to the integrated command structures of NATO, but on all substantive issues the two countries would collaborate or at least consult regularly and in depth.

New tensions and a second reconciliation under Giscard

The Franco-American relationship turned sour once again in 1973–4. Both the Yom Kippur war and efforts to develop a united Western reaction to the subsequent oil shock played substantial roles in this period of crisis, exacerbated by Henry Kissinger's attempt to force the European Community to consult with Washington on all external issues before

---

[2] Jean-Paul Cointet, Bernard Lachaise, Gilles Le Béguec, and Jean-Marie Mayeur (eds.), *Un politique: Georges Pompidou* (Paris: PUF, 2001).
[3] Georges-Henri Soutou, "President Pompidou, the Ostpolitik and the Strategy of Détente," unpublished typescript.
[4] Georges-Henri Soutou, "Georges Pompidou and US–European Relations," in Marc Trachtenberg (ed.), *Between Empire and Alliance: America and Europe During the Cold War* (New York: Rowman & Littlefield, 2003), pp. 157–200.

reaching decisions (the US secretary of state's so-called Year of Europe). But there was another, underlying cause to the rift: the Soviet–American SALT negotiations and especially the Nixon–Brezhnev Agreement on June 22, 1973, for "the prevention of a nuclear war." This agreement was understood in Paris as tantamount to a Soviet–American condominium over Europe. This was, by the way, a rather un-Gaullist concern: France was not opposing a Western bloc, but was regretting that the West was not enough of a bloc!

Despite these deep differences, Pompidou managed to keep the new rift within manageable limits (against the more aggressive views of some of his ministers). Most significantly, he instructed Foreign Minister Michel Jobert to negotiate the Ottawa Declaration, subsequently passed by the Atlantic Council on June 19, 1974, some weeks after Pompidou's untimely death. That declaration substantially resolved the outstanding issues, including the relationship between the European Economic Community (EEC) and the United States, and officially acknowledged the value to the Alliance of the French and British deterrents. Under the trying circumstances, the Ottawa Declaration was a substantial accomplishment; indeed, it remained the basis of relations between France and NATO until the end of the Cold War.[5] Still, the Franco-American relationship remained tense. After 1972, Pompidou increasingly feared both Soviet–American détente and the acceleration of German *Ostpolitik*, believing that western Europe might become the victim of either an American–Soviet condominium or a German–Soviet one. In his view, the only possible answer for Paris to those mounting dangers was the further development of the European Community, including establishing it with a strong identity that extended to foreign policy and defense, while at the same time retaining the absolute independence of the French deterrent and refusing to rejoin the integrated structure of NATO.

Thus at the very end of his term Pompidou reverted to an increasingly orthodox version of Gaullism. As a result, relations between Paris and Washington remained frosty; it was not until after the election of Valéry Giscard d'Estaing that a closer and more cordial relationship was restored. Elected in May 1974, Giscard was the head of the Républicains indépendants and thus the leader of the pro-American part of the French *bourgeoisie*. He met with President Ford on the island of Martinique on December 14–16, 1974; there the two men agreed to overcome previous

---

[5] Ibid.

differences about energy policies and also decided to continue secret Franco-American relations concerning nuclear cooperation.[6]

Of course, Giscard had no desire to break with the Gaullist mantra of "national independence," nor could he have done so had he wished to (since the Gaullist party represented an essential part of his parliamentary support). Indeed, the lack of a parliamentary majority that genuinely supported his foreign policy was Giscard's bane throughout his time in office. On the other side of the aisle, the Socialist Party, reconstituted after 1970, had itself become much less Atlanticist than previously, even allying itself with the Communists in 1972. Hence, there was no longer a majority on the left or the right, or even a potential majority of the center, that actively favored accommodation with the United States; the domestic political situation was in this sense even more constraining than it had been during the presidency of de Gaulle. But despite this evolution of domestic affairs during Giscard's presidency, bilateral cooperation with the United States once again became quite close. In Africa, for example, in the Kolwezi operation of 1978, Washington and Paris worked together to stem Soviet advances.[7]

During this period, Paris upgraded cooperation with NATO, as an expression of Giscard's new strategic doctrine – a doctrine that was much less opposed than previously to the American concept of graduated deterrence. Thus Giscard implicitly admitted that the security of France was linked to that of its neighbors, and did not exclude the possibility of French participation in NATO's forward defense. He even conceded the possible eventual use of French tactical nuclear weapons within the framework of NATO strategy, rather than exclusively in defense of French territory as part of a purely national deterrence strategy. At his instruction, conversations were held between General Méry, the French military chief of staff, and General Alexander Haig, NATO's military commander, and procedures were established for eventual cooperation in nuclear planning. Another positive contribution to the Atlantic alliance took place at the Guadeloupe Summit of January 1979, when Giscard helped negotiate the "dual-track" decision about intermediate-range missiles in answer to the Soviet SS-20s (that is, the decision to pursue negotiations with Moscow and simultaneously to prepare for the

---

[6] Samy Cohen and Marie-Claude Smouts, *La politique extérieure de Valéry Giscard d'Estaing* (Paris: Presses de la FNSP, 1985); and Valéry Giscard d'Estaing, *Le pouvoir et la vie* (Paris: Cie 12, 1991), vol. II, pp. 187–192.

[7] Michael Ledeen and William Lewis, *Débâcle: l'échec américain en Iran* (Paris: Albin Michel, 1981).

installation of American Pershing II missiles and cruise missiles in Europe should those negotiations fail).[8]

In short, Giscard succeeded in both restoring and expanding the Franco-American reconciliation first engineered by Pompidou in 1969–70. France still did not return to the integrated command of NATO, but the consequences of the 1966 rift were largely overcome. This reconciliation was accomplished despite strong opposition from Gaullist quarters. Still, from the very beginning of President Jimmy Carter's term in 1977, French relations with Washington once again soured. Fortuitous external circumstances managed to check the consequences of this breakdown in relations, but the breach was never fully repaired.

New problems, but no new reconciliation

There were several reasons for the new breakdown in relations. To begin with, there was a strong Gaullist reaction against the closer links to NATO, complicating Giscard's domestic situation. In addition, however, the French president had evident misgivings about the ability of Carter to manage the "new Cold War." Later Giscard desired, in close agreement with Chancellor Helmut Schmidt of Germany, to save détente and to cushion western Europe from the consequences of both the Afghan crisis and mounting tensions in eastern Europe.[9]

Of these many and somewhat contradictory impulses, Giscard retrospectively stressed – in his memoirs, *Le pouvoir et la vie* – the doubts he had about Carter's ability to withstand Soviet pressure. But at the time he expressed much more forcefully his disagreement with the American president's wish to inject some basic moral and liberal values into the East–West relationship, and to pressure Moscow on those points. As Giscard told *Newsweek* on July 25, 1977:

What seems clear in Mr. Carter's foreign policy is that he has introduced a fresh ideological dimension. This undoubtedly met certain needs – such as nonproliferation, arms limitations and human rights – just as it met some of my own preoccupations, but it has compromised the process of détente. The question now arises whether or how new ideological themes can be applied without provoking negative reactions.

---

[8] Giscard d'Estaing, *Le pouvoir et la vie*; and Georges-Henri Soutou, *L'alliance incertaine: les rapports politico-stratégiques franco-allemands, 1954–1996* (Paris: Fayard, 1996), pp. 351–369. On the dual-track decision, see also chapter 8 in this volume.

[9] Giscard d'Estaing, *Le pouvoir et la vie*, vol. II, pp. 198–201, 404–409, 409–438, 454–457, and 469.

What Paris did not realize at the time was that Carter, despite his often-hesitating stance, was beginning to change the rules of the Cold War. With his insistence upon human rights and genuine disarmament, while at the same time modernizing the American armed forces, his policies laid the foundation for a rejection of the détente of the Nixon–Kissinger era and movement toward a new policy framework that ultimately proved much more threatening to the stability of the Soviet system. But Giscard's attitude toward Carter has a deeper explanation, true also of most French leaders during the Cold War, as I explain in the next section.

In any event, with the election of François Mitterrand in May 1981, Giscard lost whatever opportunity he may have had to mend fences with the Americans. Mitterrand's agenda did not include any closer links to NATO, and French foreign and strategic policy regarding the United States and the Atlantic alliance returned to a kind of Gaullist orthodoxy tinged with leftist ideology. This did not prevent Mitterrand from colla-borating closely with the United States at times, but his aim was to redress the balance with the Soviet Union in the last, difficult stages of the Cold War – not, as with Giscard d'Estaing, to advance the basis of the trans-atlantic community. Instead, the main thrust of Mitterrand's foreign policy, as with de Gaulle, was to preserve France's freedom of action by carefully balancing American and Soviet influence. With the Cold War's end, Mitterrand likely believed that NATO would soon be disbanded; thus he vigorously pursued the aim of a European foreign policy and defense identity outside NATO. But in this he was no more able than de Gaulle had been to overcome the opposition of Germany, and for that matter of most of France's European partners. Thus Franco-American relations remained in a state of more or less cordial deadlock from around the end of Giscard's term until Chirac's gambit in 1995, as I discuss later in this chapter. Washington was unable to bring France back into the fold, but France was likewise unable to unite Europe behind it to redress the transatlantic imbalance.[10]

The French Cold War agenda: rhetoric versus reality

These oscillations between periods of Franco-American tension and episodes of cooperation are probably best explained by the real agenda, as opposed to public rhetoric, of France during the Cold War. This secret agenda precluded a wholehearted and permanent cooperation with Washington, but at the same time French ulterior motives were not

---

[10] Soutou, *L'alliance incertaine*, pp. 371–378.

entirely incompatible with American policies and did not prevent a cautious cooperation on topics of common interest. These motives, which could never be frankly acknowledged, had to do with fears about Germany and desire for a closer and more prestigious bilateral relationship with the United States.

The first of these ulterior motives is best encapsulated by the notion of "double security." This meant in the first place security against Germany, or at least a counterweight against the growing German influence, through the division of the country. This remained a central fact of the French international environment and hence of French policy until the end of the Cold War. But Paris also relied upon West Germany, firmly embedded in the European Community and NATO, as a useful pillar for French security against what was, at least since 1947–8, perceived as France's second big security problem: the Soviet Union and the expansion of Soviet communism. Hence, double security entailed dividing Germany against itself while enlisting the assistance of Germany's western half against the USSR.[11]

A second ulterior motive of French policy was the wish to retain a tacit reinsurance against Germany in Moscow: to ensure that the Soviet Union could be counted upon to prevent German reunification and to resist, or at least to balance, any German–American relationship that became too close – a permanent fear in Paris since 1950. After all, the Soviets had signed the Potsdam agreements, which the French were now defending tooth and nail (because they formed the legal basis of French superiority over Germany) against the more relaxed attitude of the Anglo-Saxons. In addition, until the very end of the Cold War, the Soviets regularly let Paris know that Moscow was amenable to such tacit cooperation, and even tried to bring France at least indirectly into their orbit. Indeed, many in Paris expressed periodic interest in upgrading the Soviet relationship; this was especially evident immediately after the death of Stalin, during de Gaulle's presidency, during the 1970s, and once again at the end of the Cold War. The trick for successive French governments, and more generally for French diplomacy, was to nibble at the Russian bait sufficiently to encourage continued Soviet resistance to German reunification and to help Paris escape the embrace of the German–American couple, without actually getting hooked.[12]

---

[11] Geneviève Maelstaf, *Que faire de l'Allemagne? Les responsables français, le statut international de l'Allemagne et le problème de l'unité allemande (1945–1955)* (Paris: Ministère des Affaires Etrangères, 1999).

[12] Soutou, *L'alliance incertaine*; and Georges-Henri Soutou, "De Gaulle's France and the Soviet Union from Conflict to Détente," in Wilfried Loth (ed.), *Europe, Cold War and Coexistence, 1953–1965* (London: Frank Cass, 2003), pp. 173–189.

The third part of the unspoken agenda was to maintain as far as possible a strong bilateral (as opposed to a NATO-based) relationship with Washington. This was deemed necessary for practical reasons, including nuclear cooperation with the United States and more general bilateral cooperation in new technologies. Likewise, Pompidou and Giscard realized perfectly the importance of Franco-American cooperation for the defense of French interests in the fields of international trade and finance.[13] But most importantly, a prominent Franco-American relationship was intended to demonstrate France's continued significance in world politics. Paris resented the American–British special relationship and strove to achieve the same status for itself in Washington. Even de Gaulle desired this, and until late 1962 he tried to upgrade the Franco-American relationship in the framework of a trilateral directorate (with London and Washington) of the Atlantic alliance.

As a consequence, there was sufficient overlap between French and American interests that relations were tolerably good as long as Washington agreed to maintain a bilateral dialogue with Paris, did not try to privilege the German–American dialogue, and followed a prudent policy with Moscow – that is to say, a policy that was firm but that also promoted détente without trying to achieve a Soviet–American super-power condominium above the heads of the Europeans. This convergence of interests explains the good understanding (at least initially) between Pompidou, Nixon, and Kissinger, since all three were disquieted by German *Ostpolitik*; it also accounts for the difficulties between Giscard d'Estaing and Carter, whom Giscard accused of being both too lax and too ideological in his relations with Moscow as well as too ready to further German ambitions. Much the same could be said about the relationship between Mitterrand and Reagan, although Mitterrand, like de Gaulle, was something of an exception to this stylized account of French foreign policy proclivities. But the main point is that there was frequently sufficient tacit convergence between the positions of Paris and Washington to keep recurrent bilateral tensions in check.

But there were indeed exceptions to the French agenda as I have outlined it. De Gaulle, and to a lesser extent Mitterrand, had in mind a different system of European security, a system that would have relied on a special Franco-Soviet relationship in order to control the German problem (with the United States pushed to the periphery). Within that framework, there was no overlap between French and American interests, and hence no buffer on bilateral tensions. De Gaulle's insistence on such

---

[13] Soutou, "Georges Pompidou and US–European Relations."

an approach to France's international relations largely explains Franco-American difficulties between 1963 and 1969. As for foreign policy under Mitterrand, until the coming of Gorbachev, the main emphasis was to balance the influence of the Soviet Union. But after 1985, Mitterrand hoped to balance Reaganism with the help of a reforming USSR; only the speedy demise of Soviet communism prevented a looming clash with Washington.[14]

But, even for Pompidou and Giscard, the circumstances of the Cold War were essential for a tolerably good Franco-American relationship. After all, the Cold War arrangements promoted by the United States within the NATO framework were highly beneficial for France: the partition of Germany helped resolve one set of concerns, while the American security guarantee at last achieved with the Atlantic alliance in 1949 had been sought by Paris since 1919. Whether the French foreign policy agenda described above was advisable or judicious in the long term is a question I do not address in this chapter. But it is evident that the end of the Cold War quickly changed the assumptions underlying such an approach.

Failed reconciliation under Chirac

The Cold War ended, as I have suggested, with Franco-American relations in poor shape, having been in a state of low-level crisis since the latter portion of Giscard's presidency and throughout Mitterrand's two presidential terms. But shortly after assuming office in 1995, President Jacques Chirac suggested a solution which would have put Franco-American and transatlantic relations on a much better institutional footing. Since the 1960s, the French had repeatedly tried to form a European security identity alongside and outside NATO, and Chirac realized that this was not acceptable to France's partners (especially Germany). He decided to break the deadlock by having France rejoin NATO as a full partner and then by promoting a European defense identity inside rather than outside the Atlantic alliance.

Chirac's proposal, put forward in 1995 and 1996, would have fully returned France to NATO's integrated command structure, which France left in 1966; NATO in turn would recognize the existence of a European identity inside the Alliance and set up a special European chain of command inside the different NATO staffs, allowing the Europeans to use NATO assets in operations in which the Americans chose not to

---

[14] Soutou, *L'alliance incertaine.*

participate. That compromise was accepted and promulgated by the Atlantic Council in Berlin in June 1996,[15] but it ultimately failed because of a major disagreement between Paris and Washington about the commanding officer for NATO's Mediterranean forces, headquartered in Naples. The Americans wanted to retain the position (the American admiral in Naples is also the commander of the Sixth Fleet), while the French felt it should go to a European admiral.

Beyond that outward disagreement, the real reason for this new Franco-American controversy lay in diverging ulterior motives on both sides. Almost certainly France wished to retain, through an agreement with NATO promoting a European defense set-up, a greater weight in Washington for Paris than for Berlin, and to continue to distinguish itself from its eastern neighbor by emphasizing its enduring world role at the highest level of the Alliance, on a par with Washington and London.[16] On the other side, Washington was convinced it should keep a tight grip on NATO as an instrument of regional and global security against the new threats arising after the end of the Cold War, consistent with the "New Concept for NATO" adopted in Washington on April 25, 1999. It bears noting that this New Concept explicitly opened the possibility of out-of-area action for NATO forces acting without a UN mandate, a feature of the new strategy that the French tried hard to tone down.

In any event, the tentative Franco-American agreement of 1996 ultimately failed.[17] Of course, that failure did not prevent close Franco-American cooperation in Bosnia in 1995 and in Kosovo in 1999. But the lack of a real solution to deep-seated Franco-American differences, including coming to grips with the relationship between NATO and a European foreign policy and defense identity, greatly contributed to the transatlantic break over Iraq in 2002–3.

Thus, from 1963 to the present, the Franco-American relationship has been characterized by three deep rifts or ruptures but only two genuine reconciliations. Pompidou succeeded in mending fences with the Americans following de Gaulle's tempestuous presidency, but by 1973–4 relations between Paris and Washington were once again in crisis. Giscard built upon the legacy of the Ottawa Declaration, authorized by Pompidou shortly before his death, to achieve a second reconciliation with the Americans, culminating with the double-track decision of 1979. But Giscard's relations with Carter were never good, and by the end of the French president's term the bilateral relationship was again in peril. It

[15] Ibid., pp. 423–429.
[16] Article by Lothar Rühl in the *Neue Zürcher Zeitung* of November 30–December 1, 1996.
[17] Gilles Delafon and Thomas Sancton, *Dear Jacques, Cher Bill* (Paris: Plon, 1999).

remained so until the election of Jacques Chirac, who sought to return France to NATO on the basis of a new understanding within the Alliance regarding the role of a European defense identity. But Chirac's proposal did not succeed, and the Franco-American relationship remained mired in a low-level crisis until tensions erupted in the run-up to the war in Iraq.

The current crisis: from tacit convergence to differing worldviews

We have now at our disposal fairly well-developed accounts of the Franco-American crisis at the UN in the spring of 2003, sufficient to address ourselves to the underlying issues.[18] The real question is the following: was the crisis a conjunctural accident, due simply to a major difference of views about the way to handle the Iraq question, or was it a structural problem? Official commentary and many private specialists favor the first interpretation, together with an emphasis on the inherent differences between American "unilateralism" and the multilateralism extolled by France. Certainly during the Iraq crisis, the United States showed little regard for the three major international organizations it had set up or contributed to setting up after 1945 – the United Nations, NATO, and the European Union – by acting outside the framework of the first two and playing upon the divisions within the third. American foreign policy is therefore the object both of serious scientific debate in France[19] and of heated controversies.[20] But things go much deeper than the

---

[18] For example, Kenneth R. Timmerman has published a severe indictment of the French attitude in *The French Betrayal of America* (New York: Crown Forum, 2004). See especially the first chapter. In my view, the best and most balanced exposition is to be found in Charles Cogan, *French Negotiating Behavior: Dealing with La Grande Nation* (Washington, DC: United States Institute of Peace Press, 2003), pp. 186–214; in it, Cogan shows clearly that the Franco-American rift did not result only from a clash of views about the problem of Iraq's disarmament, but instead reflected deeper-seated differences of worldviews and negotiating behaviors. Cogan's account would seem to be supported by Hans Blix's book, *Disarming Iraq* (London: Bloomsbury, 2004).

[19] For instance, the very good book by Pierre Hassner and Justin Vaïsse, *Washington et le monde: dilemmes d'une superpuissance* (Paris: CERI/Autrement, 2003); or recent issues of the major journals *Commentaire* (100, Winter 2002–3; 101, Spring 2003; 102, Summer 2003), *Politique Internationale* (99, Spring 2003; 100, Summer 2003) and *Politique Étrangère* (98, Spring 2003); see also the special issue "Les Amériques et nous" of the journal *Outre-Terre: Revue Française de Géopolitique*, 5, 2003; Lawrence F. Kaplan and William Kristol, *The War over Iraq: Saddam's Tyranny and America's Mission* (San Francisco: Encounter Books, 2003), has been translated into French, with an introduction by François Heisbourg (*Notre route commence à Bagdad*, Paris: Saint-Simon, 2003).

[20] See a very intelligent and forceful condemnation of American "imperial" policy in Gabriel Robin, "Sens et enjeu de la guerre d'Iraq," *Géopolitique* 82 (April–June 2003), pp. 3–10. A well-argued justification of the French position is André Bonnet, *Iraq: le veto français* (Paris: Les Dossiers de France Demain, 2003).

quite real differences about the problem of a UN mandate for Iraq and so-called American unilateralism, which itself is not a new development but a permanent tendency.

Of course, the present transatlantic crisis is not the first, and the most serious earlier crises were sooner or later resolved – usually tolerably quickly. The same thing might occur this time, but there are good reasons to doubt it, because both the international environment and French policy have changed deeply in recent years. After years in the making, the current Franco-American rift, as opposed to the recurrent tensions of the Cold War period, is most probably a lasting reality. There is no real reconciliation in view, for four reasons: differing theories of foreign policy, diverging geopolitical interests, a disturbing tendency on both sides of the Atlantic to frame these differences in ideological terms, and, at least in France, the erosion of a domestic political context that was once reasonably supportive of – or at least not inimical to – bilateral cooperation.

Foreign policy theory

The first reason is that the French have recently experienced a sea change in their view of international relations: they no longer see their interest lying in close bilateral Franco-American cooperation, even on terms favorable to France. This represents an important shift from what all French leaders, including de Gaulle, have tried to achieve since 1945 (or even since 1919). Present French foreign policy is in this respect of course a development of the Gaullist policy of national independence, but it goes much further. Even for de Gaulle himself, there was still some sort of useful relationship with the United States, despite all the differences between Paris and Washington, if only as guarantor of last resort; this was true of his foreign policy even after the crisis of 1963. But present French foreign policy is in this respect different even from the course outlined by Jacques Chirac in 1995–6.

The term "multipolarity" goes to the heart of the matter. A quick perusal of the Quai d'Orsay website, where all official pronouncements and foreign policy speeches by the president and the minister for foreign affairs since 1990 are listed, should be sufficient to make the point.[21] Once there, one can search for particular words or expressions. Such an exercise reveals that the word "multipolaire" appeared in 152 speeches or

---

[21] See http://www.doc.diplomatie.fr.

declarations by Jacques Chirac between his assumption of office in 1995 and the end of July 2003.

What is the French understanding of multipolarity? In the bipolar world of the Cold War, there were two "blocs." France refused to belong definitively to either of the two, but was instead aligned with the West, recognizing that the United States was essential to maintaining peace and the bipolar balance. Indeed, French leaders quite happily nurtured the national interest within that framework, with the American security guarantee enabling the policy of "double security" toward Germany and the USSR, as well as a kind of tacit reinsurance that Moscow would balance discreetly both the United States and Germany. But today the bipolar world order no longer exists, and therefore these considerations no longer obtain. Instead, in the French view, the role played by the United States has changed: it has become unilateralist if not outright imperialistic, and it is no longer interested in, and has even turned against, the UN, NATO, and a unified Europe. (The irony of the fact that Paris at times was no strong supporter of at least the first two of those institutions does not escape some commentators.)[22]

Current American foreign policy is therefore seen as dangerous, because it leads to a "clash of civilizations" and to instability. This policy therefore has to be resisted in the framework of a "multipolar world," that is to say a world where there will be several major actors besides the United States, and major alliances that will not include the United States. Among these global players and partnerships will be a European Union with a strong foreign policy identity under the guidance of the Franco-German partnership (which, by the way, has been strongly revived since the autumn of 2002); a Paris–Berlin–Moscow axis; China; India; and enhanced links between France (and therefore Europe) and Africa. It should be stressed that despite some superficial convergence, this vision is fundamentally different from the world system recently advocated by Henry Kissinger, a system of interlocking regional balances in which the United States would play a cooperative but central role in all regions.[23] For the French, "multipolarity" is not meant to enhance or even to modify the global role of the United States, but to reduce it, because American power and policy are currently regarded as excessive and unbalanced.[24]

[22] See for instance Jean-Claude Casanova, "De Charles de Gaulle à Jacques Chirac," *Le Monde*, July 25, 2003.

[23] Henry Kissinger, *Does America Need Foreign Policy? Toward Diplomacy for the Twenty-First Century* (New York: Simon & Schuster, 2001).

[24] See, for instance, Chirac's words during a joint press conference with Putin and Schröder in St. Petersburg, on April 11, 2003, Quai d'Orsay website (see n. 21).

Even so, official American reactions to these French views have been excessive. For example, at the end of June 2003, the Bush administration's national security advisor, Condoleezza Rice, condemned multipolarity as an outmoded remnant of the past, "a necessary evil that sustained the absence of war but did not promote the triumph of peace." She added that something different, under American leadership, must take its place.[25] But such a response does not do justice to the thinking in Paris, where the government is articulating a much more sophisticated and intellectually valid vision than Rice's comments suggest.[26] As President Chirac explained in Brussels on April 29, 2003:

When we watch the evolution of the world, we see that in a quite natural way a multipolar world is taking shape, whether we wish it or not; it is an unavoidable development. Not only the United States and Europe, but also China, India, and South America will form new groupings in the near future, that is to say in the next fifty or hundred years. Links between those groupings will have to be strong if clashes are to be avoided, especially between groupings with the same culture – that is, mainly between Europe and the United States. But, for the sake of balance, it will be necessary that a strong Europe and a strong United States be linked together by a strong pact, that is a pact resting on their common culture.

That is what we defend, and that means of course that relations between Europe and the United States will be complementary, amounting to a partnership – of course between equal partners, or there is no partnership and it is another kind of world. It is not the world that France recognizes and wishes.[27]

Thus, while the dispute with the United States is certainly the focus of recent attention, the French position on multipolarity is better understood in the framework of debates within France about the possible evolution of the global political system. For French realists, states will retain their international role; for idealists, transnational forces and phenomena will supersede the former international system of relations among nation-states and ensure final peace. Within the realist school, theorists imagine that only political hegemony, not benevolent social forces, could usher in world peace, and hegemony has to be absolutely resisted – with the United States being the aspiring hegemon at present (the "hyperpower," as described by Hubert Védrine). But most French

---

[25] William Pfaff, "Atlantic Divide," *International Herald Tribune*, July 3, 2003.

[26] For a very elaborate presentation of his views on this subject, stressing the development of a multipolar world resting on a set of common values and on a system of international democracy, one must refer to a 62-page interview Dominique de Villepin gave the journal *Politique Internationale*: "Diplomatie et action, entretien avec Dominique de Villepin," Supplement to *Politique Internationale* 102 (Winter 2003–4), pp. 5–62. See also Dominique de Villepin, *Un autre monde* (Paris: L'Herne, 2003).

[27] Official English translation on the Quai d'Orsay website (see n. 21).

analysts do not believe that the world system would long tolerate a hegemon, even a benevolent one. Hence, multipolarity is both a desirable objective and, in all likelihood, a lasting fact of international life.[28]

On top of that, the tradition of French diplomacy since before 1945 has been to call for a multilateral approach to problems, to support the United Nations and the Security Council, and to take into account regional situations as well as economic and social imbalances as major factors of world tensions. According to that tradition, the aim of policy should be to go to the roots of problems; hence, international life is not a series of crises to be solved one by one, but a complex mix of long-term structural problems that needs to be addressed with continuity and persistence. Of course, the articulation of these views has often been self-serving, French policy has not always been a model of consistency, and France has frequently failed to convince its partners with these arguments – at least until recently. But such inconsistencies are typical of foreign policy, and not only in France. The point is that Paris generally frames its policy actions within a consistent and coherent worldview that has significant crossparty appeal to the French.[29]

Geopolitical interests

The second important factor underlying increasing Franco-American tensions goes beyond diverging theories of international relations and has to do instead with very real geopolitical factors. French geopolitical interests and aims have remained basically the same since de Gaulle: to take the leadership of Europe through a strong Franco-German link and thus by proxy to retain world influence, an influence that is political but also economic and cultural. But the end of the Cold War, German reunification, the collapse of the Soviet Union, the continued evolution of Germany and of Russia, and the perceived change in American foreign policy have modified the French game, or at least, if not the goal of the game, its rules. In particular, the United States is no longer considered to be a useful ally, or even a sort of reinsurance of last resort, but instead to be the main obstacle to the achievement of French goals.

The first of these goals is the achievement of a European defense and foreign policy identity, an aim going back to de Gaulle and reaffirmed by

[28] Thierry de Montbrial, *L'action et le système du monde* (Paris: PUF, 2002); Jean-Baptiste Duroselle, *Tout empire périra: une vision historique des relations internationales* (Paris: Armand Colin, 1982).

[29] Daniel Vernet, "Le vieux dilemme de la diplomatie française," *Le Monde*, September 26, 2003.

Mitterrand with the Maastricht Treaty.[30] This aim was relaunched on November 22, 2002, with a new Franco-German proposal to the European Union suggesting the adoption of a clause of mutual assistance between members of the EU and the building of a core group of countries willing to collaborate more closely in matters of security and defense; the joint proposal also suggested an increase in armaments cooperation.[31] This led to a summit meeting in Brussels between the leaders of France, Germany, Belgium, and Luxembourg at the end of April 2003, endorsing those proposals and suggesting the set-up of a European military staff independent of NATO.

Of course, it was widely noted that the Brussels summit took place without the participation of Great Britain, despite the fact that its military contribution would be essential and that Prime Minister Blair had been instrumental in restarting the idea of a European defense with the Saint-Malo Declaration of December 1998 (signed by Blair and Chirac).[32] Blair's absence from the Brussels summit was of course a result of the deep European rift induced by the Iraq crisis, and it is certain that a majority of European countries are not willing to follow the French lead if it means setting up a European defense system outside NATO. At the same time, American leaders are too complacent in believing that France is not making headway in this respect: it is enough to read Articles 39 and 40 of the European Constitutional Treaty, agreed at the June 2004 European Summit, to realize that the idea of a common European foreign and defense policy is making real progress even if most European countries still do not wish it either to contradict or to supersede NATO.

Thus, when Tony Blair did finally meet with Chirac and Schröder in Berlin on September 20, 2003, he extended a hand – albeit prudently – toward the two other countries on the matter of European defense.[33] While Blair plainly still resists any European arrangement that might contradict NATO, it is nonetheless clear that things are moving. At the European summit of Brussels in December 2003, an agreement was reached that did not go as far as setting up a true operational staff for the EU independent of NATO, as the French and the Germans had envisioned in April, because Great Britain opposed it. But it was decided to form an operational nucleus inside the already existing European staff,

---

[30] Soutou, *L'alliance incertaine;* Nicole Gnesotto, *La puissance et l'Europe* (Paris: Presses de la FNSP, 1998).

[31] See Henri de Bresson and Daniel Vernet in *Le Monde* of November 26, 2002.

[32] Laurent Zecchini in *Le Monde,* May 29, 2003, and Isabelle Lasserre in *Le Figaro,* July 14, 2003.

[33] "The European Union and NATO: A Lull Between the Storms," *Economist,* September 27, 2003.

which advises the European Council on strategic matters. That nucleus will provide operational plans for the national commands in charge of operations (as in the recent European operation in the Democratic Republic of Congo, under French command). So the European Union is inching progressively toward an independent command capability.

Another main direction of French geopolitical policy is developing a close relationship with Russia. Jacques Chirac, on January 10, 2003, mentioned "the vitality of our [Franco-Russian] strategic partnership," and added, "France was striving for the establishment of an ambitious strategic partnership between Russia and the European Union, with France in the vanguard." In July 2002, a "council for security coopera-tion" was established between the two countries, with foreign and defense ministers to meet every six months. Cooperation in matters of space and aeronautics (including the project of a common advanced fighter) is thriv-ing.[34] There are also ideas for further promoting a Paris–Berlin–Moscow axis.[35] The leaders of the three countries now meet regularly, and their common approach toward Iraq still holds, despite frequent prognostica-tions that either Germany or Russia (or both) would soon veer toward Washington.

More generally, the French believe that the problems of Europe call for, in addition to the further development of the European Union, much closer cooperation between the three major countries of the continent. This prescription applies to energy, trade, and European security, but also to practical and complex problems such as the Kaliningrad enclave. In any case, the French are quite comfortable with a revitalized great powers diplomacy, especially as this stands a better chance of enhancing the role of Paris than does a common European foreign policy (a goal that is still at some distance and whose substance France might have trouble controlling in the more and more complex institutional framework of the enlarged European Union).

A third strategic direction is the establishment of substantial links with North Africa, both to keep an eye on developments there and to give more weight to France at the international level. During his visit to Algeria in March 2003, President Chirac insisted on the special nature of Franco-Algerian cooperation as a leading factor in the establishment of a close

---

[34] Philippe Migault, "Après EADS, Sukhoï s'allie avec Dassault," Le Figaro, June 21–22, 2003; Patrick de Saint-Exupéry, "Un trio chiraquien pour sceller l'axe de sécurité franco-russe," Le Figaro, July 8, 2003; Marie-Pierre Subtil, "Paris et Moscou affichent leurs convergences 'jusqu'au moindre détail,'" Le Monde, July 10, 2003; "Chère Russie," Le Monde, July 11, 2003.

[35] "Declaration from Russia, Germany and France," on March 5, 2003, Quai d'Orsay website (see n. 21).

relationship between the European Union and North Africa. He under-lined the fact that one Frenchman in six has a personal relationship to Algeria, either as a French refugee after 1962, a descendant of French refugees, or as an Algerian immigrant. He further underscored the "links established between the two countries by Islam, the second religion in France"[36] – factors that, I might add, were certainly not without effect on Paris' attitude in the Iraq crisis. Also in March 2003, in a speech to the students of Oran University, Chirac forcefully condemned theories about "the clash of civilizations" and extolled the role of the United Nations, as well as positing the principle of cultural diversity as a buffer against the spread of globalization. Two weeks earlier, Foreign Minister Dominique de Villepin had stressed the concept of a partnership between the European Union and North Africa, and stated that France, despite the enlargement of the EU toward the east, would "make sure that Europe's relation with the Mediterranean remains a strategic priority."[37]

Still another strategic direction that Paris is nurturing is relations with sub-Saharan Africa, where Chirac and de Villepin have decided to reen-gage France after the relative disengagement of the 1990s.[38] Accordingly, Paris has been instrumental in the recent engagement of the European Union in Congo, with two aims: to promote a "strategic presence of Europe in Africa," and to set an example for European military opera-tions outside NATO.[39]

Ideology

The third important factor behind current differences between Paris and Washington is ideology. Neither de Gaulle, Pompidou nor Giscard d'Estaing ever felt or expressed the view that basic values differ across the Atlantic. Indeed, during all major crises (Berlin and Cuba, for example), de Gaulle stressed the basic solidarity between Europe and the United States, "her daughter." But this is no longer the case: the

---

[36] Speech to the Algerian parliament on March 3, Quai d'Orsay website (see n. 21).

[37] On February 17, to the Institut national de la Magistrature, in Algiers, Quai d'Orsay website (see n. 21). Non-French readers should be aware that all these topics strike a deep chord in many French people, particularly the youth. If they doubt me, I invite them to give a course on current affairs, as I have done for years, to an audience of about 150 second-year university students and watch the reactions, keeping in mind that French universities rely on a system of mass education that is representative of society at large.

[38] Speech by de Villepin to the Institut des Hautes Etudes de Défense Nationale, June 13, 2003, Quai d'Orsay website (see n. 21).

[39] Lothar Rühl, "Vorwärtsverteidigung und globale Ordnung," *Neue Zürcher Zeitung*, August 9–10, 2003.

French consider themselves and Europe at large to represent a culture and a worldview quite different from that of the "Anglo-Saxons." And this sense of cultural separation goes beyond the well-known disputes about the death penalty, the environment, and the International Criminal Court. As Olivier Mongin, director of the well-known journal *Esprit*, has written (in an article provocatively entitled "Which Values? For Which Europe?"):

In order to inscribe the European Union in world history, it is necessary to promote specific values setting it apart from those values which an imperial post-Cold War strategy is forcing on the other side of the Atlantic.[40]

It is enough to read de Villepin's speech to representatives of the Freemasons on the 275th anniversary of Freemasonry (June 25, 2003) to understand that his conception of "European identity" relies on a set of values – "a modern and rejuvenated humanism" resting on "justice, solidarity, and responsibility" – that sets it apart from what is understood, at least in France, as "American" or "Anglo-Saxon liberalism."[41]

All this has much to do with the perceived need to defend a French model against the disruptive forces of "globalization" and "communitarization" (with the latter phenomenon often linked with the heavy immigration that has taken place since the beginning of the 1970s). And this attack on the French model is seen as part of the self-serving agenda of "Anglo-Saxon" powers.[42] Indeed, the resentment of American (or Anglo-Saxon) influence is all the greater because the French model – republican, centralized, statist, and Jacobin – is regarded as under attack from various different quarters, some of which are routinely confused with one another. These multiple sources of attack include the forces of ultra-liberalism and globalization, putting into question the validity of the French economic and social model; the growing importance and scope of the European Union, with deep consequences for the French constitutional order; the growing tendency toward a form of regionalism that is basically opposed to the centralization of the French state; and the growing impact of multiculturalism, feminism, and immigration on French culture and the French legal system. This latter point stems from mounting pressure in many quarters for the legal recognition of special social groups, a development that is absolutely contrary to the basic principle that the French state recognizes only individual citizens

[40] *Le Monde*, June 18, 2003.   [41] Quai d'Orsay website (see n. 21).
[42] Georges-Henri Soutou, "France, Nations and Empires from the Nineteenth Century to the Present Day: Between Jacobin Tradition, European Balance of Power and European Integration," in Henry Cavanna (ed.), *Governance, Globalization and the European Union: Which Europe for Tomorrow?* (Dublin: Four Courts Press, 2002, pp. 69–86).

and only equal, individual rights, with no legal possibility to support affirmative action or to distinguish the legal status of any special cultural, sexual, or ethnic groups. All these factors tend to contribute to the French ascribing, whether rightly or wrongly, their current problems to the rise of the "global" and "communitarian" model, which many French believe to be the result not only of social evolution but also of the agenda of Great Britain and the United States.[43] This belief and the resentment that accompanies it go to the roots of French self-perceptions.

Domestic politics

Finally, the institutional evolution of French political life also matters.[44] Under Pompidou and Giscard d'Estaing, there was a strong constituency for good Franco-American relations, and this constituency had representation in the spectrum of French political parties. Even if it did not constitute a majority, that constituency could exert considerable leverage. Indeed, one of the reasons for de Gaulle's failure to win the referendum of April 1969, which led to his resignation, was the opposition of important parts of French society and political elites to his American policies. And whatever the views of Pompidou and Giscard d'Estaing, both needed the support of right-of-center Atlanticists to retain a majority in parliament.[45]

But this constituency no longer exists, or at best is too widely dispersed to be influential. From polls and through conversations, one could guess that approximately one-third of French political elites do not desire permanent tension with Washington. But on the right, since a majority of UDF members (the former Giscardians) joined the new UMP party of Jacques Chirac, which is basically the old Gaullist party, they now have little leverage on major issues of foreign affairs: having burned their own boat, they cannot leave the one in which they now sit. As for moderate Socialists, most of whom are by no means anti-American (even if the current American administration has, generally speaking, few supporters in France), they cannot hope to regain power without allying themselves with the Communists, the Greens, and the ultra-left, all groups opposed to the United States as a matter of principle.

As a result, there is as of now no possible domestic political arrangement, either on the left or on the right, for a real refoundation of Franco-American

---

[43] Ibid.

[44] For a parallel analysis of developments within the context of American political institutions, see chapter 4 in this volume.

[45] In the case of Pompidou, see Cointet, et al., *Un politique: Georges Pompidou*. For Valéry Giscard d'Estaing see Jean-Jacques Becker, *Crises et alternances 1974–2000* (Paris: Le Seuil, 2002).

and Franco-Atlantic relations. This has to do with the evolution of French politics described here, but also with the recent evolution of French society as suggested in the previous section. On the latter point, a long period of high unemployment has destroyed the brief and quite new acceptance of liberalism that was present for a few years around 1990. In addition, recent immigration has further undermined the constituency for positive relations with Washington. The outlook in France is generally much more influenced by Third World considerations nowadays, such as support of the Palestinians and hostility toward the capitalism of rich countries, than it has been previously. The constituency for those views stems largely from immigrants, the ultra-left, the Communists, and a major part of the Socialists, with deep inroads even further to the right or the far right. The Franco-American rift has thus probably become a structural rather than a cyclical problem within French politics.

The day after

The difficulties of the coalition occupying Iraq are regarded by many French as vindicating their government's hostility to the war.[46] There is intense interest in ongoing debates in Washington about whether President Bush underrated terrorist threats prior to September 11 and then diverted resources needed against Bin Laden into an unnecessary war with Saddam Hussein.[47] One can hardly expect most French to be any less severe in their judgments on these matters than are the American media that informed people in France follow.[48]

Of course, the French government wisely refrained from gloating. During spring 2004, one even witnessed a narrowing of the gap between American and French views, particularly about the future role of the UN in Iraq.[49] (This is true even if most French are convinced that, because of the Americans' difficulties, it is Washington, not Paris, that is doing most

---

[46] See for instance Rémy Ourdan in *Le Monde* of April 9 and 11, 2004.

[47] See for instance the April 9 issue of *Le Figaro*, and *Le Monde* of April 10, 13, and 20, 2004.

[48] The *International Herald Tribune*, *Time*, and *Newsweek* are widely followed; the *Wall Street Journal* is much less read. The relevant books that came out in early 2004, for instance Richard A. Clarke's *Against All Enemies* (New York: Free press, 2004), were reviewed in the French press (see, e.g., Patrick Jarreau in *Le Monde*, March 26, 2004). Clarke's book is due to come out translated into French at Albin Michel (*Contre tous les ennemis*).

[49] Christian Müller, "Détente zwischen Paris und Washington: Vermehrte Flexibilität in der Irak-Frage," *Neue Zürcher Zeitung*, January 20, 2004; Corine Lesnes, "M. De Villepin annonce une 'phase différente' dans les relations franco-américaines," *Le Monde*, February 8–9, 2004; Laurent Zecchini, "Paris et Berlin ne s'opposeront pas à un rôle accru de l'OTAN en Europe," *Le Monde*, February 10, 2004.

of the narrowing.)[50] Some commentators note that France has no interest in an American failure in Iraq; the best outcome would therefore be for the United States to recognize its mistakes and change course, in cooperation with Europe.[51] Others suggest that the French as a whole recognize that they went too far in their opposition to the United States, that France and Germany isolated themselves in Europe, and that now both Berlin and Paris need to mend fences with Washington.[52] This would seem to be overly sanguine: the majority view in France remains an "I told you so" attitude, with some commentators equating Dominique de Villepin's speech at the United Nations with de Gaulle's 1966 speech in Phnom Penh condemning the Vietnam War.[53]

Elsewhere, the difficulties of Tony Blair, the Madrid bombings and subsequent electoral defeat of Aznar, and similar developments have been mostly interpreted as a series of defeats for Washington; these events are seen as the first signs of the unraveling of the occupying coalition, and as the beginning of a reconciliation between "Old" and "New" Europe along the lines advocated from the beginning by Paris and Berlin. The forward march toward a closer European Union, on this reading, has become much easier with the (supposed) appearance of unified European public opinion, based in part on the growing view that Europe and the United States really are different. Institutional progress should enable the EU to fight terrorism more efficiently, employing methods different from the American ones, and also to call more effectively for an alternative American policy.[54]

Thus, while the French government is keeping a more low-key profile these days, one should not infer a change of basic orientation. Paris is resting its case, but one senses no change in its basic geopolitical tenets.

---

[50] Corine Lesnes, "Frappée à Bagdad, l'Amérique tente d'impliquer les Nations Unies," *Le Monde*, January 20, 2004.

[51] Justin Vaïsse, "L'enfer des bonnes intentions," *Le Monde*, April 18–19, 2004.

[52] John Vinocur in the *International Herald Tribune* of April 10–11, 2004.

[53] Charles Lambroschini, *Le Figaro*, April 2, 2004.

[54] For examples of these views, see Pierre Avril in *Le Figaro*, March 29, François Heisbourg in Le Monde, March 27, and Alexandrine Bouilhet in *Le Figaro*, March 27–28, all 2004. See also an interview with Dominique Reynié, a political science professor, in *Le Figaro Magazine* of April 24, 2004: "L'opinion européenne est née un an avant l'élargissement!" Prospects for an alternative American policy were regarded as heavily dependent on the election of Senator John Kerry as president, on whom the French press dedicated mostly glowing reports and who was supposed, once elected, to adopt the Venusian world outlook of "Old Europe"; see for instance the magazine supplement of *Le Monde*, February 29, 2004, titled "JFK." That matters might have been more complicated if Senator Kerry had indeed been elected is little understood; for an analysis, see John Vinocur, "Europe in for a Letdown if It's Counting on Kerry," *International Herald Tribune*, March 30, 2004.

For instance, in March 2004, Paris and Berlin agreed upon a document called "Strategic Partnership for a Common Future with the Middle East," later adopted by the European Council. Drafted as an answer to the "greater Middle East" plan of President Bush, this document stresses the necessity to respect the identity of each country in the region and warns against any hasty and oversimplifying approach – an evident if implicit criticism of the American plan.[55] Likewise, Chirac's April 2004 visit to Moscow evidenced the continuing closeness of the Franco-Russian relationship, at least as seen from Paris.[56]

In short, if the French tone is softer than in 2003, underlying differences with the American approach remain. The only real sign of movement is a recent reexamination of the French position about the relationship between a European defense system and NATO, which I address in the concluding section.

Prospects for change

If changes in France's international position and preferences, in the French self-conception, and in domestic political arrangements all tend to undermine the relationship between Paris and Washington, then what circumstances might conspire to produce a more positive bilateral relationship?

For one thing, one may doubt whether France will achieve much success along the present lines of its foreign policy. True, Prime Minister Blair now seems to take much more seriously the concept of a European defense system. But, in the final analysis, Germany does not share the French foreign policy agenda: while Berlin certainly wishes to redress the balance inside the Alliance, it will not be anxious to create a new imbalance that benefits Paris. Meanwhile, even if French officials genuinely envision a Franco-German axis to move Europe in the direction of a greater international assertiveness, there are important segments of French public opinion that have strong doubts about this model and especially about Germany. These critics, or potential critics, believe that Berlin wants to mold the European Union along the lines of the German federal model – a policy aimed at furthering Germany's interests, but with great dangers for the unity and stability of France.[57]

---

[55] Laurent Zecchini in *Le Monde*, March 4, 2004.
[56] Laure Mandeville, "Les relations entre Paris et Moscou au beau fixe," *Le Figaro*, April 3–4, 2004.
[57] As the success of the essay by Yvonne Bollmann, *Ce que veut l'Allemagne* (Paris: Bartillat, 2003), testifies.

The French still favor a core group of countries forging ahead inside the EU (*groupes pionniers*), in order for integration to proceed in the wake of the enlargement and also to retain more French influence in the expanding union, but the Germans have let it be known that they no longer accept that view and instead are calling for a large Europe (including Turkey) organized along more federal lines. A major crisis for the Franco-German relationship is therefore looming.[58] Meanwhile, Russia will continue to play its own game and not unduly antagonize Washington.[59]

The lack of any real results deriving from France's current policy might eventually induce a change of mind, although this may take quite some time.[60] But it is important to note that France's present antagonism toward the United States serves the useful political goal of rebuilding national unity; thus, the failure of the new policy orientation to achieve its major putative objectives may not prove fatal. Indeed, in order to transform what are at present minority views in favor of improved relations with the United States into a new mainstream approach in France, several additional conditions or circumstances will be necessary.

First and foremost, there should be a welcome change of public spirit when the present period of economic troubles, social turbulence, and difficult and much disputed reforms abates. Second, the further development of the common fight against terrorism may change public perceptions. Franco-American cooperation never ceased on this front despite all the tensions of the Iraq War, but this fact was not sufficiently appreciated. It is not widely known, for instance, that during the summer of 2003 French Special Forces joined their American counterparts around Kandahar, Afghanistan, and have been for all purposes integrated with them.[61] Furthermore, France itself could at any time become subject to terrorist attacks; if that happens, there might be a powerful call for more cooperation with Washington.

---

[58] Pierre Bocev in *Le Figaro*, March 1, 2004.

[59] Daniel Vernet, "La Russie face à l'hégémonie américaine," *Le Monde*, July 30, 2003.

[60] Indeed, from the beginning, many noted French experts disputed the wisdom of the French policy and argued for the repair of Franco-American relations and for a better understanding of American aims and motives. See, e.g., Dominique Moïsi, "Une diplomatie qui n'a pas accru notre prestige," *Le Monde*, June 17, 2003; Alexandre Adler, "Multipolarité et politique des Blocs," *Le Figaro*, July 1, 2003; Casanova, "De Charles de Gaulle à Jacques Chirac"; Thierry de Montbrial, "Les Etats-Unis contre l'Europe puissance," *Le Monde*, August 1, 2003. Thérèse Delpech drew "three lessons," each quite lucid, from the Iraq crisis ("Bagdad: trois leçons pour une crise," *Politique Internationale* 100 [Summer 2003].) Pascal Cuche even risked the blasphemous title "Iraq: And If France Was Wrong?" ["Irak: et si la France s'était trompée?], *Politique Etrangère* 99 (Summer 2003), pp. 409–422.

[61] Patrick de Saint-Exupéry in *Le Figaro*, August 13, 2003.

A third precondition is to find a solution to the problem of the relationship between the EU's fledgling defense organization and NATO, because it is there that the French ambition of a *Europe puissance* has created the most transatlantic problems since de Gaulle. There are some recent positive developments to note, including Paris' apparent acceptance that the buildup of a European defense system will not be accepted by its partners if it appears to threaten NATO and the Euro-American relationship.[62] A balance might therefore eventually be struck between a NATO that evolves and becomes more efficient at peace-keeping, and a developing European defense organization that cannot substitute for NATO but should certainly supplement it, as everyone agrees. There is a growing and welcome tendency to consider those questions on their practical merits rather than in ideological terms.[63]

But the fourth precondition is a change in the American mindset, including a renewed capacity for official Washington to express a view of the world that is both workable and convincing for French elites. Americans should realize that, if many Europeans regard the present French course as excessive, they nevertheless desire the articulation and development of a new transatlantic balance. This is certainly the case for Germany, where even leading scholars well known as longstanding Atlanticists make the point quite forcefully.[64] Washington should therefore realize that the move toward further European integration – both geographic and functional – is, though slow, now probably unstoppable. Failure to recognize this fact undermines the prospects for deeper transatlantic cooperation, which will certainly have to be based on some new formulation of the balance between Europe and the United States.[65]

---

[62] As President Chirac himself has put it, there is "no longer an opposition between the EU and NATO": Laurent Zecchini, *Le Monde,* April 22, 2004.

[63] Interview of Marc Perrin de Brichambaut, head of the Delegation for Strategic Affairs at the Defense Ministry, *Le Figaro,* April 19, 2004; Laurent Zecchini, *Le Monde,* March 4, 2004. More generally, Paris seems to have come to the conclusion that the UN, the EU, and NATO could cooperate on important geopolitical tasks, first of all in the Middle East, as they did, after all, in the former Yugoslavia.

[64] For instance, Helga Haftendorn, *Deutsche Aussenpolitik zwischen Selbstbeschränkung und Selbstbehauptung* (Munich: DVA, 2001), p. 445; Michael Stürmer, *Die Kunst des Gleichgewichts: Europa in einer Welt ohne Mitte* (Berlin: Propyläen, 2001).

[65] See Roger Cohen, *International Herald Tribune,* April 30–May 2, 2004. That there is still a long way to go is evidenced by Zbigniew Brzezinski's book, *The Choice: Global Domination or Global Leadership* (New York: Basic Books, 2004). Although the author wants to criticize current American foreign policy, his views are still far from what many Europeans are willing to accept, for his prescription for "global leadership" by the United States is quite strong indeed. See the critical review by William Pfaff in the *New York Review of Books,* April 8, 2004.

6   Security exporters: Germany, the United States, and transatlantic cooperation

Hubert Zimmermann

The transatlantic crisis over the Iraq War presented many surprises to observers of European–American relations. One of the most unexpected developments, and the one that made this crisis very different from earlier transatlantic disagreements, was the line taken by Germany. Since World War II, it had always been among the strongest supporters of the United States in the global arena. Though it frequently disagreed with specific American policies, Germany always expressed its disapproval cautiously, qualified by statements underlining the preeminence of the transatlantic alliance. In 2002–3, however, it was at the forefront of European opposition to the course pursued by the Bush administration, and it actively tried to build an international coalition with the goal of undermining American efforts to obtain international legitimacy for the war in Iraq. Germany's chancellor was reelected after a campaign in which he capitalized heavily on condemning American policies.

This is not the only development indicating an astonishing transformation of the basic tenets of Germany's international policy. Since World War II, Germany had been fundamentally opposed to participating in military operations outside the NATO alliance's territorial space (so-called out-of-area operations); support for US-led campaigns in international trouble spots was limited to financial and logistical assistance. Yet at this very moment, Germany is the second- or third-largest provider of peacekeeping forces in the world, a striking change within a very short period.[1]

In short, Germany seems on its way to becoming a different actor in world politics: less inhibited and more inclined to formulate policies that disregard the interests of its closest allies. Recent episodes of brinkmanship in EU policies show that this tendency is not confined to transatlantic

---

[1]   In July 2004, German soldiers were active in the following missions, and in the following numbers: KFOR (Kosovo): 3,280; ISAF (Afghanistan): 1,970; Operation Enduring Freedom (Afghanistan/Horn of Africa/Kenya): 300; Active Endeavour (Mediterranean): 430. See http://einsatz.bundeswehr.de/einsatz_aktuell/index.php, accessed July 5, 2004.

relations. How can these momentous transformations be explained? Are they the result of the 1998 switch from a Conservative-led government to a coalition of the Social Democrats with the Green Party? Or is the Kaganite explanation correct, locating differences in international policy preferences across the Atlantic in different national characters shaped by vast power inequalities?[2] Does the Iraq crisis reflect the natural reaction of a country that defines itself as a "civilian power" to the unilateralism of the Bush administration?[3] Are these changes inevitable, as many realist and neorealist observers argue, since after the Cold War the German–American alliance has lost its fundamental *raison d'être*?

None of these explanations is sufficient to account for the changes outlined above. Instead, the key change in German–American relations (as well as EU–US relations) is the continuing shift from a relationship based on *acceptance of American leadership* toward one of *collaboration among equal partners*. Why? To an extent unprecedented in the postwar era, Germany and the United States now pursue structurally similar international policies. Since the end of the Cold War, Germany has become an *exporter of security* abroad, whereas previously it had been an *importer of security* from the United States.[4] Thus the fundamental policy objectives and policy tools of the United States and Germany in the international system are becoming more alike, as both seek to address security threats by intervening abroad – politically, economically, and militarily. Germany is slowly equipping itself with the same broad range of policy instruments as the United States and is therefore incrementally able to pursue similar operations (albeit on a much smaller scale). Within Europe, Germany's move in this direction has been the most pronounced, though other countries have certainly undergone a similar transformation. But due to its crucial place in the fabric of European institutions, Germany will be the decisive actor in determining how these changes will affect the future direction of common European defense efforts and the intensity of cooperation with the United States. Whereas the general thrust of British and French policy remains more or less consistent with their traditional roles, Germany's transformation will make the crucial difference "after Iraq."

---

[2] Robert Kagan, *Of Paradise and Power: America and Europe in the New World Order* (New York: Knopf, 2003).

[3] Sebastian Harnisch and Hanns W. Maull (eds.), *Germany as a Civilian Power? The Foreign Policy of the Berlin Republic* (Manchester: Manchester University Press, 2001).

[4] This distinction is also made by Daniel S. Hamilton, *German–American Relations and the Campaign Against Terrorism* (Washington, DC: AICGS, 2002, http://www.aicgs.org/publications/PDF/hamilton.pdf), p. 10. There it is, however, not used as a conceptual instrument.

This chapter begins by sketching a basic conceptual framework to guide the analysis of this transformation in German–American relations. I then trace the nature of transatlantic cooperation during the Cold War era, focusing on the concept of burden-sharing, and analyze the structural transformation of mutual relations during the 1990s that has led to functionally similar roles for these two states within the international system. While this transformation might result either in increasing alienation or in a new form of collaboration based on equality, I conclude that the latter is more likely due to the persistent network of common institutions and the nature of common challenges that require cooperation. Germany and the United States share similar threat perceptions, and the Federal Republic remains strongly attached to transatlantic institutions. This fact, plus Germany's weight within European institutions, makes it rather unlikely that the European Security and Defence Policy (ESDP) will develop as a balancing force to US power. However, in order for this optimistic prognosis to obtain, the German and American governments must actively engage domestic constituencies in order to bridge the gap between different institutional practices shaped in part by cultural factors.

Structural change and burden-sharing

The rift in the transatlantic alliance and the refusal by key American allies to support the US campaign in Iraq have demonstrated that the core concept traditionally underpinning the alliance – burden-sharing within a framework of more or less automatic acceptance of American leadership – has had its day. NATO, whose working principle was transatlantic cooperation in the task to contain the Soviets (as well as, inside the West, the Germans), is in a deep crisis. On both sides of the Atlantic, widespread support is voiced for a policy in which the United States and Europe "go it alone" and pursue strategies of selective alliances instead of embarking on the complicated and time-consuming process of devising a common strategy toward the global issues of the twenty-first century. Dissolution of the former institutional framework and the gradual decoupling of Europe and the United States seem possible (as the ongoing debate about the withdrawal of American troops from US bases in western Europe shows). According to some voices, this trend, which would amount to a fundamental rupture in transatlantic relations, is inevitable, desirable, or both.

Neorealist theory in particular predicted that the end of the Cold War would result in the slow dissolution of the transatlantic alliance.[5]

---

[5] For more on this subject, see chapter 3 in this volume.

American hegemony would give way to a situation in which new great powers (such as Germany and Japan) emerge, reassert their role in the international system, and engage in balancing behavior to safeguard their position in an anarchic environment of self-help.[6] In this interpretation, a competitive transatlantic relationship results from the fact that the supreme power against which such balancing behavior would have to be directed is, at least for the foreseeable future, the United States. This neorealist interpretation is helpful insofar as it emphasizes structural change in the international system as the main factor accounting for the remodeling of Germany's international policies.[7] However, the decisive factor in this respect is less the disappearance of the Soviet threat than it is Germany's belated assumption of a new functional role in the system. Once we add domestic, ideological, and institutional factors to the mix, it is not at all certain that the transformation of German foreign policy described above will lead to balance-of-power rivalry between the United States and Germany.

I use the concept of "burden-sharing" as a lens that helps one to bring these multiple considerations into focus. Attention to the burden-sharing debate in the Atlantic alliance is useful inasmuch as it encompasses not only the military side of the power equation but the economic dimension as well. A more limited focus on purely military capacity perhaps too quickly suggests a state of American *hyperpuissance* and leads almost automatically to the conclusion that the United States would be better served by unilateral policies.[8] But the broader concept of burden-sharing consistently points to the economic underpinning of every allied projection of power, since joint undertakings by two or more states necessarily involve a search for a formula to divide both the political and economic costs thereof. Furthermore, the burden-sharing focus integrates the domestic dimension into the analysis, since it implies that a major task for governments is to extract from their electorates the necessary (and potentially massive) resources that projects based on common purpose and interests require. This extractive challenge draws attention to the difficulties inherent in reaching an understanding of the nature of joint tasks, including the critical question of who will execute them and who will pay for them. Finally, burden-sharing is also inextricably linked to

---

[6] Kenneth Waltz, "The Emerging Structure of International Politics," *International Security* 18:2 (Autumn 1993), pp. 44–79.

[7] By accepting this insight, I necessarily disagree with the "civilian-power" approach and its insistence on the essential continuity of German foreign policy from the Cold War era to the present.

[8] Charles Krauthammer, "The Unipolar Moment Revisited," *The National Interest* 70 (Winter 2002–3), pp. 5–17.

power-sharing,[9] as the current debate on European participation in Iraq's postwar reconstruction clearly shows.

Burden-sharing during the early Cold War

After September 11, the American government called upon its European allies to share the burden of a common fight against global terrorism. This appeal was based on the experience of the Cold War, during which the United States and Europe had established a comprehensive relationship at the core of which lay the concept of burden-sharing. The rationale underlying this strongly institutionalized framework was not only the struggle against the communist bloc; it also included sustained efforts to create stable economic conditions within "the West" so as to insulate the allies from the threat of political extremism and to prevent the sorts of dislocations wrought by the economic crisis of the 1930s.[10] Thus transatlantic burden-sharing encompassed a broad range of issues: the provision of military security, the shared management of international monetary and trade policy, and even "ideological" burden-sharing – that is, European political support for the United States' global policy, providing the latter with enhanced international and domestic legitimacy.

Many US postwar policies toward Europe can be described in terms of burden-sharing. In the period immediately after World War II, the American government and public expected that the unprecedented wartime involvement in European affairs could be terminated and that the American troops would be sent home. However, leaders such as Secretary of State Dean Acheson soon realized that a sustained American commitment and strong political leadership would be necessary to prevent the establishment of Soviet hegemony in Europe and to resist any resurgence of German nationalism.[11] This commitment was not intended to last for eternity, however. The expectation was that American military and economic support would help the Europeans to pull together, reconstruct their economies, and provide the means for their own defense, thus eventually allowing the United States to cut its overseas presence to a minimum.[12]

---

[9] Andrew B. Denison, *Shades of Multilateralism: US Perspectives on Europe's Role in the War on Terrorism* (Bonn: ZEI Discussion Paper No. 106, 2002), p. 10.

[10] G. John Ikenberry, "The Political Foundations of Atlantic Order," in Hall Gardner and Radoslava Stefanova (eds.), *The New Transatlantic Agenda: Facing the Challenges of Global Governance* (Aldershot, UK: Ashgate, 2001), p. 20.

[11] Geir Lundestad, *"Empire" by Integration: The United States and European Integration, 1945–1997* (Oxford: Oxford University Press, 1998).

[12] However, US decision-makers in this period remained divided as to whether this should result in a truly independent Europe or a continuing situation of American political preponderance, due to the US nuclear monopoly.

A crucial step in this endeavor was the rearmament of Germany.[13] Only the manpower provided by this former enemy could serve as the necessary conventional component of a flexible defense structure. However, neither German rearmament nor the parallel economic reconstruction of western Germany was acceptable to the rest of Europe without guarantees of continued American involvement. Albeit reluctantly, the United States had to "export" additional security to Europe: the nuclear guarantee against the Soviets was supplemented by the guarantee (in the form of American troops) against Germany's resurgence.[14] The United States thus assumed the final responsibility for the security of Europe. But considerable resources were necessary to execute this task, with the result that a core American interest in the management of interallied affairs became more burden-sharing by its European partners. The resulting dialogue kept transatlantic institutions busy throughout the Cold War and after.

The policy of double containment eventually led to the construction of a vast network of military and quasi-military installations not only in Germany but in almost every west European country. NATO thus became an "entangling" alliance: the ongoing presence of such an important part of the American military in Europe necessitated a continuing process of consultation aimed at the resolution of numerous strategic, logistical, financial, and legal problems. The cost of the bases was shared among host and stationing countries. The German government in particular made available huge training areas, constructed barracks, and – in the so-called status-of-forces agreements – granted US and British troops a whole series of privileges that continue to exist today.[15]

Cold War burden-sharing was not limited to the military field. Germany and the other European allies also supported American policies diplomatically by generally acting as a bloc on issues related to the overall conflict with the Soviet Union – for example, by presenting a united front in the United Nations and by supporting anti-communist regimes throughout the world. Throughout this period, the principle of American leadership remained at the core of the Alliance. While there was a plethora of opinions among the NATO partners regarding the most

---

[13] Christopher Gehrz and Marc Trachtenberg, "America, Europe, and German Rearmament, August–September 1950," in Marc Trachtenberg (ed.), *Between Empire and Alliance* (Lanham, MD: Rowman & Littlefield, 2003), pp. 1–32.

[14] France was thus a major importer of security, with the creation of the French *force de frappe* only partially mitigating this fact; see chapter 5 in this volume.

[15] For a description, see James R. Golden, *NATO Burden-Sharing: Risks and Opportunities* (Washington, DC: Praeger, Washington Papers 96, 1983), p. 61.

appropriate East–West policies, in critical moments (as during the Cuban missile crisis, for example) even the most critical allies of the United States rallied behind it.

The military-political framework of NATO necessitated regular consultations among Western leaders on key political and strategic questions. But a corresponding network of economic institutions was developed as well, which likewise required constant attention. The Bretton Woods formula of liberalizing trade while controlling international capital markets (famously described by John Ruggie as "embedded liberalism")[16] required constant action by state authorities and necessitated the construction of multiple institutional platforms to serve as consultation and decision-making arenas. Some of these institutions had been designed during the war (the International Monetary Fund and the World Bank, for example), but others were negotiated in its aftermath and in the shadow of East–West confrontation; these latter included the Organisation for European Economic Co-operation (or OEEC, later transformed into the OECD) and the General Agreement on Tariffs and Trade. It was the United States that took the lead in establishing this dense multilateral network of institutions regulating international trade and finance,[17] as American preponderance permitted the United States to act as a benign hegemon in overcoming collective-action problems. The management of the fixed-rate exchange system in particular necessitated intense consultation and financial burden-sharing, including rather frequent bailouts of currencies that came under pressure. Financial decision-makers from both sides of the Atlantic met each other on a regular basis and thus developed a shared outlook;[18] this was an important asset when the questions associated with burden-sharing developed into very serious problems in the Alliance.

Such problems were not long in coming. As early as the middle and late 1950s, as the recovery of the European states progressed and the costs of the Cold War mounted, American governments became increasingly weary of the defense burden. President Eisenhower frequently voiced his frustration about the situation that had emerged: "These other NATO powers cannot go on forever riding on our coat-tails … All of these nations seem to be trying to figure out how little they themselves can

---

[16] John Ruggie, "Embedded Liberalism in the Postwar Economic Order," *International Organization* 36 (1982), pp. 379–415.

[17] Mark Pollack, "Unilateral Europe, Multilateral America?," in John Peterson and Mark Pollack (eds.), *Europe, America, Bush: Transatlantic Relations in the Twenty-First Century* (London: Routledge, 2003), p. 119.

[18] Charles A. Coombs, *The Arena of International Finance* (New York: Wiley, 1976).

do and how best to leave us to do the rest of the job."[19] In addition to rising criticism within Congress regarding the seemingly interminable nature of large-scale American commitment to Europe's defense, there were growing economic tensions across the Atlantic. Among these was the role of the Allies in providing support for the US dollar. Balance-of-payments deficits induced by the vast American military and economic commitments abroad threatened the dollar's stability; a core issue concerned the foreign exchange cost of the massive American troop commitment abroad, most of which was located in Germany. In a series of highly contested negotiations, the Germans eventually agreed to "offset" these costs by investing heavily in American weaponry, buying US treasury bonds, intervening in currency markets on behalf of the dollar, and creating a foreign aid program that supported US allies in need such as Turkey or Greece.[20] Germany also began providing substantial economic support for Israel, supplementing and partly supplanting US aid.[21]

However, the more responsibilities that countries such as Germany assumed, the more they felt entitled to influence decision-making in an alliance that was dominated by the Americans. This development was reflected in the debate on nuclear-sharing in the 1950s and early 1960s;[22] more generally, the Germans were hesitant to share Cold War burdens further if this would not entail increased political power-sharing. No lasting solution to this problem was found. Nevertheless, the Alliance, founded as it was on common norms and institutions, proved sufficiently cohesive to manage the countless skirmishes generated by the Americans' demands for more burden-sharing and the Europeans' demands for more power-sharing. Temporary and politically sustainable solutions were agreed upon, even if they often made little economic sense.[23] Meanwhile, the principle of American leadership remained uncontested; the questions concerned instead how this principle would be practiced, not the fact or necessity of American preeminence.

---

[19] Memorandum of Discussion at the 390th NSC Meeting, December 11, 1958, US Department of State, *Foreign Relations of the United States*, 1958–1960 series, vol. 2, pp. 368–369.

[20] Hubert Zimmermann, *Money and Security: Troops, Monetary Policy, and West Germany's Relations with the United States and Britain, 1950–1971* (Cambridge: Cambridge University Press, 2002).

[21] Institut für Zeitgeschichte, *Akten zur Auswärtigen Politik der Bundesrepublik Deutschland 1971* (Munich: Oldenbourg, 2002), vol. III, Doc. 365.

[22] Marc Trachtenberg, *A Constructed Peace: The Making of the European Settlement, 1945–1963* (Princeton: Princeton University Press, 1999).

[23] Simon Duke, *The Burdensharing Debate: A Reassessment* (London: Macmillan, 1993).

Vietnam, the Nixon shocks, and Afghanistan

The system of mutual burden-sharing entered a sustained crisis during the Vietnam War. The Johnson administration was unable to extract troop commitments for the war from its European allies, though some financial help was forthcoming.[24] But Vietnam was the first massive transatlantic disagreement concerning the nature of common tasks. Parallels with the 2003 Iraq crisis abound, although at that time even the British did not offer the United States direct military support. Frustrated by Europe's unhelpfulness, Congress became an increasingly active player in the burden-sharing debate. A 1966 congressional resolution sponsored by Senator Mike Mansfield called for a massive reduction of US troops in Europe, initiating an endless series of similar demands based on the argument that the Europeans were not contributing enough to common tasks.[25] American administrations used these initiatives to extract additional offset payments, especially from Germany. But US officials were determined to retain their autonomy in foreign policy decision-making and successfully resisted any force reductions mandated by Congress.

While the Mansfield initiatives did not result in decisive cuts in US troop levels abroad, they did signal the firm anchoring of the burden-sharing debate in the American domestic political arena. Until the 1990s, however, the East–West conflict provided US administrations with at least a potential argument to neutralize domestic opposition to the sacrifices deemed necessary to sustain the Alliance. As a general matter, European support for Washington's policies abroad helped successive US governments convince the American public of the benefits of costly international engagements. The external threat thus helped contain the potentially disruptive burden-sharing debate, which, particularly given the American system's propensity for frequent changes in domestic political constellations, might have led to an early disintegration of the postwar network of transatlantic institutions.

The early 1970s witnessed continued turbulence in the Alliance. Despite the durability of the US military commitment, mutual doubts about Cold War policies (on the one hand Nixon's détente, on the other Brandt's *Ostpolitik*) intensified the bad feelings. The strains in transatlantic relations were further magnified by President Nixon's 1971 decision to decouple the

---

[24] Germany, for example, was the largest donor of foreign aid to South Vietnam; see Wilfried Mausbach, "European Perspectives on the War in Vietnam," *German Historical Institute Bulletin* 30 (2002), pp. 71–86.

[25] Phil Williams, *The Senate and US Troops in Europe* (London: Palgrave, 1985).

dollar from gold, thereby unilaterally shifting the burden of monetary adjustment onto the backs of American allies. It was in the context of mounting concerns about Atlantic political and monetary relations that Germany had supported the first plan for a common European currency, at the Hague Summit in December 1969; renewed calls for formulating a common European foreign policy also date from this period. However, from the start, the United States expressed strong reservations about any project that might lead to a duplication of NATO defense structures. The preferred US policy approach was by that time clearly burden-sharing under American leadership: withdrawal from Europe was no longer considered an option, but neither was treating the Alliance as a collaboration among equal parties.

The mutual disenchantment of the 1970s was partly remedied by the Soviet invasion of Afghanistan in 1979, triggering a new hot phase of the Cold War. In the wake of the Soviet action, most west European governments provided (despite considerable protest in their countries) bases for the forward stationing of intermediate-range ballistic missiles; indeed this became a major factor in the fall of the Schmidt government in Germany. In addition, in 1982, Washington and Bonn signed a Wartime Host Nation Agreement, stipulating that the United States could use German units for rear-area logistical support in wartime.[26] Meanwhile, the debate about burden-sharing continued. In the 1980s, against the background of substantially increased defense spending under the Reagan administration, Congress again sponsored a series of initiatives which exhorted the allies to step up their efforts lest the United States take compensatory measures.[27] However, the Cold War framework for transatlantic relations proved resilient, and no major changes in the Alliance took place before the 1990s.

The end of the Cold War and the demise of burden-sharing

The 1991 Gulf War was a final highlight of traditional burden-sharing. Thirty-two countries provided considerable troop support, and affluent countries such as Japan, Germany, and Saudi Arabia footed a large part of the bill.[28] After the successful campaign, the administration of George Bush, Sr., extended an offer to the Germans to become a "partner in leadership."[29] The transatlantic declaration of February 1990 called for

---

[26] Duke, *The Burdensharing Debate*, p. 76.
[27] Ibid., pp. 76–81.   [28] Ibid.
[29] Deutsche Einheit, *Sonderedition aus den Akten des Bundeskanzleramts* (Munich: Oldenbourg, 1998).

regular and systematic consultation between Europe and the United States, and resulted in a huge increase of meetings by officials. The New Transatlantic Agenda (NTA), which was signed at the Madrid summit in December 1995, listed a wide range of common goals for collaborative efforts, including promoting stability in eastern Europe and the Middle East, trade liberalization, combating terrorism and nuclear proliferation, safeguarding access to energy resources, protecting the environment, supporting the transformation of states such as China and Russia, and strengthening the international economic system.[30] This gave rise to a series of optimistic statements regarding the creation of a new transatlantic partnership.[31] Would the Atlantic alliance now be transformed from burden-sharing under American leadership to a framework for collaboration among genuine equals?

The results of the NTA did not meet these high expectations. One reason for this disappointment was that the United States still resisted the development of a European defense force that would be independent of NATO, fearing a potential waste of efforts. Madeleine Albright famously warned against the "three D's": de-coupling, discrimination, and duplication.[32] Attempts to restructure the Alliance so as to integrate the ESDP into NATO structures failed, partly due to American resistance to sharing facilities and command posts.[33] Influential voices in Washington argued that the Kosovo campaign demonstrated only too clearly that too much cooperation with too many allies leads to diminished military efficiency.[34] Equally unhelpful to any stable cooperation schemes were American domestic politics in the second Clinton administration, which at times seemed to immobilize the government.[35]

A final important factor precluding the negotiation of a new institutional framework was the substantial divergence among the approaches of leading EU member states to the potential relationship between NATO and ESDP. In Germany, the traditional emphasis on a continued strong American presence in Europe remained resilient, in contrast to French plans to build up a European counterweight to the United States. Indeed,

---

[30] Mark Pollack and Greg Shaffer (eds.), *Transatlantic Governance in the Global Economy* (London: Rowman & Littlefield, 2001).

[31] Kevin Featherstone and Roy Ginsberg, *The United States and the European Union in the 1990s: Partners in Transition* (London: Palgrave Macmillan, 1993).

[32] "The Right Balance Will Secure NATO's Future," *Financial Times*, December 7, 1998.

[33] Jolyon Howorth, "Foreign and Defence Policy Cooperation: European and American Perspectives," in Peterson and Pollack, *Europe, America, Bush*, p. 15.

[34] Frederic Bozo, "The Effects of Kosovo and the Danger of Decoupling," in Jolyon Howorth and John T. S. Keeler (eds.), *Defending Europe: The EU, NATO and the Quest for Autonomy* (London: Palgrave, 2003), pp. 61–80.

[35] Most obviously with the impeachment proceedings against the president.

most European governments did not see an urgent need for European defense capabilities that could operate autonomously of NATO or the United States: a continuation of traditional security arrangements under American leadership embodied both less risk and less cost. Thus, at the end of the Clinton administration and the onset of George W. Bush's presidency, a well-known series of mutual grievances dominated most aspects of transatlantic relations.[36] While mutual cooperation continued at lower levels of government, there was no strong political push on either side of the Atlantic to put the ambitious goals of the NTA into effect.

From security deficit to surplus: the transformation of German foreign policy

The preceding review of burden-sharing during the Cold War and in its immediate aftermath leads to the following observations. First, a mix of military and financial burden-sharing was essential to both the formation and the maintenance of the transatlantic alliance. Economics and politics were closely intertwined, and transatlantic burden-sharing became embedded in a number of common institutions. Second, due to the vast military superiority of the United States and especially the security "deficit" in Europe, the burden-sharing debate was framed in terms of European acceptance of American leadership. This was a natural consequence of the very different functional roles played by the United States and Europe throughout the Cold War. Third, the Cold War helped to keep domestic opposition to transatlantic ideological, political, and economic burden-sharing at bay. Put differently, the Cold War limited the "ratification costs" of burden-sharing agreements on both sides of the Atlantic. But beginning in 1989 the external threat of communism began to vanish rather quickly, and with it the opportunity to stifle opposition to support of the Alliance.

Much of the acrimony in the recent crisis derived from the absence of this erstwhile restraining effect on domestic debate. In addition, however, a further decisive change in Atlantic relations was occurring, as Germany slowly began to assume a role within the international system that had previously been almost unimaginable: as a supplier of security to neighboring regions. This switch to a far more active stabilizing role was provoked by the transformation of the Warsaw Pact countries and the disintegration of Yugoslavia. As German defense minister Rühe put it in

---

[36] See chapter 2 in this volume for a brief summary.

May 1994, "If we do not export stability now, we will sooner or later be seized by instability."[37]

In the context of reunification, Germany took a leading role in the stabilization of central and eastern Europe, including enormous financial transfers. Traditional roles in the Atlantic alliance were briefly reversed, with Germany calling on its allies to assume a greater share of this huge cost. The results of shared efforts across the Atlantic remained limited, however, largely because of the different mechanisms through which the United States and Europe pursued their policies, namely NATO and the EU. *Ad hoc* cooperation was the rule, as Lily Gardner Feldman has shown succinctly;[38] a more genuinely coordinated EU–US policy toward eastern Europe was thwarted by different institutional cultures. In part, this reflected different domestic contexts. The United States is characterized by greater demands for transparency and relatively short electoral cycles, a combination geared toward the production of immediately visible results; the EU, on the other hand, acting with less public debate, can often afford a longer-term perspective.[39]

Despite these institutional and cultural differences, Germany continued to press for "multilateralization" of its stabilization policy toward central and eastern Europe;[40] both EU and NATO enlargement became leading elements in this strategy. To a certain extent, these policies corresponded to Germany's traditional pattern of pursuing international objectives mainly by economic means and within a multilateral framework. However, to many observers it was clear that the export of political stability as a core strategic interest would sooner or later entail more than simply humanitarian and economic aid. Sooner or later, exporting stabilization would necessitate military engagement abroad, a development that would collide with the deeply ingrained reticence of most Germans to engage troops in out-of-area actions.[41]

---

[37] Rühe continued as follows: "We therefore have to enforce the concept of stability transfer, which consists of two core elements: integration and cooperation" (speech in Oxford, Bulletin des Presse- und Informationsamts der Bundesregierung, vol. 47 [1994], p. 422 [my translation]).

[38] Lily Gardner Feldman, "The European Union's Enlargement Project and US–EU Cooperation in Central and Eastern Europe," in Fran Burwell and Ivo Daalder (eds.), *The United States and Europe in the Global Arena* (London: Macmillan, 1999), pp. 44–82.

[39] Hubert Zimmermann, "Governance by Negotiation: The EU, the United States and China's Integration into the World Trade System," in Stefan Schirm (ed.), *Global Economic Governance* (London: Palgrave, 2003), pp. 67–86.

[40] Deutsche Einheit, *Sonderedition aus den Akten des Bundeskanzleramts*, Doc. 344.

[41] Nina Philippi, "Civilian Power and War: The German Debate About Out-of-Area Operations 1990–1999," in Harnisch and Maull, *Germany as a Civilian Power?*, pp. 49–67.

The breakup of Yugoslavia glaringly exposed this dilemma. Germany quickly assumed a leading role in the Western response to this conflict; but diplomatic efforts, in conjunction with economic and humanitarian aid, were in the end followed by military engagement. The decisive moment was the Kosovo war, in which the German military participated despite the absence of a legitimizing UN resolution. This radical change in Germany's international policies had clearly been foreshadowed by less spectacular steps, such as peace-keeping in Bosnia and participation in NATO out-of-area operations with AWACS aircraft, and each of these incremental steps had sparked heated national controversies over the future course of German foreign policy.

The basic question in each of these instances was whether Germany would become an active exporter of security, employing all available instruments to that end, and thus fundamentally transform its international role, or instead remain an observer (and occasionally a financier) of such activities. The left and the center left of the political spectrum advocated continuing abstinence from a more active international role, primarily for historical reasons. Conservatives usually supported a more active German foreign policy; however, apart from a small group of traditional nationalists, this support was framed mainly as obligation necessitated by the transatlantic partnership – and by the dogma that Germany should never stand alone – rather than as a new strategic undertaking.[42] Thus the conservative argument was typically framed in traditional and Atlanticist terms. However, the logic of Germany's new structural position gradually superseded the historically induced self-conception of the Federal Republic as a purely civilian power – that is, as a nation that would go to war only in self-defense and that would share the costs of the more activist policies of its Alliance partners exclusively through economic and logistical means. Instead, Germany's painful decisions to send peacekeeping forces first to Bosnia, then Kosovo, then Macedonia, opened the door to further expansions of this role.[43]

But, from the beginning, a paramount consideration was the embedding of these missions in both Atlantic and European frameworks. As a consequence, Germany was a strong proponent of NATO and EU involvement in the Balkans; and, while transatlantic cooperation in that region proved complicated and too slow in its deliberations to prevent massive

[42] Marianne Takle, "Toward a Normalisation of German Security and Defence Policy: German Participation in International Military Operations," *ARENA Working Papers* 02:10 (2002), pp. 7–8, www.arena.uio.no/publications/wp02_10.htm.

[43] See n. 1.

human rights violations, in the end the United States and Europe were able to develop a mutually acceptable division of labor. Strikingly, this division of labor put the Americans more and more in the role of junior partners, and gave the EU the primary responsibility for the stabilization of this region.[44] By extending the carrot of future EU membership, the European Union – following the German lead – has become the major exporter of stability in the region.

Some analysts see in this pattern a blueprint for transatlantic cooperation in the twenty-first century.[45] Whether that proves to be the case or not, the Balkan wars and the history of the transformation of eastern Europe draw attention to a fundamental change of the greatest significance for the burden-sharing debate: during the 1990s, western Europe as a whole (and Germany in particular) became an exporter of security. During the Cold War, the most basic west European interest was its territorial defense, with fundamentally different roles assigned to the United States (as a security supplier) and its European allies (as security consumers). Given these roles, American leadership was functionally logical: Europe agreed to follow the American lead, and to share the costs of the American presence, because it was not able to produce the security "imported" from the United States on its own. The core roles assigned to the United States and Europe within the Alliance, and their international positions more generally, were strikingly different. But this has begun to change, and will continue to do so, as the functional roles of the United States and Europe within the international system have converged.

 Both American and European political leaders now regard the neutralization of potential threats located abroad as a core interest of their international security policies. While it is true that their strategies continue to differ at the margins, this is primarily because of differences in their geopolitical positions and continuing imbalances in their capacities. But the essential fact is that both the EU and the United States are now able to pursue a wide range of broadly similar policies in much the same business – that is, the business of exporting security – and therefore transatlantic relations have necessarily shifted from widespread acceptance (even if it was sometimes grudging) of American leadership to calls for a collaboration among genuine equals, with shared leadership.

---

[44] John Peterson, "The US and Europe in the Balkans," in Peterson and Pollack, *Europe, America, Bush*, pp. 92–94.
[45] James Dobbins et al., *America's Role in Nation-Building: From Germany to Iraq*, MR-1753 RC (Santa Monica: RAND, 2003), pp. 87–128.

Leadership requires willing followers, and the functional basis for asymmetrical US leadership of the Atlantic partnership is gone.[46]

The most striking case of this shift in functional roles is Germany. Spurred by the transformation of eastern Europe and by the Yugoslav wars, Germany moved gradually toward an eventual wholehearted embrace of the role of security exporter, including an astonishingly rapid move from absolute opposition to out-of-area military operations to acceptance of a new role as one of the largest providers of military and policing forces to troubled areas throughout the globe. German defense minister Peter Struck summarizes this shift in one of his favorite quips: "The defense of Germany starts at the Hindukush [sic]."[47] Likewise, the new German defense policy guidelines of March 2003 reflect this change toward out-of-area defense: "Defense as it is understood today means more than traditional defense operations at the national borders against a conventional attack. It includes the prevention of conflicts and crises, the common management of crises and postcrisis rehabilitation. Accordingly, defense can no longer be narrowed down to geographical boundaries, but contributes to safeguarding our security wherever it is in jeopardy."[48]

The manifestations of this fundamental shift are ubiquitous. Since autumn 2003, the German government and the conservative opposition parties have debated a law which would lead to more rapid decision-making for Bundeswehr deployments abroad, with the objective of shortening the presently time-consuming process of obtaining parliamentary approval. The talks are presently blocked (as of July 2004), since the left wing of the Social Democratic Party and the Greens are alarmed by the degree of executive discretion in sending troops abroad. The trend, however, is clear.[49] Elsewhere, consider Chancellor Schröder's (not very realistic) declaration in spring 2002 that Germany would participate in a UN peacekeeping mission in the Israel–Palestine conflict – a proposal that was not well received in either Tel Aviv or Washington.[50] Taken

---

[46] The exception to this rule is large-scale military intervention, for which the EU is clearly unfit. However, as will be shown later, the objectives and scope of such interventions have taken on a completely new character, particularly after 9/11, which tends to neutralize this "disadvantage."

[47] See for example Defense Minister Struck's speech at the conference "Impulse 21 – Berlin Forum on Security Policy" on June 23, 2003, http://www.bmvg.de/archiv/reden/minister/print/030623_eroeffnungsrede_englisch.php.

[48] Bundesministerium der Verteidigung, *Defence Policy Guidelines*, May 24, 2003, http://eng.bmvg.de/pic/pdf/sicherheit/030521_VPR-english.pdf.

[49] See http://www.deutsches-wehrrecht.de/WR-AktuelleMeldungen_Text.html#Entsendegesetz.

[50] "Kurswechsel in der deutschen Israelpolitik?," *Neue Zürcher Zeitung*, April 11, 2002.

together, these developments and others suggest an utterly new role for German foreign policy. And they raise the same question posed in its most blatant form during the Iraq crisis: what does this new role mean for the future of the transatlantic alliance and for German–American relations? Will the future be characterized by a widening rift or a new form of cooperation?

The Iraq crisis: rival worldviews

A few days after the attacks of September 11, former president George Bush, Sr., drew attention to the importance of American allies: "Just as Pearl Harbor awakened this country from the notion that we could somehow avoid the call to duty and defend freedom in Europe and Asia in World War II, so, too, should this most recent surprise attack erase the concept in some quarters that America can somehow go it alone in the fight against terrorism or in anything else for that matter."[51] This sort of thinking was reflected in the comprehensive diplomatic efforts of the US government after the terrorist attacks.

However, soon it became clear that key American leaders were not thinking in terms of a new entangling alliance based on the premise that, in the long run, the United States would be unable to eradicate the terrorist threat on its own. As the American defense secretary, Donald Rumsfeld, famously wrote: "This war will not be waged by a grand alliance united for the single purpose of defeating an axis of hostile powers ... Instead it will involve floating coalitions of countries ... the mission will define the coalition – not the other way around."[52] Despite the invocation of NATO's Article 5, the Americans fought the Afghanistan campaign without involving the Alliance – though peace-keeping immediately after the war was a thoroughly multinational enterprise, with NATO eventually taking over the command of the International Stabilization Force for Afghanistan (ISAF). This provoked intense debates in Germany, and Chancellor Schröder had to resort to a vote of confidence to obtain a parliamentary majority.[53] Germany then made a substantial commitment to a region where its direct interests seemed rather negligible; the paramount consideration was not only solidarity with the United States but also the recognition of the borderless nature of modern terrorism.

---

[51] "World Leaders List Conditions on Cooperation," *New York Times*, September 19, 2001.

[52] Donald Rumsfeld, "A New Kind of War," *New York Times*, September 27, 2001.

[53] In a less politicized environment, however, the support of the conservative parties would have resulted in overwhelming approval for the Afghanistan mission.

But the Iraq War represented an entirely different situation. Apart from the British, only very small (essentially symbolic) units were provided by the non-American members of the so-called coalition force. Even a full year after the conclusion of "major hostilities," Germany continued to balk at American demands for a traditional burden-sharing relationship based on acceptance of US leadership, insisting instead on power-sharing as a condition for its help. The major reason for this unprecedented refusal was that, as Thomas Risse has put it, the American action "violate[d] some constitutive norms on which the transatlantic community has been based for more than fifty years."[54] These are in particular procedural norms of mutual consultation and policy coordination, now usually subsumed under the label of multilateralism. Germany strongly emphasizes these norms, and Chancellor Schröder has mentioned this specifically: "Consultation cannot consist in getting a call with two hours' advance notice, and being told 'we are marching in.'"[55] The absence of the Cold War constraint gave him the opportunity to transform his indignation into a successful election issue. American policy during the Iraq crisis also ran into Germans' new perception of their country, and of other European countries, as net exporters of security, and of the necessity of transforming the Atlantic alliance into a collaboration among true equals. As the German defense minister put it, "We have learned to think of our security in a global dimension ... And this path has unavoidably influenced the character of transatlantic relations. It points toward a partnership of equals in the future."[56]

For a long time, the debate about allied participation in the reconstruction of Iraq, however, remained couched in the old terms of pure burden-sharing (as called for by the American side) or pure power-sharing (on the French side). The United States initially refused to grant larger roles in Iraq's reconstruction either to countries that opposed the war or to the UN, due to suspicions that such help would come only in order to get more contracts and economic benefits.[57] While this position was understandable from a psychological standpoint, it fundamentally misunderstood the new nature of international cooperation. Reassessments of the Iraq crisis by the

---

[54] Thomas Risse, *Beyond Iraq: Challenges to the Transatlantic Security Community*, AICGS/German–American Dialogue Working Paper Series (Washington, DC: AICGS, 2003, http://www.aicgs.org/publications/PDF/risse.pdf), p. 15.

[55] Quoted in: "Hände weg," *Der Spiegel*, September 5, 2002, my translation.

[56] Peter Struck, "Perspectives of a Renewed Transatlantic Partnership," speech in Berlin, November 3, 2003, http://www.bmvg.de/archiv/reden/minister/031103_struck_wams.php, accessed November 9, 2003, p. 2., author's translation.

[57] "US Abandons Idea of Bigger UN Role in Iraq Occupation," *New York Times*, August 14, 2003.

German government stress this point strongly: "[Differences] should not be interpreted as the beginning of the end of a virtual transatlantic harmony, but rather as the expression of a desirable political emancipation and a partnership of equals. The decisive point is something else: common actions require comprehensive and intense dialogue, and a corresponding coordination regarding the available options. This has suffered in the past years. Those who do not talk, or do not want to talk, cannot act jointly. It's as simple as that."[58] The "institutionalization of power"[59] thus remains at the core of Germany's self-understanding of its new role as exporter of security, just as it was in earlier self-assessments of the German role of shouldering burdens in the transatlantic and European frameworks of the Cold War.

Prospects for German–American relations in the twenty-first century

Plainly there are major differences in the worldviews of Berlin and Washington. Despite these differences, however, two factors will very likely lead to the continuation and reaffirmation of close German–American cooperation in security policies: common interests based on shared threat perceptions, and the continuity of mutual institutions that are strongly valued by Germany. Both these factors mitigate the possibility of escalating disagreements. The dispute about Iraq got out of control because Schröder unleashed domestic forces in a way that was unthinkable during the Cold War; the major and urgent task for both sides now is to create mechanisms that are able to constrain the potential for populist policies to undermine common institutions.

Consider first perceived threats. German, European, and American threat perceptions are remarkably similar, as a comparison of the Federal Republic of Germany's defense policy guidelines, the European security strategy, and the US National Security Strategy shows;[60] the top priorities in these documents are the need to stabilize failed societies in order to prevent terrorism, and to limit proliferation of weapons of mass

---

[58] Struck, "Perspectives of a Renewed Transatlantic Partnership," p. 8.

[59] Peter J. Katzenstein, "Uniting Germany in an Integrating Europe," in Peter J. Katzenstein (ed.), *Tamed Power: Germany in Europe* (Ithaca: Cornell University Press, 1997), p. 3.

[60] For Germany's defense policy guidelines, see Bundesministerium der Verteidigung, *Defence Policy Guidelines*. For the European security strategy, see the webpage of the Italian EU Presidency, http://www.ueitalia2003.it/EN/, accessed June 30, 2004. For the US security strategy, see the George W. Bush administration's National Security Strategy document of September 2002 (http://www.whitehouse.gov/nsc/nss.html).

destruction. Iraq, which combines both these characteristics, will not long remain the only case of nation-building requiring transatlantic collaboration. Instead, 9/11 has ushered in an age of unparalleled interventionism, based on recognition that decomposing states and brutal dictatorships breed threats whose effects are not confined to immediately neighboring regions. As a consequence, the nature of military interventions has changed since the Cold War. States and their elites are no longer the only targets; rather, the transformation of whole societies is now part of the challenge, and this provides the capabilities of the EU with new salience.

A recent comparative analysis of nation-building since 1945 demonstrated that multilateral efforts, although complex and time-consuming, generally achieve more thoroughgoing transformations at lesser cost than do unilateral efforts.[61] As is well known, European capabilities for purely military action are rather limited. As discussed before, this might suggest a division of labor in which the United States, due to its military superiority, does the fighting while the Europeans are left with the task of cleaning up afterwards – that is, nation-building and post-hostilities peace-keeping. Certainly the latter capacities are where the comparative advantage of the Europeans lies (although the 2002–3 Artemis mission in the Congo demonstrates a new readiness by the Europeans to engage militarily abroad). Still, the continued existence of complementary capabilities suggests continued prospects for transatlantic cooperation in response to the new security threats emanating from Iraq and elsewhere.

An important example is shared intelligence and police cooperation. Since September 11, US–European collaboration in this area has greatly intensified;[62] and given the transnational character of the terrorist threat, the necessity of further steps is self-evident. Here again, the changes in the international system outlined earlier help explain the European switch from primarily inward-looking policies aimed at the containment of internal security threats to the new focus on threats emanating from outside Europe. In Germany's case, counterterrorism policies used to be managed by the Ministry of the Interior and were very much directed against the destabilization of society from the inside, whether by right-wing or left-wing subversives. However, the combination of 9/11, the March 2004 Madrid train bombings, and the April 2002 terrorist attack on German tourists in Tunisia has underlined the inadequacy of counterterrorist policies limited to German territory. Germany now fully embraces international prevention of terrorism in European as well as transatlantic frameworks, and it added a provision to its penal code

---

[61] Dobbins et al., *America's Role in Nation-Building*, p. xxv.
[62] Hamilton, "German–American Relations and the Campaign Against Terrorism," p. 3.

that allows the prosecution of individuals suspected of planning terrorist acts abroad.[63] German–American cooperation is demonstrated by the frequent meetings of the US Secretary of Homeland Security, Tom Ridge, and the FRG minister of the interior, Otto Schily, that have resulted in increasing institutionalized mutual cooperation in this field – and probably the importation into the United States of some German concepts of organizing internal security against terrorist threats.[64]

Given the increasing Europeanization of crime prevention efforts, collaboration between the EU and the United States will first supplement and then partly supplant such examples of bilateral cooperation. For example, two agreements were recently signed between the United States and the EU broadening mutual legal assistance and facilitating the extradition of suspected criminals. These agreements replaced the previous arrangement of fifteen bilateral treaties between the United States and the individual EU member states;[65] the new agreements came on top of an already much improved system for information exchange between American and European police forces and prosecutors.[66] The scope for cooperation in the nonproliferation issue has been further demonstrated by the fall 2003 agreement reached between the EU and Iran on the suspension of the latter's uranium-enrichment program. In these negotiations, the EU assumed the role of the "good cop" while the United States stressed that in case of noncompliance it would take action at the UN Security Council.[67] Germany, which has a long tradition of close relations with Iran, joined the UK and France in this multilateral effort to export security.

The culminating point of transatlantic collaboration might eventually take the form of a lasting solution to the Israel–Palestine problem. The EU has been a major contributor to the Palestinian authority and some neighboring countries, such as Lebanon and Jordan, for some time; this role was initially encouraged by the United States, according to the logic

---

[63] Peter J. Katzenstein, "Same War – Different Views: Germany, Japan, and Counterterrorism," *International Organization* 57 (Fall 2003), pp. 731–760.

[64] Institutionalized security cooperation now includes, among other things, regular meetings of officials and experts and a common multilateral policy toward the international standardization of new technologies. For more details, see the webpage of the Bundesinnenministerium, http://www.bmi.bund.de.

[65] "Ausbau der Rechtshilfe EU–USA," *Neue Zürcher Zeitung*, June 25, 2003.

[66] There are, however, limits to this type of cooperation due to differing institutional legacies. For example, the EU reserved to itself the right to refuse extradition if the suspect is a potential candidate for the death penalty, since all EU members have outlawed the death penalty. Likewise, there are open questions about how these agreements will relate to the contested International Criminal Court.

[67] "Iran Still Under Pressure to Give Arms Assurance," *Financial Times*, October 22, 2003.

of Cold War burden-sharing.[68] The EU's Barcelona Process complemented the Madrid peace talks and American high-level diplomacy, exploiting the EU's comparative advantage.[69] At present, given Israel's substantial mistrust of the EU, Europe is sidelined in the peace process. European ambiguities regarding an active and unequivocal commitment to the continued existence of the state of Israel will of course have to be resolved. But if and when that happens, Germany, with its history of diplomatic, military, and economic support of Israel, might eventually play an important role as an honest broker.[70]

All in all, there is a compelling case for transatlantic cooperation across a broad range of issues. Given these common interests, Andrew Moravcsik has called for a "new transatlantic bargain" in which the European and American resources would complement each other.[71] He provides a list of desirable common policies; however, there is little discussion of how these would come about, reflecting a rationalist credo that the existence of similar interests will automatically result in cooperation. This is unlikely. Instead, the emergence of a new transatlantic identity, a common comprehensive strategy, and a strengthening of the existing institutional network will be necessary. A constructive relationship will require a stronger Common Foreign and Security Policy in Europe and, subsequently, the acceptance by American leaders and public alike of the "division of labor that accompanies institutional arrangements."[72] Common institutions that incorporate common values and permit necessary dialogue are preconditions to solving unavoidable conflicts, as recent institutionalist research has made abundantly clear.[73] They also help create the requisite common identity, emerging through the repeated process of resolving conflicts, to tackle collective-action

---

[68] Volker Perthes, "The Advantages of Complementarity: The Middle East Peace Process," in Gardner and Stefanova, *The New Transatlantic Agenda*, p. 104.

[69] "Given Europe's strong interdependence and more diversified relations with the region as well as the predilection of European policies for the creation of multilateral networks and their focus on societal actors, Europe will, in general, be the better interlocutor for such low-level diplomatic or semi-diplomatic activities": ibid., p. 113.

[70] Greg Caplan, *A Transatlantic Approach to the Middle East Conflict: Do We Have Enough in Common?*, AICGS/DAAD Working Paper Series (Washington, DC: AICGS, 2003, http://www.aicgs.org/publications/PDF/caplan.pdf), pp. 21–22.

[71] Andrew Moravcsik, "Striking a New Transatlantic Bargain," *Foreign Affairs* 82:4 (July–August 2003), pp. 74–89.

[72] Alice Ackermann, "Why Europe and America Don't See Eye to Eye," *International Politics* 40 (March 2003), p. 122.

[73] Thomas Risse, "Constructivism and International Institutions: Toward Conversations Across Paradigms," in Ira Katznelson and Helen V. Milner (eds.), *Political Science: State of the Discipline* (New York: W. W. Norton, 2002), pp. 597–629.

problems successfully.[74] Even the US National Security Strategy of September 2002 accepts this point.[75]

Within Germany, all the available public statements from the government and, even more strongly, from the opposition suggest that multilateralism and specifically cooperation with the United States remain at the core of German foreign policy.[76] Despite a multitude of voices predicting the end of transatlantic institutions, the "ties that bind" will not disappear so quickly. A key example is the institution that has entangled Germany and the United States more than any other, the American troop presence. Reports to the effect that American troops would be relocated from Germany to a more forthcoming ally – Poland, for example – were carried by major newspapers during the Iraq War and in the period immediately preceding it.[77] Most of these reports suggested that a further vital pillar of the Alliance was about to disappear. The more sensational accounts, however, were wrong with respect to both the motivations for these plans and the facts on the ground. Plans for these changes were underway well before the transatlantic rift of 2003; they reflect decisions to relocate some forward-based troops in response to new strategic priorities. Further, the bulk of the current deployment will remain in their current locations, since important bases such as Ramstein (which will even be enlarged) can be removed only at a very high cost.[78] Moreover, since the admission of ten new EU members in spring 2004, a relocation of the troops to Poland would still mean that the troops are on EU territory; thus, this major factor linking the United States and Europe will remain. After all, within the EU, it is Germany, Britain, Italy, and the new member states from central and eastern Europe that are the most

---

[74] On the notion of collective-action problems in alliances, see, most prominently, Mancur Olson and Richard Zeckhauser, "An Economic Theory of Alliances," *Review of Economics and Statistics* 48 (1966), pp. 266–279.

[75] "There is little of lasting consequence that the United States can accomplish in the world without the sustained cooperation of its allies and friends in Canada and Europe": National Security Strategy of the United States, 2002, p. 25.

[76] "The transatlantic partnership remains the bedrock of our security. Now and in the future, there can be no security in and for Europe without the United States of America. Germany will continue to make a substantial contribution to the transatlantic partnership ... the Bundeswehr will conduct armed operations only together with allies and partners in a UN, NATO and EU context": Bundesministerium der Verteidigung, *Defence Policy Guidelines*, May 24, 2003, pp. 9–10. For statements from the Christian Democrats, see, for example, "Beschluss des Bundesvorstands: die aussenpolitischen Interessen Deutschlands," April 28, 2003 (http://www.cdu.de/politik-a-z/parteitag/beschluss_240403.pdf).

[77] For example, Hans Binnendijk, "A New Strategic Basis for US Forces in Europe," *International Herald Tribune*, April 28, 2003.

[78] "Interview with SACEUR J. L. Jones," *Süddeutsche Zeitung*, July 12, 2003.

powerful advocates of continuing American involvement in European security.

In short, the major danger for the Alliance is not to be found in the new strategic environment. Quite the opposite: the biggest threat lies in unleashing domestic forces that undermine adherence to common norms and institutions. Despite the Iraq crisis, substantial majorities in both the United States and Europe strongly support a continuation of the transatlantic alliance.[79] However, the German debate about the Iraq War demonstrates that the restraining influence of the Cold War is now gone, and with it the viability of transatlantic cooperation based exclusively on agreement among government elites. A new understanding at the societal level is necessary. The European reaction to the publication of the pictures of torture of Iraqi prisoners by American soldiers at Abu Ghraib and the extraordinary acclaim accorded to people such as Michael Moore suggest that this will be a quite difficult process.

However difficult it may prove, the creation of such a new understanding is essential. Burden-sharing based on the premise of American leadership made sense until recently because only the United States was both willing and able to project the worldwide capabilities that the Alliance deemed indispensable to deter the Soviet Union. As long as the legacy of the postwar division of Europe perpetuated a state of insecurity, Germany (and by extension Europe) would have to import security from the United States, and as a consequence to cope with the burden-sharing demands made by the Americans. Indeed, it has been Germany's apprehensions about the possible damage to the transatlantic alliance that have prevented the Federal Republic from supporting the independent European security and defense policies preferred by France. But those apprehensions are now much reduced, as reflected in both official policy and popular debate. Both the United States and Europe now pursue similar roles with similar threat perceptions; it would therefore behoove governments on both sides of the Atlantic to develop a new and more responsive framework for governing their partnership. Otherwise, if the populism witnessed during the Iraq crisis gets out of control, Europe and the United States might well become rival rather than complementary exporters of security.

---

[79] See chapter 4 in this volume.

7   A bridge too far: the United Kingdom and the transatlantic relationship

William Wallace and Tim Oliver

For the past fifty years, British foreign policy has attempted to act as a "bridge" between continental European governments which (at least from the perspective of the British conventional wisdom) were parochial in their concerns, and US administrations which often forgot that their European allies had legitimately distinct interests. The end of the Cold War did not alter this stance. First John Major and then Tony Blair came into office declaring their intention to place Britain "at the heart of Europe" while also attempting to maintain what they saw as a "special relationship" with the United States.

Developments in the period from September 11, 2001, to the invasion of Iraq, and even more in the aftermath of that invasion, have severely shaken this concept of a special relationship and the whole idea of Britain as a bridge between Europe and the United States. The government – above all, Britain's strong-minded prime minister – gave strong support to American policy in Iraq; much of the prime minister's party, and a substantial segment of public opinion, equally strongly questioned the rationale for American preemption. The argument of this chapter is that Prime Minister Blair's firm support came more from his personal conviction that Saddam Hussein's regime was a threat to global security than from his commitment to transatlantic cooperation under all circumstances. It also derived from the settled British preference for seeking influence within Washington through offering public support and private criticism, in the hope of moderating the direction of American policy – to adopt a stance of "Yes, but," in contradistinction to the French stance of "No, unless."

The political success of this strategy, however, depended upon visible evidence of British influence over US policy. President George W. Bush's visit to Belfast, in April 2003, conveyed a strong message of American–British transatlantic solidarity; President Bush publicly promised that the UN would play "a vital role" in the reconstruction of Iraq after the conflict, and assured his British counterparts that Washington would press forward with the "roadmap" toward a settlement of the Israeli–Palestinian conflict. Accumulating evidence in the year after the invasion, however, that Washington was not delivering on either of these concessions to British views and interests left the British government uncomfortably committed to an American strategy in the Middle East over which it appeared to have no influence. Britain's public support for the Bush administration, Number 10 recognized, also severely compromised another prime ministerial objective, the pursuit of closer European cooperation. In the months after the invasion of Iraq, the British government attempted to rebuild relations with the French and German governments, above all on closer cooperation in defense. The depth of suspicion in Washington of French motives, however, and especially resistance within the US Department of Defense to any modification of NATO's dominant role in European security, suggested that there were many in Washington who wanted Britain to choose between its transatlantic and European links rather than to balance between them.

The "English-speaking peoples" and the special relationship

In the early postwar years, British governments stayed apart from the European integration process despite US encouragement to become more directly involved. First the Truman administration and then the Eisenhower administration attempted to push the British into full participation in the institutionalized integration which – under American sponsorship and encouragement – France, Germany, the Low Countries, and Italy were building.[1] The discovery that President Kennedy's incoming administration intended to pursue the same strategy was one of the factors that pushed Prime Minister Macmillan and his Conservative cabinet toward Britain's first application to join the European Communities, in 1961.

Britain's aloofness from continental integration in the 1950s stemmed from a number of different factors. Less than a generation earlier, Britain had maintained its independence – with American support – when Nazi Germany had overrun the continent as far as the English Channel. In the tense circumstances of 1950, with communist forces invading South Korea and a visible threat that France and the Low Countries might be overrun by Soviet forces in central Europe linking up with supporters in western Europe, it seemed self-evidently unwise for a

---

[1] Geir Lundestad, *"Empire" by Integration: The United States and European Integration, 1945–1997* (Oxford: Oxford University Press, 1998).

British government to submit its key coal and steel industries to a supra-national authority based in Luxembourg. For example, a UK Chief of Staffs paper in 1950 discussed the possibility of maintaining a redoubt on the Iberian peninsula in the event that the rest of western Europe should be overrun.[2] More generally, Britain was still an imperial power, with forces spread across the Mediterranean, the Middle East, and "east of Suez." The Commonwealth and Empire were still seen as assets to Britain's international standing, economy, and security, as they had proved during World War II. In contrast, relations with the European continent were seen as a necessary commitment but a continuing burden.

The United States had tipped the balance in continental conflicts which had threatened Britain twice in the previous forty years. By the end of World War II, the British war effort (and the British economy) had become desperately dependent on American support; but politically and militarily the Anglo-American relationship remained one in which British policy-makers saw themselves as valued junior partners, offering advice that was often taken, tempering the raw edges of American power with the nuances of Britain's global experience. Winston Churchill spoke of Britain's postwar role as resting on "three circles" of global influence: transatlantic, Commonwealth and Empire, and Europe. For him, and for other British policy-makers, there was no doubt that Britain gained most from the first of these, and least from the third. Churchill's efforts to reimagine Britain's place in the world included a two-volume *History of the English-Speaking Peoples*, linking Americans with Britons and the white emigrants of the British Commonwealth into a chain of free-minded people spreading the principles of constitutional democracy and law around the world.[3]

The United States carried immense prestige in Britain in the early 1950s as Britain's main partner and ally (and since 1949 again with substantial forces in Britain), and as the symbol of modern culture, management, and innovation. The United States, in British media and political discourse, was the land of the future; continental Europe, in contrast, with news of mass strikes and slow economic reconstruction, looked like the past. British diplomacy had played a central role in con-structing the North Atlantic Alliance, in which Britain and the United States occupied privileged positions. Anglo-American cooperation in intelligence, under the terms of the 1947 UK–US agreement on this

[2] See Paul Cornish, "The British Military View of European Security 1945–1950," in Anne Deighton (ed.), *Building Post-War Europe: National Decision-Makers and European Institutions, 1948–1963* (Basingstoke: Macmillan, 1995).

[3] Winston Churchill, *A History of the English-Speaking Peoples* (London: Cassell, 1956–58).

subject, was supplemented by naval cooperation and alliance on the ground in the Korean War. The development of US air bases in Britain, reopening wartime air force stations as staging posts to resupply American forces in Germany as well as for conventional and nuclear bombers to deter a Soviet advance across Germany, made the UK a crucial factor in maintaining a link between the North American continent and the renewed US commitment to European defense. Britain thus provided, in effect, a geographic as well as political "bridge" between the American and European continents, holding the newly imagined Atlantic Community together.

The classic era of the "special relationship," however, ended with the crisis over Suez in 1956. Anthony Eden, a British prime minister obsessed with maintaining Britain's global role and with avoiding "another Munich," negotiated a secret alliance with France and Israel to overthrow the nationalist-military regime in Egypt and thereby regain control of the Suez Canal, the linchpin of imperial Britain's global military deployment.[4] But no one in London had consulted with their partners in Washington. President Eisenhower placed greater weight on maintaining the stability of the Arab Middle East than on support for Israel or for what seemed to be an ill-judged Anglo-French intervention; the Federal Reserve withdrew support for the pound sterling on the international exchanges, there followed a run on the pound, and British withdrawal from halfway along the Suez Canal Zone was accompanied by Eden's resignation.

Both British and French political leaders drew the lesson from the Suez intervention that they could not sustain their pretensions to empire or to global standing with their own limited resources. Harold Macmillan, Eden's successor as prime minister, took great care to reestablish a mutually confident Anglo-American relationship, managing in 1957 to sign a series of agreements that gave Britain privileged access to American nuclear research and delivery systems, and the promise of continued close cooperation in foreign policy, military developments, and intelligence. This was a much more unequal "special relationship," with Britain very clearly both the dependent partner and the partner that gained most from the relationship. President de Gaulle, taking office after the collapse of the French Fourth Republic in 1957–8, attempted to claim a similar privileged position, alongside the United States and Britain, within NATO; when this was denied him, he turned to Germany to supply the resources

---

[4] Eden, as foreign secretary in 1938, had had direct experience of the Munich Agreement and its consequences, unlike the many policy-makers since then who have evoked the image of Munich to justify their behavior in other crises.

and the political support France on its own lacked. Gaullist rhetoric from then on portrayed Britain and the United States as "les Anglo-Saxons," outside Europe and opposed to European autonomy under French leadership. The British self-image of the UK as holding the two sides of the Atlantic together was thus countered by Gaullist France's insistence that the British had to choose.

Successive British governments nevertheless did their best to avoid any irrevocable choice between Atlantic and European linkages. Harold Macmillan's decision in 1961 to apply for European Economic Community membership was paralleled by the Kennedy administration's "Grand Design" to reshape the Atlantic Community as a partnership with an enlarged EEC, within the wide framework of NATO and a reshaped Organization for Economic Co-operation and Development (OECD), formerly the Organization for European Economic Co-operation. Both these initiatives were blocked by President de Gaulle, who saw Britain as a potential Trojan horse for American influence within European institutions.[5] Months of British haggling to protect Commonwealth economic interests in its accession negotiations, followed by the Nassau Agreement (which reaffirmed Britain's privileged relationship with the United States in nuclear weapons and nuclear delivery systems), provided the justification for the French leader to dismiss the British application.

The Labour prime minister, Harold Wilson, renewed Britain's application in 1967. Wilson offered closer technological cooperation with France and Germany as an incentive, only to be again refused by an entrenched, and now overtly anti-American, President de Gaulle. Maintaining Britain's international balance became particularly difficult in the years following, as the US administration pressed Britain to contribute troops to the worsening war in Vietnam. Wilson skillfully played on the opposition within his own party and among the wider public to justify his refusal to send troops, as well as playing up the contribution Britain was making to containing radical regimes by protecting Malaya and Borneo from Indonesian infiltration. The British government did not withdraw its EEC application, using the framework of the otherwise redundant seven-member Western European Union for political consultations with the six EEC states (against the opposition of France). In 1970, Edward Heath's returning Conservative government was thus able to pick up Labour's preparations for negotiated entry, in the wake of de Gaulle's resignation in 1969. British–French bilateral discussions over the next two years included defense cooperation, even

[5] Alfred Grosser, *The Western Alliance* (London: Macmillan, 1980), pp. 199–208.

potential nuclear cooperation, and the British foreign secretary took part in the new framework for European foreign policy coordination, "European Political Cooperation," well before the UK formally joined the European Communities in January 1973.

The British government thus faced from inside the EC the bitter Franco-American confrontation of 1973–4, which included Kissinger's "Year of Europe" speech, the October Middle East war, the EC's launch of the Euro-Arab Dialogue and the Ottawa Agreement of June 1974. British diplomats took the lead in drafting a "Declaration of European Identity" in the summer of 1973, in response to American demands that their European allies clarify their objectives in foreign policy cooperation. They followed the Americans into the new International Energy Agency, intended by Washington to strengthen Western coordination in the face of threats from oil-producing states; but Britain joined with the French, too, in developing the Euro-Arab Dialogue. The Conservative government, ambivalent about the balance of commitments between transatlantic and European cooperation, was succeeded in 1974 by an even more ambivalent Labour government, one that learned to value the advantages of foreign policy consultations with its continental partners but preferred to maintain sterling's global and dollar links rather than join France and Germany in launching the European Monetary System to stabilize their currencies.

The legacy of Margaret Thatcher

Margaret Thatcher did not enter office as prime minister either a confirmed Atlanticist or a settled skeptic about European integration. Her disillusionment with Edward Heath's approach as Conservative prime minister had much more to do with his acceptance of the "corporatist" framework for British economic policy – in which ministers bargained with representatives of employers and trade unions, and government subsidies supported key industries – than with his commitment to closer European cooperation. There was, of course, a link between these mindsets: the EC reflected, both in its institutions and its policies, the settled corporatism of continental economic governance to which both Christian Democrats and Social Democrats were committed, while the American economy was much closer to the economic liberalism which attracted Thatcher. After the settlement of Britain's bitter dispute over the EC budget in 1984, there was a brief period of harmony during which her government entertained hopes of extending the tide of deregulation from Britain across the continent through the 1992 program and the Single European Act. It was not until her Bruges speech of September 1988 that

Thatcher set her face against what she saw as the entrenched corporatism and centralization of the Brussels institutions and their French and German supporters.[6]

Personal relations shape political affiliations, particularly when heads of government hold office for prolonged periods. It was a tragedy that Thatcher and Chancellor Kohl, who shared many common interests and attitudes, developed such a disastrously poor relationship; Kohl's efforts to build a personal rapport, and to explain to Thatcher the particularities of German politics, only made the relationship worse.[7] In contrast, her relations with President Reagan rapidly became close, and grew closer over the eight years of his presidency – in spite of occasional sharp disagreements, as over the American failure in 1983 to forewarn their British allies of their intervention in Grenada, a former British colony and member of the Commonwealth. Thatcher and Reagan shared a robust approach to East–West relations, a commitment to free market economics, and a direct political style that contrasted with the indirection and compromise characterizing the coalition politics of continental governments and multilateral European negotiations. On coming into presidential office in January 1989, however, George Bush, Sr., signaled his determination not to listen to Thatcher with the same patience Ronald Reagan had displayed. His first European visitor was Chancellor Kohl, later described by President Bush as "a true friend ... a statesman of the highest order."[8] It was the close US–German partnership that successfully negotiated the reunification of Germany with the Soviet Union, while the British government resisted from the sidelines.

In her last two years in office, Margaret Thatcher grew increasingly antagonistic to Europe in general, and to Germany in particular. Senior members of her cabinet grew increasingly unhappy about her loss of transatlantic balance. Her negative approach to German reunification followed her instinctive resistance to closer monetary integration. Michael Heseltine's 1990 challenge for the Tory leadership rested partly on the case for more positive engagement with Britain's European partners; a deeply divided Conservative Party thereupon chose not Heseltine but John Major, seen as a potential reconciler of pro- and anti-European factions within the party.

---

[6] Margaret Thatcher, *The Downing Street Years* (London: Harper Collins, 1993), pp. 742–746.

[7] Ibid, p. 257.

[8] George Bush, Sr., on the selection of Helmut Kohl as the first recipient of the "George Bush Award for Public Service," Berlin, November 1999.

Thatcher's political legacy included a Conservative Party with a "Thatcherite" wing that was now strongly anti-European, that had developed close links during the 1980s with the rising think tanks of the American Republican right, and that shared the latter's views on free market economics and on an American-led Western alliance. Partly in response to this, the opposition Labour Party shifted from a strongly anti-European (and anti-American) stance in the early 1980s to a more open approach to European integration, which was now seen as a social democratic enterprise with which British Labour politicians and trade union leaders could be comfortable. The balance of British domestic politics, however, had been tipped in the opposite direction by changes in the ownership of British print media. Thatcher had encouraged Rupert Murdoch's acquisition of the *Sun*, *The Times*, the *News of the World*, and the *Sunday Times*, altogether some 40 percent of British national newspaper circulation, which played a crucial role in breaking the power of the unions over the British press; but it also brought into British politics a more combative style of journalism that combined a commitment to open markets with deep antagonism to the regulatory regimes of the EC/EU. Together with the entrenched nationalism of the *Daily Mail* and the transfer of the *Daily Telegraph* from the traditionally Conservative Berry family to the Canadian Conrad Black, a devotee of the Commonwealth and the idea of the English-speaking peoples who was also close to Reagan's White House, this built a pro-American and anti-European bias into British politics.

On a wider front, changing religious factors within the UK were having an impact on Britain's approach to the Middle East. Margaret Thatcher's north London parliamentary seat, Finchley, contained one of the highest proportions of Jewish voters in Britain. The leaders of Britain's Jewish community, though deeply committed to Israel, had however been closer to Israel's Labor elite than to the Likud governments of the 1980s, and had many doubts about the expansionist policies of the Israeli right and about their actions in the occupied West Bank. Conservatives in Britain were also attempting to attract votes from within Britain's now substantial and socially conservative Muslim community (though the overwhelming majority of Britain's 1.5 million Muslims, as is typical of recent immigrants starting with little, voted for the Labour Party). A growing number of wealthy Arabs were acquiring second homes in southern England, and Arabs were starting to become a major force within British horse-racing and a visible presence within London's social and financial elites. Religious affiliation among Britain's new right was high-church Anglican or, rejecting the liberal trend within the Church of England, Roman Catholic; with few exceptions, the British Conservative Party was drifting away from the strict Protestantism of Ulster Unionism, the closest movement in the United Kingdom to the evangelical churches of the American South. There was thus no influential constituency within Britain for the strong pro-Israeli image of Middle Eastern politics that developed within the United States in these years.

John Major, Thatcher's successor as prime minister, attempted to recapture the traditional sense of balance between Britain's continuing transatlantic loyalties and its growing engagement with Germany, France, and institutionalized Europe. "My aims for Britain in the Community can be simply stated," he declared in March 1991: "I want us to be where we belong – at the very heart of Europe, working with our partners in building the future."[9] Chancellor Kohl went out of his way to cultivate this new face in European conservative politics, hoping to extend the established Franco-German partnership into a triangular relationship with Britain. With Lady Thatcher (as she had now become) still in the background, however, proclaiming a sharpened message of Atlantic solidarity and European perfidiousness to British and American audiences, Major found it increasingly difficult to maintain his preferred course. The Euroskeptic "bastards," as he bitterly described them, in his cabinet held him back from playing the European role to which he aspired.[10] In the final stages of negotiating the Maastricht Treaty of the European Union, in December 1991, he felt it necessary to phone Michael Howard, the secretary of state for employment in his own cabinet, to check the acceptability of the terms he proposed with his party's Thatcherite wing.[11] His second administration limped to its end in 1997 unable to agree on the British position toward the next EU Intergovernmental Conference, and with other EU governments delaying the conclusion of what became the Amsterdam Treaty until after the British election.

The Anglo-American special relationship after Margaret Thatcher, and after the Cold War, retained special elements in military and intelligence matters. The United Kingdom provided a fully equipped armored division for the US-led force which expelled Saddam Hussein from Kuwait in 1991, more than any other NATO ally. French efforts to match Britain's contribution exposed shortages of deployable troops and equipment, resulting in a smaller French division for the allied forces' northern flank. Prime Minister Major led in committing troops to northern Iraq, after the conflict, to protect Iraqi Kurds from Saddam Hussein.

---

[9] Speech given at the Adenauer Haus in Bonn, March 1991.
[10] See "Major Hits Out at Cabinet," *Observer*, July 25, 1993.
[11] Anthony Seldon, *Major: A Political Life* (London: Weidenfeld & Nicolson, 1997), p. 247.

The British government's touch was less sure in handling the disintegration of Yugoslavia, a crisis which the Bush administration had signaled was for its European allies to manage. Anti-Europeans within the Major cabinet insisted that this was better left to continental powers; hesitant intervention saw Britain first refuse to commit troops, and then contribute troops (alongside France and others) to a UN force, before uncomfortably acquiescing to American-led negotiations between the parties to the conflict, the Dayton Conference of November 1995.

Experience of fighting alongside French forces in Bosnia had, however, tipped attitudes within the British military toward pursuing closer cooperation with France. Michael Portillo as defence secretary, though an avowed Euroskeptic, agreed to establish a joint Air Wing with his French counterparts in 1995. The British government had attempted to reconcile closer European cooperation in foreign policy and defense with the continued superiority of the NATO framework since the end of the Cold War and the negotiation of the Maastricht Treaty. Relations between London and Washington cooled with the election of a Democratic president, the more so because of allegations (firmly denied) that the British government had assisted the Republican campaign by helping to investigate Bill Clinton's behavior as a student in Oxford during the Vietnam War. From 1993 to 1997, therefore, the Conservative government found itself without close and confident partners on either side of the Atlantic.

New Labour and Old Europe

When the Labour Party regained office in May 1997, it had been out of power for eighteen years. Few of its senior members had ministerial experience; its new prime minister had not been elected to Parliament until 1983. Tony Blair and many of those around him were marked by their recollections of the early 1980s: an unelectable Labour Party, ideologically anti-American and anti-European, in thrall to unruly party activists and unable to reach out to a wider electorate. "New Labour" was a self-conscious break with Labour's past; Blair's efforts to "modernize" his party, building on the more cautious efforts of his two predecessors, led him to adopt a style in both domestic and foreign policy that sometimes pitched him explicitly against the language and instincts of his own party members. In particular, his style of leadership tolerated little dissent, especially in contentious areas such as foreign policy.[12]

---

[12] Nicholas Jones, *The Control Freaks* (London: Politico's, 2001).

Most traumatic for the party leadership had been their unexpected failure to win the 1992 general election, the third campaign they had fought since they had lost office in 1979, against a divided and uncertain Conservative government. The Murdoch press's claim that "It woz the *Sun* wot won it"[13] for the Conservatives against the earlier trend of the election campaign led Tony Blair to cultivate Rupert Murdoch by flying to the latter's island retreat in Australia in July 1995 to assure him that Labour would abandon its plans to reduce his News International's position within the British media.[14] The Labour leadership was cautious in its whole presentation of policy between 1992 and 1997, traumatized by its 1992 defeat and uncertain that it could guarantee victory in the next election. Blair was clear that the anti-Americanism of "old Labour" had cost it support in the media and among uncommitted voters; its past reputation for instinctive anti-Americanism now required it to keep as closely in step with the White House as possible. Close relations with the Clinton White House were, however, easy to develop. The success of the Clinton campaign in projecting a moderate image to uncommitted voters provided a model of the "Third Way" that Blair and his advisors sought to promote: a Third Way between free market economics and corporatist social democracy that was also implicitly for New Labour a middle path between Atlanticism and commitment to European integration.[15]

While in opposition, Blair had put explicit emphasis on his party's regained European credentials. As he told the 1994 Labour Party Conference, the first after he became party leader, "I will never allow this party to be isolated or left behind in Europe."[16] Labour's manifesto for the 1997 general election stressed cooperation within Europe, together with "strong support for NATO," but said more about the future of the Commonwealth than about relations with the United States – or about policy toward the Middle East. Labour's first efforts in office were to differentiate itself from its predecessor by setting out an "ethical foreign policy," oriented beyond the Euro-Atlantic world: emphasizing human rights, tighter controls on arms sales, and the reestablishment of a separate Department for International Development.[17]

---

[13] *Sun*, April 1992.

[14] In addition to the two national dailies and national Sunday newspapers that News International owned, it was building a dominant position in satellite television, including Sky News.

[15] See Tony Blair, *New Britain: My Vision of a Young Country* (London: Fourth Estate, 1996).

[16] Peter Riddell, *Hug Them Close: Blair, Clinton and the Special Relationship* (London: Politico's, 2003), p. 75.

[17] For a detailed discussion of the New Labour government's initial approach to foreign policy, see Richard Little and Mark Wickham-Jones, *New Labour's Foreign Policy: A New Moral Crusade?* (Manchester: Manchester University Press, 2000).

Tony Blair personally found it easy to be at home on both sides of the Atlantic. He was the first British prime minister since Harold Macmillan to speak good French, a legacy from student days in Paris. While the French Socialist prime minister, Lionel Jospin, was suspicious of the centrist drift of the Third Way, the German Social Democrats looked to ally with the incoming Labour government in building a broad international consensus for a "modernizing" agenda. The Clinton White House loved debating broad ideas; a succession of Third Way seminars and "think-ins" (or "wonkathons," as a White House spokesman once called them) on both sides of the Atlantic from 1997 to 1999 built closer relations among center-left parties and their leaders. Time was even found to discuss the Third Way at NATO's fiftieth-anniversary celebrations.

The key issues that underpinned Third Way debates were globalization and how it was transforming domestic politics. The Third Way, however, did not give much guidance on the hard questions of foreign policy outside Europe, particularly toward the intractable issues of the Middle East region. On relations between Israel and Palestine, there was a broad consensus across British politics that a two-state solution was the only acceptable outcome, that Jewish settlements across the West Bank and Gaza should be withdrawn, and that Britain and its European partners should play a role in assisting the development of a Palestinian state alongside Israel. The British press gave sympathetic coverage to Palestinian as well as Israeli perspectives; right-wing Americans protested that there was now a structural bias against Israel within the British media.[18] Meanwhile, British forces continued to operate in the Gulf region following the Iraqi expulsion from Kuwait in 1991, helping to enforce UN sanctions against Saddam Hussein's regime in close cooperation with US air forces. This reflected the settled assumption of the previous Conservative government that Britain should demonstrate its value to Washington as its most loyal and militarily capable ally wherever possible, outside the NATO area as well as within it. This was not an assumption that Labour challenged on its return to office.

Tony Blair had little experience of foreign policy before he became prime minister. But he had a deeply moral view of world politics, derived partly from his personal religious faith, from which he developed in office a strongly held vision of Britain's responsibilities in the world. He set out his approach most explicitly in a speech delivered in Chicago in April

[18] Some in Washington went further, alleging that British reporting suffered from "structural anti-Semitism" (personal information from off-record discussions in Washington, 2000–1). Conrad Black's newspapers, at least, offered an alternative (pro-Likud) line.

1999, in the context of the contested Western intervention in Kosovo, in which the British government was arguing for military commitment on the ground against American preference for air bombardment and limited commitment on the ground:

This is a just war, based not on any territorial ambitions but on values. We cannot let the evil of ethnic cleansing stand. We must not rest until it is reversed. We have learned twice before in this century that appeasement does not work. If we let an evil dictator range unchallenged, we will have to spill infinitely more blood and treasure to stop him later.

In facing this and other challenges, he went on to say,

the EU and US should prepare to make real step-change in working more closely together. Recent trade disputes have been a bad omen in this regard. We really are failing to see the bigger picture with disputes over the banana regime or [airplane engine] hushkits or whatever else. There are huge issues at stake in our co-operation. The EU and the US need each other and need to put that relationship above arguments that are ultimately not fundamental ...

Many of our problems have been caused by two dangerous and ruthless men – Saddam Hussein and Slobodan Milosevic. Both have been prepared to wage vicious campaigns against sections of their own community. As a result of these destructive policies both have brought calamity on their own peoples. Instead of enjoying its oil wealth Iraq has been reduced to poverty, with political life stultified through fear ...

America's allies are always both relieved and gratified by its continuing readiness to shoulder burdens and responsibilities that come with its sole superpower status. We understand that this is something that we have no right to take for granted, and must match with our own efforts. That is the basis for the recent initiative I took with President Chirac of France to improve Europe's own defense capabilities ...

For the first time in the last three decades we have a government that is both pro-Europe and pro-American. I firmly believe that it is in Britain's interest, but it is also in the interests of the US and of Europe.[19]

This was a foreign policy program that encouraged and supported American military engagement in support of ambitions that were far beyond Britain's capability to achieve. It also expressed renewed confidence that the European and American dimensions of British foreign policy could be reconciled, that there was a continuing community of values across the Atlantic, and that Britain was well placed to hold the two sides together in promoting those shared values in an unstable world. Finally, it was a definition of foreign policy framed in ethical terms and explicitly opposed to Saddam Hussein's regime, provided some four

---

[19] Tony Blair, "Doctrine of the International Community," Chicago, April 24, 1999, http://www.number-10.gov.uk/output/Page1297.asp, accessed May 2004.

years before George W. Bush assumed office. But reconciling these different ambitions was never likely to prove easy. In particular, Britain had moved away from France and Germany the previous year in supporting the United States on the withdrawal of UN arms inspectors from Iraq (in the face of active obstruction of their efforts), a tightening of the sanctions regime, and an increase in air patrols and in the suppression of hostile air defenses across Iraq.

The evidence suggests that Blair had been convinced by the intelligence reports to which he gained access as prime minister that the Iraqi regime – and Saddam Hussein as its dominating figure – was a threat to world order, and had to be contained. Paddy Ashdown, then the leader of the British Liberal Democrats, was closely consulted by Blair on the Kosovo intervention; he recalls in his diaries a talk with Blair in November 1997 where all the prime minister could talk about was Saddam and weapons of mass destruction. "I have now seen some of the [intelligence] stuff on this. It really is pretty scary. He is very close to some appalling weapons of mass destruction. I don't understand why the French and other [sic] don't understand this. We cannot let him get away with it. The world thinks this is gamesmanship. But it's deadly serious."[20] Unlike his European counterparts, Blair, and the British government, saw in these reports a growing threat; this perception was shared with the United States, with which the gathering and exchange of information were still based upon the UK–US Agreement on Intelligence Cooperation.

In perceiving the Iraqi regime as a threat, the prime minister was well ahead of his party, and of much of his own government. The "old" left of the Labour Party was anti-imperialist by instinct and suspicious of attempts to forcibly impose Western values on the regimes of developing countries. Though it had been his foreign secretary, Robin Cook, who had launched the concept of an ethical foreign policy in the summer of 1997, Blair's Chicago speech was prepared in the Prime Minister's Office, with scarcely any consultation with the Foreign and Commonwealth Office (FCO) on the other side of Downing Street. Blair's foreign policy style was intensely personal. Important initiatives were led from within the Prime Minister's Office; here, as in other areas of Labour policy, the cabinet as a collective entity played little part.[21] The prime minister depended on his own rhetorical skills to carry his party with him, devoting a major part of his speech to the Labour Party

[20] Paddy Ashdown, *Ashdown Diaries: 1997–1999* (London: Penguin Books, 2001).
[21] See John Kampfner, *Blair's Wars* (London: Free Press, 2003); Peter Stothard, *Thirty Days: An Inside Account of Tony Blair at War* (London: HarperCollins, 2003).

Conference in October 2000 to justifying the stance he had taken in foreign policy as he argued to his activists that "standing up for Britain means knowing we are stronger with the US if we are stronger in Europe, and stronger in Europe if we are stronger with the US."[22]

The balancing initiative that demonstrated Blair's commitment to closer European cooperation came in the autumn of 1998, when he introduced a number of proposals on closer defense cooperation at an informal meeting of EU heads of government, and followed those with a bilateral initiative with President Chirac at Saint-Malo. Building on the positive experience of Franco-British cooperation on the ground in Bosnia, the two leaders proposed to bridge the longstanding gap between British loyalty to NATO and French commitment to European military autonomy by promoting closer EU defense cooperation within the wider NATO framework. Reactions in Washington reflected the entrenched suspicion of French motivations that marked the US defense establishment. British participation provided some reassurance to US policy-makers, and British negotiators made sure that their American counterparts were kept fully informed as the initiative moved forward. The Vienna European Council in December 1998 welcomed the proposals, and the Helsinki European Council the following December agreed a set of targets for a future European Rapid Reaction Force, together with a small military staff attached to the EU Council Secretariat.[23]

Like John Major before him, however, Tony Blair found it difficult to maintain a balance which involved as full a commitment to closer European cooperation as to Atlantic solidarity. He had fewer Euroskeptics in his party, certainly, but the press which he cultivated was largely North American by ownership and affiliation, and maintained its long-established anti-European bias. It would have required a sustained political effort to alter British public attitudes to the European Union; the bitter antagonism of Thatcher's final years as prime minister had been sustained by her supporters in the Conservative Party and the press since then. But there was no equivalent to the Chicago speech in Paris or Berlin; the prime minister felt inhibited by the hostility of the media from spelling out a British vision for European integration. Similar caution about public reaction had led the incoming government to rule out reversing Conservative opt-outs on the Schengen Agreement, which lifted internal border controls within EU states, and on proposals for

[22] For the full text of Tony Blair's speech to the 2000 Labour Party Conference, see the Guardian Online, http://www.guardian.co.uk/labour2000, accessed May 2004.

[23] See Helsinki European Council, Presidency Conclusions, December 10–11, 1999, http://europa.eu.int/council/off/conclu/dec99/dec99_en.htm.

monetary union, now moving ahead toward the introduction of a single currency. The 1998 defense initiative was therefore vital to demonstrate that the Labour government differed from its predecessor in its approach to the European continent – and that Labour ministers had to tread delicately between the mutual suspicions of Washington and Paris.

Divergent developments in the American and continental European economies also pulled Labour ministers – and British opinion – back toward a transatlantic orientation. The contrast between the dynamism of the US economy in the late 1990s and slow growth in Germany, France, and Italy reinforced old images of America as the future and Europe as the past. British investment flowed into North America, while continental governments resisted deregulation and foreign ownership; indeed, the successful takeover of Mannesmann by Britain's Vodafone caused a political furor in Germany. While Peter Mandelson, Blair's confidant within the government on the Third Way, cultivated links with social democrats in Germany and the Netherlands, Gordon Brown as chancellor of the Exchequer was becoming increasingly critical of European economic governance and vocally enthusiastic about American patterns of innovation. Just as Margaret Thatcher had attempted to carry her Anglo-Saxon agenda of deregulation onto the European level, so Blair and Brown pressed their continental colleagues to accept the so-called Lisbon Agenda, agreed at a European Council under the Portuguese presidency in 2000, "to become the most competitive and dynamic knowledge-based economy in the world, capable of sustainable economic growth with more and better jobs and greater social cohesion," by 2010.[24]

September 11 and after

Blair's government had learned from the Major government's mistakes during the 1992 presidential election campaign; British officials had made contacts with George W. Bush's team during the 2000 campaign, and worked on the assumption of continuing good relations as the new administration prepared to take office. The Blair government was committed to maintaining a stable balance between the USA and Europe, whatever administrations and governments came and went. Poor personal relations with Chirac had not been allowed to damage the Franco-British partnership beyond repair; anticipated difficulties with incoming Republicans should similarly be managed.

[24] See Lisbon European Council, Presidency Conclusions, March 23–24, 2000. http://www.bologna-berlin2003.de/pdf/PRESIDENCY_CONCLUSIONS_lissabon.pdf.

There was nevertheless much initial suspicion about the Bush administration within the British elite, and even considerable criticism within the press. Neoconservatives who had visited London in the months before the new administration took office had made it clear that they had no sentimental attachment to Britain, and that the British government would be judged by how loyally it followed the vigorously asserted American line.[25] Controversy over the US election outcome only strengthened the doubts of those within the Labour Party who were in any event both happier and more familiar with a Democratic administration. Washington's unilateralist rhetoric unsettled a government that was deeply committed to multilateral cooperation and international institutions; dismissal of the Kyoto Protocol on global warming and renewed commitment to missile defense added to the dismay. Prime Minister Blair was determined, however, to ensure that good relations were established with the new president and his team, even using the good offices of an old school friend, Bill Gammell, who had gone into the oil industry and become an acquaintance of George W. Bush, to ease initial exchanges.[26]

The two leaders' first meeting, at Camp David in February 2001, was not easy; but the British team had prepared carefully, and the prime minister appears to have returned to London reinforced in the view that a British voice within Washington was needed to moderate the American approach to world politics. The aggressive responses of successive EU heads of government to President Bush on climate change at the EU/US summit in Gothenburg in June 2001 made clear that transatlantic understanding would not be easy. Plainly, Britain's "bridge" function would be even more necessary to hold European and American leaders together as this new administration settled in.

Transatlantic relations were immediately transformed by the events of September 11. Other European governments were as vigorous as the British in offering support and sympathy; for the first time, their assembled representatives within NATO invoked Article 5 of the Atlantic Treaty, doing so on behalf of the United States. In keeping with Britain's established role as the most dependable American ally, British forces were mobilized in support of the US intervention in Afghanistan. British Special Forces operated with US counterparts; British air-tankers provided refueling to a substantial number of aircraft

---

[25] John Bolton, who became under secretary of state for arms control in the George W. Bush administration, led a team from the American Enterprise Institute around London in September 2000, propounding a clear message that the Bush foreign policy would be "America first."

[26] Riddell, *Hug Them Close*, pp. 134–135.

from the US carrier fleets; a Royal Navy task force comprising the aircraft carrier HMS *Illustrious*, an amphibious assault ship, two other warships, three submarines armed with cruise missiles, and seven auxiliary vessels was deployed to the Indian Ocean; and over 1,800 UK troops led and coordinated the initial deployment of the International Stabilization Force for Afghanistan.[27] France also offered its forces to the Americans, and Special Forces from several European states, including Germany, were deployed in Afghanistan.[28]

As has now become clear, the trauma of September 11 enabled the hawks within the Bush administration to pursue a larger preexisting, neoconservative agenda: the remaking of the Middle East, including regime change in Iraq followed also by Iran and Syria. So it was that President Bush's State of the Union message in January 2002 identified Iraq and Iran, with North Korea, as part of an "axis of evil." For his part, Tony Blair did not need convincing of the need to tackle Iraq. He had, after all, been convinced of the Iraqi threat to world order over the previous years and had actively engaged the UK in limited armed conflict against Iraq in Operation Desert Fox. But the rest of his government, his party, and his public – who had not been privy to the intelligence reports or their interpretation – were much less convinced that now was the time to force regime change on Iraq.

A key difficulty in approaching war in Iraq lay with the prime minister's style of government and managing of foreign policy. Like Thatcher, a previous dominant prime minister, Blair has had a distant relationship with the FCO, though his staff in Downing Street included a number of people from the diplomatic service. During the Iraq War, the UK did not have an ambassador in Washington, with most contact run on a Downing Street–White House link. While distant from the FCO machine, the prime minister did have the full support of the foreign secretary, Jack Straw.[29] The rest of the cabinet was marginally involved. Full cabinets have little time for broad discussion, but there was little attempt to open informed discussions in cabinet committees. The Ministerial Committee on Intelligence was bypassed and never met in the run-up to Iraq. There were only occasional Defence and Overseas Policy Committee meetings. That Blair keeps information and decisions to himself and the small group of people who surround him has become a

---

[27] See Ministry of Defence, *Performance Report 2001/2002*, November 2002, http://www.mod.uk/publications/performance2001, accessed May 2004.

[28] See the US State Department's "Allied Contributions to Common Defence," available at http://www.defenselink.mil/pubs/allied_contrib2002/02-Chptr2/02-Chptr_2tx.html.

[29] Although John Kampfner in *Blair's Wars* (pp. 301–304) argues that Straw wobbled in his commitment to war in Iraq.

recurring theme in criticisms of his administration. This situation led the Prime Minister's Office to promote a case for solidarity with the United States in moving toward intervention in Iraq that was based upon incomplete reports and inadequate intelligence, relying on management of the press and of Parliament to carry its case.

When Blair and Bush met at the latter's ranch in Texas in early April 2002, the president made it clear that he intended to intervene militarily in Iraq; and the prime minister made it clear (privately) that he would commit the British to the same objective.[30] But the Blair and the Bush administration agendas were nevertheless different; and the modifications to US rhetoric and to the rationale it presented for intervention, which Blair needed if he was to carry a reluctant party and public, only accentuated those differences. US officials were comfortable with sidelining the UN, brushing aside the inspection process, and being seen as bringing democracy to the Middle East. Downing Street, on the other hand, needed legitimization for intervention through the UN, and visible efforts to revive the Middle East peace process in order to carry domestic support and to keep lines open to its continental partners.

The prime minister had invested a good deal of political time and capital in building a relationship of trust with this Republican administration; after September 11, he gained increasing popularity and prestige within the United States as a leader who stood four-square with the Americans, and indeed one who could articulate the case for standing up to terrorists more fluently than their president. But the US administration appears to have done little to make it easier for Blair to rally his own government or his country behind him. In a divided administration, the reasonable case that Colin Powell could put to British listeners was repeatedly undermined by others in the Pentagon and elsewhere.[31] It remains unclear whether Donald Rumsfeld's suggestion in March 2003 that the United States would be willing to go ahead without the British was intended to be helpful. The "Quartet" initiative on Arab–Israeli peace negotiations had Powell's commitment, alongside Javier Solana on behalf of the EU (and the UN and the Russians); but Powell did not represent the consensus of the Bush administration on relations with Israel, and counterpressures from the Christian right on Republican Party strategists and congressmen were strong.

The State Department and Colin Powell were willing to try to build multilateral support through the UN, so helping the British to maintain a

---

[30] Ibid., p. 167.
[31] See Bob Woodward, *Plan of Attack* (New York: Simon & Schuster, 2004), pp. 128–129, 148–153, 174–176, 226, 411, and 415.

dialogue with the skeptical French and other European governments. But, again, Powell's position was repeatedly undermined from elsewhere within Washington by harsher language and explicit commitment to remove Saddam Hussein, whatever the UN Security Council might say.[32] Resolution 1441 was the best that the State Department and the British government could achieve in building a Security Council consensus; the ambiguities built into this multilateral compromise, however, left much room for American hawks on one side, and French and German leaders on the other, to interpret it in contradictory ways, with the UN inspectors caught in between.

So it was that the British government slipped toward presenting a case for intervention in Iraq that was based on evidence it knew to be thin, to justify support for an American administration that wanted to intervene for different reasons. From this difficult position Blair found himself facing a series of crises and dilemmas. The "doctored dossier" – "Iraq – Its Infrastructure of Concealment, Deception and Intimidation," from February 2003 – was shown to have been plagiarized from various sources, most notably from a Californian student's thesis. Blair's cabinet was sidelined by a prime minister who increasingly consulted with a small cadre of top officials and advisors. The parliamentary Labour party was also uneasy at the lack of reliable evidence, with some rebel MPs seeking to use the situation to oust Blair as party leader and prime minister. In the end, the whole untidy process led to the resignation of two cabinet ministers (Robin Cook, former foreign secretary and then leader of the House of Commons, and Clare Short, secretary of state for international development), to the largest back-bench rebellion the Labour government had ever suffered, and to the suicide of Dr. David Kelly, an expert on weapons of mass destruction within the Ministry of Defence, and two official inquiries. The British government went to war in Iraq alongside its American allies; but it went with a deeply divided country and a crisis in relations with its European neighbors. Estimates of the numbers of people who marched on February 3, 2003, against a British intervention in Iraq range from 750,000 to 2 million – perhaps the largest demonstration that London had ever seen. Local Labour parties were reporting membership losses.

Relations were just as uneasy with the continental governments that New Labour had attempted to cultivate over the previous five years. The German Social Democrats, who had followed domestic public opinion in taking an increasingly hostile line on US policy toward Iraq in the 2002

---

[32] See ibid., especially pp. 148–153 and 174–176.

election campaign, had moved from their earlier friendly relations with British Labour to renewed Franco-German partnership. Schröder had visited London soon after his reelection to discuss transatlantic differences with Blair, but the British prime minister could not bridge the gulf between American imperatives and German doubts. Indeed, his assurance to President Bush that he could bring Schröder and the Germans on board, and his subsequent failure to do this, displayed the problems inherent in his belief that he could act as a bridge across the Atlantic.[33] Franco-British relations were also stormy. The relationship between Blair and Chirac was never easy; Chirac saw Blair as a rival as much as a potential partner.[34] Nor had Blair achieved a good relationship with the French Socialist leader and prime minister Lionel Jospin. The defeat of Jospin in the French presidential elections of 2002 and the ending of "cohabitation" resulted in a more self-confident Chirac, determined to assert French interests in Gaullist style. Events reached a climax at a Brussels EU summit in October 2002 when Blair and Chirac clashed angrily, and publicly, after Blair challenged a Franco-German agreement on EU common agricultural policy reform. As a consequence of "le row," as it became known, Chirac cancelled the annual Franco-British summit due to be held at Le Touquet.[35] The following January, France and Germany marked the fortieth anniversary of the Elysée Treaty with a grand celebration. The Franco-German axis which Blair had worked so assiduously to break now appeared to be alive and kicking, and kicking in the direction of "les Anglo-Saxons."

A meeting to discuss defense in Brussels in April 2003 between France, Germany, Belgium, and Luxembourg again signaled the idea of an alternative to NATO and transatlantic cooperation. However, Britain, France, and Germany were at the same time developing a trilateral relationship over defense and foreign policy issues. Similarly, the EU's draft "Security Strategy Document,"[36] circulated in June 2003, reflected French and British perspectives on a more active and more global approach to foreign policy. While British and French leaders clashed on transatlantic relations and Iraq, their officials nevertheless continued to discuss the creation of a common European armaments agency, and cooperation in the design and building of aircraft carriers. These

---

[33] See Kampfner, *Blair's Wars*, p. 242.

[34] Chirac appears to have seen this conflict as personal as well as political, and according to reports from British intelligence was out to undermine Blair. See Philip Stephens, *Tony Blair: The Making of a World Leader* (New York: Viking, 2004), p. 226.

[35] See ibid., pp. 224–226.

[36] European Council, "A Secure Europe in a Better World: The European Security Strategy," December 2003, http://ue.eu.int/uedocs/cms_data/docs/2004/4/29/European%20Security%20Strategy.pdf, accessed May 2004.

developments were all set against the impending enlargement of the European Union and the entry of mainly pro-NATO and pro-American east European states. "New Europe," as Defense Secretary Donald Rumsfeld of the United States termed this group, very much included the UK, set against the "Old Europe" of a Franco-German axis.

Within the UK, the situation for Blair remained. The failure to locate weapons of mass destruction (WMD) – the whole basis upon which Blair had justified military action against Iraq – has plagued him more than it has the Bush administration, which saw and presented the Iraq War as more than just about WMD. The Hutton Inquiry into the death of Dr. David Kelly – a UK weapons expert who had given an unauthorized interview to a BBC reporter during which he supposedly stated that intelligence on WMD had been "sexed up" by Downing Street – cleared the prime minister and those around him, but left a negative impression of the style with which Blair and his government had approached the war in Iraq.[37] Not long after the publication of the Hutton Report, Blair established the "Review of Intelligence on Weapons of Mass Destruction," commissioned in February 2004 and chaired by Lord Butler, to investigate the way intelligence material had been gathered and why no weapons of mass destruction had been found.[38] Yet it was so tightly circumscribed in its objectives that the Liberal Democrats refused to participate and the Conservatives withdrew after only a few weeks. In such a context, President George W. Bush's visit to London in November 2003 was viewed with great trepidation by those in Westminster. Such has been the unease with appearing too close to President Bush that, as of late 2004, the prime minister has not yet found the time to collect his Congressional Medal of Honor.

Throughout the lead-up to war, Blair had sought three assurances from Bush: that the reconstruction of Iraq would be handled in an effective, efficient, and responsible way; that postwar Iraq would involve the UN; and finally that Bush would address the Israel–Palestine issue. To manage an effective reconstruction of Iraq, the Pentagon appointed retired Lieutenant-General Jay Garner, whose main area of expertise was missile defense. Widespread looting and increased lawlessness signaled an almost complete collapse of the state apparatus and civil society. The increasing number of attacks against US and allied forces, and the lack of US military preparation or capabilities for handling this, revealed the Pentagon's failure to plan for postwar reconstruction.

---

[37] For full transcripts and details of the Hutton Inquiry, see http://www.the-hutton-inquiry.org.uk.
[38] For further details, see http://www.butlerreview.org.uk.

On the second point, of involving the UN, early indications were that the United States would do so. When President Bush visited Belfast in April 2003, in a political gesture to his most important ally he spoke of a "vital role" for the UN, stating "vital role" no less than eight times in one press conference. But this does not appear to be what the Pentagon wanted, and the UN was given only an auxiliary role until an attack on its Baghdad headquarters forced it to withdraw. This has been particularly difficult for Blair, who from the beginning was keen to maintain the principles of multilateral support and of legitimation through UN approval and engagement.

It was on Israel–Palestine that Blair initially appeared to have made some progress. However, the state of the "Middle East roadmap" as it stands in 2004 leaves this looking like an empty gain. President Bush's approval in April 2004 of the Israeli plan for withdrawal from Gaza effectively discarded the roadmap that Blair thought he had helped commit Bush to. It was this change in approach to the Palestinian–Israeli conflict that provoked fifty-two retired prominent British diplomats to sign an open letter to the Prime Minister, stating their frustration at the approach he was taking. The letter, which many felt reflected the opinions of the majority of the British diplomatic community, criticized the approach taken to Iraq and how "the conduct of the war in Iraq has made it clear that there was no effective plan for the post-Saddam settlement." It further criticized the level of force employed in countering resistance, noting the use of "heavy weapons unsuited to the task in hand." It urged the prime minister to take a more determined approach to the policies of the United States with which the UK disagreed. It concluded:

We share your view that the British Government has an interest in working as closely as possible with the US on both these related issues [Iraq and Israel–Palestine], and in exerting real influence as a loyal ally. We believe that the need for such influence is now a matter of the highest urgency. If that is unacceptable or unwelcome there is no case for supporting policies which are doomed to failure.[39]

Is transatlantic balance still possible?

Like so many other British prime ministers since World War II, Tony Blair has become increasingly preoccupied by foreign policy. In six years,

[39] "A Letter to Blair: Your Middle East Policy Is Doomed, 10/19/2004 6:23PM," *Independent*, April 27, 2004; full text at http://argument.independent.co.uk/commentators/story.jsp?story=515676, accessed May 2004.

he has committed British forces to Operation Desert Fox, Kosovo, Sierra Leone, Afghanistan, and the 2003 Iraq War. Such a preoccupation has presented similarly numerous problems. His commitment to a multilateral international order, his determination to play a more positive role in European politics, and his pursuit of a close partnership with the United States have never knitted together as neatly as he would like. In particular, his double commitment to Europe and the United States has impaled him on the horns of the diplomatic dilemma that has caught so many British prime ministers before him. On the one hand, the historical relationship with the United States has brought significant gains, but the experience of Iraq calls into question how much longer this is sustainable when little is given in return by the Americans. The Europeans, on the other hand, have been divided and frequently portrayed as weak, with Euroskepticism remaining a strong impulse in British domestic political debate.

While Blair did not need much convincing of the need to attack Iraq, the British public did. Few argued more passionately and compellingly the case for military action than Blair. His belief in his ability to convince led him to engage in discussions at every level and expose himself to intense criticism. In the view of Clare Short, who resigned as secretary of state for international development, Blair saw the issue of WMD as an "honourable deception."[40] While his role as an "ambassador," often putting the argument more forcefully than anybody from the United States, gave him access to the White House, he often appeared to be taking responsibility for things he could not control. We have already noted how he failed to secure a US commitment to full involvement of the United Nations, its increasing involvement only coming to pass because of the problems the United States and the UK have faced in the day-to-day running of Iraq. This failure endangered his leadership and his government and encouraged rebellion within his own party. The price paid was to inject a further level of distrust among the French and other European partners about Britain's real intentions in the EU. It destroyed any real chance of his winning a referendum on the euro in the near future; winning the referendum on the EU constitution, to which he had agreed in early 2004 in order to take the wind out of the sails of the Conservative campaign for the European elections, also looked an insuperable task. The European elections in June 2004 saw significant gains for the UK Independence Party, which is committed to taking Britain out of the EU. The European dimension of

---

[40] Clare Short before the House of Commons Foreign Affairs Committee, June 17, 2003, available at http://www.Publications. parliament.UK/pa/cm 200203/cmselect/cmfaff/813/30617a10.htm, accessed December 2004.

Blair's foreign policy now seemed as unpopular with the public as the American.

Blair remains committed to the concept of Britain as a "bridge" across the Atlantic; he does not appear to consider this concept irrecoverably damaged by the events of 2003. However, as former British foreign secretary, Sir Malcolm Rifkind, pointed out, "any bridge will be very unstable if it leans too much in one direction."[41] Gerhard Schröder similarly noted that traffic across the bridge nearly always seemed to be in one direction.[42] Playing this bridging role is becoming increasingly difficult, with its success depending on the attitude of Washington toward working with other members as key partners and through NATO as a whole. In the aftermath of the Iraq War and occupation, it looks unlikely that Washington elites will attach sufficient importance to partnership with European governments to be willing to modify American foreign policy, however active British ministers and officials may be in attempting to persuade them that this is worthwhile.

---

[41] Sir Malcolm Rifkind, "The Special Relationship Between the United States and the United Kingdom – Is It Special?," speech at the London School of Economics, November 18, 2003.

[42] Riddell, *Hug Them Close*, p. 142.

8 The richest and farthest master is always best: US–Italian relations in historical perspective

Leopoldo Nuti

"If we have to make do with a mock Europe ... or ... with some Anglo-French *pastiche*, then it would be better not to play the game and to support the Atlantic Community instead · · · Italy not being able to be independent by herself, and Europe being unable to proceed with a real integration, then 'the richest and farthest master is always best.'"[1] In February 1963, when the process of European integration seemed to be on the verge of collapse as a consequence of the initiatives of President Charles de Gaulle of France, Ambassador Roberto Ducci summed up in this brilliant if cynical definition the role of the United States as the lodestar of Italian foreign policy. Aligning with the United States inside the Atlantic alliance was singled out by Ducci as the best possible option for Italy if the process of European integration were derailed and European relations were to revert to the traditional pattern of national power politics. That game, Ducci implicitly warned, was one that Italy had already tried and lost, and should not be tempted to play again; instead, siding with the strongest power provided the best chance for a return to the foreground of the European political landscape.

Ducci's words capture in a nutshell the importance that the United States has assumed in the history of Italy's international relations since World War II. Some of the reasons for this were closely connected with the Cold War and the international system in which Italy found itself after World War II, but others have deeper roots; this explains the ever growing role that the United States has played in Italy's foreign policy even after the dissolution of the blocs and throughout the 1990s, up to the beginning of the new century. This chapter will explore some of these causes by focusing on the dramatic impact of World War II on Italy's international standing, by providing some examples of the relevance of the United States for Italian policy-makers at various stages of the Cold War, and

---

[1] Letter from Ambassador Ducci to Foreign Minister A. Piccioni, February 4, 1963, in Archivio Centrale dello Stato (ACS), Archivio La Malfa, b. 75, f. "La grossa questione dell'Inghilterra." The ambassador's message echoes a Tuscan proverb.

by looking at the evolution of the relationship in the years that followed the end of the Soviet Union. In the final section, I address the policy of the Berlusconi government in the Iraqi crisis, trying above all to provide an answer to the question whether its actions during the showdown between Washington and Paris/Berlin were consistent with or diverged from previous trends of Italian foreign policy.

The external dimension: the United States and postwar Italian foreign policy

In order to understand why the United States assumed such importance for Italy in the postwar period, one must start with the traumatic experience of World War II, from which Italy emerged in a shambles. The armistice between Italy and the Allied powers on September 3, 1943, is of fundamental importance to any understanding of postwar Italian politics, both domestic and external. Among its many consequences, the 1943 disaster left Italy a weakened power, totally isolated in a hostile and resentful environment. This, for a country that since its inception had suffered from a severe inferiority complex vis-à-vis the other major European powers, and that had made the pursuit of parity the hallmark of its foreign policy, was the worst of all possible worlds.

The ramshackle Italian state that was eventually reassembled in the last two years of the war, therefore, was constantly striving to reassert itself as a normal member of the international community by shedding the formal trappings of inferiority deriving from its status as a defeated country.[2] First it demanded a role as cobelligerent against Nazi Germany; then it tried to avoid the punitive aspects of the peace treaty; then it asked for their revision; and finally it started pushing for membership in all the international organizations that the Western world was trying to set up (with the initial, significant exception of the Western Union, to which the United States was not a party).[3]

Italian diplomacy had few cards to play. The European scenario after World War II was likely to be dominated by two powers, France and Britain, which certainly would not soon forget the "stab in the back" of 1940; Germany was likely to remain in a weakened condition for a long time, and the Soviet Union was a dangerous and unknown entity. For a

---

[2] For an enlightening analysis of Italian revisionism, see Ilaria Poggiolini, "Italian Revisionism After World War II: Status and Security Problems, 1947–1957," in R. Ahmann (ed.) *The Quest for Stability: Problems of Western European Security 1918–1957* (Oxford: Oxford University Press, 1993), pp. 327–359.

[3] The Western Union was created in 1948; it became the Western European Union in 1954, with the signing of the Treaty of Paris, at which point both Italy and West Germany joined.

while, some Italian diplomats considered a flirtation with the USSR to exert pressure on the Western allies and soften their attitude, but it soon became clear that this game was too risky. That left the United States as the only lever available to Italian diplomacy to regain some of its previous standing. Not only did the United States not regard Italy as a traditional enemy, and not only did the American public not harbor any hostile sentiments toward it, but the warm feelings of the Italian-American community for its old homeland were a precious asset for Italian foreign policy. True, this factor may be overrated, but by the end of World War II Italian-Americans were an influential lobby that no American politician could afford to neglect. The search for a preferential relationship with Washington, therefore, actually began before the end of World War II and continued through the onset of the Cold War: the postwar fear of Soviet expansionism strengthened it, but did not create it. The armistice and the cobelligerence that followed it had, in short, a twofold consequence for postwar Italian thinking, revealing Italy's powerlessness but also showing a possible escape from the country's predicament through cultivating the relationship with Washington.

The importance of the relationship with the United States in the construction of postwar Italian foreign policy was also enhanced by Washington's growing support for the process of European integration after 1947. The American pressures for an integrated Europe allowed Italy to reconcile its own inclination to promote the same cause with its aspiration to build a stable and privileged Atlantic relationship. Fully aware of Italy's almost complete powerlessness, De Gasperi and Sforza had come to realize the utter futility of another attempt to play the game of power politics. They imagined instead a Europe whose states would gradually merge their sovereignties into a supranational entity spanning a fully renovated, peaceful continent, an outcome that would accord with certain ideals and at the same time conveniently make Italian inferiority irrelevant in terms of traditional measurements of power. The Europe imagined by the Italian statesmen of the early postwar years, therefore, was a singular combination of idealism and realism, firmly entrenched in its Atlantic framework, with the United States as supreme guarantor both of its security and of the impossibility of returning to the old European balance of power. Clearly, such a project dovetailed quite nicely with the American vision of a strong, federated Europe that would help the United States share the burdens of containing the Soviet Union in the coming Cold War.

Desiring on the other hand to avoid an excessively passive relationship with Washington, Italian diplomacy reached the conclusion that building up a powerful Europe would be the best way to avoid being relegated to mere satellite status. Atlanticism and Europeanism were therefore perceived as mutually reinforcing elements of a single policy that would allow Italy to recover its place in a new Europe while relying on the safety net offered by the relationship with the United States. The contradiction in this design would become evident only when European integration threatened to take a wrong turn, and to move outside the Atlantic cocoon in which it was originally conceived.

The internal dimension: the United States and Italian domestic politics

The second consequence of the wartime disaster was that it left Italy internally chaotic, in what many observers perceived as bordering on a prerevolutionary stage. Would the monarchy survive the defeat, or would it be dropped by a war-weary Italian populace that blamed the king as much as it did Mussolini for the war, the armistice, and their catastrophic effects? Would the collapse of previous institutions pave the way for the creation of a republic or for a revolutionary uprising that would sweep away all remnants of the past and radically transform Italian politics and society? Fears of the latter outcome were widely shared in Italy, and long before the war was over many an appeal had been issued by the Italian elites to Washington and London: unless the Allies lent a helping hand, the Italian domestic balance of power was likely to be subverted at the end of the war, and the winner of the resulting struggle could be the Communist Party. Once again it was Washington, and not London, that proved to be the key partner for stabilizing Italian politics; Great Britain was too closely associated with the deposed Italian monarch, Vittorio Emanuele III, and with the most conservative sectors of Italian society. Washington, though, gradually worked out an alternative policy that gambled on the success of a more democratic, reformist-oriented party to stem the possible tide of a Communist victory. The Christian Democrats of Alcide De Gasperi fit this role only partially, but – if only for the lack of any better option – they eventually delivered almost half a century of reasonably satisfactory cooperation with Washington.[4] As the tensions of the early postwar years crystallized in the permanent fractures of the Cold War, Washington's interest in keeping Italy away from a possible Communist government thus became an enduring

---

[4] On the uneasy relationship of the United States with the Christian Democrats, see Mario Del Pero, *L'alleato scomodo: gli USA e la DC negli anni del centrismo (1948–1955)* [The Inconvenient Ally: The USA and the Christian Democrats in the Age of Centrism (1948–1955)](Rome: Carocci, 2001).

feature of the relationship between the two countries – an interest, one hastens to add, that Italian politicians were fully aware of, and were not averse to exploiting. Even the Communist threat, then, real or inflated as it might have been, became a powerful tool in the search for a preferential relationship. Thus, the final stage of the war and the onset of the Cold War helped to enmesh the United States further into Italian affairs, and to strengthen its role as a key reference point for moderate, centrist Italian political forces.[5]

Some examples from the Cold War

Of course, Italy's partnership with the United States was not always smooth and easy. On the contrary, there were several attempts to manipulate the relationship in order to satisfy Italian interests more completely, and these sometimes led to frictions with Washington – in particular with respect to policy in the Mediterranean and the Middle East. But this took place inside an overall framework in which the United States played a pivotal role in the orientation of Italy's foreign *and* domestic policies. Italian politicians have been quick to grasp the possible multiple advantages of playing the American card at the right moment, as the following examples demonstrate.

NATO entry

An obvious initial example is the difficult decision taken by De Gasperi and Sforza to ask for Italian inclusion in the Atlantic pact, a crucial feat that, once successfully accomplished, achieved several results at once. Becoming a member of the Alliance restored some parity to Italy's international standing only four years after the end of the war and two years after signing a rather punitive peace treaty; it also aligned Rome firmly with Washington, strengthening the country's security and removing all previous doubts about a possible Italian flirtation with neutrality in the Cold War. But, while taken primarily to secure Italy's international position, the Atlantic choice had the additional benefit of sealing the orientation of the country's domestic system for the next

---

[5] On the perception of the Communist threat, see in particular Ennio Di Nolfo, "The United States and Italian Communism: World War II to the Cold War," *Journal of Italian History* 1:1 (1978), pp. 74–94; Ennio Di Nolfo, *Vaticano e Stati Uniti: dalle carte di Myron Taylor 1939–1952* [The Vatican and the United States: From the Documents of Myron Taylor 1939–1952] (Milan: F. Angeli, 1978); James E. Miller, *The United States and Italy, 1940–1950: The Politics and Diplomacy of Stabilization* (Chapel Hill: University of North Carolina Press, 1984).

fifty years – a consequence that its leftist opponents were very much aware of, and strenuously resisted.

Finally, it is also important to note that the Atlantic choice was taken after Italy had decided *not* to become one of the founding members of the Brussels treaty with which France, the UK, and the three Benelux countries created the Western Union, the original nucleus of west European security, in March 1948. While there were a number of reasonable motives for the Italian decision to opt out – ranging from the need to avoid such a crucial choice barely a month before the dramatic political elections of April 1948, to some rather clumsy attempts to drive a bargain in return for Italian participation – the fact remains that Italy refused to enter a *purely European* defense system but enthusiastically joined a *transatlantic* one just eleven months later.

Suez

This Atlantic orientation was further confirmed at the time of the 1956 Suez crisis, when France and Britain decided to settle their scores with the Egyptian president Gamal Nasser through a military intervention that Washington strongly opposed. Italy found itself aligned with the United States in condemning this initiative at the UN and in criticizing the position of its European allies at a very sensitive moment; after all, Rome and Paris were negotiating the final phase of the EEC and Euratom treaties. Shortly afterwards, Italy launched its so-called neo-Atlanticist policy in the Mediterranean. The aim was to develop a policy of rapprochement toward the moderate Arab regimes and keep them within the Western fold, thus preventing the Soviet Union from taking advantage of the power vacuum left by the Franco-British defeat. Once again, that ambitious design was based on the notion that a new, bolder Italian policy in the Mediterranean would be possible only if it was carried out with US support. Together Italy and the United States, as the only two powers untainted by the charge of neocolonialism, might have a chance of succeeding in the effort.[6]

The Jupiter deployments

A crucial strategic decision taken in 1958 is among the clearest examples of this pattern of relying on the United States and the Atlantic alliance to achieve a number of goals that cut across both the international and

---

[6] For an analysis of Italy's Mediterranean policy, including the Suez crisis, see Alessandro Brogi, *L'Italia e l'egemonia americana nel Mediterraneo* [Italy and American Hegemony in the Mediterranean] (Florence: Nuova Italia, 1996).

domestic dimensions of Italian politics. In July 1958, Prime Minister Fanfani personally communicated to President Eisenhower his willingness to deploy in Italy the new Jupiter intermediate-range ballistic missiles (IRBM), thus making Italy the first NATO country in continental Europe to accept the new generation of nuclear weapons that Washington had offered to its allies at the NATO Council of the previous December.

There were a number of reasons for the Italian prime minister's willingness to do this, most of which pertained to the foreign policy realm. In particular, the deployment would give Italy a nuclear status of a sort and would improve its international prestige at a time when nuclear issues formed the core of the Atlantic debate over the best defensive posture for the West. Faced by the challenge of a deterioration in its status by Britain's acquisition of a national nuclear deterrent and by the French intention to rapidly follow the British example, Rome had been deprived of a possible alternative to a national nuclear choice when a project for trilateral nuclear cooperation with Bonn and Paris (never very promising anyway) was terminated by General de Gaulle in June 1958. This left Italy with the NATO option and the relationship with Washington as the only instrument that would allow it to match the nuclear status of its European counterparts, unless it decided to launch a costly (both economically and politically) national nuclear program of its own.

Through most of 1957 and early 1958, moreover, Italian diplomats had been terribly concerned by the possibility that a solution to the German question would be negotiated by a quartet made up of the victors of World War II. This would obviously have excluded Italy and thereby confirmed its inferiority vis-à-vis Great Britain and, even more painfully, France. The prospect of suddenly stepping up Italy's position by the quick acceptance of the missiles, therefore, was immediately grasped by Italian statesmen, who did not lose any time in reminding the Allies that Italy's acceptance of the risks involved in the deployment turned it into an indispensable partner in any future negotiations on European security – including negotiations about Germany. "This," wrote the Italian ambassador to the Atlantic Council in a memo to the prime minister, "is the best political card which Italy has in its hand, and our relations with the United States will be positively influenced by it." And in another dispatch he penned another, even more revealing, remark:

This is why Italy's position in NATO vis-à-vis Washington is at its zenith . . . [Accepting the missiles] increases the assistance we provide to the United States, as well as the risks our country runs in case of war. We could almost say that for the time being we are getting closer to the atomic club than France: not because we produce the atomic warheads, but because we accept them on our soil.

I believe this to be a strong enough argument, both in order to defuse any attempt at building a directorate and to demand a more active Italian participation in the formation of the common policy inside the [Alliance's] Council and Committees.[7]

In short, accepting the missiles entailed major consequences for Italy's external position. As an incoming prime minister with an ambitious agenda, however, Fanfani might also have had his own personal reasons for accepting the deployment. When he met with President Eisenhower, his new Cabinet had barely been completed, but it was already said to have quite a bold foreign policy program; rumors circulated in Rome that the new Italian prime minister supported a more assertive Italian policy in the Middle East and, more generally, toward all of the newly independent countries of the Third World. Furthermore, it was known that Fanfani intended to conduct a sweeping purge of the high ranks of the Ministry of Foreign Affairs in order to make it a more amenable tool of his policy. Last but not least, Fanfani was expected to adopt some audacious domestic policy initiatives in order to prepare the ground for a rapprochement with Pietro Nenni's Socialist Party, which hitherto had been perceived as a threat to the country's foreign policy because of its longstanding alliance with the Communist Party.

Fanfani probably thought the IRBM decision would keep his new political program from being interpreted as anti-American or as a weakening of the country's Atlantic orientation. By deploying the missiles, he was showing both to the United States and to his possible domestic partners, namely the Nenni Socialists, that any deal they might work out together would not alter the country's international policy, which would be firmly locked into an Atlantic framework by the presence of the missiles. In addition, Fanfani was fully aware of the extensive support – both overt and covert – the United States had provided to his party and to his own personal faction during the previous years, and he may have wanted to show his benefactors that he deserved the trust they had placed in him. Thus, not only did he personally tell Eisenhower of his approval of the Jupiters, but during the subsequent negotiations for the deployment of the missiles he intervened at least twice to remove major roadblocks and to help steer the discussions to a successful

---

[7] The Italian Ambassador to the Atlantic Council to Prime Minister Fanfani, November 24 and December 19, 1958, both in Archivio Storico Ministero Affari Esteri (ASMAE), Fondo Ambasciata di Parigi 1951–1958, b. 84, f. R-11. In September 1958, president Charles de Gaulle of France tried to get US and British approval for a scheme to create a trilateral Franco-British-American directorate or leadership group within the Atlantic alliance. His efforts elicited irate responses from the Italian government and many of the other member countries.

conclusion.[8] Clearly, the search for a preferential relationship with Washington spanned the whole range of his possible motivations, from building up Italy's standing to guiding the domestic debate in the desired direction.

The 1963 crisis

Yet another example of Italy's inclination to go Atlantic can be seen in the government's reaction to the great crisis of January 1963, which prompted Ambassador Ducci to write the scathing remark quoted at the beginning of this chapter. Throughout the previous two years, Italy had tried to mediate between the new European policy of General de Gaulle and Macmillan's cautious attempt to bring Britain inside the EEC, while Italian diplomats had tried to reconcile the French ideas of the Fouchet Plan with their own vision of Europe. Yet when the crisis burst out after de Gaulle's twin salvoes of January 1963, which derailed the negotiations for British accession and seemed to threaten the future of the Atlantic community itself, the Italian Ministry of Foreign Affairs had no doubts about which way to go. Following the French road, concluded an assessment written inside the ministry in February 1963, would risk an even greater crisis and leave Italy without the protection of the US atomic umbrella. The twin pillars of Italian foreign policy, the paper continued, should remain loyalty to the Atlantic alliance, the true cornerstone of Italian security which should not be jeopardized by any anti-American Europeanism, and loyalty to the idea of European integration with a view to the creation of a federated Europe, in cooperation with the United States in a broad Atlantic partnership. It was in Washington, concluded the report, that the answers to most problems could be found, and there that they should be sought.[9]

Pershing II and Cruise missile deployments

Lest it be thought that this pro-American orientation was solely a pre-rogative of the Christian Democrats or a byproduct of the Cold War environment of the frigid 1950s, one need only look at the similar

[8] Leopoldo Nuti, "Dall'operazione *Deep Rock* all'operazione *Pot Pie*: una storia documen-tata dei missili SM 78 Jupiter in Italia" ["From Operation Deep Rock to Operation Pot Pie: A Documentary History of SM 78 Jupiter Missiles in Italy"], *Storia delle Relazioni Internazionali*, 11/12:1 (1996–7) and 2 (1996–7), pp. 95–138 and 105–149.
[9] Ministero degli Affari Esteri, *Considerazioni su di una possibile azione in relazione alla crisi di Bruxelles*, February 23, 1963, ACS, Archivio La Malfa, b. 75, f. "La grossa questione dell'Inghilterra."

behavior of two other prime ministers, a Christian Democrat and a Socialist, some twenty years later. Both Francesco Cossiga and Bettino Craxi, between 1979 and 1983, followed a course similar to Fanfani's to strengthen the country's foreign policy after a period in which the deterioration of Italy's political system and the rising threat of domestic terrorism had significantly lowered the country's international standing. Italian diplomacy, in particular, had been stung by Rome's exclusion from the Guadeloupe Summit of January 1979, when the United States, France, Britain, and West Germany had taken important decisions about the future of the Atlantic alliance. Thus, when the time came to implement the Guadeloupe decisions and NATO began to discuss the deployment of a new category of long-range theater nuclear forces, namely the Pershing II and Cruise missiles, the Cossiga government rapidly spread the word that it would be ready to host the new weapons.

While Cossiga's decision was mostly dictated by the need to bolster Italy's foreign policy with a move that would be strongly approved in Washington, the Socialist leader Bettino Craxi played a more sophisticated game. Craxi's own role, as a matter of fact, was crucial not once but twice. In the late months of 1979, Craxi first signaled his assent to future deployment of the new weapons system, at a moment when the support of his Socialist Party was indispensable if the Italian parliament was to give its preliminary approval to the North Atlantic Council's eventual decision of December 12, 1979. Even though at that time his party was not a member of the majority coalition and usually abstained when the government presented its initiatives to the parliament, Craxi skillfully managed to overcome its vocal internal opposition and led it to vote in favor of the NATO decision to deploy the new missiles.[10] Thus, not only did he help the government achieve a remarkable result, he also signaled that the Italian Socialists now had a leader who would not waver when faced with the responsibility of taking important, and controversial, international decisions.

A few years later, in the tense summer of 1983 – shortly after becoming the first Socialist prime minister in Italian history – Craxi again displayed his full Atlantic reliability by declaring, in his very first speech after assuming office, that Italy would fulfill the pledge made by the Cossiga government in December 1979. He further asserted that, if the disarmament negotiations with the Soviet Union did not reach a positive conclusion, his government would indeed deploy the missiles, which in the meantime had become the central feature of a heated political debate in

[10] Lelio Lagorio, *L'ultima sfida: gli euromissili* [The Ultimate Challenge: Euromissiles] (Florence: Loggia de' Lanzi, 1998).

the streets and in national parliaments throughout western Europe. By repeating, on his first trip to Washington, his firm intention to accept the missiles, and by making good on this promise shortly thereafter – in spite of an increasingly tense and difficult domestic situation – Craxi allowed Italy to recover some of the prestige that it had lost in the mid- and late 1970s. Indeed, the Italian decision to deploy the Cruise missiles played a crucial role in the implementation of the whole NATO project, since Germany's chancellor, Helmut Schmidt, had made clear that the Italian acceptance of the new weapons would be quite influential – almost a precondition for the German deployment – thus turning Italy into a real pivot of the whole Atlantic design.

At the same time, Craxi was certainly aware of the deep implications for Italian domestic politics of his dual gestures of 1979 and 1983. By his stance on this critical issue, he had made clear to the White House that he could be as strong an Atlanticist as any Christian Democrat, thus using the test of Atlantic firmness against both his Communist enemies and his Christian Democratic allies. The decision to deploy the missiles, moreover, was only part of a policy that aimed, first, at implementing an overall vision of modernization of the country that cut across both foreign and domestic policies, and, second, at relegating to the past the difficult and somewhat ambiguous cooperation with the Communist Party – the *compromesso storico* – that had been the main feature of Italian politics in the 1970s. What was at stake in Italy in 1983, in other words, was not only the deployment of the new weapons, but the overall political orientation of the forces that would rule the country for the near future.[11]

Sigonella and Tripoli

Finally, the stability of the relationship with Washington was paradoxically confirmed by the most tense confrontations that any Italian government ever had with the United States, the twin crises of 1985 and 1986. In October 1985, in the so-called Sigonella crisis, the US Delta Force and the Italian *carabinieri* almost shot it out at the Sigonella airport in Sicily to decide who should take charge of the Palestinian terrorists just captured after hijacking the Italian cruiser *Achille Lauro* and murdering in cold blood one of its passengers, a handicapped American citizen of Jewish descent. At stake was not just a matter of principle about the jurisdiction over foreign citizens in Italian territory, but a tense dispute between Rome

---

[11] L. Nuti, "Italy and the Battle of the Euromissiles," in Olav Njolstad (ed.), *The Last Decade of the Cold War: From Conflict Escalation to Conflict Transformation* (London: Frank Cass, 2004), pp. 332–359.

and Washington about the best course of action in dealing with the growing tensions in the Middle East and Mediterranean basin; Craxi and his foreign minister, Andreotti, were in the midst of a protracted effort to engage the moderate Arab states and the Palestinian Liberation Organization's (PLO) Yasser Arafat in a constructive dialogue to stabilize the region, and were critical of the more bellicose attitude of the Reagan administration, which they regarded as jeopardizing the whole initiative.

For similar reasons, in April 1986 the Italian government criticized the US decision to carry out a bombing raid in retaliation for a terrorist attack clearly linked to Libya's Muammar Qaddafi, then regarded as one of the main sponsors of the wave of terrorism sweeping across Europe.[12] In the public imagination, these two episodes, and particularly Sigonella, became the symbols of a new, different type of relationship ("more mature," as one sometime reads) between Italy and the United States. In this view, an Italian politician with a stiffer backbone, Bettino Craxi, had finally stood up to the United States, which had been allowed to develop some very bad habits due to forty years of Italian servility. This may well have been the case, and certainly Craxi had personal courage that was lacking in many previous Italian leaders. But it is significant that, at the time of the crisis, and not far from the Sigonella airport, the more than one hundred Cruise missiles deployed since the previous year stood as a pointed reminder of US–Italian cooperation. In other words, perhaps Craxi could afford to challenge what he regarded as the most unpalatable expressions of US foreign policy because the underlying relationship with Washington was so firm.

After the Cold War: *plus ça change* ...

In the 1990s, the centrality of the United States for Italian foreign policy survived almost unaltered despite momentous transformations of the international system and of Italy's own internal political structure. That said, Italy's Atlantic orientation gradually lost much of its domestic significance. With the end of the Cold War, gone is the climate of "international civil war" that so closely linked the evolution of domestic Italian politics to the oscillations of the bipolar confrontation. This is not to say that taking a pro- or anti-American stance has now become purely a matter for disputes among foreign policy experts, without any repercussions for the country's internal political debate. To the contrary, throughout the 1990s, there has

---

[12] Alessandro Silj (ed.), *L'alleato scomodo. I rapporti tra Roma e Washington nel Mediterraneo: Sigonella e Gheddafi* [The Inconvenient Ally. Relations Between Rome and Washington in the Mediterranean: Sigonella and Gaddafi] (Milan: Corbaccio, 1998).

been a steadily growing antagonism to American foreign policy among the radical left, mirrored by a somewhat ruthless exploitation of Italy's "friendship" with Washington by the new right and in particular by the Berlusconi government. Still, the contemporary foreign policy debate lacks the deep sense of belonging to opposite international camps which cut across Italian politics during the bipolar confrontation.

Even though the domestic implications of a pro-American foreign policy changed significantly with the end of the Cold War, the transformation of the international system has not altered the basic aim of Italian foreign policy: to maintain a careful balance between its European and Atlantic dimensions. In a new international environment whose contours and features are still to be defined, there has been a careful effort by Italian diplomacy not to abandon those habits that have worked reasonably well in the past. Washington remains the center of the Italian diplomatic universe, and it is difficult to find in the Italian foreign policy of the 1990s any effort to rebalance the American preponderance by consorting with other powers. The opposite seems to have been the case: the traditional attention to the relationship with Washington remained more or less constant throughout the decade to retain a counterweight against any attempts to develop a European security framework outside its original Atlantic shell, and in which Italy would probably be confined to a less and less relevant role. Italian foreign policy throughout the 1990s, therefore, seems to have followed the pattern described by Frank Ninkovich in a different context, where he pointed out that many of the international structures created during the Cold War were not merely a response to US–Soviet rivalry, but also addressed older and more fundamental issues of the international system.[13] Just as Italy has, since 1943, looked for an external guarantor to balance its inferiority vis-à-vis its European partners, Rome is likely to continue to look to the United States as an important source of support, Cold War or no Cold War.

Again, examples of this attitude are not hard to find. A prominent one occurred at the beginning of the 1990s, during the protracted debate about the possible development of a defense capacity for the European Union that would complement its economic dimension. Unsurprisingly, Italy took a favorable stance toward the creation of a European security identity; indeed, one of the first European statesmen to suggest merging the existing Western European Union (WEU)[14] into the future European

---

[13] Frank Ninkovich, "The United States, NATO, and the Lessons of History," in Dean J. Kotlowski (ed.), *The European Union: From Jean Monnet to the Euro* (Athens: Ohio University Press, 2000), pp. 203–212.
[14] Formerly the Western Union, as mentioned above.

Union was Italian foreign minister Gianni De Michelis, in September 1990, during the Italian presidency of the European Community. Even if this initial enthusiasm was somewhat toned down in the following weeks by De Michelis himself and by Prime Minister Giulio Andreotti, who made clear that a common foreign and security policy was only a medium-term project and therefore did not pose any immediate threat to NATO, Italy promoted the initiative for several months. By early 1991, when France and Germany declared their support for the development of an "organic" link between the EU and the WEU, Italy reiterated its interest in a common European system of security and defense, implying an ambitious schedule for integrating the WEU into EU structures.[15]

Given this initial support, it is all the more remarkable that just a few months later Italy signed a joint declaration with Great Britain, whose reaction to the proposals for a WEU/EU merger had been increasingly critical. The statement, issued on October 4, 1991, articulated a remarkable compromise between the two opposing visions of the WEU that had developed in the previous months, one pan-European and the other Atlanticist:

The WEU should be entrusted with the task of developing the European dimension in the field of defence, [and] it will develop its role in two complementary directions: as the defence component of the Union and as the means to strengthen the European pillar of the Alliance.[16]

The Italian rapprochement with London can be explained by a number of factors. First and foremost, by early February 1991, the administration of George Bush, Sr., had made clear its concern about the development of a WEU dependent only on the EU, which could marginalize NATO as the provider of European security.[17] Clearly, such a powerful reminder from the United States that the construction of Europe should not become a tool for weakening the Atlantic alliance was bound to have a deep impact on Italian diplomacy. The effect of the American démarche

---

[15] Mika Luoma-aho, "'Arm' Versus 'Pillar': The Politics of Metaphors of the Western European Union at the 1990–1991 Intergovernmental Conference on Political Union," *Journal of European Public Policy* 11:1 (February 2004), pp. 106–127. On this issue, see also Willem Frederik van Eekelen, *Debating European Security, 1948–1998* (The Hague: SDU Publishers, 1998), and Holly Wyatt-Walter, *The European Community and the Security Dilemma 1989–1992* (London: Macmillan, 1997).

[16] "An Anglo-Italian Declaration on European Security and Defence in the Context of the Intergovernmental Conference on Political Union," *Europe Documents*, October 5, 1991, pp. 1–2.

[17] See, for example, the March 1991 intervention by Deputy Assistant Secretary of State for European Affairs James Dobbins – the so-called Dobbins démarche – as discussed in Geir Lundestad, *The United States and Western Europe Since 1945: From "Empire" by Invitation to Transatlantic Drift* (Oxford: Oxford University Press, 2003), p. 243.

was then heightened by the events of the summer of 1991, when the attempted coup against Mikhail Gorbachev in the Soviet Union and the early signs of the impending disintegration of Yugoslavia reminded everybody how dangerous it would be to separate the United States from Europe at a stage when "the new world order" was in such a state of flux.

Thus, by the fall of 1991, Italy was ready to side with Britain and make clear that the functions of the new, revitalized WEU should be entirely compatible with the preservation of the Atlantic alliance.[18] The eventual compromise reached in the Maastricht Treaty, Article J.4, made it clear that the future of the WEU lies inside the European Union, but also added that the EU's policy should be fully compatible with "the common security and defence policy" defined by the Atlantic framework.

In the following months, the Italian preference for such an Atlantic orientation, allowing for a continuous US political presence in European affairs, was also apparent in the aloofness displayed by the Italian military toward the next steps of Franco-German military rapprochement – for example, the creation of the Eurocorps. It was, after all, an Italian officer who dryly commented that the main result of the "gesticulations" of the Eurocorps had been to have the German *Panzergrenadieren* parade along the Champs Elysées some fifty years later.[19] Nor did this orientation change much throughout the rest of the decade, as was confirmed by the open support for the American, versus the French, position during the 1996–7 debate about naming a French officer as commander-in-chief of NATO's Southern Command. In February 1997, both the Italian foreign and defense ministers clearly defended the US refusal to cede the AFSOUTH Command to the French.[20]

While these diplomatic skirmishes illustrate the Italian inclination to maintain a close relationship with Washington, this preference is most evident in the support that Italy gave to the NATO interventions in the wars of the former Yugoslavia. When, at the margins of the Helsinki meeting of the Conference on Security and Cooperation in Europe, a debate arose in July 1992 about which organization would be best suited to enforce the embargo, Italy is said to have mediated between the French

---

[18] Roberto Aliboni, "Il dibattito sulla politica europea di sicurezza e difesa" ["The Debate on European Policy on Security and Defense"], Istituto Affari Internazionali, *L'Italia nella politica internazionale, 1993* (Rome: SIPI, 1993), pp. 142–154.

[19] Carlo Jean, "La nostra sicurezza nel mondo balcanizzato" ["Our Security in a Balkanized World"], *Limes* 4 (1994), pp. 201–212; Maurizio Cremasco, "L'Italia e la sicurezza internazionale" ["Italy and International Security"], in Istituto Affari Internazionali, *L'Italia nella politica internazionale, 1994* (Roma: SIPI, 1994), pp. 63–79.

[20] Roberto Menotti, "Italy and NATO: The Unsinkable Carrier and the Mediterranean," *What Italy Stands For – Limes* (Washington, DC: Center for Strategic and International Studies, 1997), pp. 15–29, in particular pp. 20–23.

request for an all-European force and the US pressure to reassert the primacy of NATO.[21] Above all, it was in the subsequent combat missions that Italy revealed the significance it attached to the relationship with Washington. Despite serious domestic criticism, which will be discussed below, and despite previous political and economic connections with the Serbian government, the Italian cabinet pledged its support for NATO's armed interventions both in Bosnia (in Operation Deliberate Force, August to September 1995) and in the much more dramatic and trouble-some Kosovo air campaign (March to June 1999). These displays of Italy's Atlantic orientation were not unproblematic: while many Italians regarded intervention favorably, as the only means to stop the bloodshed, other were deeply uneasy about NATO's resort to force in a theater so dangerously close to Italian territory.

The intervention in Kosovo in particular, in the spring of 1999, raised domestic problems for the government even within its own parliamentary majority, eventually forcing it to rely on the support of the opposition to carry out its participation in the NATO campaign. But Italian participa-tion was seen by many as a test of the reliability of the first government led by a former member of the Communist Party. As Prime Minister Massimo D'Alema himself made clear in his memoirs about the war, there were doubts in Washington about the sincerity of his government's international alignment, or at least about its capacity to play a significant role in time of crisis. In the early months of his premiership, these doubts had been strengthened by severe tensions with the United States, espe-cially over the case of the Kurdish leader Abdullah Ocalan. The decision of the D'Alema government to participate in the war, though prompted by the gruesome behavior of the Belgrade regime toward the Kosovar population, also served to prove to the United States the prime minister's personal credibility as a legitimate partner and his full reliability as a member of the pro-Western, moderate left.[22] In the end, Italy took part in both NATO campaigns and ended up as one of the major participants

---

[21] Virgilio Ilari, "La politica militare italiana" ["Italian Military Policy"], in Istituto Affari Internazionali, *L'Italia nella politica internazionale, 1993*, pp. 203–229, in particular p. 228. For the overall French efforts to engage the WEU in Yugoslavia, see Sonia Lucarelli, *Europe and the Breakup of Yugoslavia: A Political Failure in Search of a Scholarly Explanation* (The Hague: Kluwer Law International, 2000); Thierry Tardy, *La France et la gestion des conflits yougoslaves (1991–1995): enjeux et leçons d'une opération de maintien de la paix de l'ONU* [France and the Management of the Yugoslav Conflicts (1991–1995): Stakes and Lessons from a UN Operation to maintain the Peace] (Brussels: Bruylant, 1999).

[22] Massimo D'Alema, *Kosovo: gli italiani e la guerra* [Kosovo. The Italians and the War] (Milan: Mondadori, 1999); see also Lamberto Dini, *Tra Casa Bianca e Botteghe Oscure: Fatti e retroscena di una stagione alla Farnesina* [Between the White House and the Botteghe Oscure. Behind the Scenes of a Season at the Farnesina] (Milan: Guerini e Associati, 2001).

in the postwar peacekeeping missions, with Italian troops playing a significant role in stabilization and reconstruction.

Finally, shortly after the first NATO intervention in the Balkans, the importance of the Atlantic alliance was reinforced by a frustrating *a contrario* demonstration. At the time of the Albanian crisis of 1997, when that country seemed on the verge of collapse and Italy tried to mobilize its European allies to prevent a total breakdown of Albanian society and an ensuing mass exodus of refugees to Italian shores, Rome was left completely isolated. The WEU, which was then experiencing its umpteenth relaunch, turned a deaf ear to the Italian requests, forcing Rome to initiate its own coalition of the willing under the codename Operation Alba. In the security field, Europe was plainly not yet adequate for Italy's defense needs.

The policies of the Berlusconi government

Since the elections of 2001, the government of Silvio Berlusconi seems to have toned down the customary display of Italian support for European integration, emphasizing instead close personal relations with the leaders of key countries such as the United States, Russia, Great Britain, and Spain (at least while Aznar was in power). Rumors that the Italian prime minister was disdained as an unpleasant parvenu by some of his European partners may have played a role in the choice of an Atlantic, rather than European, orientation for the new government's foreign policy, but the growing reliance on the United States is not just the result of personal pique. Rather, it must be gauged against the background of an ideological preference for a return to a more assertive style of foreign policy and as part of a larger design aimed at bolstering the prime minister's image both at home and abroad. At the same time, this personal diplomacy enables Italy to maintain a higher international profile even while remaining aloof from renewed efforts by Paris and Berlin to relaunch their European dialogue and to strengthen and intensify their cooperation.

Examples of this strategy can be found in the readiness displayed by the Italian government to align the country with almost every initiative taken by the United States even before the shock of September 11. As early as March 2001, when the new US administration signaled its interest in the accelerated creation of an anti-missile system, Italy was one of the European countries to display interest in the project regardless of its potentially disruptive implications for arms control. After Berlusconi's election victory in June 2001, support for this US initiative began to grow as the new government's foreign policy gradually took shape. The new defense minister, Antonio Martino, gave a ringing endorsement of the project in the fall of 2001, not only declaring that he fully shared the rationale for the initiative, but adding that, paradoxically, the US proposal "responded more to the defensive needs" of countries like Italy than to those of the United States.[23]

Then came the traumatic shock of 9/11. It was immediately clear that security issues would be afforded a much higher priority in the international system and that among the pivotal regions for the confrontation with terrorism would be the Mediterranean and the Middle East, areas traditionally at the center of Italian foreign policy and interests. This profound change in the international environment ended up reinforcing an existing trend toward Italian cooperation with the United States in foreign policy. After 9/11, the Berlusconi government went to great lengths to demonstrate Italy's readiness to participate in the war against terror: in November 2001, the Italian parliament approved naval participation in Operation Enduring Freedom and shortly afterwards agreed to send ground troops as well. On October 2, 2002, this commitment was significantly increased by a contingent of about 1,000 troops, deployed from March to September 2003, turning Italy into one of the major contributors to the mission in Afghanistan. Italian soldiers were therefore engaged in one of their most dangerous, complicated, and risky missions since the end of World War II.[24]

Later, during the dramatic escalation of the Iraqi crisis, the Italian government showed itself more willing than many of its European counterparts to support the administration of George W. Bush in stepping up the pressure against the regime in Baghdad. By late 2002, Berlusconi underlined his support for US intervention, even if he hastened to add that Italy supported a UN resolution to provide the necessary mandate and international legitimization. In early 2003, Italy helped isolate the Franco-German diplomatic counteroffensive by refusing to be drawn into their maneuver and instead joining seven other countries in signing a letter to the *Wall Street Journal* in support of the policy of the Bush administration. This decision was crucial at least in symbolic terms: had Rome sided with Berlin and Paris, the three largest powers at the core of European integration would have aligned against Washington.

Italy nevertheless found itself in a difficult spot when the United States and its closest allies decided to go to war without a second UN resolution

---

[23] "Missile Defense: A Challenge and an Opportunity for Transatlantic Cooperation," remarks by Admiral Giampaolo Di Paola, Secretary General of Defense and National Armaments Director, Ministry of Defense, Italy Transatlantic Cooperation on Missile Defense, Rome, October 1–2, 2003.

[24] Stato Maggiore della Difesa, *Ufficio Generale del Capo di Stato Maggiore – Ufficio Pubblica Informazione*, "Task Force Nibbio," available at www.difesa.it.

backing their intervention. The Berlusconi government was placed in the embarrassing position of maintaining support for Washington without actually participating in the war, since anti-war rallies were already drawing hundreds of thousands of demonstrators in the streets and squares of Italy. At the same time, however, there was also clear resentment inside Italian diplomatic circles of the Paris–Berlin axis that is perceived – just as Ducci perceived de Gaulle's initiatives in 1963 – as having little to do with real European integration and much to do with old-fashioned power politics. The *bon mot* that began circulating within the ranks of Italian diplomats was to call the Chirac–Schröder declaration an example of "Franco-German unilateralism," throwing back at the two European partners their condemnation of the Bush administration. Later, when the war was over, Italy quickly decided to send in its troops to do what they are best at: peace-keeping. In doing so, Rome chose to support Washington in the rebuilding of war-torn Iraqi society. Neither the large-scale attacks on the Italian base at Nassiriya, resulting in a high number of casualties, nor the kidnapping and cruel slaughter of hostages have so far (as of July 2004) deterred the government from keeping Italian soldiers in Iraq, and the Berlusconi government seems likely to retain its American orientation.

Continuity or change?

Does Berlusconi's pro-American foreign policy represent a critical break with Italian foreign policy tradition? Yes and no. Today's positive Atlantic predisposition, even if its tone is distinctive, actually represents the continuation of an important element of Italy's overall postwar foreign policy. On the other hand, downgrading the European pillar of Italian foreign policy represents a more conspicuous shift from times past. What is striking is not the Berlusconi government's support for the Bush administration, but its failure to balance that support with the customary enthusiasm for deeper European integration.

Hints that the Berlusconi team would be less committed to Europeanism than previous governments were already perceptible from its earliest steps, with the initial refusal to support the European arrest warrant and the development of the A400 transport aircraft. After the resignation of Foreign Minister Renato Ruggiero, however, the trend became clearer. Ruggiero had been appointed to reassure those who suspected an anti-European drift in the government, and his resignation reinforced those suspicions. At the very least, there has been a clear shift from the previous identification of Italy's European policy with the federalist approach to evident support for the intergovernmental one. This is mostly due to the composition of the government. Of the four major forces that support it, one (Alleanza Nazionale) has never made a secret of its Gaullist sympathies and of its disdain for federalism; two others (Forza Italia and La Lega Nord) are anti-government, anti-regulation parties (the latter often with demagogic, populist overtones) that despise laws whether they come from Rome or Brussels. This leaves only the heirs of the old Christian Democrats (the Catholic UDC, or Union of Christian Democrats) to keep alive a very feeble federalist flame inside the government. To this is added the impact of generational change: with memories of World War II fading into the past, the new ruling class has little or no understanding of the idealistic roots of the European project and is less inclined to support it than were its predecessors. This has resulted in a more practical, business-like approach to European integration.

This is not to say that Italy has totally neglected the European dimension of its foreign policy. It has not, if only because it held the presidency of the EU when many expected the member states to approve the Constitutional Treaty drafted in the previous months by the Giscard convention. Italy also demonstrated, in particular by the active participation of its military in these initiatives, a continuous interest in building up a European Rapid Reaction Force as well as in the broader process of constructing a European Security and Defence Policy. Yet there is clearly a difference in intensity between the government's European and American policies, and this change in attitude toward European matters seems to have affected the Italian capacity to maneuver between Paris and Washington. It is in Europe, after all, that Rome can reap the possible benefits of pro-American alignment, and this is why previous Italian governments always took pains to avoid deepening the chasm between the Atlantic and the European pillars of their foreign policy.

Even in the crisis over Iraq, Italy supported couching any US action in a UN framework, thus avoiding an open clash within the Atlantic alliance. When push came to shove, however, Berlusconi clearly sided with Washington, and previous difficulties with Berlin and Paris returned to the fore. Isolated from its European partners, however, Italy has nowhere to go and few benefits to reap if and when Paris and Berlin decide to mend fences with Washington and London, as seemed to be happening on the Normandy beaches on the sixtieth anniversary of the landing.[25] Playing

---

[25] Giuseppe Sacco, "Tra Europa e mare aperto: un'agenda per il nostro governo" ["Between Europe and the Deep Blue Sea: An Agenda for Our Government"], *Limes* 5 (2002), pp. 75–86.

the American card, in other words, requires a degree of attention to the European dimension that the Berlusconi government, in its often over-stated support of all things American, has neglected.

A second element of change in the wider context of Italian foreign policy is the Berlusconi government's approach to Mediterranean and Middle Eastern issues. Before the Six Day War, the tradition of Italian foreign policy was to keep a balanced attitude between Israel and the Arab countries. Since then, Italian diplomacy has worked for a solution to the dispute by trying to cultivate the moderate Arab leaders, helping to turn Arafat and the PLO into respectable partners that would support the peace process. Even at the tensest moments of its relations with the Arab world (and there have been some tense moments indeed), the Italian inclination was to mediate rather than take an outspoken position; no Italian government has ever taken such an openly pro-Israeli stance as the current one has. True, some parties inside the government (such as Alleanza Nazionale) had to atone for their fascist past, and particularly the racial laws of 1938–9; but this is not enough to explain their support of the policies carried out by the Sharon government in the past few years. Such a shift in Italian foreign policy can be explained mostly by the desire to ally Italy as strongly as possible with Washington in the very region that in the past, for example in the mid-1980s, had been the source of the most serious misunderstandings between Italy and the United States. This pattern is repeated in Berlusconi's surprising declaration about the possibility of bringing Turkey and even Israel inside the EU.

Still, much of the perceived shift under Berlusconi may perhaps be a change in style and tone more than in substance. This has less to do with foreign policy than with the general style of Berlusconi as a leader: in order to survive in the domestic context, his coalition must constantly inflame the political debate and use provocative tones to create tensions in the opposition and, by keeping it under pressure, render it incapable of debating the issues. By framing the debate over Iraq or over US foreign policy more generally in highly ideological terms, the Berlusconi govern-ment is keeping the opposition at bay while at the same time providing a rallying point for its own forces.

By placing the foreign policy of the Berlusconi government in the general context of the history of US–Italian relations over the past forty years, elements of continuity seem to prevail, even if some conspicuous alterations have taken place. In particular, it is remarkable that two governments – those of D'Alema and Berlusconi – that had very little else in common felt it necessary to side with the United States on such controversial issues as Kosovo and Iraq. These episodes reveal an almost structural inclination to keep looking to Washington with the same intensity with which most Italian political forces also look over the Alps or across the Mediterranean. This in turn suggests that, at least for the foreseeable future, the richest and farthest master is likely to keep playing a major role in Italian foreign policy, much as it has for the past fifty years.

Part III

Prospects for the Alliance

9   The Iraq crisis and the future of the Western alliance

Marc Trachtenberg

In January 1963, Konrad Adenauer, the chancellor of the Federal Republic of Germany, came to Paris to sign a treaty of friendship with France. This was an event of considerable political importance. The German government, it seemed, had decided to form a kind of bloc with the France of President Charles de Gaulle, a country which for some time had been pursuing a policy with a distinct anti-American edge. Indeed, just one week before Adenauer's visit, de Gaulle had risen up against the United States. He had announced that France was going to veto Britain's entry into the European Common Market. If the British were allowed in, de Gaulle argued, continental Europe would eventually be absorbed into a "colossal Atlantic Community, dependent on America and under American control," and this France would not permit.[1] The German government seemed to share de Gaulle's sentiments. How else could its willingness to sign a treaty with France at that particular point possibly be interpreted?

The Americans were enraged by what France and Germany had done, and the Kennedy administration, then in power, decided to take a very hard line. The Europeans, President Kennedy felt, could not be expected to pursue a pro-American policy simply because of what the United States had done for them in previous years. "We have been very generous to Europe," he told the National Security Council on January 22, 1963, "and it is now time for us to look out for ourselves, knowing full well that the Europeans will not do anything for us simply because we have in the past helped them."[2] They would come around, in his view, only if the most intense pressure were brought to bear. The United States would

---

A more fully footnoted version of this article, with direct links to the text of many of the sources cited, is available online (http://www.polisci.ucla.edu/faculty/trachtenberg/useur/iraqcrisis.html).

[1] Press conference of January 14, 1963, in Charles de Gaulle, *Discours and messages*, vol. IV (Paris: Plon, 1986), p. 69.

[2] Notes on remarks by President Kennedy before the National Security Council, January 22, 1963, US Department of State, *Foreign Relations of the United States* [*FRUS* hereafter], 1961–1963 series, vol. 13, p. 486.

threaten to pull its military forces out of Europe. The Europeans would be forced to make a choice. It would be made clear to them that they could not have it both ways. If they wanted to be fully independent politically, they would also have to be fully independent militarily – that is, they would have to provide for their own defense.

Kennedy had made the same point a few months earlier in a meeting with the famous writer André Malraux, French minister of culture and a de Gaulle confidant. "A Europe beyond our influence – yet counting on us – in which we should have to bear the burden of defense without the power to affect events" – this, the president thought, just could not be.[3] De Gaulle, he warned, "should make no mistake: Americans would be glad to get out of Europe."[4] And this, it should be noted, was no idle threat. The United States, in Kennedy's view, did not need Europe. As he told his top advisors on January 25, 1963, "we can take care of ourselves and are not dependent upon European support."[5]

West Germany, exposed to Soviet power as it was, was the primary target of this policy. "There is not much we can do about France," Kennedy said, "but we can exert considerable pressure on the Germans."[6] And that pressure could be exerted in one and only one way. "The threat of withdrawing our troops," the president thought, "was about the only sanction we had."[7] It was made abundantly clear to the Germans that, if they wanted American military protection, they could not pursue an "independent," Gaullist, anti-American policy. Those warnings had the desired effect. Forced to choose, the Germans in 1963 chose the United States.[8]

In January 2003, another German chancellor, Gerhard Schröder, met in Paris with another French president, Jacques Chirac. The two men had come together to celebrate the fortieth anniversary of the Franco-German Elysée Treaty, but they took advantage of the occasion to adopt a common position on the most important foreign policy issue of the day, the question of a possible war on Iraq.

For months, it had been clear that the United States had been heading toward war with that country. US policy had been laid out, for example, in a major speech Vice President Dick Cheney gave on August 26, 2002.

---

[3] Kennedy–Malraux meeting, May 11, 1962, *FRUS* 1961–1963, vol. 13, p. 696.
[4] *Ibid.*
[5] NSC Executive Committee meeting, January 25, 1963, *FRUS* 1961–1963, vol. 13, p. 490.
[6] *Ibid*, p. 489.
[7] NSC Executive Committee meeting, February 5, 1963, *FRUS* 1961–1963, vol. 13, p. 178.
[8] For a fuller account of this story, see Marc Trachtenberg, *A Constructed Peace: The Making of the European Settlement, 1945–1963* (Princeton: Princeton University Press, 1999), pp. 303, 369–379.

For Cheney – and there was no doubt that he was speaking for the president – the Iraqi threat was growing, and it was important to deal with it sooner rather than later. The Iraqi dictator, Saddam Hussein, had "systematically broken" all the agreements he had entered into at the end of the Gulf War in 1991. He had promised at that time that Iraq's nuclear, biological, and chemical weapons would be destroyed, and an inspection regime had been set up to make sure that those promises were honored. But work on those forbidden weapons had continued. Iraq had "devised an elaborate program" to keep the inspectors in the dark. The inspection regime had thus not been able to guarantee that Iraq's weapons of mass destruction (WMD) programs had been shut down permanently. Given the nature of the threat, it was vitally important, Cheney said, to take action before it was too late.[9] And this, one should note, was not just the view of a right-wing clique that had somehow managed to hijack government policy. A number of key senators and respected elder statesmen (including former secretaries of state Henry Kissinger, George Shultz, and James Baker) took basically the same general line.[10]

This was the policy that first Germany and then France came to oppose, and to oppose in a very direct and public way. Chancellor Schröder, in the heat of an electoral campaign, made it clear by the beginning of September 2002 that he was against a war with Iraq no matter what. He would oppose war even if the UN Security Council authorized a military operation.[11] German opinion was heavily anti-war, and it seemed that Schröder had decided to try to win what was by all accounts a close election "by running against America."[12]

The French position at that time was more ambiguous. In September 2002, it seemed that the French government might be willing eventually to approve the use of force if Iraq were given one last chance to come clean about its weapons programs and to destroy whatever forbidden weapons it still had. The US government had decided, after a serious internal debate, to try to work through the United Nations, and the French

---

[9] Remarks by the Vice President to the Veterans of Foreign Wars 103rd National Convention, August 26, 2002, http://www.whitehouse.gov/news/releases/2002/08/20020826.html.

[10] See especially Henry Kissinger, "The Politics of Intervention: Iraq 'Regime Change' Is a Revolutionary Strategy," *Los Angeles Times*, August 9, 2002; George Shultz, "Act Now," *Washington Post*, September 6, 2002; James A. Baker, "The Right Way to Change Iraq's Regime," *International Herald Tribune*, August 26, 2002.

[11] Steven Erlanger, "German Leader's Warning: War Plan Is a Huge Mistake," *New York Times*, September 5, 2002.

[12] Steven Erlanger, "For Now, Trading Allies for Votes," *New York Times*, September 14, 2002, and Peter Finn, "Ruling Coalition Wins Narrowly in German Vote: Strong Anti-War Stance Helps Schroeder Defeat Conservatives," *Washington Post*, September 23, 2002.

foreign minister, Dominique de Villepin, had proposed a possible course of action. At a lunch with Secretary of State Colin Powell, de Villepin "floated the idea of having two resolutions," one that would demand that Iraq disarm, to be followed by a second authorizing military action if Iraq failed to comply. "Be sure about one thing," Powell told his French colleague. "Don't vote for the first, unless you are prepared to vote for the second." And "Villepin assented, officials who were there said."[13]

A resolution was adopted and the Iraqis allowed the UN inspectors, who had left in 1998, to come back in. But, as Chirac himself would admit, Iraq was not "sufficiently cooperative."[14] For the French, however, this did not mean that the time for military action had come. Instead, the Chirac government dug in its heels. Its opposition to American policy hardened. In January, when Chirac and Schröder met in Paris, France basically aligned its policy with that of Germany: the two countries had come together to oppose the United States.[15]

Their efforts focused on the UN Security Council. The basic tactic was to insist that the use of force against Iraq would be legal only if the Security Council gave its consent, and at the same time to do what they could to make sure the Security Council would not authorize US action, not for quite some time at any rate. In that way, a US military operation would come across as illegitimate; the hope was that, rather than engage in what would be branded an illegal use of force, the Americans would back down and war would be avoided. So for six weeks after the Paris meetings, according to one of the best-informed discussions of this affair, Chirac and Schröder "worked the phones, visited foreign capitals and called in diplomatic chits. Their goal: nothing less than the reining in of what they saw as a rogue superpower. The German ambassador to the UN boasted in one confidential e-mail to colleagues at his foreign ministry that their strategy was to isolate the US and make it 'repentantly come back to the [UN Security] Council,' seeking compromise."[16]

---

[13] Steven Weisman, "A Long, Winding Road to a Diplomatic Dead End," *New York Times*, March 17, 2003, and Marc Champion, Charles Fleming, Ian Johnson, and Carla Anne Robbins, "Allies at Odds: Behind US Rift With Europeans. Slights and Politics: Schröder and Chirac Discover How Popular Tweaking a Superpower Can Be," *Wall Street Journal*, March 27, 2003. These two articles are the best descriptions of this story that have appeared so far.

[14] Chirac interview with TF1 and France 2, March 10, 2003, http://www.diplomatie.gouv.fr/actu/bulletin.gb.asp ?liste=20030311.gb.html.

[15] Luc de Barochez, "Jacques Chirac and Gerhard Schröder se prononcent pour un règlement pacifique: front franco-allemand sur la crise irakienne," *Le Figaro*, January 23, 2003. See also the text of the joint Chirac–Schröder press conference and joint television interview, both of January 22, 2003.

[16] Champion et al., "Allies at Odds."

It was clear that what was at stake was of absolutely fundamental importance. For the German foreign minister, Joschka Fischer, what was at issue was nothing less than the "question of a new world order after the end of the Cold War."[17] And many Europeans opposed the idea of an American-dominated world order – an order which they saw as based on the strength and will of a single extraordinarily powerful country. In their view – and one comes across countless articles in the European, and especially the French, press based on premises of this sort – the USA was a lawless state, an arrogant, overbearing, presumptuous power, a country that no longer felt any obligation to play by the rules, a country that relied on brute force to get what it wanted. And in this view, Europe, in standing up to the United States, was championing a very different kind of policy. Europe was standing up for law and for justice, for a "multipolar world," a more balanced world, a world in which there were limits to what any single country could do.

US leaders obviously did not view things the same way. From their point of view, the whole idea of an Iraq armed with weapons of mass destruction, especially nuclear weapons, was intolerable. They took it for granted that the threat of force, or perhaps even the actual use of force, was the one thing that might prevent Iraq from moving ahead with its weapons program. But the German government wanted to rule out the use of force no matter what. "In the twenty-first century," Foreign Minister Fischer said, "you can't use war to force disarmament."[18] And the French, especially after January, seemed to take much the same line. "War," President Chirac said over and over again, "is always the worst of solutions."[19] For the US government, which was inclined to view a nuclear-armed Iraq as the "worst of solutions," the Germans and even the French had apparently opted for what was in the final analysis a policy of appeasement. And many Americans deeply resented both the sort of anti-US rhetoric coming out of Europe and the sort of policy the French and German governments were pursuing, especially from January 2003 on. The Bush administration was particularly angry with the French for (in its view) having led the United States down the garden path. The French government, it felt, had essentially reneged on the deal de Villepin and Powell had worked out in September: a "senior administration

[17] Quoted in "More Europe," *Der Spiegel*, March 31, 2003.
[18] Fischer interview with *Stern* magazine, March 5, 2003.
[19] See, for example, Chirac and Schröder interview with Olivier Mazerolle and Ulrich Wickert, January 22, 2003, and Chirac–Schröder joint press conference, January 22, 2003.

official" later told reporters that the diplomatic process "had been going well" until "France stabbed the United States in the back."[20]

On the surface, the crisis seemed to blow over fairly quickly. US leaders threatened that the French would pay a price for their behavior, but it soon became clear that they had only trivial reprisals in mind. Chirac had warned the east Europeans that their support for the United States during the crisis would "reduce their chances" of entering the European Union.[21] But the Americans at no point warned France and Germany that their actions were putting their alliance with the United States at risk. For Kennedy in 1963, the threat to withdraw the American troops from Europe, and thus effectively to end the alliance, was the only real sanction the Americans had. But forty years later, the Bush administration made no such threat. The Americans, in fact, were soon stressing their continuing commitment to the NATO system, and indeed soon both sides were more or less trying to sweep all the problems that had emerged under the rug.[22]

My basic premise here is that this is not a healthy way of dealing with the issue. I think that some basic questions that emerged during the crisis need to be discussed openly and seriously. So instead of focusing on the question of how US policy in the run-up to the Iraq War is to be assessed, or how the policies of the various allied governments are to be judged, I want to try to analyze some of the fundamental issues that this episode brought to the surface. How much of a problem, first of all, would the development of a mass destruction capability by a regime like that of Iraq in 2002 have actually posed? Aren't nuclear weapons, and their biological and perhaps chemical equivalents, essentially unusable, when both sides in a conflict are armed with them? Wouldn't the development of an Iraqi nuclear capability have led to mutual deterrence and thus to a relatively stable strategic relationship? To the extent that an Iraqi capability of this sort would have posed serious problems, couldn't the Iraqis have been prevented permanently from developing such forces through nonmilitary

[20] David Sanger, "Bush Links Europe's Ban on Bio-Crops with Hunger," *New York Times*, May 22, 2003. See also Alexandra Stanley, "Two Disciples Spread Word: The End is Near," *New York Times*, March 17, 2003; Elisabeth Bumiller, "US, Angry at French Stance on War, Considers Punishment," *New York Times*, April 24, 2003; Elaine Sciolino, "France Works to Limit Damage from US Anger," *New York Times*, April 25, 2003; and especially Weisman, "Long, Winding Road," and Champion et al., "Allies at Odds."

[21] Chirac's remarks were widely reported in the press. See, for example, Ian Black, "Threat of War: Furious Chirac Hits Out at 'Infantile' Easterners," *Guardian* (London), February 18, 2003. For the remarks themselves, see Chirac press conference, February 17, 2003, http://www.elysee.fr/cgi-bin/auracom/aurweb/search/file?aur_file=discours/2003/CP030217.html.

[22] James Dao, "Powell Says to the French, Yes … But Not All Is Forgiven," *New York Times*, May 23, 2003.

means? Couldn't an inspection regime have done the trick? And if the control regime wasn't up to the job, would it be legitimate for a country to act essentially on its own, without first getting explicit UN Security Council authorization? Was unilateral action impermissible under international law, and is a country that dealt with the problem in that way to be branded a law-breaker? These are not the only important issues that need to be dealt with, but they are important enough, and they are the ones I want to focus on here.

The question of deterrence

There is no question, in my mind at any rate, that the weapons of mass destruction issue – not so much what the Iraqis actually had, but what they were in all probability going to have if no action were taken – lay at the heart of the Iraq crisis.[23] The US government would have been willing to live with the Saddam Hussein regime if it had not thought that this regime had active nuclear, biological, and chemical weapons programs. Even the claim that Iraq had various ties with terrorist groups would not in itself have warranted military action if it had been clear that the regime had honored its commitments and had abandoned all programs for the production of forbidden weapons.[24] And although no such weapons were found in Iraq in the postwar period, and although in all probability none will ever be found, it does not follow from that that the Bush administration's concern with this issue was artificially trumped up to rationalize a policy

[23] To be sure, this view is not universally accepted. In France, for example, a March 2003 poll showed that only 3 percent of those questioned thought the main motivation of the United States for going to war was to "disarm Iraq"; 49 percent thought it was to "take control of Iraq's petroleum resources" (http://www.ifop.com/europe/sondages/opinionf/ jgtirak.asp). Indeed, many people have claimed, especially after no such weapons were actually found in Iraq, that the argument about Iraqi weapons of mass destruction was artificially trumped up, to serve as a pretext for a war that the Bush administration wanted to conduct for other reasons. But the fact that an assessment turned out to be mistaken is no proof that it was simply fabricated, and there are many reasons why the argument that the Bush administration was lying on this matter is simply implausible. Henry Kissinger, for example, made one key point in a September 2003 interview: "I attended many closed hearings in Washington, and it is impossible to imagine that representatives of the US administration constantly lied to each other at such hearings when they were talking about Iraqi weapons of mass destruction" (Y. Verlin and D. Suslov, "Henry Kissinger: Iraq Is an Exception, Not the Rule," *Nezavisimaya Gazeta*, September 17, 2003). For the basic point that the "US intelligence community's belief that Saddam was aggressively pursuing weapons of mass destruction pre-dated Bush's inauguration, and therefore cannot be attributed to political pressure," see Kenneth Pollack's important article, "Spies, Lies, and Weapons: What Went Wrong," *Atlantic Monthly*, January–February 2004, pp. 78–92.

[24] See, for example, Kenneth Pollack, *The Threatening Storm: The Case for Invading Iraq* (New York: Random House, 2002), pp. xxii, 153–158.

of "regime change" that had an entirely different basis. The fear was real; even the German and French authorities believed that Iraq had active programs for the development of those prohibited weapons. In early 2002, August Hanning, the head of the German equivalent of the CIA, the BND, said that his agency thought that the Iraqis would "have an atomic bomb in three years."[25] In February 2003, Hanning and other BND officials reportedly told a Bundestag committee that they "believed Iraq had mobile laboratories capable of developing and producing chemical and biological weapons."[26] And in a March 10, 2003, interview, President Chirac himself referred to an "Iraq which obviously possessed weapons of mass destruction, which were in the hands of an indisputably dangerous regime and consequently posed a definite threat to the world."[27] Indeed, the most reasonable inference to be drawn from the story of the UN inspection system in the 1990s was that Iraq was determined to move ahead in this area – to do whatever it could get away with. The control regime, of course, had kept it from moving ahead as quickly as it would have liked, but as that regime unraveled, it seemed that nothing would stop it from going ahead with those programs.

But would it have mattered all that much if Iraq had been able to build even a strong nuclear force? Wouldn't the US government have been able to deter the Iraqis from ever actually using those weapons against American targets or against any of their neighbors? If so, why would an Iraqi nuclear capability have posed a problem? If nuclear weapons are good only for defensive purposes, then why shouldn't countries be allowed to acquire them (or their equivalents)?

In the United States, the most serious criticism of US policy in the crisis turned on this one absolutely fundamental point: that is, on the argument that nuclear weapons cannot be used for coercive purposes – on the idea that in a conflict neither the Iraqis nor their adversaries would have dared to use their nuclear weapons against each other. Indeed, the claim is that they would not even have dared to use nonnuclear forces in a major way. The use of force would have been too risky, given the nature of the weaponry both sides had. If Iraq had acquired nuclear weapons,

---

[25] Quoted in Jeffrey Goldberg, "The Great Terror," *New Yorker*, March 25, 2002 (toward the end of the article). Note also the evidence from non-US sources cited in Julian Borger, "Saddam 'Will Have Nuclear Weapons Material by 2005,'" *Guardian* (London), August 1, 2002. Richard Butler, the former UN chief weapons inspector, was quoted there as saying that "there is now evidence that Saddam has reinvigorated his nuclear weapons programme in the inspection-free years."

[26] Article in the German weekly *Focus* quoted in Agence France Presse report, February 2, 2003. See also "What Now, Mr. President?," cover story, *Der Spiegel*, February 17, 2003.

[27] Chirac interview with TF1 and France 2 (excerpts), March 10, 2003, http://www.diplomatie.gouv.fr/actu/bulletin.gb.asp?liste=20030311.gb.html.

the prospect of nuclear escalation, this argument runs, would have led to a stable peace, just as it (supposedly) had during the Cold War.

A number of leading American international relations scholars argue along these lines, but I think they're wrong.[28] If Iraq had developed a nuclear capability, it could, I think, have readily been used for coercive purposes. It could easily have been made clear to the Americans – not by making a direct threat, but (in order to reduce the risk of retaliation) in the guise of a simple prediction – that a continuing American presence in the Gulf, for example, would have led to continuing terrorist attacks against the United States. It is often assumed, of course, that Iraq could never have implemented such a strategy, because the United States could have made it clear that any such attack would have led to a devastating counterattack: Iraq would essentially have been wiped out if anything of that sort had been attempted. And administration officials have repeatedly warned that the use of massive countercivilian weapons against the United States would lead to extremely harsh retaliation. In an article published during the 2000 presidential campaign, for example, Condoleezza Rice, later President Bush's national security advisor, wrote that if countries like Iraq and North Korea acquired weapons of mass destruction, those weapons would be "unusable, because any attempt to use them will bring national obliteration."[29] But if top officials honestly believed that they were truly unusable, the US government could have looked on calmly as such states acquired those kinds of capabilities. The fact that it was willing to go to extraordinary lengths to prevent a country like Iraq from being able to build forces of that sort shows that it understood that a massive counterattack would not be automatic, and that the deterrent effect is therefore far from absolute.

And why is it less than absolute? Suppose the Iraqis developed a nuclear arsenal and adopted a coercive strategy of the sort I just described, and suppose the United States did not accede to whatever demands the Iraqis put forward. And then suppose a bomb or two were exploded on American soil. How then would the US government respond? Would it simply destroy Iraq, even if there were no proof the Iraqi government was behind the attacks? Presumably if the United States

---

[28] The most important example is the argument Kenneth Waltz develops in the chapters he wrote in a book jointly authored with Scott Sagan, *The Spread of Nuclear Weapons: A Debate Renewed* (New York: Norton, 2003). For a critique, see the review I wrote of this book, "Waltzing Toward Armageddon," published in *The National Interest* (Fall 2002), pp. 144–152; a better version of that review is available online, http://www.polisci.ucla.edu/faculty/trachtenberg/cv/prolif.doc.

[29] Quoted in "Serving Notice of a New America That Is Poised to Strike First and Alone," *New York Times*, January 27, 2003.

were attacked in this way, the Iraqis would have gone to great lengths to conceal their responsibility. *Direct* threats would not have been issued, and the operation would have been conducted clandestinely, perhaps with a foreign terrorist organization serving as a vehicle of attack. The Americans would have their suspicions, but in the absence of evidence it might be very hard to hold the Iraqis accountable – at any rate in a way that would warrant the destruction of their whole country. Even if the preponderance of evidence strongly suggested that the Iraqis were responsible, it is by no means certain that the US government would retaliate by killing millions of Iraqi civilians – innocent by its own reckoning – above all if it believed that such an attack would have led to additional Iraqi counterattacks against the United States or its allies. Would more limited operations – for example, a conventional attack aimed at the overthrow of the Iraqi government – be possible in such a case? If the Iraqis had any nuclear weapons at all, the United States might be very reluctant to launch an attack against a regime whose back was against the wall. Given all these considerations, it would not be absurd or irrational for Iraq to judge that the risks were limited and thus to opt for a coercive strategy. And indeed there is a good chance that such a strategy, if adopted, would have the desired effect. The Americans, anticipating the problems they would face, might give way and allow themselves to be pushed out of the Gulf, or indeed out of the Middle East as a whole. But there would also be a certain probability, in such circumstances, that these devastating weapons would actually have been used, by one or both sides.

All of this may sound somewhat speculative, but it is important to note that the US government was actually concerned with problems of this sort. Indeed, one of the main reasons why nuclear proliferation was thought to be a problem had to do with the fact that it was understood that even small nuclear arsenals could be used to support a coercive policy. Thomas Schelling, for example, in a top-secret report written for the US government in 1962, had considered the possibility of "extortionate use" by countries with small nuclear arsenals. He noted that countries might profitably adopt a policy of exploiting that kind of threat; and he thought in particular that the "strategy of anonymous attack" needed to be examined.[30]

The same sort of concern (but focusing on the threat posed by biological and not nuclear weapons) surfaced during the Gulf crisis in 1990. The CIA at that time warned that it could not "rule out that Iraq may have

---

[30] Schelling Study Group Report, "Report on Strategic Developments over the Next Decade for the Inter-Agency Panel," October 12, 1962, pp. 51–55 (pp. 54–55 for the quotations), in National Security Files, box 376, John F. Kennedy Library, Boston.

contingency plans to use biological weapons covertly." Iraq, it thought, "could attack targets out of range of even its missiles by using special forces, civilian government agents, or foreign terrorists to hand-deliver biological or chemical agents clandestinely."[31] The point about clandestine attack came up again in 2002 as the Iraq problem again began to heat up. Secretary of Defense Donald Rumsfeld, for example, told a congressional committee that the United States needed to be concerned about the threat posed by Iraqi biological weapons (BW). Such weapons, he said, were "simpler to deliver" than nuclear weapons, and could readily be "transferred to terrorist networks, who could allow Iraq to deliver them without Iraq's fingerprints."[32] Charles Duelfer, formerly deputy head of UNSCOM, the UN inspection organization for Iraq, and an acknowledged expert in this area, had made the same kind of point in congressional testimony earlier that year. "BW," he said, "is the most difficult present threat posed by Iraq. They certainly have the capacity to deploy it clandestinely or through surrogates should the regime so decide."[33] In fact, before the Gulf War the Iraqis had themselves suggested that Arab terrorists in the West could serve as instruments of attack.[34]

So the problems an Iraqi nuclear capability would have posed were very real, especially in a world where large-scale terrorism was a fact of life.

Inspections: a viable solution?

The prevailing view in the United States during the Iraq crisis was that Saddam Hussein had to be prevented from acquiring a nuclear capability or its equivalent. Many Europeans were also disturbed by the prospect of nuclear or even biological weapons in the hands of the Iraqi dictator. And those attitudes were by no means absurd. But it was one thing to recognize that a serious problem existed and would have to be dealt with, and quite another to say that an invasion of Iraq was the only solution. And indeed those who opposed military action generally argued that a peaceful solution was within reach, and that an inspection regime was a viable alternative to war.

---

[31] Avigdor Haselkorn, *The Continuing Storm: Iraq, Poisonous Weapons, and Deterrence* (New Haven: Yale University Press, 1999), p. 68.

[32] Donald Rumsfeld, testimony before House Armed Services Committee, September 18, 2002, http://www.defenselink.mil/speeches/2002/s20020918-secdef2.html.

[33] Charles Duelfer, "Weapons of Mass Destruction Programs in Iraq," testimony before the Subcommittee on Emerging Threats and Capabilities, US Senate Armed Services Committee, February 27, 2002, http://www.senate.gov/~armed_services/statemnt/2002/Duelfer.pdf.

[34] See Haselkorn, *Continuing Storm*, pp. 67–68, and Lawrence Freedman and Efraim Karsh, *The Gulf Conflict, 1990–1991: Diplomacy and War in the New World Order* (Princeton: Princeton University Press, 1993), pp. 52, 344–345.

But does that view really stand up to analysis? If the use of force were ruled out (as the Germans, for example, wanted), why would the Iraqis have complied with an effective inspection regime? And how could inspections have provided any effective guarantee that Iraq no longer had any stockpiles of forbidden weapons, nor any programs for the development of such weapons, when the Iraqi government could easily prevent well-informed Iraqis from talking openly with the inspectors? Perhaps on occasion violations would be uncovered, but if those discoveries had no consequences for the regime beyond the destruction of the forbidden material that had been found, how much of a deterrent effect would the inspection regime actually have?[35] In the view of US specialists, and not just people connected with the Bush administration, "an inspection regime that fails to give us high confidence that it is successfully uncovering and blocking any serious WMD development is worse than no regime at all."[36] If nothing were uncovered, people would say that this proves there was nothing to be found and that further action would therefore be unwarranted. If the inspectors, however, did find something, the Iraqis would destroy it, and that would be the end of it. In such a case, people would say that this again proved that "inspections were working" and that there was therefore no basis for military action. In either case, the effect of the inspection regime would be to shield Iraq and enable it to go ahead with its clandestine weapons programs essentially with impunity.

During the crisis, problems of this sort – the problems related to the forcible disarmament of Iraq – did not receive anything like the attention they deserved. There was not enough attention given on either side of the Atlantic to what might be called the theory of an inspection regime. There was not enough attention given in 2002 to the history of the inspection regime in the 1990s, and to the lessons that might be drawn from that story. Most of the Americans familiar with that story had come to the conclusion that inspections had not worked.[37] It was important at that point to try to understand why they had failed; it was important in that

---

[35] See Robert Gallucci's discussion of the inspection regime as it actually functioned during the UNSCOM period. The basic rule was, he points out, "if you find it, you get to destroy it; if you don't destroy it, we get to keep it" (quoted in Jean Krasno and James Sutterlin, *The United Nations and Iraq: Defanging the Viper* [Westport, CT: Praeger, 2003]), p. 80. Gallucci was deputy executive director of UNSCOM, and is currently dean of the School of Foreign Service at Georgetown University.

[36] Robert Gallucci testimony, 107th Congress, 2nd session, US Senate Foreign Relations Committee, "Hearings to Examine Threats, Consequences and Regional Considerations Surrounding Iraq," July 31, 2002, p. 66, http://frwebgate.access.gpo.gov/cgi-bin/getdoc.cgi ?dbname=107_senate_hearingsamp;docid=f:81697.pdf.

[37] See, especially, Charles Duelfer, "The Inevitable Failure of Inspections in Iraq," *Arms Control Today* 32:7 (September 2002).

context to try to deal with the question of how a new inspection regime could possibly succeed. But the US government did not push the issue: it did not push the advocates of inspections onto the defensive, by demanding to know how the new regime that was proposed would overcome the problems that had led to the failure of the old regime. And, in Europe, there was no great interest in examining the issue carefully: if an inspection regime was the alternative to war, what point was there to questioning the viability of such a regime?

So the issue was not dealt with seriously by either side, and the American government, in particular, did not handle this question very skillfully. But the fact that it did not make its case very effectively did not prevent many Americans close to these issues from sensing the problems with the notion that one could deal with the situation by reestablishing an inspection regime. For one thing, they viewed it as odd, to say the least, that the French, who had done their best to weaken the control regime in the 1990s, were now presenting themselves as the champions of inspections.[38] And in Europe, although people rarely went into these issues in great depth, it was widely believed that the Americans were much too quick to give up on inspections. But this is the sort of issue that can be analyzed in a relatively sober way. And to do that, one of the main things we need is a serious political history of the control issue – that is, inspections plus sanctions – from 1991 to 2003, preferably based in large part on captured Iraqi documents. The war may be over, but how Europeans and Americans feel about each other might depend to a certain extent on how issues of this sort are resolved, and one can at least try to think these issues through in the light of the empirical evidence.

The United States and international law

One of the most serious charges leveled against the United States in the European press, and indeed by some European governments, was that the American government was not acting in accordance with international law. Those charges were echoed by an important body of American opinion; many international law scholars, in particular, saw things in much the same way. The standard argument was that, largely as a result of the United States' own efforts, a legal system had come into being at

---

[38] For the US view on this point, see especially Fareed Zakaria, "Message to the Foot-Draggers," *Washington Post*, September 24, 2002: "The dust from the Persian Gulf War had not settled when the French government began a quiet but persistent campaign to gut the sanctions against Iraq, turn inspections into a charade and send signals to Saddam Hussein that Paris was ready to do business with him again."

the end of World War II. That system, embodied in the UN Charter and based on the principle of the sovereign equality of all states, had "served as the framework of international relations for the past half century."[39] The UN regime had established real limits on the use of force; international politics had been "legally domesticated"; instead of a world of unconstrained violence, one had a world based at least to some extent on the rule of law – that is, on respect for basic legal principles.[40]

But now it seemed that the Bush administration was determined to take whatever measures it felt were needed to deal with developments which in its view threatened American security, whether those measures were lawful or not. The US government felt free to act "preemptively" – that is, to deal with developing threats through military action well before attacks on the United States were actually mounted.[41] It would not respect the sovereign rights of countries it viewed as hostile to do whatever they wanted on their own territory – not if those countries shielded terrorists, or were developing weapons that might pose a threat to the United States, and especially not if those two threats were combined. And it would feel free to take any necessary action, in the final analysis, on its own: it felt it had the "sovereign right" to move ahead without first getting authorization from the UN Security Council. The United States, in other words, this argument runs, had broken with tradition and had opted for a "strategy of violence" – for a world in which the strong did whatever they wanted, unconstrained by any legal principle whatsoever. The United States had thus broken with the rule of law; the claim was that it was bringing about a lawless, dangerous, and exceptionally violent world.[42]

American policy toward Iraq after September 11 was interpreted in the light of what the Americans were saying about their general strategy. The US government and its supporters had little trouble coming up with a

---

[39] Tom Farer, "Beyond the Charter Frame: Unilateralism or Condominium?," *American Journal of International Law* 96:2 (April 2002), p. 360.

[40] The allusion here is to Jürgen Habermas' reference to the "civilizing achievement of legally domesticating the state of nature among belligerent nations" in an interview published in *The Nation*, December 16, 2002.

[41] For an attempt to place this strategy in historical context, see my article "The Bush Strategy in Historical Perspective," to be published in James J. Wirtz and Jeffrey A. Larsen (eds.), *Nuclear Transformation: The New US Nuclear Doctrine* (New York: Palgrave Macmillan, 2005).

[42] See, for example, Charles Lambroschini, "Le droit ne se divise pas," *Le Figaro*, February 21, 2003. Note also Chancellor Schröder's views, as paraphrased in a cover story, "More Europe," published in *Der Spiegel* on March 31, 2003, and especially the reference there to how "the law of the more powerful has replaced the law." For the views of a very eminent French student of international affairs, see Pierre Hassner, "Le retour aux guerres sans règles," *Les Echos*, October 17, 2002. Hassner makes many of these same points.

legal justification for the United States' Iraq policy. The argument was that the use of force against Iraq, a country which everyone agreed had not fully complied with the obligations it had accepted at the end of the Gulf War in 1991, had been legitimated by a whole series of Security Council resolutions, especially by Resolution 687, the famous "mother of all resolutions."[43] But whether valid or not, in a sense this was a purely technical point. The US decision to launch a military operation was bound to be interpreted in the context of the Bush doctrine. Whatever the technical legal justification, the war on Iraq was publicly justified, and is in fact to be understood, as a "preemptive" war.[44] The US government made it clear during the crisis that it felt (as Secretary of State Powell put it) that the United States had the "sovereign right to take military action against Iraq alone."[45] UN resolution or no UN resolution, the United States felt it had the right to legitimately take action of this sort.

So the real issue here has to do with that basic claim – that is, with the question of the legitimacy under international law of "anticipatory self-defense." And it is important to note that the prevailing, although by no means universal, opinion among even American students of international law is that the Bush administration view is legally untenable, and that under international law, at least as it has existed since 1945, the right of self-defense is very narrowly circumscribed.[46] According to Article 2, paragraph 4, of the UN Charter, all member states are to "refrain in their international relations from the threat or use of force against the territorial integrity or political independence of any state, or in any manner inconsistent with the Purposes of the United Nations." Under the charter, the UN Security Council would alone have the right to authorize the use of force. The one exception, provided for in Article 51 of the charter, was that states would still have the right, both individually

---

[43] See, for example, a speech given by the State Department legal advisor, William Howard Taft IV, to the National Association of Attorneys General on March 20, 2003, http://usinfo.state.gov/regional/nea/iraq/text2003/032129taft.htm.

[44] See especially the text of Vice President Cheney's August 26, 2002, speech, cited n. 9.

[45] Excerpts from Secretary of State Powell's Davos speech of January 26, 2003, published in the *New York Times*, January 27, 2003.

[46] For a strong dissenting argument, see especially the works of Michael J. Glennon: "The Fog of Law: Self-Defense, Inherence, and Incoherence in Article 51 of the United Nations Charter," *Harvard Journal of Law and Public Policy* 25 (Spring 2002), pp. 539–558; Glennon, "Preempting Terrorism: The Case for Anticipatory Self-Defense," *Weekly Standard*, January 28, 2002; and Glennon, *Limits of Law, Prerogatives of Power: Interventionism After Kosovo* (New York: Palgrave Macmillan, 2001). See also Thomas Franck, "Terrorism and the Right of Self-Defense," *American Journal of International Law* 95 (October 2001), pp. 839–843 – a reply to the charge leveled against the United States by a number of mainly German international lawyers that even the US intervention in Afghanistan against al Qaeda was unlawful.

and collectively, to defend themselves against armed attack, pending Security Council action. But that right applied only to the case of actual attack, and not, for example, to a case where attack was merely threatened. The scope for unilateral action was thus evidently very narrow; and with the one exception relating to an actual armed attack, the unilateral use of force, the argument runs, was now legally impermissible, even when what a country honestly saw as its "vital interests" were threatened.[47] A "presumption against self-help," it is said, lay at the heart of the UN system.[48] According to that interpretation, there was in fact not much that a state could do without Security Council sanction, unless it or one of its allies had actually been attacked. "With the right of self-defence in Art. 51 restricted to the case of armed attack," one scholar writes, "and with no further exception to Art. 2(4) allowing for the use of force by the individual State, the exercise of force for the enforcement of a vested right or for the purpose of ending another State's unlawful behaviour is prohibited."[49] Even reprisals were legally permissible only if they did "not involve the use of armed force."[50]

What is to be made of this whole line of argument? To get at that question, we first have to deal with a more fundamental issue: what gives a certain principle, such as the idea that military reprisals are impermissible, the force of law? How do we know that such a principle is legally binding? And those questions in turn are closely related to the general question of how international law is made, since no given principle is legally binding unless it is produced by a process that gives it the force of law. The law, after all, is not just sitting around someplace waiting to be discovered. It has to be created – and created by a process that gives people the sense that the principles that take shape are legally binding. But created by whom? Legal scholars, obviously, do not have the right to actually make the law; the principles they put forward are not legally binding simply because they say they are. And there is no world parliament, no supranational body with recognized legislative power. Even the UN General Assembly does not have the authority under the UN's own charter to actually make law. Nor does the World Court have any lawmaking power. It does not even have the right under its own statute to

[47] See, for example, Louis Henkin, *How Nations Behave: Law and Foreign Policy*, 2nd edition (New York: Columbia University Press, 1979), pp. 137, 141, 155.

[48] Ian Brownlie, *International Law and the Use of Force by States* (New York: Oxford University Press, 1963), p. 268.

[49] Bruno Simma (ed.), *The Charter of the United Nations: A Commentary*, 2 vols., 2nd edition (New York: Oxford University Press, 2002), vol. I, p. 794.

[50] Ibid.

issue legally binding interpretations of the law, except when states voluntarily agree to accept its jurisdiction.

How then is international law actually made? The only really plausible answer is that the law is made by the states themselves. "Governments derive their just powers from the consent of the governed," and in this case it is the states who are the governed, and it is they themselves who in one way or another decide on the principles they are to be governed by. It is not as though the governments of the world have had the basic principles of international law handed down to them. It is the states themselves who establish international law, by accepting in practice various principles that constrain their behavior, and especially by agreeing to treaties that define what those principles are. "International law," as the famous legal scholar Lasso Oppenheim pointed out long ago, "is a law not above but between states."[51] As a result, the community of states has to accept a given principle as law for that principle to be legally binding. Some scholars go even further. "Each nation," Hans Morgenthau, for example, says, "is bound only by those rules of international law to which it has consented."[52] And this is not just a view that only the most hardened realist theorists hold. Even someone like Louis Henkin, whose thinking was by no means rooted in the realist tradition, made essentially the same point. "In principle," he wrote, "new law, at least, cannot be imposed on any state; even old law cannot survive if enough states, or a few powerful and influential ones, reject it."[53]

It is in this context that the basic texts – above all, the UN Charter – that define the international legal order need to be interpreted. If the charter is to be taken seriously, the governments that drafted it would have had to be serious about bringing a new legal regime into being. It follows that to see what new law was really being created, one has to understand what new obligations governments at the time thought they were taking on. When they agreed to the charter, what did the founders of the United Nations think they were doing? What sorts of constraints – that is, new constraints – did they think the UN Charter would impose on their future behavior? Did they really believe that the use of force, unless it was explicitly authorized by the Security Council, would no longer be legally permissible, except in the event a state was responding to an actual armed attack on itself or an ally?

---

[51] Lasso Oppenheim, "The Science of International Law: Its Task and Method," *American Journal of International Law* 2:2 (April 1908), p. 322; see also pp. 332–333.
[52] Hans Morgenthau, *Politics Among Nations*, 3rd edition (New York: Knopf, 1961), p. 279. Morgenthau himself, one should remember, had begun his career as a student of international law.
[53] Henkin, *How Nations Behave*, p. 23.

The only way to get at the answers is to look at the historical evidence – that is, to look at evidence that throws some real light on the question of what the governments understood the charter to mean when that document was first hammered out. And to understand what they had in mind, it is important not just to look at the record of what was said publicly in the formal discussions at the conferences at which the charter was drafted. If the goal is to understand how people really felt – and not just to understand the line governments were taking in public – it is obviously essential to look at sources that were secret at the time – the records, for example, of key meetings in which responsible officials expressed their views.[54] And the most important readily available source of this sort – most important, because the US government played the leading role in drafting the charter – is the first volume in the US State Department's *Foreign Relations of the United States* series for 1945, the volume dealing with UN affairs.

What the evidence in that volume shows is that the US drafters did not believe that they were giving away very much by accepting the charter. According to John Foster Dulles, then a key member of the delegation to the conference drafting that document, the principle that would eventually become Article 2(4) of the charter gave the United States pretty much a free hand to use force whenever it liked. Under that principle, he pointed out, the member states "pledged to refrain from the use of force in a manner inconsistent with the purposes of the organization. Since the prevention of aggression was a purpose of the organization, action to prevent aggression in the absence of action by the Security Council would be consistent with the purposes of the organization." That meant that there would be no legal constraint on what the United States could do. As Senator Arthur Vandenberg, the leading Republican on the delegation, noted, Dulles' "point reduced itself to the principle that we have the right to do anything we please in self-defense."[55]

Administration representatives saw things much the same way. Leo Pasvolsky, a key State Department official concerned with UN matters, also thought that, under the charter as it was being drafted, "if the Security Council fails to agree on an act, then the member state reserves the right to act for the maintenance of peace, justice, etc." "There was certainly no statement in the text" being drafted, he said, "under which

[54] The historian's approach in this regard is somewhat at variance with that of legal scholars, who generally play down the importance of this kind of evidence. See, for example, Simma, *Charter of the United Nations*, vol. I, p. 27.

[55] Meetings of the US Delegation to the San Francisco Conference, May 4, May 7 and 8, 1945, *FRUS 1945*, vol. 1, pp. 637, 648; see also p. 593.

we would give up our right of independent action." This was not a trivial point. The British, in fact, as Pasvolsky pointed out, had been "shocked" by how expansive the "American concept of self-defense was."[56]

Indeed, Vandenberg himself had been shocked. He did not dispute the Dulles–Pasvolsky interpretation. But people, he said, "would be disillusioned beyond words" when they came to see what the plan was. He had thought that there had been "a general renunciation of the right to use force," but this too, he was told by Senator Connally, the most important Democrat in the delegation, "was not the case."[57] To be sure, the wording was not as explicit as it might have been, but that was only because it was felt that more explicit phrasing might give the Soviets too free a hand, not because the Americans were prepared to accept real limitations on their own freedom of action – above all, in the western hemisphere, an area where they claimed "preclusive rights." As Connally put it in this context: "The United States must be able to take care of itself."[58]

The UN system, moreover, was built on the assumption that the major powers would be able to act as a bloc. States might be asked to forgo the right of self-help if the larger community was able and willing to come to their aid; but if the system did not provide for their security, and if the system did not protect their rights, they could hardly be expected to abide by the rules against self-help. This rather obvious point has been made by a number of distinguished legal theorists. "It is reasonable to restrict self-help against violations of the law," Hans Kelsen wrote, "only insofar as self-help is replaced by effective collective security." And Julius Stone took it for granted that it did not make sense to rule out forceful self-help by individual states when the Security Council is unable to work as a bloc and no "effective collective measures are available for the remedy of just grievances."[59] But what is important to note here is that this point was recognized even in 1945. The Americans took it for granted that, if the UN system failed, the right of self-help would revert to the member

---

[56] Meetings of US Delegation to the San Francisco Conference, May 7 and 12, 1945, *FRUS* 1945, vol. 1, pp. 637, 677.

[57] *Ibid*, p. 637.

[58] Meetings of the US Delegation to the San Francisco, May 4 and 12, 1945, *FRUS* 1945, vol. 1, pp. 591 ("preclusive rights"), 593, 680. Note also General Embick's reference in the May 4 meeting to the need for the United States to maintain "preclusive control over this hemisphere" (p. 594).

[59] Hans Kelsen, *Principles of International Law*, 2nd edition (New York: Holt, Rinehart and Winston, 1966), p. 38; Julius Stone, *Aggression and World Order: A Critique of United Nations Theories of Aggression* (Berkeley and Los Angeles: University of California Press, 1958), pp. 93–98; the quotation is on p. 96. Note also the passage from Judge Sir Robert Jennings' partial dissent in the *Nicaragua* case, quoted in Thomas Franck, *Recourse to Force: State Action Against Threats and Armed Attacks* (New York: Cambridge University Press, 2002), pp. 62–63.

states.[60] And the official British commentary on the charter noted that "the successful working of the United Nations depends on the preservation of the unanimity of the Great Powers," that "if this unanimity is seriously undermined no provision of the Charter is likely to be of much avail," and that "in such a case the Members will resume their liberty of action."[61] Such documents show what was in the minds of the governments at the time; the language shows that they had by no means set out to build the sort of legal structure most international law scholars today assume had been brought into being in 1945. They certainly did not think that the use of force without Security Council sanction and for purposes other than defense against actual armed attack would be legally impermissible no matter how divided the great powers were – no matter how poorly, that is, the Security Council regime functioned. The states, that is, never intended to create a legal regime that would tie their hands too tightly, a regime that would be binding no matter how poorly the UN system worked.

But the law is defined not simply by the intent of the drafters. It is also to be interpreted in the light of, and indeed as a product of, subsequent state behavior. And the key point to note here is that not one of the leading powers – not one of the five permanent members of the Security Council – was prepared in practice to limit its use of force in the way the charter seemed to imply. The examples are too well known to need repeating here, but let me talk about two cases, France and post-Soviet Russia. France was particularly vociferous in condemning the US invasion of Iraq as illegal because it was undertaken without explicit Security Council authorization.[62] And yet the French themselves had frequently intervened militarily in what they view as their sphere of influence in Francophone Africa without first getting UN sanction.[63] As for post-Soviet Russia, that country has occasionally intervened (without UN

[60] Note Leo Pasvolsky's remarks in the May 12, 1945, meeting of the US Delegation to the San Francisco Conference, *FRUS* 1945, vol. 1, p. 677, which quoted on pp. 218–219; and also in the May 7 meeting, *FRUS* 1945, vol. 1, p. 639.

[61] United Kingdom, Foreign Office, *A Commentary on the Charter of the United Nations*, Cmd. 6666 of 1945 (London: HMSO, 1945), p. 17.

[62] Iraq Communiqué issued by the Presidency of the Republic, March 18, 2003.

[63] See, for example, Howard French, "France's Army Keeps Grip in African Ex-Colonies," *New York Times*, May 22, 1996; Louis Balmond (ed.), *Les interventions militaires françaises en Afrique* [The French Military Interventions in Africa] (Paris: Pedone, 1998); and Claude Wauthier, *Quatre présidents et l'Afrique. De Gaulle, Pompidou, Giscard d'Estaing, Mitterrand: Quarante ans de politique africaine* [Four Presidents and Africa. De Gaulle, Pompidou, Giscard d'Estaing, Mitterrand: Forty Years of African Policy] (Paris: Seuil, 1995). See also the revealing memoir by the head of the French intelligence service in the 1970s: Count Alexandre de Marenches (with Christine Ockrent), *Dans le secret des princes* (Paris: Stock, 1986), and translated into English as *The Fourth World War: Diplomacy and*

authorization) in what the Russians see as their sphere of influence in the "near abroad" – in Moldova, Tajikistan, and Georgia.[64] In September 2002, President Putin of Russia threatened to take military action if the Georgians did not prevent their territory from being used as a base for Chechen rebels: "Like America in Iraq, his officials claim, Russia is insisting on its right to take military action, alone if necessary, against a nation which it deems to be in breach of international law."[65] Two years earlier, Putin had made a similar threat to the Taliban authorities in Afghanistan.[66]

I bring these examples up not because I want to point to French or Russian hypocrisy in this area. Hypocrisy of this sort is perfectly normal in international politics and needs to be taken in stride. The real point has to do with the light such examples shed on the question of what international law actually is. The international legal regime is created by states, not by judges or legal scholars. But all the major states were prepared to use force without UN sanction for purposes other than self-defense, narrowly defined. It is scarcely conceivable that they would have created and sustained a legal regime that would have made them all into law-breakers.

It follows that the argument that the Americans acted "illegally" because force was used without explicit UN Security Council authorization is to be taken with a grain of salt. Indeed, it seems quite clear that this argument has to be interpreted in political terms.[67] A legal framework no one ever took too seriously in the past is now taken very seriously indeed – and from the

Espionage in the Age of Terrorism (New York: Morrow, 1992, with David Andelman as co-author). See especially, in the translated edition, pp. 129–130, for the reference to the many actions involving the use of force, including assassinations of heads of state, undertaken by France in Africa, and pp. 191–196, for a discussion of an important operation in the Central African Empire (subsequently the Central African Republic).

[64] See Andrew Bennett, *Condemned to Repetition? The Rise, Fall, and Reprise of Soviet–Russian Military Interventionism, 1973–1996* (Cambridge: MIT Press, 1999), pp. 311–321, and (for the absence of a UN mandate) pp. 318, 325–326.

[65] "Putin's Folly," *Economist* (US edition), September 21, 2002. The US government condemned the Russians for "threatening unilateral action against Chechen targets on Georgian territory" – a foolish response, given what the Americans would soon end up doing in Iraq: "Echoing Bush, Putin Asks UN to Back Georgia Attack," *New York Times*, September 13, 2002. See also "Putin Warns Georgia to Root Out Chechen Rebels Within Its Borders or Face Attacks," *New York Times*, September 12, 2002, and "Putin Has His Own Candidate for Pre-emption," *New York Times*, October 6, 2002.

[66] Franck, *Recourse to Force*, p. 66.

[67] To capture the idea that juridical arguments are framed with political goals in mind, the French have developed the concept of a "foreign juridical policy." See Guy de Lacharrière, *La politique juridique extérieure* [Juridical Foreign Policy] (Paris: Economica, 1983); and Michel Debré et al. (eds.), *Guy Ladreit de Lacharrière et la politique juridique extérieure de la France* [Guy Ladreit de Lacharrière and France's Juridical Foreign Policy] (Paris: Masson, 1989). De Gaulle himself, incidentally, during the Cuban missile crisis, explicitly supported the idea that American action was legal, even though the

US point of view, this can only be because it serves the purposes of those hostile to US policy, those who seek to use whatever instrument is at hand for bringing American power under some sort of control. By pushing a particular theory of international law, the goal, it seemed, was to limit US freedom of action, a tactic that was pursued in other areas as well. The aim, as Michael Ignatieff put it, was to tie the United States down, "like Gulliver with a thousand legal strings."[68]

But perhaps this is going too far. Governments may be cynical, but there is a serious case to be made by those who believe in the sort of legal regime they associate with the UN Charter at least as an ideal that we should try to move toward, and that case has to be examined on its own terms.

There are fundamental issues here that we need to try to grapple with. One of the most fundamental is the question of whether we really want a world in which force could be legitimately used only in response to armed attack. And the answer here is not as obvious as one might think. To rule out the use of force except in the case of armed aggression is to allow states to renege on their obligations with relative impunity. Does it make sense, for example, to have a legal system in which states in effect have the right to give shelter and support to terrorists? Does it make sense to set up a legal order that shields the law-breaker (as long as his actions do not amount to an "armed attack") and requires law-abiding states "to submit indefinitely to admitted and persistent violations of rights"?[69] Is that what we mean by the "rule of law"?

The US government, for one, never fully accepted the idea that lawless states could legitimately claim the protections of the international legal system. The "rule of law" might govern relations among states that basically accepted the international legal system. But when a country like the United States had to deal with a lawless power, a somewhat different set of rules applied. In 1941, for example, President Roosevelt rejected the German claim that the American policy of helping Britain was not in line with what was expected of a neutral power under international law. Given its own behavior, a state like Nazi Germany, he thought, had no right to demand that the United States pursue a policy

---

United States was not actually being attacked. "President Kennedy wishes to react, and to react now," he told Dean Acheson, whom President Kennedy had sent over to brief him on US policy in this affair, "and certainly France can have no objection to that since it is legal for a country to defend itself when it finds itself in danger": Acheson–de Gaulle meeting, October 22, 1962, *FRUS 1961–1963*, vol. 11, p. 166.

[68] Michael Ignatieff, "The American Empire: The Burden," *New York Times Magazine*, January 5, 2003. Josef Joffe has used the same metaphor in many recent speeches and articles.

[69] Stone, *Aggression and World Order*, pp. 97 (for the quotation), 101.

in accordance with traditional legal standards. It was absurd that one country would be bound by the rule of law, but not the other; it was absurd that international law would in effect privilege the lawless. A "one-way international law," a legal system that lacked "mutuality in its observance" – that, in his view, was utterly unacceptable. Such a system, he said, would serve only as an "instrument of oppression."[70]

There is a basic problem with the idea that we should try to outlaw the use of force except in response to armed attack. The problem is not just that it is out of touch with political reality. A more fundamental problem arises from the fact that armed conflict does not, as a general rule, result from a simple decision on the part of an aggressor to start a war. It is the outcome, generally speaking, of a political process, one that often takes many years to run its course. It is that process as a whole that needs to be controlled; it is a mistake to focus excessively on just one point in that process, the point at which the decision to use force is made. To concentrate all our legal firepower on that one point is to opt in effect for a rather unsophisticated who-fired-the-first-shot approach to the problem of war causation. It is overall policy, and not just policy at one key moment, that we should seek to influence; it is overall policy that we should therefore seek to judge; the principles we develop, the norms we come up with, should thus relate to policy as a whole. And it is by no means obvious (as the case of the 1930s shows) that policies that rule out the use of force will lead to a more stable international order. If the goal is to influence the way an international conflict runs its course – that is, to try to make sure that it runs its course in such a way that the conflict is ultimately resolved peacefully – then it may be entirely proper, and indeed necessary, that power be brought to bear. Everything depends on circumstances. That approach, as Michael Walzer points out, "opens a broad path for human judgment – which it is, no doubt, the purpose of the legalist paradigm to narrow or block altogether."[71] But that fact is reason in itself to be wary of the legalist approach to these issues.

If power plays a central role in international politics – and in certain key areas of conflict, power is still clearly of fundamental importance – then the last thing that we should want is to give people the sense that they can ignore power realities with impunity – that they are sheltered by legal norms from retaliation and that they are free to act as irresponsibly as they like. We should want people to face up to realities, to accommodate

---

[70] Franklin Roosevelt, Annual Message to the Congress, January 6, 1941, *Public Papers and Addresses of Franklin D. Roosevelt*, 1940 volume (New York: Macmillan, 1941), p. 669.

[71] Michael Walzer, *Just and Unjust Wars: A Moral Argument with Historical Illustrations* (New York: Basic Books, 1977), p. 85.

to basic realities, and in that way to bring about a relatively stable international order.

The fundamental point is that a world in which power considerations loom large is not necessarily a world of endless violence and destruction. A world based on power, in fact, has a certain stability: as the international relations theorists say, there can be "order without an orderer."[72] If international politics during the Cold War period was relatively stable, especially after 1963, it was not because the international legal system established in 1945 had taken the edge off interstate violence. It is simply a mistake to assume that "UN Charter norms" actually "served as the framework of international relations for the past half century."[73] The UN regime, in fact, counted for very little. Key elements of the international system during that period – for example, the strategy of deterrence based on the threat of retaliation on an absolutely massive scale – were in fact wildly at variance with the international legal framework as the lawyers commonly portray it. "The lawyers," as Walzer says, "have constructed a paper world, which fails at crucial points to correspond to the world the rest of us still live in," and one has to wonder whether that enterprise has done more harm than good.[74]

When people today embrace those legalist conceptions, that position is bound to have major political implications. The prominence of those legal arguments in the political discourse relating to the Iraq crisis is striking, and they played an important role in the politics of the crisis. But those arguments are far more problematic than many people believe, and a more serious analysis of the international law side of the question might lead people to rethink their positions, or at least lead them to look at things in a somewhat different light.

The crisis in the Alliance

The showdown with Iraq, Henry Kissinger wrote about a month before the war with that country broke out, had "produced the gravest crisis within the Atlantic Alliance since its creation five decades ago," and that view was shared by many observers on both sides of the Atlantic.[75] "It is possible we stand before an epochal break," German foreign minister

---

[72] This argument is developed in some detail in Marc Trachtenberg, "The Question of Realism: An Historian's View," *Security Studies*, 13:1 (Fall 2003), pp. 156–194.

[73] Farer, "Beyond the Charter Frame," p. 360.

[74] Walzer, *Just and Unjust Wars*, p. xiii.

[75] Henry Kissinger, "NATO's Split: Atlantic Alliance Is in Its Gravest Crisis," *San Diego Union-Tribune*, February 16, 2003.

Joschka Fischer declared in early March.[76] In the Iraq crisis, many European governments supported the United States to one degree or another, but European opinion was overwhelmingly opposed to what the US government was doing. The European press, and especially the French press, was full of anti-American abuse, quite unparalleled by anything one saw in the leading American journals.[77] The Iraq crisis had triggered what Josef Joffe, coeditor of *Die Zeit* and an exceptionally well-informed observer of US–European relations, called "an enormous wave of hatred against the United States."[78] The Americans, it seemed, were lawless, arrogant, and imperialistic – the French had in fact taken to referring to the United States as "the empire." After the war broke out, public opinion polls in France showed about a third of those questioned actually wanted Saddam to win.[79] Anti-American feeling in fact ran high throughout Europe. On April 7, 2003, for example, the *New York Times* carried an article on anti-Americanism in Greece. One well-known Greek critic of the United States was quoted there as calling the Americans "detestable, ruthless cowards and murderers of the people of the world."[80] And all of this had repercussions on the other side of the Atlantic. Many Americans read this sort of thing and thought to themselves: "and these people are supposed to be our *allies*? How can we be *allies* with people who feel that way about us?"

Some people say that what we saw in the run-up to the war with Iraq was just another crisis in the Alliance, not fundamentally different from the sort of thing we have seen many times in the past. I have spent many years studying US–European relations during the Cold War period, and my sense is that this view is fundamentally mistaken. This crisis *was* very different from the NATO crises of the Cold War period, even from the most serious of those crises, the crisis of early 1963. During that period, the Europeans and the Americans felt themselves basically to be on the same side. Whatever their differences, the US government and the major European governments did not question each other's basic honesty. But, in the case of the Iraq crisis, many Americans who follow these issues had

---

[76] "Rumblings of War," *Der Spiegel* (English edition), March 10, 2003.
[77] On April 8, 2003, for example, *Le Monde* carried an article with the title "Bush, obscène mécanicien de l'empire." It is inconceivable that an anti-French article with a similarly inflammatory title would have been published at the time in the *New York Times*.
[78] Quoted in Richard Bernstein, "Foreign Views of US Darken After Sept. 11," *New York Times*, September 11, 2003.
[79] Referred to in Pierre Lellouche et al., "Après la guerre, renouons nos alliances," *Le Figaro*, April 8, 2003.
[80] Anthee Carassava, "Anti-Americanism in Greece Is Reinvigorated by War," *New York Times*, April 7, 2003.

the sense that some key European allies were inclined to take sides *against* the United States – that the goal was to balance *against* the American "hyperpower," to use Hubert Védrine's famous phrase. They were struck by how quick many in Europe were to jump to what were viewed as extreme anti-American conclusions – to assume, for example, that the Americans were lying about Iraq's weapons of mass destruction – and they were struck by the fact that the charge that the US government was playing fast and loose with the truth in this area was itself rooted in a very cavalier use of the evidence.

Let me give a couple of examples of this, each involving Deputy Secretary of Defense Paul Wolfowitz. The first has to do with an interview he gave on May 9, 2003, which served as one of the bases for a story called "Bush's Brain Trust" published in the July 2003 issue of *Vanity Fair*; the story itself was released on May 29. According to that article, "Wolfowitz admitted that from the outset, contrary to so many claims from the White House, Iraq's supposed cache of WMD had never been the most compelling casus belli. It was simply one of several: 'For bureaucratic reasons, we settled on one issue, weapons of mass destruction, because it was the one reason everyone could agree on.'"[81] This gave rise to a slew of articles saying, in effect, that Wolfowitz had admitted that the WMD issue was just a "pretext" for a war.[82] But it was quite clear from the transcript of Wolfowitz's taped interview with the *Vanity Fair* writer posted on the Pentagon website that this was a gross distortion of what Wolfowitz had said. His argument was that the WMD issue had been emphasized because it was the one issue that everyone agreed would justify military action against Iraq.[83] The other incident involving Wolfowitz had to do with his supposed admission that "oil was the main reason for military action against Iraq"; again, it turns out that he had said nothing of the sort, a point that again would not have been at all hard to discover.[84] It is not difficult to understand why incidents of this sort were often seen in the United States as evidence of a deeply ingrained

---

[81] Sam Tanenhaus, "Bush's Brain Trust," *Vanity Fair*, July 2003, p. 169.

[82] For examples of articles using the word "pretext," see "Rounds of Lies," *Der Spiegel*, June 27, 2003; Pierre Marcelle, "Les menteurs," *Libération*, June 4, 2003; and Jeffrey Sachs, "The Real Target of the War in Iraq Was Saudi Arabia," *Financial Times* (London), August 13, 2003. There were articles with similar themes in the *Observer* (June 1, 2003), the *Independent* (May 30, 2003), and the *Guardian* (May 31, 2003).

[83] Paul Wolfowitz interview with Sam Tanenhaus, May 9, 2003, http://www.defenselink.mil/transcripts/2003/tr20030509-depsecdef0223.html.

[84] See, for example, the story in the *Daily Mail* (London), June 5, 2003, whose source was the German newspaper *Die Welt*. On this incident, see Sarah Baxter, "If It Makes America Look Bad, It Must Be True, Mustn't It?," *Sunday Times* (London), June 15, 2003.

anti-US bias – of an "obsessive" attitude (to use Jean-François Revel's term), one that went far beyond what the evidence actually warranted.[85] Many Americans, in other words, had the sense that there was a certain tendency in Europe in general, and especially in France, to think the worst of the United States. They were struck, for example, by the reaction in Europe to Secretary Powell's February 5, 2003, speech to the United Nations laying out the US case on Iraq. A good deal of evidence was presented and, although the Iraqis dismissed that evidence as fabricated, the speech impressed most Americans who heard it as a serious and well-thought-out statement. But the mainstream European response was very different. "To Saddam's lies we can probably add the administration's own lies" – that was how Yves Thérard reacted in *Le Figaro*, and many Europeans reacted that same way.[86] And when no forbidden weapons were found after the war, that suspicion tended to harden into an article of faith, as though a mistaken judgment was the same as a lie. That sort of reaction, as the more historically aware American commentators noted, represented quite a change from the past. In 1962, it was pointed out in this context, when the Americans offered to show de Gaulle the evidence about the Soviet missiles in Cuba, the French president said he did not need to be convinced: "great nations such as yours," he told the American envoy, Dean Acheson, "would not take a serious step if there were any doubt about evidence."[87] But that was obviously not the official French attitude during the Iraq crisis period.

What does all this mean about the future of the Western alliance? Many people think that it does not mean all that much – that these problems will blow over as other problems have in the past and that the NATO alliance will remain intact. And it is certainly true that very few people in the United States today openly question the desirability of the American alliance with Europe. Even the expansion of NATO into eastern Europe was generally supported by both political parties – although one has the sense that this support was a mile wide and an inch deep. But NATO itself is still conventionally seen as a "cornerstone" of the international order: it has been around so long that people can scarcely imagine a world without it. If they are pushed on the issue, people will say the United States needs to work with Europe to deal with problems

[85] On this point, see especially Jean-François Revel, *L'obsession anti-américaine: son fonctionnement, ses causes, ses inconséquences* [The Anti-American Obsession: Its Function, Its Causes, Its Inconsistencies] (Paris: Plon, 2002).

[86] Yves Thérard, "Powell a dit," *Le Figaro*, February 6, 2003.

[87] See Fareed Zakaria, "A Dangerous Trust Deficit," *Newsweek*, February 10, 2003. De Gaulle's remark is quoted in that piece.

like international terrorism – as though cooperation would be impossible if the Alliance were gone, and as though the Europeans would have less of an incentive to cooperate with the Americans if the American security guarantee could no longer be taken for granted.

The US government, moreover, no matter how it feels about France and Germany, is still reluctant (as I write this in June 2004) even to talk about withdrawing from the Alliance for fear of embarrassing those European governments who, defying political feeling at home, sided with the United States in the crisis. The Bush administration does not want to betray the governments who took that position. And beyond that, a whole series of considerations having to do with the unhappy course that events in Iraq have taken in the postwar period now has to be taken into account. There is a certain sense today that the US government has bitten off more than it can chew in Iraq and would like more European help to deal with the situation that has developed there. There is a certain sense that the case for war was weaker, in retrospect, than it had seemed at the time the decision to attack Iraq was being made, and that there might be more to be said for the prevailing European view than many Americans had been prepared to admit before the war. And, above all, there is a certain sense that something has to be done about the fact that feeling throughout the world has turned so sharply against the United States, and that the country perhaps needs to start rebuilding its relations with those powers who in the past had been its closest allies. For all these reasons, the US government has tended to take a rather mild line on Alliance issues in the post-Iraq War period.

But still one has to wonder about the future of the Alliance. If even the Kennedy administration, at the height of the Cold War, was prepared to withdraw from Europe during the 1963 crisis, why would a less cosmopolitan US government remain involved indefinitely – when (from the American point of view) the provocation is far greater than it was in the time of de Gaulle and Adenauer, when the need to stay in Europe has receded with the collapse of the Soviet Union and the end of the Cold War, and when the United States is seen as getting so little benefit from its continuing commitment to the security of Europe? The Kennedy administration felt the Europeans could not have it both ways – they could not pursue an anti-American policy (very mild by today's standards) and still expect to have their security rest ultimately on a system based on American power. It is not hard to imagine that, if attitudes remain as they are, the US government, no matter who is running it, will eventually reach much the same conclusion: if the Europeans want to go their own way politically, they have every right to do so, but if they do, they should not expect the United States to guarantee their security. The feeling would be (as Eisenhower once put it) that the Europeans could not be allowed to make "a sucker out of Uncle Sam."[88]

And one does sense below the surface of political discourse a certain lingering resentment toward the two most important continental allies. One is struck, for example, by Kenneth Pollack's reference, in an important article he published in the *Atlantic Monthly* in early 2004, to the "shameful performance" of France and Germany in the run-up to the war.[89] European views about the United States – and the prevailing view in the post-Iraq War period is decidedly negative – are even closer to the surface. In such circumstances, it would seem natural, in the long run, for the two sides to drift apart. Alliances, of course, are not ends in themselves, and they cannot be expected to last forever. They take shape for political reasons, and they end when political interests no longer warrant their continuation.

If it turns out that the Atlantic alliance is no longer viable, then that fact will have to be faced philosophically. Lord Salisbury, perhaps the greatest diplomatist of the late nineteenth century, once said that the "commonest error in politics is sticking to the carcasses of dead policies." The policy of maintaining the NATO alliance may indeed be a dying, if not yet a totally dead, policy and if it is, it is important to begin thinking about the sort of successor regime that should be established and how the transition to that new regime should be managed. But whether the Western alliance is to be saved or replaced by something else, the very fundamental issues the Iraq crisis has brought to the surface need to be analyzed seriously – certainly more seriously than they have been so far.

That analysis has to begin, I think, with the recognition that the core questions here have no easy or obvious answers – with the recognition, as Bernard Brodie put it when he was referring to the complex of problems relating to nuclear weapons, that we are now dealing with issues of "great intellectual difficulty, as well as other kinds of difficulty." I personally have been studying international politics for over forty years now, and the whole set of problems relating to terrorism, nuclear proliferation, biological weapons, and so on I find extremely difficult – harder to answer, harder even to deal with, than any other set of issues relating to international politics that I have ever encountered, including the nuclear issue as we understood it during the Cold War.

---

[88] Eisenhower–Norstad meeting, November 4, 1959, *FRUS* 1958–1960, vol. 7, no. 1, p. 498. Lauris Norstad was then the military commander of NATO forces.

[89] Kenneth Pollack, "Spies, Lies, and Weapons." Pollack, one should note, was by no means a blind supporter of the Bush Iraq policy. In the same paragraph that he characterized French and German behavior as shameless, he also referred to the administration's "reckless" rush to war.

In fact, the main point I am trying to make in this chapter is that the questions that we now have to deal with are extraordinarily difficult, and the answers are not nearly as obvious as people think. And if we are to get a sense of how difficult these issues are, it seems to me that some historical perspective might be of real value. We often hear people today, for example, talking about American imperialism and about NATO as an "instrument of American domination." But it would help, I think, if people remembered that the US government never wanted to create an American empire in Europe as a kind of end in itself. It would help if people remembered that in the early years of the Alliance the US government in fact wanted the Europeans to come together and provide for their own defense – that it wanted Europe to become (to use Eisenhower's phrase) a "third great power bloc" in world affairs – and that it was only when it became clear that a purely European security system was not viable that the Americans reluctantly accepted the idea of a more or less permanent US troop presence in Europe and thus of a security system based, in the final analysis, essentially on American power.[90] There is a myth that the United States had imposed itself on Europe – that from the start it had sought to dominate Europe, that NATO was a way of enabling it to control Europe, that the United States was a country whose sheer power had led it to pursue a policy of domination.[91] But the more one understands the real story, the more one is able to see how misleading and indeed how pernicious myths of that sort can be.

The Americans, of course, have a lot of thinking of their own to do – and that applies to Americans on both sides of the Iraq issue. But the Europeans are also going to have to think more deeply about this whole complex of issues. They will have to grapple with them more seriously as they come to see that the American presence in Europe can no longer be taken as an immutable fact of political life. And this is something which may well become clear to them in the not-too-distant future. If basic attitudes do not change dramatically, the two sides are almost bound to drift apart, and an American withdrawal from Europe will become a real possibility. If the Americans reach the conclusion that people in Europe are much too quick to engage in anti-American abuse and that the most important continental governments are more interested in "balancing" the American "hyperpower" than in dealing seriously with real problems, then it is not hard to imagine the United States disengaging from Europe.

---

[90] See Trachtenberg, *Constructed Peace*, pp. 147–156.

[91] Note, for example, de Gaulle's reference in passing in his memoirs to the United States as "un pays que sa puissance sollicite vers la domination": Charles de Gaulle, *Mémoires d'espoir: le renouveau* [Memories of Hope: The Renewal] (Paris: Plon, 1970), p. 222.

In 1963, President Kennedy said that the United States could "take care" of itself, and the Americans still believe that in the final analysis they do not need Europe. The point is recognized by some of the more serious European commentators. Helga Haftendorn, for example, noted in a recent article that "today the United States can easily do without NATO."[92] But, for the Europeans, a US withdrawal would open up a can of worms; a whole series of problems, relating especially to German nuclear weapons and to the relationship between Russia and the rest of Europe, would almost automatically come to the fore. Sooner or later, the Europeans are probably going to have to deal with the issue of whether they would really like the United States to withdraw – and, from their point of view, the sooner this issue is addressed, the better. And if, after due consideration, they conclude that they would like the Americans to stay, then they might want to grapple with the very difficult problems of the new world we now live in in a more serious way than they have so far.

Looking back on the run-up to the Iraq War, one cannot help but be struck by the shallowness of the discussion – not just in Europe, but in the United States as well. And my assumption here is that this was a big part of the problem – that the reason why the Iraq affair took the course it did, and the reason why US–European relations took the course they did, had a good deal to do with the way the fundamental issues were dealt with. The issues were discussed at much too superficial a level; the core issues were not argued out, with the result that in the end no real meeting of the minds was possible. But that does not mean that we cannot do better in the future. The issues that came up during the Iraq crisis are not going to go away for some time, if ever. My goal here was to show how some of them could be dealt with, but I have done little more than just scratch the surface. There is a lot more scholarly work to be done – including a lot more *historical* work – and it is about time that we started doing it.

[92] Helga Haftendorn, *One Year After 9/11: A Critical Appraisal of German–American Relations*, Thyssen German American Dialogue Seminar Series, AICGS, 2002, http://www.aicgs.org/publications/PDF/haftendorn.pdf.

10 Military competence versus policy loyalty: central Europe and transatlantic relations

Wade Jacoby

Does NATO have a future? Should it? That depends in large measure on what one thinks NATO is all about, especially now that it is no longer about defending the Fulda Gap. Some observers see the Alliance as a military "tool kit" for the United States. Others regard it as a political organization on which the United States can rely – or at least should be able to rely – for official support when it undertakes controversial missions abroad. Doubtless these are important functions, but NATO serves other purposes as well, or at least it ought to. Among these other purposes is the provision of a military framework for mutual defense against external aggressors and, at least since the 1990s, for united efforts to punish rogue leaders or bring peace to war-torn regions. These are valuable collective resources and ones that would be difficult to replace – or to rebuild.

NATO is not a "coalition of the willing"; it is an alliance. It is a military club, and the members of that club have certain military obligations toward one another. During the run-up to the Iraq War, the government of the United States made a considered judgment to downgrade those obligations – to trade away pressure on the newer NATO members to upgrade their military capabilities and competences – in exchange for displays of political loyalty to Washington in the United Nations and elsewhere.[1] In this chapter, I argue that this trade was a bad idea. The states at the heart of "new Europe" – the generally pro-American states that joined NATO during its 1999 enlargement – are not yet the kind of partners that US secretary of defense Donald Rumsfeld has publicly imagined them to be. Certainly, they are no substitute for the "old" NATO alliance.

I argue that the administration of George W. Bush asked at once too much and too little of these states. It asked too little when it downgraded

The author thanks David Andrews, Rachel Epstein, and Georges-Henri Soutou for comments on an earlier draft.
[1] Other countries – France, notably – were similarly engaged in trading favors in exchange for support of their position at the UN. Notwithstanding the ubiquity of this temptation, my focus here is on US policy toward NATO and especially its new member states.

an older demand, shared widely across NATO's membership, that the new NATO members be able to make a real military contribution to the Alliance. It asked too much when it pressured politicians with razor-thin majorities in turbulent parliamentary systems to commit to foreign policies that were deeply unpopular among their voters. While some leaders survived and others did not, the broader point is that the support for American policies in this region is less and less evident.[2] Having asked these elected officials, militaries, and their societies to do a hard thing in the short term – to support the US invasion of Iraq – Washington has distracted their focus from doing a hard thing in the long term: provide a competent military that can make a real contribution to security in Europe and beyond.

To be sure, under the right circumstances, expressions of policy loyalty to the United States can bring immediate benefits. The strongest illustration is the case of Leszek Miller, the center-left politician who resigned in March 2004 as prime minister of Poland. Miller had long been desperately unpopular at home; his approval rating was down to 7 percent at the time of his resignation, and he had faced the defection of key parliamentary allies from his coalition while pushing through austerity policies that helped the country meet its commitments to the European Union. For a politician in this situation, it must have been much more satisfying to be involved in high-profile politics alongside the United States than to try to hammer out failed domestic policies. In this, Miller was hardly alone, especially in the heady first weeks of the occupation in Iraq, when some Polish conservatives even suggested that Poland should use its links with the United States as an alternative to deeper involvement in the EU.[3] Not only was it easier to get into the coalition of the willing than into the EU, but being a policy-maker on the world stage was more rewarding than being a policy-taker on the European one.

But central and east European (CEE) governments will not always find it so attractive to follow the United States, and future US administrations should think carefully before risking the long-term vitality of the Western alliance in the pursuit of short-term objectives. Both the opportunity for CEE governments to play a key foreign policy role as a partner of the United States and the constraints inherent in being on the threshold of EU membership were due to special circumstances. The politics are likely to be quite different the next time.

[2] For details, see Anand Menon and Jonathan Lipkin, *European Attitudes toward Transatlantic Relations, 2000–2003: An Analytical Survey* (Birmingham: European Research Institute, 2003).

[3] Basil Kerski, "Zwischen Desinteresse und Misstrauen: zur Krise in den deutsch–polnischen Beziehungen," *Internationale Politik* 59:4 (2004), pp. 31–40.

This chapter uses the Czech, Polish, and Hungarian experiences to underline such a note of caution.[4] The three states that joined NATO in 1999 vary in terms of their military legacies, strategic situations, and popular attitudes toward the military. Nevertheless, they all share (along with most older NATO members) a profound reluctance to spend money on military modernization at a time when so many other domestic needs seem to deserve high priority. Because they began the transformation with militaries that were substantially inferior to those of the older NATO members, their reluctance to spend on defense has led them to build what might be called niche forces and showcase units. But these two responses are an inadequate substitute for more thoroughgoing defense reforms; and, absent such real reforms, the CEE states run the risk of being instrumentalized by the United States for foreign policy purposes while the military side of the alliance becomes increasingly hollow. The United States also runs risks with this strategy, since it cannot take either the future diplomatic support or military contributions of the CEE states for granted.[5]

The new NATO members live in a region where the current scarcity of immediate and direct security threats is fairly novel. Theirs has been a bad neighborhood, especially, though hardly exclusively, in the twentieth century. To address potential threats to their security, CEE states have several options: they can rely on their own unilateral capacity for territorial defense, on multilateral options through NATO and/or the EU, or on bilateral help from the United States (with which they all have very friendly relations). But the first option (unilateralism) has badly eroded, while the US–bilateral and EU–multilateral options are risky. While not precluding recourse to the other strategies, the CEE states have bet on NATO membership to solve their security problems. Unfortunately, they did so at a time when the United States had begun to lose interest in NATO as a military organization. To some extent, the Bush administration's view of the transatlantic relationship was congenial to the CEE

---

[4] While this account focuses on the first-wave central and east European cases of Poland, the Czech Republic, and Hungary, the case is not fundamentally different (and is in many ways stronger) if one also includes the states that joined NATO in April 2004 (Bulgaria, Estonia, Latvia, Lithuania, Romania, Slovakia, and Slovenia).

[5] While I expand on each of these points, my analysis relies on some important premises for which space constraints prohibit much discussion. These include the fact that the newer NATO members border on a host of unstable or potentially unstable states to their east; that while the newer members face security problems that cannot be resolved by military means, competent and professional armies can nevertheless make important contributions to regional stability and peace; and that, notwithstanding positive developments in the situation of ethnic minorities in CEE, significant potential ethnic problems remain unresolved and could destabilize parts of the region.

states, for they found they could play important foreign policy roles even without making serious investments in military reforms. But, as this chapter will show, the current situation is unstable enough that it should worry both American and CEE supporters of the Alliance.

CEE militaries: variable legacies, similar goals

The Czech and Hungarian militaries have four common features that are relevant to this chapter. First, the two countries share a legacy of foreign domination that diminished public support for the two armies.[6] In the twentieth century alone, the Czech military sat out potential confrontations in 1938–39 (against the Nazis), in 1948 (against the Communist coup), and in 1968 (during the Prague Spring). Whereas the Czech army did not fight, the Hungarian army did not win. Its last victory came with the occupation of Vienna in 1487. It has hosted foreign troops continuously since 1526 and fought on the losing side of both world wars, each of which resulted in significant territorial losses. Both these national militaries were deeply unpopular at the end of communism. Second, after over fifty years in the Soviet empire, each was actually only a partial military that depended upon other (Warsaw Pact) elements in order to fight. Neither state could defend its own territory or even produce the independent strategic planning that a strictly territorial defense would require. Third, like all Warsaw Pact armies, these two were cumbersome: enormous in manpower and very officer-heavy compared to Western militaries.[7] Finally, the armies were dominated by their national Communist Parties.[8]

While the Polish military shared many of these features, it differed from the Czech and Hungarian militaries in two important ways. First, if the military had often been unable to protect the Polish state, at least it had on several occasions fought bravely in the national defense. And, while the military had been significantly coopted by the party, both party and army had posed resistance to some forms of Soviet domination. Moreover, the Polish military tradition had, since the late eighteenth century, continually built on an ethos of national independence that seemed to draw strength from successive episodes of foreign

---

[6] For details, see Wade Jacoby, *The Enlargement of the European Union and NATO: Ordering from the Menu in Central Europe* (New York: Cambridge University Press, 2004), ch. 4.

[7] In these already enormous conscript armies, many officers were "cadres" around which additional reserve units would be expected to mobilize and fight.

[8] Zoltan Barany, "The Military and Security Legacies of Communism," in Zoltan Barany and Ivan Volgyes (eds.), *The Legacies of Communism in Eastern Europe* (Baltimore: Johns Hopkins University Press, 1995), pp. 101–117.

occupation.[9] After 1956, Poland was able to limit the number of Soviet garrisons in Poland, officially glorify its precommunist military history, and occasionally pursue independent foreign policy initiatives.[10] The Polish military also worked hard to conceal the extent of its involvement in domestic repression.[11] As a result, the Polish military was both much more popular and better able to plan for and execute its own territorial defense.

Despite these differences, in 1989, all three states had large national militaries. All three sought first to downsize their forces and join NATO. Hungary, which bordered all three of the disintegrating multinational states (the USSR, Yugoslavia, and Czechoslovakia), called for the Warsaw Pact's dissolution in June 1990 and requested NATO membership the next year.[12] Czechoslovakia also moved early to apply for membership; Poland was not far behind, once Germany and Poland signed two treaties solidifying the Oder–Neisse line as their common border.[13] Thus, whatever differences existed across the three states, they shared the same broad reform goals: reduce and reform the military, and get into NATO.

Enlarging NATO: the diplomatic background

One important aspect of the transatlantic connection is the ethnic ties between the United States and the CEE states. These ties are often quite strong – between 8 and 11 million Americans are of Polish heritage. One key to the recent warm US–CEE relations has been US leadership on the issue of NATO expansion, an issue that played well both with these ethnic voters in the United States and inside CEE itself. CEE elites began public discussion of NATO membership even prior to the 1991 dissolution of the Warsaw Pact;[14] by May 1992, five months after the

---

[9] Andrew Michta, *Red Eagle: The Army in Polish Politics, 1944–1988* (Stanford: Hoover Institution Press, 1990); and Michta, *The Soldier-Citizen: The Politics of the Polish Army After Communism* (London: Macmillan, 1997).

[10] Rachel Epstein, "NATO Enlargement and the Spread of Democracy: Evidence and Expectations," *Security Studies* 14:1 (Spring 2005).

[11] Michta, *Red Eagle*.

[12] When the Soviets began to pull out of Hungary in 1991, the country lost its entire air defense at a time when Serbian aircraft often violated Hungarian airspace: Zoltan Barany, "Hungary: Appraising a New NATO Member," *Clausewitz-Studien* (1998), pp. 3–31, especially p. 12.

[13] As in Hungary, Poland's border situation changed radically with the collapse of communism. Bordered in 1989 by the GDR, Czechoslovakia, and the USSR, Poland soon had seven new neighbors – none of them the same state as prior to 1989: Andrew Michta, "Poland: A Linchpin of Regional Security," in Andrew Michta (ed.), *America's New Allies: Poland, Hungary, and the Czech Republic in NATO* (Seattle: University of Washington Press, 1999), pp. 40–73.

[14] This section follows Ronald Asmus, *Opening NATO's Door* (New York: Columbia University Press, 2002); James Goldgeier, *Not Whether But When: The US Decision to*

collapse of the USSR, Presidents Havel, Wałęsa, and Antall declared that their goal was full-fledged membership in the Western alliance. The Clinton administration initially opposed any expansion of NATO that might antagonize Russia, and in 1993 it bought some time by proposing a new program for postcommunist states called the "Partnership for Peace." But, by then, a combination of factors had begun to erode Washington's opposition to enlargement: mounting Western frustration at the inability to prevent the carnage in Bosnia, direct entreaties by CEE leaders to President Clinton during the dedication of the Holocaust Museum in Washington in April 1993, episodic support for enlargement from the German government, persistent appeals by leaders of US ethnic communities (especially Polish-Americans), and growing pressure from the Republican Party. In late 1994, NATO finally announced that it would begin to study how enlargement could occur – a decision embraced warmly in CEE and bitterly denounced in Moscow.

Ultimately, Russia had to accept the reality of NATO expansion, though it received some consideration for doing so. NATO and Russia signed a pact to allow Russia to observe NATO decision-making in a "Permanent Joint Council"; in addition, the Clinton administration, in deference to Yeltsin's reelection chances, pledged not to raise any concrete plans for enlargement until after the 1996 Russian presidential election. But when Yeltsin narrowly won that election and Clinton, several months later, won his own reelection, enlargement gathered speed. At NATO's 1997 summit in Madrid, US support for a small first round of enlargement to include only Poland, the Czech Republic, and Hungary prevailed over proposals to add Romania (led by France) and Slovenia (led by Italy). The United States and the other NATO members ratified the enlargement treaty – the April 1998 vote in the US Senate was 80–19 – and the three new members officially joined on March 12, 1999.

As we will see, however, the diplomatic process was not sufficiently flanked by efforts to reform and modernize the CEE militaries. Part of the problem lay with NATO: unlike the EU, the Alliance had no significant programs to prepare the new states for membership.[15] But much of the problem lay with the CEE states themselves, which did not reform so much as simply slash spending. When then-US defense secretary William Cohen toured Hungarian military facilities shortly before Hungary

Enlarge NATO (Washington: Brookings Institution Press, 1999); George Grayson, *Strange Bedfellows: NATO Marches East* (Lanham, MD: University Press of America, 1999); Sean Kay, *NATO and the Future of European Security* (New York: Rowman & Littlefield, 1998); David Yost, *NATO Transformed: The Alliance's New Roles in International Security* (Washington, DC: United States Institute of Peace Press, 1998).
[15] Jacoby, *The Enlargement of the European Union and NATO.*

formally joined the Alliance, officials covered infrastructure and weapons with camouflage netting so that the United States "wouldn't have to see what they were getting."[16]

Soldiers and citizens

While CEE states struggled to establish credibility with NATO, their militaries struggled to establish credibility with their own citizens. Lost wars, complicity or inaction in the face of foreign interventions against their own populations, and mistreatment of conscripts had left the Czech and Hungarian militaries with very low standing in the eyes of their respective peoples. Again, the Polish case was somewhat different; the army suffered significant loss of prestige by virtue of martial law but still enjoyed relatively higher acceptance on the part of the population than did its Czech and Hungarian counterparts.

Since the end of communism, however, CEE military personnel have been treated badly in all three states. Their earnings are quite low: in 1993, 46 percent of Hungarian noncommissioned officers (NCOs), 17 percent of officers and 57 percent of civilian employees of the army (HDF) were earning wages that put them under the official poverty line.[17] In 1998, the monthly wages of Polish privates were $377, NCOs barely more at $431, and even battalion commanders made only $542.[18] This means that institutional reforms in all three states were often conducted against a backdrop of frustration and distrust on the part of the military itself.[19]

Low societal legitimacy meant that funds for genuine military reform were hard to come by, while high CEE inflation rapidly eroded defense budgets. Defense spending data from the Stockholm International Peace Research Institute (SIPRI) confirm that military budgets declined sharply in all three countries in both real and GDP terms for several years after the collapse of communism.[20] Many cuts were made without any defense concept in mind beyond shrinking the military. With pressing social and economic investment needs in a variety of other policy domains, the

---

[16] Barany, "Hungary," p. 23.

[17] Ibid. Following national conventions, this chapter refers to the Polish People's Army (PPA), the Hungarian Defense Forces (HDF), and the Army of the Czech Republic (ACR).

[18] Michta, "Poland: A Linchpin," p. 61. All dollar figures are in US dollars.

[19] The situation was much worse in Russia, where manuals were issued instructing army personnel on how to forage for food in the wild: Brian Taylor, "Russia's Passive Army: Rethinking Military Coups," *Comparative Political Studies* 34:8 (2001), pp. 924–952.

[20] Starting in 1996–97, Czech and Hungarian spending began to rise again while Polish spending, which had remained higher in the preceding years, fell slightly in GDP terms.

governments of the three states were in no mood to spend on defense. Once inside NATO, pressure to spend more on military modernization was frequently met with the argument that the current government, uncertain of its grip on power, would have to defer reform until after the next election. Of course, all European democracies spend significantly less on their militaries than does the United States, but the combination of small budgets and old equipment sometimes made actual CEE military contributions almost vanishingly small. For example, in 1999, Poland spent more per capita on defense (about $88 per person per year) than either the Czechs or Hungarians.[21] Yet this figure was just barely above the cost of moving one of the army's older T-55M battle tanks one kilometer during a training exercise – provided that none of its weapons were fired. Another illustration of the spending differential between West and East involves the Spanish–Polish comparison. Using late 1990 figures, Spain spent about $50,000 per soldier and Poland about $16,000.[22]

To the extent NATO appears to cost money, its domestic popularity drops. When United States Information Agency (USIA) pollsters surveyed CEE citizens in 1996 and asked if they would be willing to spend more money on their military in order to meet NATO standards, large majorities said no: by 74 percent to 16 percent in Poland, by 87 percent to 9 percent in Hungary, and by 84 percent to 11 percent in the Czech Republic. In other words, this reluctance to spend is not just an elite issue; the vast majority of CEE voters do not support increased spending to meet NATO obligations. Given the large number of other demands on the budgets of these countries, this reluctance is hardly surprising. Yet at this same time in Poland, over 80 percent *supported* membership in NATO.[23] This leads one to ask what these citizens thought NATO membership entailed.

But defense spending in constant US dollars remains significantly below 1989 levels in both Hungary and Poland. (No such comparison is possible for the Czech Republic, which came into existence in 1993.)

[21] This compares to $253 for Canada, $327 for Belgium, $414 for Germany, $568 for the UK, and $1,004 for the United States. The global average is $137 per capita (SIPRI, *SIPRI Yearbook: Armaments, Disarmament, and International Security* [Stockholm: Stockholm International Peace Research Institute, 2002], p. 234).

[22] Spain had 40 million people and a GDP of $568 billion; spending 1.27 percent of this GDP on defense equates to $7.2 billion for 143,450 soldiers. Poland had 39 million people, but its GDP was only $160 billion. Even a 2.06 percent commitment of its GDP resulted in only $3.3 billion, and this sum was spent on far more soldiers (206,045): Mark Yaniszewski, "Postcommunist Civil–Military Reform in Poland and Hungary: Progress and Problems," *Armed Forces and Society* 28:3 (2002), pp. 393, 401; Andrew Cottey, Timothy Edmunds, and Anthony Forster, "Beyond Prague," *NATO Review* 3 (2002), p. 2.

[23] Johanna Granville, "The Many Paradoxes of NATO Enlargement," *Current History* 98 (1999), pp. 165–170.

The Kosovo crisis

The Iraq War pattern of strong diplomatic support but thin military contributions from the CEE states was plain from the start of their NATO membership. The three new members entered in March 1999, less than two weeks before the first war in the forty-year history of the Alliance. NATO leaders' original expectations were that a short period of bombing would convince Slobodan Milošević to end Serb attacks on ethnic Albanians and accept increased Kosovar autonomy. But Milošević intensified his attacks, driving 1.3 million people from their homes.[24] Only after eleven weeks of bombing and under the growing threat of a ground invasion did Milošević capitulate. During the war's eleven weeks, new scenarios and military needs arose, and all three new NATO members faced some unexpected requests from NATO. All three states did most of what NATO asked them to do, both during Operation Allied Force and after (in terms of peace-keeping). On the other hand, they were not asked to do much, especially in terms of combat missions. Indeed, Hungary's ability even to patrol its own airspace was quite limited, amounting to about two hours per day.[25]

Polish support for NATO efforts was the most consistent. NATO asked Warsaw to accomplish two tasks: to raise the readiness of its brigade already deployed in Bosnia and to provide air transport. The second task so taxed Polish assets that it left them with no additional lift to deliver humanitarian aid, which then had to be delivered in trucks.[26] Still, Warsaw quickly and clearly pledged ground troops if they should be needed,[27] while Polish politicians supported the bombing (though former chief of general staff Thadeus Wilecki denounced it as "barbarous").[28]

By contrast, both the Czech and Hungarian governments faced serious political difficulties regarding the war. Three hundred thousand ethnic Hungarians live in the Vojvodina region of northern Serbia, while many Czechs still remember the diplomatic support of the non-Warsaw Pact Yugoslavs during the Prague Spring of 1968. To be sure, many citizens of both countries were deeply troubled by Serb behavior over the course of

---

[24] Ivo Daalder and Michael O'Hanlon, *Winning Ugly: NATO's War to Save Kosovo* (Washington, DC: Brookings Institution Press, 2000), p. vii.

[25] Hungarian MiG-29s also lacked NATO-compatible identification friend-or-foe communication gear.

[26] Jeffrey Simon, *Poland and NATO: A Study in Civil–Military Relations* (Lanham, MD: Rowman & Littlefield, 2004), p. 102.

[27] Ryan Hendrickson, "NATO's Visegrad Allies: The First Test in Kosovo," *Journal of Slavic Military Studies* 13:2 (2000), pp. 28–30.

[28] Simon, *Poland and NATO*, p. 102.

the 1990s; Hungarian foreign policy tilted heavily toward Croatia, and the country clandestinely delivered weapons to the Croatian army in 1991.[29] Yet, for many Czech and Hungarian citizens, war seemed an extreme step.

Vigorous internal debates followed, a pattern departing from a standard observation about the first fifteen years of postcommunist partisan competition. Grzymla-Busse and Jones Luong have argued that the combination of a broad cross-party consensus in most CEE states about joining the European Union and the EU's "take it or leave it" negotiating style has meant that political parties have not actually debated much over substantive policy issues.[30] Lacking substantive areas of disagreement, CEE politicians tended to debate issues of "managerial competence" in pursuing the goals with respect to EU membership that all agreed were important. But this pattern did not extend to security policy, over which party competition has been more robust and vigorous than in many other areas.[31]

Certainly during the Kosovo crisis, Hungary saw substantial if ultimately manageable differences between the government and opposition. The Fidesz government's basic position was that Hungary would support but not participate in the air strikes, and that no NATO ground invasion could be launched from Hungarian territory.[32] Fidesz backing of NATO bombing still exposed the government to criticism from the socialist opposition (MSzP), especially over whether NATO forces could launch bombing operations from Hungarian bases (as opposed to just using their airspace).[33] In fact, the MSzP's parliamentary group proposed to modify the parliamentary resolution that had given NATO unlimited access to Hungarian facilities and airspace; the motion, which was ultimately defeated, would have prevented NATO air offensives against targets in Yugoslavia from being launched from Hungarian airports. In any event, Hungary could make virtually no military contribution to the events in

[29] Zoltan Barany, "An Outpost on the Troubled Periphery," in Michta, *America's New Allies*, p. 80.

[30] Anna Grzymala-Busse and Pauline Jones Luong, "Reconceptualizing the State: Lessons from Post-Communism," *Politics and Society* 30:4 (2002), pp. 529–554.

[31] In this sense, the pluralism of CEE foreign policies may actually be a harbinger of a renewed pluralism in domestic politics now that EU membership has been achieved.

[32] Milada Vachudová, "The Atlantic Alliance and the Kosovo Crisis: The Impact of Expansion and the Behavior of New Allies," in Pierre Martin and Mark Brawley (eds.), *Alliance Politics, Kosovo, and NATO's War: Allied Force or Forced Allies?* (New York: St. Martin's, 2001), pp. 201–220.

[33] Hungary had made this distinction in February 1994, when it indicated it would close its airspace to AWACS in the event of Western bombing of Serbia. Yet Hungarian-based AWACS were involved in the shooting-down of four Serbian jets (*Financial Times*, March 3, 1994).

Yugoslavia; as a result of its poor performance, a major initiative was launched to reshape the HDF between the years 2000 and 2013.

The Czech political elite was far more openly divided about NATO policy. The Czech Social Democrats (ČSSD) were in power, and their voters were more skeptical of NATO than Hungary's Fidesz voters. Up to 62 percent of the Czech population opposed the NATO campaign in Yugoslavia, and only 25 percent of Social Democratic voters had supported NATO membership in the first place.[34] Once the bombing began, Czech voters were subjected to a flurry of contending perspectives. Bizarrely, the government of Miloš Zeman condemned the air strikes in late March 1999, claiming not to have been consulted on the action against Kosovo but to have been presented with a fait accompli decided before their formal membership. It soon came out that the government had in fact approved the strikes in the NATO Council, and it retracted its prior statement. Meanwhile, the Czech vice prime minister, Egon Lánský, declared that Milošević's ethnic cleansing of Kosovo was morally justified because of the NATO bombing, and a few ČSSD deputies traveled to Belgrade to express their support for Milošević. On the other hand, in the April 2, 1999, vote on allowing NATO to use Czech airspace, twelve of the sixteen ČSSD ministers voted yes, while the other four abstained. On April 21, the parliament approved by a wide margin the use of Czech air facilities and roads for the transit of NATO forces.[35]

Four other decisions – by the prime minister, the ex-prime minister, the president, and the foreign minister – are noteworthy. First, Prime Minister Zeman preemptively distanced the government from any ground campaign. The Czech decision to take this option off the table before NATO had formally considered it was greeted with annoyance in several NATO capitals. Second, Václav Klaus stunned many members of the Czech political establishment by denouncing the NATO bombing (as he would later the March 2003 invasion of Iraq). Third, President Havel – Klaus' bitter rival – strongly supported the bombing and "regretted only that the military action had not started earlier." Havel invoked the Munich syndrome and constantly made reference to fears of appeasing a dictator. Finally, as the ČSSD government emphasized its efforts for a diplomatic settlement, Foreign Minister Jan Kavan pushed a joint Greek–Czech peace initiative that also increased NATO frustration toward Prague. Many observers of the Czech political scene concluded

[34] Milan Znoj, "Czech Attitudes Toward the War," *East European Constitutional Review* 8:3 (1999), pp. 47–50.
[35] Vachudová, "The Atlantic Alliance and the Kosovo Crisis."

that the Kosovo crisis had underscored the extent to which both the Czech political class and public opinion had focused on the benefits of NATO membership without really dwelling on its costs.[36]

While the Czech government met its basic procedural obligations during the Kosovo bombing, those obligations were relatively light given the Czechs' geographical position. The Hungarians were asked to do more significant things and generally performed well in political terms even if their military contribution was very modest. After the Kosovo crisis, USIA polls indicated that support for NATO membership had softened in both the Czech Republic and Hungary (down seven and ten points, respectively, between 1998 and 2000).[37] Hungarians supported routine overflights and stationing NATO troops slightly more than did Czechs, while Czechs supported sending troops to defend an ally and hosting routine exercises more than did Hungarians. In Poland, on the other hand, popular sentiment was more favorable toward NATO on all these issues. Thus Czech and Hungarian attitudes differ substantially from those in Poland, and they responded negatively to initial experiences in the Alliance.

Extracting military commitments: efforts to modernize the CEE militaries

In addition to their varying political difficulties, the Kosovo crisis underscored how modest the military contributions of the three new members were likely to be. The war showed that, if these armies could not meet certain standards, they simply could not fight alongside their NATO partners. The older NATO member states therefore redoubled efforts to oblige the CEE states to modernize their militaries.

Prior to membership, two basic tools had been used. First, NATO asked the three states to complete its annual defense planning questionnaire (DPQ), an instrument that all NATO members submit every year. Second, in response to their DPQ answers, the supreme allied commander in Europe (SACEUR) set target force goals (TFG) for the new

---

[36] See Marybeth Peterson Ulrich, "Developing Mature National Security Systems in Postcommunist States: The Czech Republic and Slovakia," *Armed Forces and Society* 28:3 (2002), pp. 403–425. Vachudová and Hendrickson both emphasize the significant difference between strong Polish and, to a lesser extent, Hungarian political consensus and the Czechs' weak political consensus: Vachudová, "The Atlantic Alliance and the Kosovo Crisis"; Hendrickson, "NATO's Visegrad Allies."

[37] Brad Gutierrez, "Defense Reform in Central Europe and the Challenges of NATO Membership: The Case of Hungary," Ph.D. dissertation, Department of Political Science, University of California, San Diego (2002), p. 155.

members, who then negotiated agreements to meet these targets. For example, the Czechs negotiated thirty-one separate compatibility goals with NATO in 1999; tasks included standardizing signs and maps and providing Western instrument landing systems for their airports.[38] Reports indicate, however, that the Czechs may have met as few as half of these more technical goals.[39] For its part, the HDF made good on only about one-quarter of the 100 points for army development that had been approved in talks with NATO officials. Moreover, the projects completed tended to be small-ticket items, such as upgrades in the equipment of peacekeeping units.[40] Poland had signed up for 65 goals in anticipation of NATO membership and then added another 135 force goals and 45 long-term requirements in 2000. It completed 23 of the initial 65 goals by the time of membership, with 37 others proceeding in a satisfactory manner and 5 in serious jeopardy as of 2001.[41] Of the second round of commitments, however, only 22 had been accomplished by 2001, though most of the others were proceeding in some fashion.[42]

A third major driver of institutional change was coterminous with NATO's first enlargement. NATO's Defense Capabilities Initiative (DCI) was launched in 1999 to ensure that all NATO member countries had compatible equipment, personnel, and training.[43] The DCI is composed of representatives from all NATO countries who meet each week to "review progress and guide the process." It aims to enable NATO forces to get to out-of-area trouble spots quickly, legally, and efficiently, to support them while there, and to allow them to use the latest technology as they fight in units that may include several nationalities. While the DCI is mandatory and a challenge to all members, it was especially so for the CEE states. For example, *"there was not a single area where the Hungarian*

---

[38] Elizabeth Gleick, "Are They Up To It? A Promising Czech Soldier Says His Nation Is Not Ready for NATO," *Time*, December 15, 1997, pp. 36–37. For an extended discussion of military requirements such as modernization of the arsenal, improvement in communications, interoperability reforms, military education, language capabilities, and reform of military doctrines, see Christopher Jones, "NATO Enlargement: Brussels as the Heir of Moscow," *Problems of Post-Communism* 45:4 (1998), pp. 44–55; and Barany, "Hungary."

[39] Yaniszewski, "Postcommunist Civil–Military Reform," p. 394.

[40] *Nepszabadsag/BBC Monitoring*, August 9, 2002.

[41] Simon, *Poland and NATO*, pp. 119–20.

[42] Since 1997, Polish modernization has also been driven by a new army program known as Army 2012. Army 2012, while subject to several amendments in subsequent years, was Poland's first major reform document written around the premise of NATO membership, which allowed Poland to forgo many of the usual assets of territorial defense. Thus (as in the Czech case), certainty about NATO membership did lead to a substantial reorientation of modernization priorities: Michta, "Poland: A Linchpin."

[43] NATO, *NATO Handbook* (Brussels: NATO Office of Information and Press, 2001), pp. 50–52.

Defense Forces had achieved compatibility with NATO when the country joined the Alliance in 1999."[44]

The Prague Summit in November 2002 was another opportunity for the new member states to reaffirm their commitment to NATO, and at least some of that reaffirmation came in the form of specific new pledges. Claiming that Hungary had met less than a third of its Alliance commitments under the Orbán government, the new defense minister, Ferenc Juhasz, pledged that by 2005 Hungary would provide its own troops with protection against biological and chemical weapons, provide a rapid-reaction battalion for NATO use and logistics for a second battalion, increase air transport, and upgrade its Russian-made MI-24 assault and transport helicopters.

These modernization efforts are incremental and far from glamorous, but they are important. Whatever combat deficiencies long-time NATO members such as Germany may have, they are significantly less than those of these three new members. These difficulties were underscored during the Kosovo air campaign, in which the United States lost its first stealth aircraft in combat (after losing none despite many hundreds more sorties in the Gulf War). Why was this? Because the aircraft of some NATO members did not have appropriate identification systems, all NATO aircraft were obliged to fly in a preset formation. When Serb anti-aircraft batteries visually observed this pattern several days running, they were able to prepare for its arrival and ambush the stealth aircraft when it flew by at the customary time.

Niche forces and two-tiered forces

The preceding account has emphasized how hard it is to implement real change in national military structures, as opposed to deep cuts with no particular concept in mind. Appropriate levels and types of military spending are vexing political questions for any society but, without external pressure, the CEE states are likely to do too little in this area. Historical legacies left bloated and ineffective CEE militaries that required major transformation, but there is no significant electoral incentive for politicians to devote themselves to modernization. Nor have NATO incentives been consistently effective. Even when NATO has offered incentives

---

[44] Pál Dunay, "Civil–Military Relations in Hungary: No Big Deal," in Timothy Edmunds, Anthony Forster, and Andrew Cottey (eds.), *Democratic Control of the Military in Postcommunist Europe: Guarding the Guards* (London: Palgrave, 2002), p. 77, emphasis in original.

for reform, CEE politicians could simply pass "new" framework programs or make grand promises but then fail to implement them.

As a compromise, the Alliance has allowed both the first and second wave of new member states to develop particular specialty niches that can at least be of some use to multinational, out-of-area interventions. It has also acquiesced as CEE states built two-tiered forces in which only the NATO-dedicated showcase units meet professional standards. As these states failed to keep pace with the full range of modernization demands, they have moved toward niche forces as a fallback position, allowing them to help in NATO missions and avoid the label of security free-riders. As Stefan Füle, Czech first deputy minister of defense, put it in 2002, "We are pushing for specialization among all NATO members, especially the Europeans since no one can compete with the USA in terms of budget size. In order to accomplish this, we will require a NATO umbrella. A new army must defend national interests abroad and not at home. It must be an army capable of responding to situations that do not fall under Article 5."[45] Hungary's ambassador to NATO, Andras Simonyi, puts the point even more explicitly:

> It is nonsense to build smaller replicas of large countries' armies. Why should small countries field cripplingly expensive fighter aircraft, when the alliance has overcapacity in this area? Instead, we must look at areas of specialization. In Hungary's case, this might include engineers and troops for point defense, military intelligence, special forces, search and rescue and gendarmerie.[46]

Plans for the NATO Rapid Reaction Force – envisioned as 5,000–20,000 soldiers raised in 7–30 days and sustainable for one month – also contain an explicit division of labor. For example, Germany is to provide much of the airlift with C-17s, Norway will focus on special operations, the Dutch will emphasize smart weapons, the Romanians are to provide a mountain battalion, and the Czechs are to specialize in defense against weapons of mass destruction (WMD). In the wake of the Prague Summit in 2003, Poland also pledged support in the areas of reconnaissance and WMD defense.[47] József Bali, deputy state secretary in the Hungarian Ministry of Defense (MoD), suggested Hungary could focus on technical units like army health care or defense against WMD.[48]

Such niche strategies may make good sense. More explicit interdependence may induce more security cooperation in the region. Fiscally, rather than ask the CEE militaries to do too much (i.e., prepare for World War III) or too little (i.e., cuts without concepts), niche strategies

---

[45] Stefan Füle, Interview, *Jane's Defense Weekly* 38:8 (2002), p. 32.
[46] Andras Simonyi, Interview, *Jane's Intelligence Review* 14:7 (2002), p. 56.
[47] Simon, *Poland and NATO*, p. 141.   [48] *Nepszabadsag/BBC Monitoring*, August 9, 2002.

may allow a realistic and useful balance. Certainly niche strategies as part of a broader alliance are hardly unprecedented. For example, the Japanese military performs minesweeping functions that are vital to US Navy operations in the Pacific. And niche strategies may provide reassurance to both opponents and advocates of national militaries within the CEE societies themselves. Those who worry about the military becoming too large and assertive can be reassured by the constraints on the military that come with being embedded in an alliance of democracies and by the way that the modest forces of individual CEE states soften the security dilemma for those on its borders.[49] Those who worry that, on the contrary, the national military will simply wither away can be reassured that, no matter how thin the social commitment, NATO obligations will ensure a certain minimum level of military competence.

A second CEE response to demands for military reform is two-tiered forces in which showcase units are developed for NATO contingencies while other units are starved of funds. This trend is also understandable, but the extremes to which some CEE states have taken it makes it less defensible than the niche-forces concept. The trend toward two-tiered forces is especially clear in out-of-area peacekeeping missions, where the new NATO members have been obliged to add some capabilities to contribute to NATO missions. All CEE states have conserved on defense spending by singling out units earmarked for NATO operations for priority treatment, and some of these units are quite competent.[50] For example, Poland sent a very small elite commando unit to support the Iraq invasion – a unit that saw action alongside US forces in securing southern oil fields. Poland was also able to deploy capable units from its twelfth mechanized division as half of its 2,500 troop commitment to Iraq.[51] But building showcase units runs counter to Polish traditions and could undercut morale. Moreover, some showcase units are simply too small to contribute much to NATO. For example, Hungary designated twelve MiG-29 pilots as "NATO-qualified," though only two of them were qualified for both day and night missions.[52] The top Hungarian pilot flew 63 hours in 1997, compared to a NATO average of 160–180 hours per year for fighter pilots.[53]

---

[49] Robert Jervis, "Cooperation Under the Security Dilemma," *World Politics* 30:2 (1978), pp. 167–214.
[50] Barany, "Hungary," p. 13; Thomas Szayna and F. Stephen Larrabee, *East European Military Reform After the Cold War: Implications for the United States* (Santa Monica: Rand Corporation, 1995).
[51] *Die Welt*, November 10, 2003.   [52] Gutierrez, "Defense Reform," p. 162.
[53] See also Jeffrey Simon, "Partnership for Peace (PFP): After the Washington Summit and Kosovo," *Strategic Forum* 167 (1999), 1–5; Dunay, "Civil–Military Relations in Hungary," p. 81; Barany, "An Outpost on the Troubled Periphery," p. 86.

In short, engagement with NATO has driven CEE militaries to think much more in terms of power projection and to deemphasize defense of their national borders.[54] The danger, however, is that "the Hungarian government ends up with the worst of both worlds – a defense force incapable of defending Hungarian airspace and territory, based on low-quality, poorly trained personnel and a small rapid reaction force capable of working with NATO, but adding little military capability to that force."[55] In the Czech case, there is a "growing awareness in the MoD and the armed forces [that] the deployment of troops abroad is siphoning off too many personnel, is too expensive and is at the cost of a reduction of the fighting effectiveness of the ACR. Moreover, this is occurring at a time when only one-third of Czechs polled support Czech participation in foreign missions.[56] Poland's experience in Iraq, detailed later in this chapter, reveals similar dilemmas. In each of these states, when governments face external demands that accord poorly with the wishes of their voters, they do the minimum necessary to meet those demands.

Extracting policy commitments: Afghanistan and Iraq

Over time, NATO's initial demands that its new members raise their military competence have been largely eclipsed by the demand for policy loyalty. As NATO members came to see the full measure of the CEE defense establishments, they grew less inclined to expect a real military contribution. At the same time, NATO did ask for diplomatic support and policy loyalty. Thus, NATO's recognition of the factors blocking real defense reform led it to refashion its key demands to stress the policy loyalty of CEE states. Of course, there is no *necessary* tension between the two demands. For example, early on, Czech and Hungarian elites hoped to meet both sets of expectations by being good peace-keepers.[57] But this approach had limits for both states since foreign deployments drain

---

[54] Anthony Forster, Timothy Edmunds, and Andrew Cottey (eds.), *The Challenge of Military Reform in Postcommunist Europe: Building Professional Armed Forces* (New York: Palgrave Macmillan, 2002).

[55] Dunay, "Civil–Military Relations in Hungary," p. 64.

[56] Marie Vlachová, "Professionalisation of the Army of the Czech Republic," in Forster, Edmunds, and Cottey, *The Challenge of Military Reform in Postcommunist Europe*, pp. 41–42.

[57] Sebestyen Gorka, "Hungarian Military Reform and Peacekeeping Efforts," *NATO Review* (November 1995), 26–29; Thomas Szayna, "A Small Contributor or a 'Free Rider?,'" in Michta, *America's New Allies*, pp. 112–148.

resources from other areas of military modernization. In practice, CEE governments have found it easier to deliver policy loyalty than military competence.

Because NATO works by consensus, at the end of the day every policy has formal "unanimous" support. But, at least initially, the CEE states felt it imperative to get on board before that consensus was fully formed. As we saw above, in their first big test in Kosovo, the Hungarians and Poles essentially passed – providing air access, diplomatic support, or both – while the Czechs were considered a political liability by many member states. Later – in Afghanistan and especially Iraq – the situation became more complicated. Even without US prompting, all three of the first-wave states were very quick to support NATO's invocation of Article 5 for the United States after 9/11. This dynamic extended even beyond the three new members, as Bulgaria and Slovakia essentially pledged to act as if they were supporting Article 5 on behalf of the United States even though they were not then members of NATO. Again, however, public support for more concrete steps was much softer. Polish support for sending troops to Afghanistan eroded steadily throughout the winter after September 11. Support fell from 77 percent of those polled in September 2001 to 60 percent in October, 54 percent in November, and 45 percent in December. By February 2002, nearly as many Poles opposed sending troops (42 percent) as supported the move (47 percent).[58]

Still, loyalty is cheaper than competence – at least in the short run. Complicating the picture, however, is the fact that individual NATO states may compete for the policy loyalty of CEE states. All three new CEE members famously joined Britain, Spain, Italy, Portugal, and Denmark in publishing an open letter in support of President Bush's policy toward Iraq.[59] France and Germany, which had led the resistance to US and British policy on Iraq, interpreted this gesture as contrary to the European and, indeed, the EU line, even though the EU member states had developed no official "common position" and were deeply divided on the issue. French president Jacques Chirac nevertheless fumed that the CEE states "could hardly have found a better way" of "[diminishing] their chances of entering Europe."[60] CEE leaders reacted strongly, with Latvian president Vaira Vike-Freiberga noting that "we have not heard of any accession criterion that we can be seen but not

---

[58] Simon, *Poland and NATO*, pp. 142–143. The departure of the Polish troops was delayed and reduced so that only in March 2002 did fewer than 100 of the originally announced 300 troops deploy to Bagram Air Force Base in Afghanistan.
[59] *Christian Science Monitor*, January 31, 2003. [60] *Transitions Online*, February 24, 2003.

heard."[61] British prime minister Tony Blair and the EU commissioner for enlargement Günther Verheugen, a German, both publicly underscored the CEE states' right to speak their mind within the EU.[62]

But the story does not end there. Clearly the letter was an opportunity for CEE states to improve their standing with the United States; but Czech and Hungarian support for US policy was notably ambivalent.[63] In the Czech Republic, President Václav Havel signed the letter, giving Prime Minister Vladimir Spidla the chance to play it both ways by having the Czech Republic (but not the government) as a signatory. Havel's term expired within a week of signing the letter, and the foreign minister, Cyril Svoboda, simply noted that it was within "the president's powers" to sign the letter.[64] In Hungary, Fidesz, in opposition, criticized Peter Medgyessy's Socialist government for signing the letter without informing the parliamentary Foreign Affairs Committee and implied that this omission made the letter merely the prime minister's personal opinion. The Polish government, of course, also signed the letter, even though some Polish commentators suggested that Prime Minister Leszek Miller should have followed the Dutch example by supporting the Blair–Aznar initiative without signing the letter, as this was an awkward format for the discussion of central questions of security policy.[65]

These responses to the letter were indicative of differing national sentiments. Poland was clearly the most stalwart supporter of US policy; the Polish foreign minister had indicated by late January 2003 that Poland would take part in a war with Iraq even without a UN resolution, though only about a third of Poles supported the government's position. On the other hand, in February 2003, even under the premise of a UN mandate, only 24 percent of Czechs supported the United States and its partners in preparations for war, with 62 percent opposed. Without a UN mandate, support dropped to 13 percent and opposition rose to 76 percent. In Hungary, support for war even with a UN mandate was a mere 17 percent.[66]

Moreover, the diplomatic coup the letter represented for the United States obscured a host of little-noticed caveats. The Czech Republic, in

---

[61] *Transitions Online*, February 23, 2003.
[62] See the overview of these developments provided by Elizabeth Pond in this volume.
[63] Around the same time, Hungarian foreign minister Ferenc Juhasz even announced that, if the United States finalized a plan for missile defense, Hungary would participate in it (*Interfax Hungary Business News Service*, January 2003, p. 14).
[64] *Transitions Online*, February 3, 2003.
[65] Kerski, "Zwischen Desinteresse und Misstrauen," p. 34.
[66] *Transitions Online*, February 3, 2002. Bulgaria, the only CEE state then on the UN Security Council, indicated very early on that it would support the US position at the UN.

keeping with the niche-forces doctrine, sent a 250-person anti-chemical warfare unit to the region, but the government insisted the unit stay in its Kuwaiti base unless it was actually needed in Iraq for a WMD emergency. The Czechs also sent a 270-person hospital battalion to Iraq, though the United States and Britain reportedly covered most of the 15.5 million euro projected costs.[67] In terms of its diplomatic posture, and despite concerted last-minute pressure from President Bush personally, the Czech Republic's three-party coalition government chose not to become part of the "coalition of the willing."[68] Less than a month later, newly elected President Václav Klaus criticized the US-led invasion in the absence of a UN resolution and called the ambition to build democracy in Iraq an idea "from another planet." The US ambassador to the Czech Republic, Craig Stapleton, walked out of a meeting with Klaus soon after and quipped that the comments of "a single Czech politician" couldn't disrupt the good US–Czech relations.[69] While this statement deftly sidestepped the fact that Klaus was commander-in-chief of the Czech army, it was true that Klaus's ODS party has generally supported the government line during the war (unlike the opposition in Hungary, as we shall see). Prague later agreed to forgive about one-third of Iraq's 126 million euro debt to the Czech Republic and, in January 2004, pledged an additional 16.3 million euros for Iraqi reconstruction. It also sent about 100 military police to Iraq, in addition to the 120 Czech soldiers that remained in Afghanistan under Dutch–German and later NATO command.

Turning to Hungary, while no CEE state saw the massive demonstrations against the war that were widespread in western Europe, the approximately 10,000 who marched in Budapest were significantly more than the few thousand who marched in Prague (or the few hundred in Warsaw).[70] The government nevertheless granted the United States access to its base at Taszar once again, this time to train up to 3,000 Iraqi exiles.[71] But the major opposition party (Fidesz) seized on the poorly handled announcements about the use of Taszar for Iraqi training – it was never clear what these Iraqis were to be trained for – to cast doubt on the government's line. Fidesz, in power after the 9/11 attacks, had not provided even a symbolic Hungarian presence in Afghanistan; and, though the subsequent Medgyessy government clearly sought closer ties to the

[67] *Deutsche Presse Agentur*, April 17, 2003.   [68] *Deutsche Presse Agentur*, March 19, 2003.
[69] *Deutsche Presse Agentur*, April 10, 2003.
[70] *General Anzeiger* (Bonn), January 22, 2003; *Neue Zürcher Zeitung*, February 25, 2003.
[71] *Guardian* (London), January 24, 2003. As it turned out, far fewer Iraqi volunteers materialized, and the camp graduated fewer than 150 trainees before being dismantled, to the obvious relief of the Medgyessy government: Neil Barnett, "Hungary Reviews Defense to Mollify Critics," *Jane's Defence Weekly*, August 7, 2002, p. 6.

United States, it did not have a free hand to do so. For example, in April 2003, a US military aircraft used a Hungarian overflight clearance for the Afghanistan operation to land in Romania as part of an operation directed at Iraq (for which no permission had been sought or granted). The Hungarian parliament reacted by changing the procedures for US overflights to require seven days' advance notice (in emergencies, two days') rather than the matter of hours that US pilots were accustomed to providing.[72] Later, in May 2003, Fidesz withheld its support for deploying a 300-person peacekeeping force, which could be sent only with a two-thirds majority of parliament. The measure passed in July, though the soldiers still required US transport to reach Iraq. But, within a month, Hungarian officials stressed that they would consider a pull-out of Hungarian troops should a "warlike situation" occur.[73] In March 2004, in the wake of the Madrid bombings, Budapest initially indicated that it would reduce the Hungarian troop presence in Iraq. The Medgyessy government retreated from this position within a few days with an announcement extending their commitment until the end of 2005, but then announced in November 2004 that they would pull out all their troops.[74]

Poland played the most important role in Iraq, a role that – as Poles often reminded visitors – went back to the first Gulf War. At that time, Polish intelligence, though still a part of the Warsaw Pact, worked closely with Washington in the months before the conflict.[75] Washington chose the Polish national day, May 3, to announce that Poland would lead one of the occupation zones in Iraq. Warsaw had initially contributed the elite 200-person "Grom" unit to the war in Iraq; additional troops began to arrive throughout the summer of 2003.[76] Since September 2003, the Polish international division in south-central Iraq has consisted of about 9,200 soldiers from more than twenty nations, including 2,500 Poles, 1,600 Ukrainians, and 1,400 Spaniards. It also includes some 2,500 US soldiers and marines tasked with the main fighting missions in the zone.[77]

---

[72] *Vereinigte Wirtschaftsdienst*, April 1, 2003.

[73] *Deutsche Presse Agentur*, July 10 and August 1, 2003.

[74] *Deutsche Presse Agentur*, March 26, 2004; *New York Times*, November 16, 2004.

[75] *Süddeutsche Zeitung*, May 5, 2003. Even earlier, in the 1970s and 1980s, Poland had some 50,000 personnel in Iraq. As a result, several thousand Poles now speak Arabic.

[76] For some time, the number of Polish troops to be involved was unclear, with the defense minister at one point speaking of a force of 4,000–10,000. Similar confusion attended other key questions. Indeed, for the first few weeks, it was not clear to many observers where in Iraq the Polish zone was to be located: Kerski, "Zwischen Desinteresse und Misstrauen," p. 35.

[77] The Poles and the other foreign troops were to concentrate on infrastructure projects and general reconstruction, though the very unstable security situation has led to their involvement in several firefights and occasional attacks from insurgents. US troops retained control in the particularly sensitive town of Najaf in the Polish zone.

The Polish command has enjoyed some assistance from NATO (though not the full logistical support it requested) and even from Russia. More importantly, the United States reportedly agreed to underwrite costs of about $200 million toward Poland's participation, with the Warsaw government itself contributing only about 37 million euros.[78]

At the time of the announcement of Poland's leadership role in Iraq, US ambassador to NATO Nicholas Burns spoke of a "new power in Europe" – notwithstanding Poland's modest military contribution to the war (Australia sent far more troops) and the deep skepticism among the Polish population about US policies. Several Polish elites emphasized the opportunity to demonstrate Polish organizational abilities on a world stage, and several spoke candidly about their desires to see Polish firms win lucrative contracts in the reconstruction era. But such contracts turned out to be exceedingly hard to come by, not only for the Poles but for the other CEE states as well. Czech politicians had set a goal of 100 million euros in contracts, but as of February 2005 that target is still distant.[79] The Poles were much more ambitious, speaking of perhaps $2 billion in contracts, but they too have been disappointed by the decisions thus far. Along with Bush's rejection of President Aleksander Kwasniewski's direct personal appeal for an end to visa obligations for Polish visitors to the United States, the failure to reap any concrete benefits from their involvement has resulted in a noticeable cooling of talk about the transatlantic relationship serving as a substitute for closer ties to Europe.[80]

Meanwhile, the rising sense of danger in the region further eroded the already low popular support for sending Polish troops to Iraq.[81] Though Polish elites have so far generally stood by the United States, President Kwasniewski admitted that he felt "misled" by US claims about WMD in Iraq. Polish officials also had to deal with skepticism about their role from both Germany and France, which Rumsfeld had famously deemed part of "Old Europe." Already stinging from press characterizations as an American "lap dog," "vassal," or even "Trojan donkey," Polish officials embarrassed themselves shortly after the commencement of their mission with what turned out to be an overly hasty public condemnation of France for selling Roland-type rockets to Iraq as late as 2003. Upon

[78] *Süddeutsche Zeitung*, July 31, 2003, and March 15, 2004.

[79] As of this writing, the Czechs have received one contract for 30 million euros, and a Czech firm now 70 percent owned by a US firm received another contract to deliver 1,500 trucks: *Wirtschaftsblatt*, January 17, 2004.

[80] Poland also assumed a much more cooperative stance in the renewed discussions that generated a deal on a draft European Constitutional Treaty: Kerski, "Zwischen Desinteresse und Misstrauen."

[81] *Frankfurter Rundschau*, August 29, 2003.

closer inspection, the rockets discovered by Poland turned out to be more than fifteen years old and the engraved date "2003" the year to which they were guaranteed.[82]

A much more important blow to Poland's operations came with the March 2004 Spanish announcement that the newly elected Zapatero government would pull Spain's 1,400 troops out of Iraq, a move completed in May 2004. Though Poland's defense minister, Jerzy Szmajdzinski, noted that US troops would fill the void, he nevertheless expressed hope that a UN resolution might induce more countries to send troops.[83] In January 2005, outgoing Ukrainian president Leonid Kuchma then tasked his government's foreign and defense ministers to plan the withdrawal of Ukrainian troops during the first half of 2005.[84] Poland is also drawing down. In the wake of the Iraqi elections, the Polish Ministry of Defense announced plans to cut their troops to 1,700.[85]

Military commitments and policy commitments

Ironically, CEE states have benefited from the fact that many Americans seem to have concluded that NATO is no longer a serious military organization. Certainly, the Bush administration appeared to believe that it made more sense to ask the new NATO members for loyalty to American policy than to badger them endlessly to make their defense institutions sound and their militaries competent. Demands for policy loyalty are compatible with the niche forces and, though to a lesser extent, the showcase forces now being developed; both trends permit the United States to fulfill its desire for a broader coalition of the willing and the CEE states to demonstrate that willingness given limited means. Given this greater emphasis on policy loyalty, even states like Bulgaria are invited to join NATO – although their military readiness is below even what was evident in the Czech Republic and Hungary and far below Poland's.

Of course, policy commitments can also entail costs. For the CEE states, the specter of recurrent political rifts within NATO à la Iraq

---

[82] *Frankfurter Rundschau*, October 7, 2003. Poland then suffered another embarrassment when a *Los Angeles Times* investigation reported on Saddam Hussein's successful effort right up to 2001 to buy from Polish scrap-dealers almost 400 Soviet-era rocket engines and parts to illegally extend the range of some of his missiles: Jeffrey Fleishman and Bob Drogin, "The Weapons Files: Iraq Sought Poland's Scrap for Edge," December 31, 2003.

[83] *Frankfurter Rundschau*, April 20, 2004.

[84] *Interfax*, January 10, 2005.

[85] BBC Monitoring, January 4, 2005.

poses the danger that they may be caught between the competing demands of a distant superpower and of the medium-sized powers that dominate their immediate neighborhood. Given the deep divides between Europe and the United States on issues such as the International Criminal Court (ICC), should NATO fall apart or drift farther toward irrelevance then the CEE states will be forced to choose ever more often between their distant patrons in the United States and their local patrons within Europe. The United States will not win all of these stand-offs. In July 2003, Romania was the only CEE country to sign a nonextradition treaty with the United States exempting US military personnel from prosecution before the controversial ICC; in response, the Bush administration cut military aid to thirty-five other states (many from CEE) by a total of $50 million.

This could be a precursor of more serious rifts. Indeed, minor cuts in aid are not the real danger for the CEE states; more serious is the fact that they have cast their security lots in with NATO. In doing so at a time of fiscal crisis, they have moved substantially away from the kind of stand-alone forces that could comprise a reasonable national army in what has been, in historic terms, a bad neighborhood. If NATO loses its stabilizing and integrating capacity in Europe, that will be a high price for CEE states to pay. To be sure, warm bilateral relations with the United States would be of immeasurable help in a true crisis. But betting on the long memory of an embattled, distracted, and increasingly isolated superpower carries with it some real risks.

In short, a breakdown in the Atlantic alliance is not likely to serve the long-term interests of either Washington or the central European states. Whatever its current frustrations with Europe, the United States should think twice before attempting to replace the existing transatlantic relationship with a new and very partial one built around "New Europe."[86]

---

[86] A review of recent proposals can be found in Alan Henrikson, "Why the United States and Europe See the World Differently: An Atlanticist's Rejoinder to the Kagan Thesis," *European Union Studies Association Newsletter* 16:3 (2003), pp. 1–10; see also Henry Kissinger, *Does America Need a Foreign Policy? Toward a Diplomacy for the Twenty-First Century* (New York: Simon & Schuster, 2001).

11 Is Atlanticism dead?

David M. Andrews

Can the political institutions that once formed the backbone of the anti-Soviet alliance long endure after the fall of the common enemy? Did the crisis of 2002–3 portend the demise of the Atlantic partnership? If so, what are the likely consequences? Wrestling with these questions, the contributors to this volume arrive at a range of conclusions. Some common themes emerge, however.

Regardless of where blame lies for the recent debacle – and the contributors differ sharply on that question – there is a shared sense that the project of building and maintaining an Atlantic community is at serious risk. As outlined in the introduction to this volume, the Alliance's strategic purpose is unclear and its domestic support greatly weakened in a number of key countries. The simultaneous fading of strategic clarity and erosion of domestic support is no accident. Only a rearticulation of the partnership's central meaning, in terms that correspond more closely to the desires of citizens and of organized interests on both sides of the Atlantic, will suffice if the Alliance is to thrive in the new century.

But, while the Atlantic mood has improved, it is hardly clear that national leaders will choose to revitalize the Alliance. The combination of tangible challenges and diffuse benefits poses a substantial deterrent. While the nexus of domestic and international politics during the Cold War generally reinforced Atlanticism, or at least resisted strategic decoupling, the political dynamics in a number of NATO's leading states are no longer balanced toward support of the Alliance even in moments of profound international crisis.

To better understand this problem, this concluding chapter summarizes and synthesizes key observations from the preceding contributions. While my own contribution to this volume dwelt at some length on the significance of changes in the international context of the Atlantic partnership for national strategies in the leading member states, here I focus instead on the relationship between international and domestic politics within the Alliance. After outlining how these forces have played out on both sides of the Atlantic, I then turn to the prospects for Atlanticism in the early twenty-first century.

The domestic–international nexus

The introduction to this volume outlined the implicit bargain that informed Alliance politics during most of the Cold War. Understanding that bargain requires differentiating between political rhetoric and actual public policy. For example, while they may have periodically criticized American policy, during the Cold War European governments generally refrained from actively opposing US policy activism around the world. The United States likewise refrained from undermining the project of European integration, including some regional and global arrangements that were plainly contrary to the narrow interests of sectors of the American economy. Both sides complained vigorously about the inequities they perceived in the resulting state of affairs, and sometimes they even explored alternative frameworks. The results of these explorations, however, were inevitably the same: while the precise terms of the Atlantic bargain were periodically modified, the underlying bargain endured.

This endurance can be attributed to the influence of important domestic interests that held a real stake in Atlanticism. The nature of those interests varied, with different coalitions supporting the Alliance at different moments in each of NATO's leading states. But when particular domestic interest groups sought to overturn fundamental elements of the Atlantic bargain, national leaders could generally rely on other, counterbalancing constituencies to mobilize and, at a minimum, to offset the costs of Atlanticism. As a consequence, the price for reaffirming the anti-Soviet partnership was generally not overwhelming.

But the crisis over Iraq was different. In this case, as tensions rose and critics of the Alliance's underlying precepts became increasingly vocal, in many NATO members offsetting constituencies either mobilized very slowly or failed to mobilize at all. Put differently, the costs of managing the Alliance were not successfully contained. Instead, deep divisions emerged between the United States and several of its major European allies, especially France and Germany.

Policy in the United States

For many observers, and certainly for Elizabeth Pond, the crisis over Iraq was mostly the result of the Bush administration's assertive foreign policy style. European leaders were so alienated by this new and aggressive approach that the system became crisis-prone. In particular, the White House's deep and continuing censure of Gerhard Schröder, after the German chancellor had retained his job following an election campaign capitalizing heavily on anti-Bush sentiment, helped drive the somewhat reluctant German leader into the arms of Jacques Chirac – two men who had never previously been particularly cordial. There followed a substantial hardening of the French position on Iraq, in exchange for Germany realigning its positions on a series of European issues to better suit French tastes. The result was the debacle at the United Nations Security Council, where the United States proved unable to secure the votes of more than a handful of the international body's membership in support of its policy of regime change in Baghdad.

There is much to be said for this analysis. Though most Europeans were skeptical about the new president from the beginning, some members of the Bush team seemed to court controversy and to savor quarrels with their European counterparts, regularly ignoring diplomatic niceties and apparently going out of their way to insult other nations' representatives and policies. This was not true of all members of the president's entourage, of course. But it soon became evident that the Bush administration spoke with many voices on foreign policy, and that several of these voices – in particular those of Vice President Richard Cheney, Secretary of Defense Donald Rumsfeld, and Deputy Secretary of Defense Paul Wolfowitz – were going to be loud and caustic.

Insider accounts suggest that the internal debate within the Bush administration was at times as intense as its Atlantic counterpart. Why? In part because foreign policy had become a central prize in an ideological battle between the traditional realists who have generally dominated American external relations under Republican administrations and *arriviste* neoconservatives. The Bush administration contained both, and at times different factions prevailed. The traditionalists, if not multilateralists as a matter of principle, had nevertheless come to accept the politics of international coalition-building as a necessary means to accomplish many important policy ends. For the neoconservatives, on the other hand, multilateralism itself, in many if not all of its guises, represented a dangerous infringement on American constitutional processes and protections. Competition between these two camps resulted in uneasy and somewhat brittle policy stances, with a bias toward unilateral action not only when necessary but as a matter of course.

Still, a bit of perspective is in order. In the United States, foreign policy unilateralism has been a perennial tendency; although the current absence of a serious peer competitor makes this propensity all the more tempting, the impulse itself is hardly novel. One puzzle of the recent episode, though, is that the Bush administration could remain popular while pursuing a foreign policy that was distinctly at odds with the mainstream of American public opinion. A substantial majority of Americans favored close ties with Europe throughout the Cold War, and support for such policies actually reached new highs following 9/11. Why then was the White House able to preside over, and indeed to a substantial degree even to provoke, the greatest transatlantic crisis in half a century without suffering an immediate loss of popular support?

For Miles Kahler, the answer to this question lies both in the particular circumstances of the Bush presidency and in longer-term trends evident in both major American political parties. The tragedy of 9/11 created an opportunity for Bush, as the sitting president, to pursue a vigorous policy response; indeed the more vigorous the better, from the public's standpoint. But the essence of the Bush team's response was to placate the Republican Party's political base rather than to embrace the broad and continuing support for close transatlantic ties in the middle of the political spectrum. Why? Because that centrist support, though wide, has typically been quite weak. There are very few votes to be had in the "apathetic internationalism" of the center; there are substantial votes to be mobilized, however, at either end of the political spectrum, as one appeals to the relatively militant activists of either the Republican or the Democratic Party. Increasingly, both the major parties have turned foreign policy into a partisan issue; thus the policy debate that once stopped "at the water's edge" now extends across the Atlantic and beyond.

Thus, the American political system has come to reflect European party politics more closely: it has become more partisan and more ideologically coherent. As a consequence, and especially in the absence of a strategic imperative such as maintaining the Alliance in the presence of a threat from a hostile superpower, American foreign policy is likely to be both more extreme and more unstable. Appeals from the business community, which generally favors close transatlantic relations, could moderate these tendencies, as will the occasional employment of "triangulating" strategies by political leaders hoping to capture centrist constituencies. But the overall thrust of both presidential and especially congressional politics is now much more directed toward partisan activists than it is anchored in the ideological center; the Atlantic relationship is a potential casualty.

Policy in Europe

As Geir Lundestad reminds us, political change has not been limited to the American side of the Atlantic. The governments of France and Germany chose to resist American leadership during the run-up to the Iraq War not merely in their rhetoric but as a matter of official state policy. Those decisions were made possible by the more permissive security situation, but they are also indicative of changing domestic politics within those states – in particular, generational change and the presence of large Muslim populations. Furthermore, the institutions of the European Union are at last beginning to extend effectively into the realm of security affairs. The enormous power differential between the United States and its European partners encourages this latter development, which, though slow, is already evident and will become more so in years to come. The development of a collaborative defense capability is bound to produce changes in Europe's collective foreign policy stance, placing further pressure on Atlantic relations. These pressures are already evident in Washington's bilateral relations with Europe's major capitals.

Franco-American relations have always been complex, not least because so much of the relationship was premised on unspoken elements of the agendas of both governments. Georges-Henri Soutou describes the tacit consensus that informed official French attitudes during most of the Fifth Republic. This multifaceted program called for exploiting American security guarantees against perceived threats while seeking "reinsurance" from a variety of sources, including the Soviet Union, in the event the United States defaulted on its commitments. Such a nuanced approach was always prone to crisis, and from the 1960s onward there has been a series of rifts and reconciliations within this troubled partnership. Franco-American relations have, in fact, been in a state of low-level crisis since the late 1970s, never having fully recovered from the falling-out between Jimmy Carter and Valéry Giscard d'Estaing; efforts to reestablish a closer partnership during the mid-1990s came to nought. It is in that historic context that the events of 2002 and 2003 must be understood.

But while serious crises have in the past prompted efforts to restore good relations, reconciliation after the Iraq debacle may prove more difficult. This is not only because of the depth of ill-will that the episode generated or even because of those changes in the international system that tend to undermine support for American policy. The most obvious of these changes is, of course, the end of the Cold War; during that sustained conflict, there was a strained but functional convergence between the underlying agendas of the French and American governments. But now the French are much more likely to see American power as a problem to be addressed than a condition to be exploited. This is reflected both in the general refrain of multipolarity that has come to dominate French conceptions of a desirable and balanced international system, and in specific objectives of French foreign policy that are likely to clash, on an increasing number of occasions, with American interests.

In addition to these external considerations, however, there are specific changes in the character and conduct of French domestic politics that are likely to undermine the Atlantic relationship still further. Chief among these is the increasingly polarized organization of the major political parties. As elsewhere, support for the Atlantic relationship is strongest in France's political center; but the amalgamation of Giscard's former party into a broad umbrella group of the right is likely to deprive centrist voters of a decisive voice in the formulation of foreign policy. The absence of an organized constituency in the political center will likewise require moderate Socialists to rely on alliances with the Communists, the Greens, or the ultra-left in order to rule. As a result, there is no domestic political arrangement currently on offer that could support a real refoundation of Franco-American relations along constructive lines. As long as Paris and Washington remain the central interlocutors of the Atlantic dialogue, then, we can expect at least periodic flare-ups.

Hubert Zimmermann too is concerned about the rising influence of domestic political forces that were previously more restrained. In his view, the greatest danger to Atlantic cooperation, and specifically to German–American relations, is the unleashing of populist forces that make genuine cooperation difficult if not impossible – in other words, exactly the sort of behavior that characterized Gerhard Schröder's 2002 election campaign. The absence of the security constraint makes such appeals possible, and the wide differences between German and American worldviews make them electorally desirable. There is a real danger, therefore, that postunification Germany's break with Washington will become more or less permanent.

On the other hand, there are some underappreciated reasons to believe that this will not be the case. One such reason has to do with shared perceptions of the threats posed by the new security environment. Despite sharp divergence on other matters, on the key issue of threat assessment, Germany's official defense policy guidelines do not differ substantially from those of the Bush administration's National Security Strategy. Both Washington and Berlin identify failed states and access to weapons of mass destruction as primary sources of concern; and both agree as well that the solution to this joint problem will require policies aimed at broad social transformation, not simply alliances of convenience with the dictator of the moment. In addition, Germany's deep psychological attachment to multilateral institutions, even if not shared by the George W. Bush administration, nevertheless provides both sides with a basis for developing an eventual *modus vivendi*.

More generally, Germany's transformed situation provides an unexploited opportunity for collaborative efforts with the United States to pursue common objectives. The end of the Cold War not only ended Germany's profound reliance on security from abroad, and especially from the United States; the years that followed German reunification also saw the emergence of a domestic political consensus that the Federal Republic should become a major exporter of security. As a result, Germany is now a leading supplier of peacekeeping forces to troubled regions across the globe, an extraordinary transformation of its role during the Cold War. This changed situation and newly developed capacity, however, make it even more essential for Washington to develop a framework for collaboration with Berlin, and with the other states of the European Union, that shares the benefits as well as the costs of international political leadership; otherwise the Atlantic powers risk working at crosspurposes.

In the United Kingdom, unlike Germany, the end of the Cold War did not fundamentally change the context and orientation of foreign policy. Postwar British governments have engaged in almost continuous efforts to serve as a bridge between Europe and the United States, helping each to understand the perspective and legitimate concerns of the other. Since the fall of the Berlin wall, this approach has remained at the heart of British policy under the governments of both John Major and Tony Blair. But as William Wallace and Tim Oliver point out, the period from September 11, 2001, through the invasion of Iraq has severely shaken the concept of the "special relationship," and of the whole idea of Britain acting as a bridge between the United States and Europe.

In fact, Blair's staunch support for the Bush administration's policy of removing Saddam Hussein from power was only partly rooted in his commitment to transatlantic cooperation; it derived as well from his personal conviction that the Baghdad regime represented a genuine threat to global security. But this conviction was framed within the British government's traditional preference to seek influence within Washington by offering public support while restricting criticism to private settings. Blair's strategy of responding to the Bush administration with "yes, but" in the run-up to the war, in contrast to Paris's "no, unless," therefore made strategic sense; but it lacked widespread public support. The long-term prognosis for basing Britain's relationship with the United States on such an unpopular policy will depend on the fruits that it produces. These may yet prove to be considerable. In the short term, however, London has alienated its European partners without having demonstrated any great leverage over policy in Washington.

Rome, like London, chose to support the war in Iraq. Italy's predilection for a close relationship with the United States predates the Cold War; World War II left the Italian state in a greatly weakened position, both domestically and internationally, and periodically reemphasizing the link with Washington has served a succession of Italian governments well on both fronts. As Leopoldo Nuti explains, the Atlantic partnership helped keep the far left out of power, an objective of the Christian Democratic right; demonstrating loyalty to that partnership has likewise helped the moderate left to identify itself as a force capable of governing responsibly. Externally, keeping the European project embedded in an Atlantic framework has helped Italy to resist domination by its European partners, and especially by France. Thus, while relations with the United States have sometimes been testy, the dissolution of the USSR had less consequence for the Italian–American relationship than it did for either French or German relations with the United States. The fear of Soviet domination was never a central motivation for Italian support of the Atlantic alliance, and hence the disappearance of that threat has not significantly altered Italian foreign policy priorities.

It should come as no surprise, then, that Silvio Berlusconi has proved willing to ally himself so firmly with the administration of George W. Bush, both on the Iraq War and on other issues. That Rome's support for Washington has been accompanied by a marked cooling of the Italian state's enthusiasm for various aspects of European integration (i.e., the growth of supranational institutions and policies), on the other hand, represents a genuine break with the past. Traditionally the Atlantic and European impulses have been carefully balanced, and both have been made to serve Italy's strategic interests: Rome has sought compensation, at both the European and Atlantic levels, for the national state's internal and external weaknesses. Italian policy is now unbalanced in that, while support for some aspects of European integration remains strong (e.g., military cooperation), the government's support for Europe more generally has weakened. This weakening reflects the particular composition of the governing coalition, however, and may not outlast it.

The Alliance under stress

To summarize, the collapse of the Soviet empire weakened the external discipline on Alliance members, especially in the United States and Germany. Meanwhile, changes in the organization of domestic politics in France and the United States, and in political discourse in Germany and the United Kingdom, have further raised the domestic costs of successfully managing the Alliance. In Italy, by contrast, the domestic political situation has actually reinforced the establishment's traditional pro-American bias, although a backlash could be mounting.

But what about the benefit side of the ledger? What utility does the Alliance provide in the absence of a common foe? Marc Trachtenberg examines the new security environment closely. In his view, the situation is genuinely new, complex, and ultimately confusing. Stateless actors, sometimes working in collaboration with hostile governments, operate in a setting where both weapons of mass destruction and the means to deliver them can be acquired with relative ease. No agreement exists as yet, either within the individual members of the Alliance or among them, about how best to deal with this state of affairs.

In this new security environment, and absent an expert consensus about the most appropriate response to Saddam's continued defiance of existing Security Council resolutions, almost any policy toward Iraq was bound to be controversial. That said, Trachtenberg argues that the Bush administration's policy was, on the whole, a thoughtful effort to come to grips with the changed security situation – a situation that, after all, had resulted in the destruction of a considerable portion of downtown Manhattan and an unprecedented attack on the headquarters of the American civilian defense leadership. As such, the policy deserved at least the respectful attention and close examination of the United States' most trusted allies.

But Trachtenberg believes that American policy never received the type of attention and examination it deserved in Europe, and was instead subjected to a campaign of intense vilification. The deep and troubling questions associated with the new security environment were never seriously addressed; instead, debate raged about American motives for removing Saddam, which resulted in a degradation of international discourse. The United States was branded as a lawless vigilante, and indeed as a major threat to international security. These charges had little basis in international law as it has actually been understood and practiced, and for senior officials of some of the United States' closest and most longstanding allies to make such inflammatory remarks necessarily opened the door to even more exaggerated claims by other actors. More valuable would have been a careful examination of the rival claims advanced on the one hand by the United States and Britain regarding the strategic necessity of armed enforcement of the UN's longstanding resolutions regarding Iraq, and on the other hand the view advanced most forcefully by France and Germany regarding the viability of a continued regime of international inspections – an approach Trachtenberg finds deeply suspect. But instead of deliberative discussion, transatlantic debate quickly degenerated into a degree of invective unprecedented in the history of the Alliance.

Trachtenberg's assessment of responsibility for the Atlantic crisis differs in almost every particular from Pond's, as discussed earlier; yet a robust synthesis is possible. The Bush administration's cavalier attitude on a host of international issues well before 9/11 had indeed poisoned the well of Atlantic dialogue, and the White House's rapid return to this policy style after only a brief interlude deepened the existing dismay of European governments. As a result, US policy toward Iraq rarely received a fair hearing in the European media or in public policy discussions, and was instead often – even typically – made subject to caricature. To a substantial degree, two parallel conversations took place: an American (and to a certain degree Anglo-American) one about how best to disarm Iraq, and a continental European one about how best to police the world's self-appointed policeman. Each paid lip service to the other's concerns, but plainly subordinated these to its own central interests. Rarely were both of these questions engaged seriously and simultaneously.

The resulting discourse was typically shallow and often coarse, leading Trachtenberg to wonder if genuine and productive Atlantic dialogue on issues of real moment remains possible. If not, the consequences will be significant. Trachtenberg regards eventual American withdrawal from the Alliance and the end of Washington's postwar guarantee of European security as, though hardly inevitable, real possibilities. This prospect should therefore be faced philosophically, he argues, and without undue sentimentality. Part of the preparation for such an eventuality would include contingency planning for an appropriate successor regime, and for a smooth transition to the same.

Wade Jacoby assesses the balance sheet somewhat differently. While preparations to deter and, if necessary, to confront a single, awesome opponent no longer constitute the *raison d'être* of the Alliance, the Atlantic community still benefits from maintaining a framework for joint military action. Absent such a framework, efforts to punish leaders of rogue states or to bring peace to war-torn regions will be severely hampered. "Coalitions of the willing" may on occasion be helpful, but primarily for political rather than military reasons; if the aim is genuine armed capacity on the ground (and in the air), then such fleeting partnerships are no substitute for a real military alliance that permits substantial coordination among well-equipped and well-trained units.

Yet NATO at present lacks many of these qualities, and as a consequence of the war in Iraq the situation is only likely to get worse. Jacoby documents how the Bush administration's efforts to secure diplomatic support for its policy toward Baghdad included relaxing previous demands on the new NATO members from central and eastern Europe to bring their national militaries into line with Alliance standards. These commitments had always been onerous for cash-strapped governments, and Jacoby's case studies of Poland, Hungary, and the Czech Republic reveal how little progress had been made in upgrading their military competence even before the war in Iraq. But external pressure for additional improvements has now been relaxed, as the White House in effect traded away long-term joint military capacity for short-term political support. Such bargains are understandable; similar deals helped cement the international coalition that went to war against Iraq in 1991. But Washington's credibility is already stretched thin in Warsaw, Budapest, and Prague; even the continued rhetorical support of these governments is far from assured. Meanwhile, another unhappy consequence of the Atlantic crisis is that expected improvements in NATO's military capacity now have to be discounted.

The future of the Atlantic community

The obstacles to continued cooperation among the Atlantic allies are real; overcoming them will not be easy. In my contribution to this volume, I played the role of objective analyst in outlining the sources and character of those obstacles. In concluding, let me now assume the role of policy advocate.

While abstract historical forces help shape the fate of nations, they do not determine them. One of the many aims of diplomacy is to construct cooperation out of the raw materials of state interests. Understood in this light, the Atlantic crisis over Iraq was a massive diplomatic failure – a failure that reflects well on no one. But there remains the potential to restructure the Alliance in accordance with a vision of shared interests and shared responsibilities. Leaders from both sides of the Atlantic can still forge a new understanding corresponding more closely to the contemporary needs of the Alliance members, if they choose to do so.

Such an understanding might result in a renewed European "invitation," to use Geir Lundestad's evocative term, for continued US engagement in European security matters, and a corresponding restatement of traditional American support for continued European integration. If so, there will undoubtedly be important qualifications to both these commitments. So be it. Far better to delineate the shape of the future Atlantic partnership than to allow it to become a casualty of war, and of the bickering of policy underlings.

At present, though, official attitudes toward these essential questions remain unclear precisely because leaders at the highest levels have permitted them to become so. This neglect does their collective publics a disservice. The Alliance is a patrimony; citizens should hold their governments responsible if this legacy is squandered. The Atlantic partnership has survived past crises intact, even if it was transformed in the process. It can do so again, given the political will to accomplish this objective.

References

Ackermann, A., "Why Europe and America Don't See Eye to Eye," *International Politics* 40 (March 2003), 121–136.

Aliboni, R., "Il dibattito sulla politica europea di sicurezza e difesa" ["The Debate on European Policy on Security and Defense"], in Istituto Affari Internazionali, *L'Italia nella politica internazionale, 1993* (Rome: SIPI, 1993), 142–154.

Ambrose, Stephen E., *Eisenhower: The President* (New York: Simon & Schuster, 1984).

American Political Science Association, Committee on Political Parties, "Toward a More Responsible Two-Party System: A Report of the Committee on Political Parties," *American Political Science Review* 44:3 (1950), part 2, supplement.

Andrews, D., "The United States and Its Atlantic Partners: The Evolution of American Grand Strategy," *Cambridge Review of International Affairs* 17:3 (October 2004), 421–436.

Art, R. J., *A Grand Strategy for America* (Ithaca: Cornell University Press, 2003).

Ashdown, P., *Ashdown Diaries: 1997–1999* (London: Penguin Books, 2001).

Asmus, R., *Opening NATO's Door* (New York: Columbia University Press, 2002).

"Rebuilding the Atlantic Alliance," *Foreign Affairs* 82:5 (September–October 2003), 20–31.

Bacevich, A. J., *American Empire: The Realities and Consequences of US Diplomacy* (Cambridge: Harvard University Press, 2002).

Bailes, A. J. K., "NATO's New Response Force," *Transatlantic Internationale Politik* 4:1 (Spring 2003), 25–29.

Balmond, L. (ed.), *Les interventions militaires françaises en Afrique* [French Military Interventions in Africa] (Paris: Pedone, 1998).

Barany, Z., "Hungary: Appraising a New NATO Member," *Clausewitz-Studien* (1998), 3–31.

"The Military and Security Legacies of Communism," in Z. Barany and I. Volgyes (eds.), *The Legacies of Communism in Eastern Europe* (Baltimore: Johns Hopkins University Press, 1995), 101–117.

"An Outpost on the Troubled Periphery," in Michta, *America's New Allies*, 74–111.

Becker, J. J., *Crises et alternances 1974–2000* (Paris: Le Seuil, 2002).

Bennett, A., *Condemned to Repetition? The Rise, Fall, and Reprise of Soviet–Russian Military Interventionism, 1973–1996* (Cambridge: MIT Press, 1999).

Bergner, J. T., *The New Superpowers: Germany, Japan, the US and the New World Order* (New York: St. Martin's Press, 1991).

Binder, S. A. "The Dynamics of Legislative Gridlock, 1947–1996," *American Political Science Review* 93:3 (September 1999), 519–533.

Blair, T., *New Britain: My Vision of a Young Country* (London: Fourth Estate, 1996).

Blix, H., *Disarming Iraq* (London: Bloomsbury, 2004).

Bollmann, Y., *Ce que veut l'Allemagne* (Paris: Bartillat, 2003).

Bonnet, A., *Iraq: le veto français* (Paris: Les Dossiers de France Demain, 2003).

Bouton, M. and Page, B. (eds.), *Worldviews 2002: American Public Opinion and Foreign Policy* (Chicago: Chicago Council on Foreign Relations, 2002).

Worldviews 2002: Topline Data from US Public Survey (Chicago: Chicago Council on Foreign Relations, 2002).

Bozo, F., "The Effects of Kosovo and the Danger of Decoupling," in J. Howorth and J. T. S. Keeler (eds.), *Defending Europe: The EU, NATO and the Quest for Autonomy* (London: Palgrave, 2003), 61–80.

Braithwaite, R., "End of the Affair," *Prospect* (May 2003).

Brogi, A., *L'Italia e l'egemonia americana nel Mediterraneo* [Italy and American Hegemony in the Mediterranean] (Florence: Nuova Italia, 1996).

Brownlie, I., *International Law and the Use of Force by States* (New York: Oxford University Press, 1963).

Brzezinski, Z., *The Choice: Global Domination or Global Leadership* (New York: Basic Books, 2004).

"The Premature Partnership," *Foreign Affairs* 73:2 (March–April 1992), 67–82.

"Where Do We Go from Here?" *Transatlantic Internationale Politik* 4:3 (Fall 2003), 3–10.

Buchanan, P. J., *A Republic, Not An Empire: Reclaiming America's Destiny* (Washington, DC: Regnery Publishing, 2002).

Caplan, G., "A Transatlantic Approach to the Middle East Conflict: Do We Have Enough in Common?," AICGS/DAAD Working Paper Series (Washington, DC: AICGS 2003).

Carter, R. G., "Congress and Post-Cold War US Foreign Policy," in J. M. Scott (ed.), *After the End: Making US Foreign Policy in the Post-Cold War World* (Durham: Duke University Press, 1998), 108–137.

Chalmers, M., "The Atlantic Burden-Sharing Debate: Widening or Fragmenting?," *International Affairs* 77:3 (2001), 569–585.

Churchill, W., *A History of the English-Speaking Peoples* (London: Cassell, 1956–8).

Clarke, R. A., *Against All Enemies* (New York: Free Press, 2004).

Cogan, C., *French Negotiating Behavior: Dealing with La Grande Nation* (Washington, DC: United States Institute of Peace Press, 2003).

Cohen, S. and Smouts, M. C., *La politique extérieure de Valéry Giscard d'Estaing* (Paris: Presses de la FNSP, 1985).

Cointet, J. P., Lachaise, B., Le Béguec, G. and Mayeur, J. M. (eds.), *Un politique: Georges Pompidou* (Paris: PUF, 2001).

Coombs, C. A., *The Arena of International Finance* (New York: Wiley, 1976).

Cooper, R., *The Breaking of Nations: Order and Chaos in the Twenty-First Century* (London: Atlantic, 2003).

The Post-Modern State and the World Order (London: Demos, 1996).

Cornish, P., "The British Military View of European Security 1945–1950," in A. Deighton (ed.), *Building Post-War Europe: National Decision-Makers and European Institutions, 1948–1963* (Basingstoke: Macmillan, 1995).

Cottey, A., Edmunds, T. and Forster, A., "Beyond Prague," *Nato Review* 3 (2002), 1–5.

Cremasco, M., "L'Italia e la sicurezza internazionale" ["Italy and International Security"], in Istituto Affari Internazionali, *L'Italia nella politica internazionale, 1994* (Roma: SIPI, 1994), 63–79.

Cuche, P., "Iraq: And If France Was Wrong?" ["Irak: et si la France s'était trompée?"], *Politique Etrangère* 99 (Summer 2003), 409–422.

Daalder, I. H. and Lindsay, J. M., *America Unbound: The Bush Revolution in Foreign Policy* (Washington, DC: Brookings Institution Press, 2003).

Daalder, I. and O'Hanlon, M., *Winning Ugly: NATO's War to Save Kosovo* (Washington, DC: Brookings Institution Press, 2000).

D'Alema, M., *Kosovo: gli italiani e la guerra* [Kosovo: The Italians and the War] (Milan: Mondadori, 1999).

Davis, J. W., "Victims of Success? Post Victory Alliance Politics," NATO Research Fellowship Final Report (2000), http://www.nato.int/acad/fellow/98-DO/davis.pdf.

de Gaulle, C., *Discours et Messages*, vol. IV (Paris: Plon, 1986).

Mémoires d'espoir: le renouveau [Memories of Hope: The Renewal] (Paris: Plon, 1970).

de Lacharrière, G., *La politique juridique extérieure* [Juridical Foreign Policy] (Paris: Economica, 1983).

de Marenches, A. and Ockrent, C., *Dans le secret des princes* (Paris: Stock, 1986), translated into English, with Andelman, D., *The Fourth World War: Diplomacy and Espionage in the Age of Terrorism* (New York: Morrow, 1992).

de Montbrial, T., *L'action et le système du monde* (Paris: PUF, 2002).

"Franco-American Relations: A Historical-Structural Analysis," *Cambridge Review of International Affairs* 17:3 (October 2004), 451–466.

Debré, M., et al. (eds.), *Guy Ladreit de Lacharrière et la politique juridique extérieure de la France* [Guy Ladreit de Lacharrière and France's Juridical Foreign Policy] (Paris: Masson, 1989).

Del Pero, M., *L'alleato scomodo: gli USA e la DC negli anni del centrismo (1948–1955)* [The Inconvenient Ally: The USA and the Christian Democrats in the Age of Centrism (1948–1955)] (Rome: Carocci, 2001).

Delafon, G. and Sancton, T., *Dear Jacques, Cher Bill* (Paris: Plon, 1999).

Delpech, T., "Bagdad: trois leçons pour une crise," *Politique Internationale* 100 (Summer 2003).

Denison, A. B., *Shades of Multilateralism: US Perspectives on Europe's Role in the War on Terrorism* (Bonn: ZEI Discussion Paper No. 106, 2002).

DeSipio, L., *Counting on the Latino Vote: Latinos as a New Electorate* (Charlottesville, VA: University of Virginia Press, 1996).

Destler, I. M., "Congress and Foreign Policy at Century's End: Requiem on Cooperation?," in L. C. Dodd and B. I. Oppenheimer (eds.), *Congress Reconsidered*, 7th edition (Washington, DC: CQ Press, 2001), 315–333.

Deutsche Einheit, *Sonderedition aus den Akten des Bundeskanzleramts* (Munich: Oldenbourg, 1998).

Di Nolfo, E., "The United States and Italian Communism: World War II to the Cold War" *Journal of Italian History* 1:1 (1978), 74–94.

Vaticano e Stati Uniti: dalle carte di Myron Taylor 1939–1952 [The Vatican and the United States: From the Documents of Myron Taylor 1939–1952] (Milan: F. Angeli, 1978).

Dini, L., *Tra casa bianca e botteghe oscure: Fatti e retroscena di una stagione alla Farnesina* [Between the White House and the Botteghe Oscure: Behind the Scenes of a Season at the Farnesina] (Milan: Guerini e Associati, 2001).

Dobbins, J., et al., *America's Role in Nation-Building: From Germany to Iraq* MR-1753 RC (Santa Monica, CA: RAND, 2003).

Duelfer, C., "The Inevitable Failure of Inspections in Iraq," *Arms Control Today,* 32:7 (September 2002).

Duke, S., *The Burdensharing Debate: A Reassessment* (London: Macmillan, 1993).

Dunay, P., "Civil–Military Relations in Hungary: No Big Deal," in T. Edmunds, A. Forster, and A. Cottey (eds.), *Democratic Control of the Military in Postcommunist Europe: Guarding the Guards* (London: Palgrave, 2002), 64–87.

Duroselle, J. B., *Tout empire périra: une vision historique des relations internationales* (Paris: Armand Colin, 1982).

Ehrman, J., *The Rise of Neoconservatism: Intellectuals and Foreign Affairs, 1945–1994* (New Haven, CT: Yale University Press, 1995).

Epstein, R., "NATO Enlargement and the Spread of Democracy: Evidence and Expectation," *Security Studies* 14:1 (Spring 2005).

Farer, T., "Beyond the Charter Frame: Unilateralism or Condominium?," *American Journal of International Law* 96:2 (April 2002), 359–364.

Featherstone, K. and Ginsberg, R., *The United States and the European Union in the 1990s: Partners in Transition* (London: Palgrave Macmillan, 1993).

Feldman, L. G., "The European Union's Enlargement Project and US–EU Cooperation in Central and Eastern Europe," in F. Burwell and I. H. Daalder (eds.), *The United States and Europe in the Global Arena* (London: Macmillan, 1999), 44–82.

Forster, A., Edmunds, T. and Cottey, A. (eds.), *The Challenge of Military Reform in Postcommunist Europe: Building Professional Armed Forces* (New York: Palgrave Macmillan, 2002).

Franck, T., *Recourse to Force: State Action Against Threats and Armed Attacks* (New York: Cambridge University Press, 2002).

"Terrorism and the Right of Self-Defense," *American Journal of International Law* 95 (October 2001), 839–843.

Freedman, L. and Karsh, E., *The Gulf Conflict, 1990–1991: Diplomacy and War in the New World Order* (Princeton: Princeton University Press, 1993).

Frum, D., *The Right Man* (New York: Random House, 2003).

Fukuyama, F., "Has History Restarted Since September 11?," John Bonython Lecture at the Centre for Independent Studies, Melbourne, Australia, August 8, 2002.

Gaddis, L., "History, Grand Strategy, and NATO Enlargement," *Survival* 40:1 (1998), 145–151.

Gehrz, C. and Trachtenberg, M., "America, Europe, and German Rearmament, August–September 1950," in M. Trachtenberg (ed.), *Between Empire and Alliance* (Lanham, MD: Rowman & Littlefield, 2003), 1–32.

Gimbel, J., *The American Occupation of Germany* (Stanford: Stanford University Press, 1970).

Giscard d'Estaing, V., *Le pouvoir et la vie* (Paris: Cie 12, 1991).

Glennon, M. J., "The Fog of Law: Self-Defense, Inherence, and Incoherence in Article 51 of the United Nations Charter," *Harvard Journal of Law and Public Policy* 25 (Spring 2002), 539–558.

Limits of Law, Prerogatives of Power: Interventionism After Kosovo (New York: Palgrave Macmillan, 2001).

Gnesotto, N., *La puissance et l'Europe* (Paris: Presses de la FNSP, 1998).

Golden, J. R., *NATO Burden-Sharing: Risks and Opportunities* (Washington, DC: Praeger, Washington Papers 96, 1983).

Goldgeier, J., *Not Whether But When: The US Decision to Enlarge NATO* (Washington, DC: Brookings Institution Press, 1999).

Gordon, P. H. and Shapiro, J., *Allies at War: America, Europe, and the Crisis over Iraq* (New York: McGraw-Hill/Brookings Institution Press, 2004).

Gorka, S., "Hungarian Military Reform and Peacekeeping Effort," *NATO Review* (November 1995), 26–29.

Grant, L., "America's Liberal Jews," *Prospect* 84 (March 2003), 52–54.

Granville, J., "The Many Paradoxes of NATO Enlargement," *Current History* 98 (1999), 165–170.

Grayson, G., *Strange Bedfellows: NATO Marches East* (Lanham, MD: University Press of America, 1999).

Grosser, A., *The Western Alliance* (London: Macmillan, 1980).

Grzymala-Busse, A. and Jones Luong, P., "Reconceptualizing the State: Lessons from Post-Communism," *Politics and Society* 30:4 (2002), 529–554.

Guérot, U., Kaiser, K., Koopmann, M., Lefebvre, M., de Montbrial, T., Defarges, P. M. and Stark, H., "Deutschland, Frankreich und Europa: Perspektiven" [Germany, France, and Europe: Perspectives], DGAP-Analyse No. 21 (German Council on Foreign Relations and the French Institute of Foreign Relations, January 2003).

Gutierrez, B., "Defense Reform in Central Europe and the Challenges of NATO Membership: The Case of Hungary," Ph.D. dissertation, Department of Political Science, University of California, San Diego (2002).

Haftendorn, H., *Deutsche Aussenpolitik zwischen Selbstbeschränkung und Selbstbehauptung* (Munich: DVA, 2001).

One Year After 9/11: A Critical Appraisal of German–American Relations, Thyssen German American Dialogue Seminar Series, AICGS, 2002, http://www.aicgs.org/publications/PDF/haftendom.pdf.

Hamilton, D. S., *German–American Relations and the Campaign Against Terrorism* (Washington, DC: AICGS, 2002).

Harnisch, S. and Maull, H. W. (eds.), *Germany as a Civilian Power? The Foreign Policy of the Berlin Republic* (Manchester: Manchester University Press, 2001).

Haselkorn, A., *The Continuing Storm: Iraq, Poisonous Weapons, and Deterrence* (New Haven: Yale University Press, 1999).

Hassner, P., "Friendly Questions to America the Powerful," *In the National Interest* 1:2 (Fall 2002).

"The United States: The Empire of Force or the Force of Empire?" (Paris: Chaillot Paper 54, European Union Institute for Security Studies, September 2002).

Hassner, P. and Vaïsse, J., *Washington et le monde: dilemmes d'une superpuissance* (Paris: CERI/Autrement, 2003).

Hendrickson, R., "Nato's Visegrad Allies: The First Test in Kosovo," *Journal of Slavic Military Studies* 13:2 (2000), 25–38.

Henke, K. D., *Die amerikanische Besetzung Deutschlands* [The American Occupation of Germany] (Munich: Oldenbourg, 1995).

Henkin, L., *How Nations Behave: Law and Foreign Policy*, 2nd edition (New York: Columbia University Press, 1979).

Henrikson, A., "Why the United States and Europe See the World Differently: An Atlanticist's Rejoinder to the Kagan Thesis," *European Union Studies Association Newsletter* 16:3 (2003), 1–10.

Holsti, O. R., "Public Opinion and Foreign Policy," in R. J. Lieber (ed.), *Eagle Rules? Foreign Policy and American Primacy in the Twenty-First Century* (Upper Saddle River, NJ: Prentice Hall, 2002), 16–46.

"Public Opinion and US Foreign Policy After the Cold War," in J. M. Scott (ed.), *After the End: Making US Foreign Policy in the Post-Cold War World* (Durham: Duke University Press, 1998), 138–169.

Holsti, O. R. and Rosenau, J. N., "Liberals, Populists, Libertarians, and Conservatives: The Link Between Domestic and International Affairs," *International Political Science Review* 17:1 (1996), 29–54.

"The Political Foundations of Elites' Domestic and Foreign Policy Beliefs," in E. R. Wittkopf and J. M. McCormick (eds.), *The Domestic Sources of American Foreign Policy* (Lanham, MD: Rowman & Littlefield, 1999), 33–50.

Horsefield, J. K. (ed.), *The International Monetary Fund, 1945–1965*, vol. III, *Documents* (Washington, DC: International Monetary Fund, 1969).

Howorth, J., "Foreign and Defence Policy Cooperation: European and American Perspectives," in Peterson and Pollack, *Europe, America, Bush*, 13–27.

"France, Britain and the Euro-Atlantic Crisis," *Survival* 45:4 (Winter 2003/4), 173–192.

Ikenberry, G. J., *After Victory: Institutions, Strategic Restraint, and the Rebuilding of Order After Major Wars* (Princeton: Princeton University Press, 2001).

America Unrivaled: The Future of the Balance of Power (Ithaca: Cornell University Press, 2002).

"The Political Foundations of Atlantic Order," in H. Gardner and R. Stefanova (eds.), *The New Transatlantic Agenda: Facing the Challenges of Global Governance* (Aldershot, UK: Ashgate, 2001), 17–29.

Ilari, V., "La politica militare italiana" ["Italian Military Policy"], in Istituto Affari Internazionali, *L'Italia nella politica internazionale, 1993* (Roma: SIPI, 1993), 203–229.

Institut für Zeitgeschichte, *Akten zur Auswärtigen Politik der Bundesrepublik Deutschland 1971* (Munich: Oldenbourg, 2002), vol. III.

Jacobson, G. C., "Party Polarization in National Politics: The Electoral Connection," in J. R. Bond and R. Fleisher (eds.), *Polarized Politics: Congress and the President in a Partisan Era* (Washington, DC: CQ Press, 2000), 9–30.

Jacoby, W., *The Enlargement of the European Union and NATO: Ordering from the Menu in Central Europe* (New York: Cambridge University Press, 2004).

Jean, C., "La nostra sicurezza nel mondo balcanizzato" ["Our Security in a Balkanized World"], *Limes* 4 (1994), 201–212.

Jervis, R., "Cooperation Under the Security Dilemma," *World Politics* 30:2 (1978), 167–214.

Joffe, J., "Who's Afraid of Mr. Big?," *The National Interest* 64 (Summer 2001), 43–52.

Jones, C., "Nato Enlargement: Brussels as the Heir of Moscow," *Problems of Post-Communism* 45:4 (1998), 44–55.

Jones, N., *The Control Freaks* (London: Politico's, 2001).

Jones-Correa, M., "Latinos and Latin America: A Unified Agenda?," in T. Ambrosio (ed.), *Ethnic Identity Groups and US Foreign Policy* (Westport, CT: Praeger, 2002), 115–130.

Kagan, R., "America's Crisis of Legitimacy," *Foreign Affairs* (March–April 2004), 65–87.

Of Paradise and Power: America and Europe in the New World Order (New York: Knopf, 2003).

"Power and Weakness," *Policy Review* 113 (June–July 2002, http://www.policyreview.org/JUNO2/Kagan.html).

Kahler, M., "The United States and Western Europe: The Diplomatic Consequences of Mr. Reagan," in K. A. Oye, R. J. Lieber, and D. Rothchild (eds.), *Eagle Resurgent? The Reagan Era in American Foreign Policy* (Boston: Little, Brown and Company, 1987), 297–333.

Kampfner, J., *Blair's Wars* (London: Free Press, 2003).

Kampfner, J. and Riddell, P., "Blair's Five Wars," *Prospect* 91 (October 2003), 40–43.

Kaplan, L. F. and Kristol, W., *The War over Iraq: Saddam's Tyranny and America's Mission* (San Francisco: Encounter Books, 2003).

Katzenstein, P., "Same War – Different Views: Germany, Japan, and Counterterrorism," *International Organization* 57 (Fall 2003), 731–760.

"Uniting Germany in an Integrating Europe," in P. Katzenstein (ed.), *Tamed Power: Germany in Europe* (Ithaca: Cornell University Press, 1997), 1–48.

Kay, S., *NATO and the Future of European Security* (New York: Rowman & Littlefield, 1998).

Kelsen, H., *Principles of International Law*, 2nd edition (New York: Holt, Rinehart and Winston, 1966).

Kennedy, C. and Bouton, M., "The Real Trans-Atlantic Gap," *Foreign Policy* 133 (November–December 2002), 66–74.

Kerski, B., "Zwischen Desinteresse und Misstrauen: zur Krise in den deutsch–polnischen Beziehungen," *Internationale Politik* 59:4 (2004), 31–40.

Khalizad, Z., *From Containment to Global Leadership? America and the World After the Cold War* (Santa Monica: RAND Corporation, 1995).

King, D. C., "The Polarization of American Parties and the Mistrust of Government," in J. S. Nye, Jr., P. D. Zelikow, and D. C. King (eds.), *Why People Don't Trust Government* (Cambridge: Harvard University Press, 1997), 155–178.

Kissinger, H., *Diplomacy* (New York: Simon & Schuster, 1994).

Does America Need a Foreign Policy? Toward a Diplomacy for the Twenty-First Century (New York: Simon & Schuster, 2001).

"What Kind of Atlantic Partnership?," *Atlantic Community Quarterly* 7 (1969), 18–38.

Kitfield, J., "Damage Control," *National Journal*, NATO Enlargement Daily Briefs, Op-Eds (July 18, 2003).

Klau, T., "France and Germany: A Re-Marriage of Convenience," US–France Analysis Series, Brookings Institution (January 2003, http://www.brookings.edu/usfrance/analysis/index.html).

Kornelius, S., "Joschka Fischer's Long Journey," *Transatlantic Internationale Politik* 4:3 (Fall 2003), 49–54.

Krasno, J. and Sutterlin, J., *The United Nations and Iraq: Defanging the Viper* (Westport, CT: Praeger, 2003).

Krauthammer, C., "The Unipolar Moment Revisited," *The National Interest* 70 (Winter 2002–3), 5–17.

Krzeminski, A., "Poland's Home Is Europe," *Transatlantic Internationale Politik* 4:3 (Fall 2003), 65–68.

Kull, S., *Americans on Terrorism: Two Years After 9/11*, Program on International Policy Attitudes (PIPA) and Knowledge Networks (September 9, 2003).

Seeking a New Balance: A Study of American and European Public Attitudes on Transatlantic Issues (Washington, DC: Program on International Policy Attitudes, Center for International and Security Studies, University of Maryland, June 26, 1998).

Kull, S. and Destler, I. M., *Misreading the Public: The Myth of a New Isolationism* (Washington, DC: Brookings Institution Press, 1999).

Kupchan, C. A., *The End of the American Era: US Foreign Policy and the Geopolitics of the Twenty-First Century* (New York: Knopf, 2002).

"The End of the West," *Atlantic Monthly* 290:4 (November 2002), 42–44.

"The Rise of Europe, America's Changing Internationalism, and the End of US Primacy," *Political Science Quarterly* 118:2 (Summer 2003), 205–231.

Lagorio, L., *L'ultima sfida: gli euromissili* [The Ultimate Challenge: Euromissiles] (Florence: Loggia de' Lanzi, 1998).

Lambert, R., "Misunderstanding Each Other," *Foreign Affairs* 82:2 (March–April 2003), 62–74.

Layne, C., "The Unipolar Illusion: Why New Great Powers Will Arise," *International Security* 17:4 (Spring 1993), 5–51.

Ledeen, M. and Lewis, W., *Débâcle: l'échec américain en Iran* (Paris: Albin Michel, 1981).

Lerman, A., "Sense on Antisemitism," *Prospect* 77 (August 2002), 34–39.

Lieven, A., "Speaking Up," *Prospect* 86 (May 2003), 24–27.

Lind, M., "The Israel Lobby," *Prospect* 73 (April 2002), 22–29.
Made in Texas: George W. Bush and the Southern Takeover of American Politics (New York: Basic Books, 2003).
Lindley-French, J., *Terms of Engagement: The Paradox of American Power and the Transatlantic Dilemma Post-11 September* (Paris: Chaillot Papers, European Union Institute for Security Studies, May 2002).
"The Ties That Bind," *NATO Review* (Autumn 2003, http://www.nato.int/docu/review/2003/issue 3/english/art 2.html).
Lindsay, J. M., "The New Apathy: How an Uninterested Public Is Reshaping Foreign Policy," *Foreign Affairs* 79:5 (September–October 2000), 2–8.
Lipset, S. M., *American Exceptionalism* (New York: W. W. Norton, 1996).
Little, R. and Wickham-Jones, M., *New Labour's Foreign Policy: A New Moral Crusade?* (Manchester: Manchester University Press, 2000).
Lucarelli, S., *Europe and the Breakup of Yugoslavia: A Political Failure in Search of a Scholarly Explanation* (The Hague: Kluwer Law International, 2000).
Lundestad, G., *The American "Empire"* (Oxford: Oxford University Press, 1990).
"Empire" by Integration: The United States and European Integration, 1945–1997 (Oxford: Oxford University Press, 1998).
"'Empire by Invitation' in the American Century," *Diplomatic History* 23:2 (Spring 1999), 189–217.
"Empire by Invitation? The United States and Western Europe, 1945–1952," *Journal of Peace Research* 23:3 (1986), 263–277.
The United States and Western Europe Since 1945: From "Empire" by Invitation to Transatlantic Drift (Oxford: Oxford University Press, 2003).
Luoma-aho, M., "'Arm' Versus 'Pillar': The Politics of Metaphors of the Western European Union at the 1990–1991 Intergovernmental Conference on Political Union," *Journal of European Public Policy* 11:1 (February 2004), 106–127.
Maelstaf, G., *Que faire de l'Allemagne? Les responsables français, le statut international de l'Allemagne et le problème de l'unité allemande (1945–1955)* (Paris: Ministère des Affaires Etrangères, 1999).
Marcellin, R., *L'importune vérité* (Paris: Plon, 1978).
Mausbach, W., "European Perspectives on the War in Vietnam," *German Historical Institute Bulletin* 30 (2002), 71–86.
Meacham, J., *Franklin and Winston: An Intimate Portrait of an Epic Friendship* (New York: Random House, 2003).
Mead, W. R., *Special Providence: American Foreign Policy and How It Changed the World* (New York: Century Foundation, 2002).
Mearsheimer, J., "Back to the Future: Instability in Europe After the Cold War," *International Security* 15:1 (July–August 1990), 5–56.
Menon, A. and Lipkin, J., *European Attitudes Towards Transatlantic Relations, 2000–2003: An Analytical Survey* (Birmingham: European Research Institute, 2003).
Menotti, R., "Italy and NATO: The Unsinkable Carrier and the Mediterranean," *What Italy Stands For – Limes* (Washington, DC: Center for Strategic and International Studies, 1997), 15–29.

Michta, A. (ed.), *America's New Allies: Poland, Hungary, and the Czech Republic in NATO* (Seattle: University of Washington Press, 1999).

"Poland: A Linchpin of Regional Security," in Michta, *America's New Allies*, 40–73.

Red Eagle: The Army in Polish Politics, 1944–1988 (Stanford: Hoover Institution Press, 1990).

The Soldier-Citizen: The Politics of the Polish Army After Communism (London: Macmillan, 1997).

Miller, J. E., *The United States and Italy, 1940–1950: The Politics and Diplomacy of Stabilization* (Chapel Hill: University of North Carolina Press, 1984).

Moravcsik, A., "Striking a New Transatlantic Bargain," *Foreign Affairs* 82:4 (July–August 2003), 74–89.

Morgenthau, H., *Politics Among Nations*, 3rd edition (New York: Knopf, 1961).

NATO, *NATO Handbook* (Brussels: NATO Office of Information and Press, 2001).

Nincic, M., Rose, R. and Gorski, G., "The Social Foundations of Adjustment," in P. Trubowitz, E. O. Goldman, and E. Rhodes (eds.), *The Politics of Strategic Adjustment: Ideas, Institutions, and Interests* (New York: Columbia University Press, 1999), 176–209.

Ninkovich, F., "The United States, NATO, and the Lessons of History," in D. J. Kotlowski (ed.), *The European Union: From Jean Monnet to the Euro* (Athens: Ohio University Press, 2000), 203–212.

Nordlinger, E., *Isolationism Reconfigured: American Foreign Policy for a New Century* (Princeton: Princeton University Press, 1995).

Nuti, L., "Dall'operazione *Deep Rock* all'operazione *Pot Pie*: una storia documentata dei missili SM 78 Jupiter in Italia" ["From Operation Deep Rock to Operation Pot Pie: A Documentary History of SM 78 Jupiter Missiles in Italy"], *Storia delle Relazioni Internazionali* 11/12:1 (1996–7) and 2 (1996–7), 95–138 and 105–149.

"Italy and the Battle of the Euromissiles," in O. Njolstad (ed.), *The Last Decade of the Cold War: From Conflict Escalation to Conflict Transformation* (London: Frank Cass, 2004), 332–359.

Nye, J. S. Jr., *The Paradox of American Power: Why the World's Only Superpower Can't Go It Alone* (Oxford: Oxford University Press, 2002).

Olson, M. and Zeckhauser, R., "An Economic Theory of Alliances," *Review of Economics and Statistics* 48 (1966), 266–279.

Oppenheim, L., "The Science of International Law: Its Task and Method," *American Journal of International Law* 2:2 (April 1908), 313–356.

Pells, R., *Not Like Us: How Europeans Have Loved, Hated and Transformed American Culture Since World War II* (New York: Basic Books, 1997).

Perthes, V., "The Advantages of Complementarity: The Middle East Peace Process," in H. Gardner and R. Stefanova (eds.), *The New Transatlantic Agenda: Facing the Challenges of Global Governance* (Aldershot, UK: Ashgate, 2001), 103–121.

Peterson J., "The US and Europe in the Balkans," in Peterson and Pollack, *Europe, America, Bush*, 85–98.

Peterson, J. and Green Cowles, M., "Clinton, Europe and Economic Diplomacy: What Makes the EU Different?," *Governance* 11:3 (July 1998), 251–271.

Peterson, J. and Pollack, M. A. (eds.), *Europe, America, Bush: Transatlantic Relations in the Twenty-First Century* (London and New York: Routledge, 2003).

Pew Research Center for the People and the Press, *The 2004 Political Landscape: Evenly Divided and Increasingly Polarized* (November 5, 2003, http://people-press.org).

"America's Image Further Erodes, Europeans Want Weaker Ties" (March 18, 2003, http://people-press.org).

Views of a Changing World (June 2003, http://people-press.org).

Philippi, N., "Civilian Power and War: The German Debate About Out-of-Area Operations 1990–1999," in Harnisch and Maull, *Germany as a Civilian Power?*, 49–67.

Poggiolini, I., "Italian Revisionism After World War II: Status and Security Problems, 1947–1957," in R. Ahmann (ed.), *The Quest for Stability: Problems of Western European Security 1918–1957* (Oxford: Oxford University Press, 1993), 327–359.

Pollack, K., "Spies, Lies, and Weapons: What Went Wrong," *Atlantic Monthly* January–February 2004, 78–92.

The Threatening Storm: The Case for Invading Iraq (New York: Random House, 2002).

Pollack, M., "Unilateral Europe, Multilateral America?," in Peterson and Pollack, *Europe, America, Bush*, 115–127.

Pollack, M. and Shaffer, G. (eds.), *Transatlantic Governance in the Global Economy* (London: Rowman & Littlefield, 2001).

Pond, E., *Friendly Fire: The Near Death of the Transatlantic Alliance* (Washington, DC: Brookings Institution Press, 2004).

Posen, B. R. and Ross, A. L., "Competing Visions for US Grand Strategy," *International Security* 21:3 (Winter 1996), 5–53.

Program on International Policy Attitudes, *Americans on Globalization* (Washington, DC: Center for International and Security Studies, University of Maryland, March 28, 2000).

Quinlan, J. and Chandler, M., "The US Trade Deficit: A Dangerous Obsession," *Foreign Affairs* 80:3 (May–June 2001), 87–97.

Revel, J. F., *L'obsession anti-américaine: son fonctionnement, ses causes, ses inconséquences* [The Anti-American Obsession: Its Function, Its Causes, Its Inconsistencies] (Paris: Plon, 2002).

Rice, C., "Promoting the National Interest," *Foreign Affairs* 79:1 (January–February 2000), 45–62.

Riddell, P., *Hug Them Close: Blair, Clinton and the Special Relationship* (London: Politico's, 2003).

Risse, T., *Beyond Iraq: Challenges to the Transatlantic Security Community*, AICGS/ German–American Dialogue Working Paper Series (Washington, DC: AICGS 2003).

"Constructivism and International Institutions: Toward Conversations Across Paradigms," in I. Katznelson and H. V. Milner (eds.), *Political*

Science: State of the Discipline (New York: W. W. Norton, 2002), 597–629.

Robin, G., "Sens et enjeu de la guerre d'Iraq," *Géopolitique* 82 (April–June 2003), 3–10.

Rohde, D. W., "Partisanship, Leadership, and Congressional Assertiveness in Foreign and Defense Policy," in D. Deese (ed.), *The New Politics of American Foreign Policy* (New York: St. Martin's Press, 1993), 76–101.

Roosevelt, F., *Public Papers and Addresses of Franklin D. Roosevelt*, 1940 volume (New York: Macmillan, 1941).

Ruggie, J., "Embedded Liberalism in the Postwar Economic Order," *International Organization* 36 (1982), 379–415.

"The Past as Prologue? Interests, Identity, and American Foreign Policy," *International Security* 21:4 (Spring 1997), 89–125.

Sacco, G., "Tra Europa e mare aperto: un'agenda per il nostro governo" ["Between Europe and the Deep Blue Sea: An Agenda for Our Government"], *Limes* 5 (2002), 75–86.

Schelling Study Group Report, "Report on Strategic Developments over the Next Decade for the Inter-Agency Panel," National Security Files, Box 376, John F. Kennedy Library, Boston (October 1962).

Schlesinger, A. Jr., "Eyeless in Iraq," *New York Review of Books* (October 23, 2003), 24–27.

Schwartz, T. A., *Lyndon Johnson and Europe: In the Shadow of Vietnam* (Cambridge: Harvard University Press, 2003).

Scott, F. and Osman, A., "Identity, African-Americans, and US Foreign Policy: Differing Reactions to South African Apartheid and the Rwandan Genocide," in T. Ambrosio (ed.), *Ethnic Identity Groups and US Foreign Policy* (Westport, CT: Praeger, 2002), 71–91.

Seldon, A., *Major: A Political Life* (London: Weidenfeld & Nicolson, 1997).

Silj, A. (ed.), *L'alleato scomodo. I rapporti tra Roma e Washington nel Mediterraneo: Sigonella e Gheddafi* [The Inconvenient Ally. Relations Between Rome and Washington in the Mediterranean: Sigonella and Gaddafi] (Milan: Corbaccio, 1998).

Simma, B. (ed.), *The Charter of the United Nations: A Commentary*, 2 vols., 2nd edition (New York: Oxford University Press, 2002).

Simon, J., "Partnership for Peace (PFP): After the Washington Summit and Kosovo," *Strategic Forum* 167 (1999), 1–5.

Poland and NATO: A Study in Civil–Military Relations (Lanham, MD: Rowman & Littlefield, 2004).

SIPRI (Stockholm International Peace Research Institute), *SIPRI Yearbook: Armaments, Disarmament, and International Security* (Stockholm: SIPRI, 2002).

Skidelsky, R., "Imbalance of Power," *Foreign Policy* 129 (March–April 2002), 46–55.

Smith, T., *Foreign Attachments: The Power of Ethnic Groups in the Making of American Foreign Policy* (Cambridge: Harvard University Press, 2000).

Soutou, G. H., *L'alliance incertaine: les rapports politico-stratégiques franco-allemands, 1954–1996* (Paris: Fayard, 1996).

"De Gaulle's France and the Soviet Union from Conflict to Détente," in W. Loth (ed.), *Europe, Cold War and Coexistence, 1953–1965* (London: Frank Cass, 2003), 173–189.

"France, Nations and Empires from the Nineteenth Century to the Present Day: Between Jacobin Tradition, European Balance of Power and European Integration," in H. Cavanna (ed.), *Governance, Globalization and the European Union: Which Europe for Tomorrow?* (Dublin: Four Courts Press, 2002), 69–86.

"Georges Pompidou and US–European Relations," in M. Trachtenberg (ed.), *Between Empire and Alliance: America and Europe During the Cold War* (New York: Rowman & Littlefield, 2003), 157–200.

"President Pompidou, the Ostpolitik and the Strategy of Détente," unpublished typescript.

Stephens, P., *Tony Blair: The Making of a World Leader* (New York: Viking, 2004).

Stone, J., *Aggression and World Order: A Critique of United Nations Theories of Aggression* (Berkeley and Los Angeles: University of California Press, 1958).

Stothard, P., *Thirty Days: An Inside Account of Tony Blair at War* (New York: Harper Collins, 2003).

Stürmer, M., *Die Kunst des Gleichgewichts: Europa in einer Welt ohne Mitte* (Berlin: Propyläen, 2001).

Szabo, S., *Parting Ways: The Crisis in German–American Relations* (Washington, DC: Brookings Institution Press, 2004).

Szayna, T., "A Small Contributor or a 'Free Rider?,'" in Michta, *America's New Allies*, 112–148.

Szayna, T. and Larrabee, F. S., *East European Military Reform After the Cold War: Implications for the United States* (Santa Monica: RAND Corporation, 1995).

Takle, M., "Towards a Normalisation of German Security and Defence Policy: German Participation in International Military Operations," *ARENA Working Papers* 02:10 (2002, http://www.arena.uio.no/publications/ wp02_10.html).

Tardy, T., *La France et la gestion des conflits yougoslaves (1991–1995): Enjeux et leçons d'une opération de maintien de la paix de l'ONU* [France and the Management of the Yugoslav Conflicts (1991–1995): States and Lessons from a UN Operation to Maintain the Peace] (Brussels: Bruylant, 1999).

Taylor, B., "Russia's Passive Army: Rethinking Military Coups," *Comparative Political Studies* 34:8 (2001), 924–952.

Thatcher, M., *The Downing Street Years* (London: Harper Collins, 1993).

Thomas, H., *The Suez Affair* (Harmondsworth: Penguin Books, 1970).

Timmerman, K., *The French Betrayal of America* (New York: Crown Forum, 2004).

Trachtenberg, M., "The Bush Strategy in Historical Perspective," to be published in James J. Wirtz and Jeffrey A. Larsen (eds), *Nuclear Transformation: The New US Nuclear Doctrine* (New York: Palgrave Macmillan, 2005).

A Constructed Peace: The Making of the European Settlement, 1945–1963 (Princeton: Princeton University Press, 1999).

History and Strategy (Princeton: Princeton University Press, 1991).

"The Question of Realism: An Historian's View," *Security Studies* 13:1 (Fall 2003), 156–194.

"Waltzing to Armageddon?," *The National Interest* (Fall 2002), 144–152.

Trubowitz, P., *Defining the National Interest: Conflict and Change in American Foreign Policy* (Chicago: University of Chicago Press, 1998).

Ulrich, M. P., "Developing Mature National Security Systems in Postcommunist States: The Czech Republic and Slovakia," *Armed Forces and Society* 28:3 (2002), 403–425.

United Kingdom, Foreign Office, *A Commentary on the Charter of the United Nations*, Cmd. 6666 of 1945 (London: HMSO, 1945).

Vachudová, M., "The Atlantic Alliance and the Kosovo Crisis: The Impact of Expansion and the Behavior of New Allies," in P. Martin and M. Brawley (eds.), *Alliance Politics, Kosovo, and NATO's War: Allied Force or Forced Allies?* (New York: St. Martin's, 2001), 201–220.

van Eekelen, W. F., *Debating European Security, 1948–1998* (The Hague: SDU Publishers, 1998).

Vedrine, H. and Moïsi, D., *France in an Age of Globalization*, translated by P. H. Gordon (Washington, DC: Brookings Institution Press, 2001).

Villepin, D., *Un autre monde* (Paris: L'Herne, 2003).

"Diplomatie et action, entretien avec Dominique de Villepin," *Supplement to Politique Internationale*, 102 (Winter 2003–4), 5–62.

Vlachová, M., "Professionalisation of the Army of the Czech Republic," in Forster, Edmunds, and Cottey, *The Challenge of Military Reform in Postcommunist Europe*, 34–48.

Wallace, W. and Musu, C., "The Focus of Discord? The Middle East in US Strategy and European Aspirations," in Peterson and Pollack, *Europe, America, Bush*, 99–114.

Wallander, C. A., "Institutional Assets and Adaptability: NATO After the Cold War," *International Organization* 54:4 (2000), 705–735.

Walt, S. M., *The Origins of Alliances* (Ithaca: Cornell University Press, 1987).

Waltz, K. N., "The Emerging Structure of International Politics," *International Security* 18:2 (Autumn 1993), 44–79.

"Structural Realism After the Cold War," *International Security* 25:1 (Summer 2000), 5–41.

Theory of International Politics (New York: McGraw-Hill, 1979).

Waltz, K. N. and Sagan, S., *The Spread of Nuclear Weapons: A Debate Renewed* (New York: Norton, 2003).

Walzer, M., *Just and Unjust Wars: A Moral Argument with Historical Illustrations* (New York: Basic Books, 1977).

Wauthier, C., *Quatre présidents et l'Afrique. De Gaulle, Pompidou, Giscard d'Estaing, Mitterrand: Quarante ans de politique africaine* [Four Presidents and Africa. De Gaulle, Pompidou Giscard d'Estaing, Mitterrand: Forty years of African Policy] (Paris: Seuil, 1995).

Williams, P., *The Senate and US Troops in Europe* (London: Palgrave, 1985).

Wilson, W., *War Messages*, 65th Congress, 1st Session, Senate Doc. No. 5, Serial No. 7264 (Washington, DC, 1917).

Wilzewski, J., "Back to Unilateralism: The Clinton Administration and the Republican-Led Congress," in M. Dembinski and K. Gerke (eds.), *Cooperation or Conflict? Transatlantic Relations in Transition* (New York: St. Martin's Press, 1998), 23–43.

Wohlforth, W. C., "The Stability of a Unipolar World," *International Security* 21:1 (Summer 1999), 1–36.

Woodward, B., *Bush at War* (New York: Simon & Schuster, 2002).

Plan of Attack (New York: Simon & Schuster, 2004).

Wyatt-Walter, H., *The European Community and the Security Dilemma 1989–1992* (London: Macmillan, 1997).

Yaniszewski, M., "Postcommunist Civil–Military Reform in Poland and Hungary: Progress and Problems," *Armed Forces and Society* 28:3 (2002), 385–402.

Yost, D., *NATO Transformed: The Alliance's New Roles in International Security* (Washington, DC: United States Institute of Peace Press, 1998).

Zimmermann, H., "Governance by Negotiation: The EU, the United States and China's Integration into the World Trade System," in S. Schirm (ed.), *Global Economic Governance* (London: Palgrave, 2003), 67–86.

Money and Security: Troops, Monetary Policy, and West Germany's Relations with the United States and Britain, 1950–1971 (Cambridge: Cambridge University Press, 2002).

Znoj, M., "Czech Attitudes Toward the War," *East European Constitutional Review* 8:3 (1999), 47–50.

Index

Kennedy
& France   202.

Trans.
  Summary   263

265 → cur.

70
76

57